The Case for Affirmative Action
for Blacks in Higher Education

The Case for Affirmative Action for Blacks in Higher Education

JOHN E. FLEMING

GERALD R. GILL

DAVID H. SWINTON

Institute for the Study of Educational Policy
Howard University

Published for ISEP by
Howard University Press
Washington, D.C.
1978

Printed in the United States of America

Library of Congress Cataloging in Publication Data

Fleming, John, 1944–
   The case for affirmative action for Blacks in higher education.

   Bibliography: p.
   Includes index.
   1. Afro-Americans—Education (Higher) 2. Affirmative action programs—United
States. I. Gill, Gerald R., 1948–   joint author. II. Swinton, David H., joint
author. III. Title.
LC2781.F56   379   78-19553
ISBN 0-88258-076-0 cloth
ISBN 0-88258-075-2 pbk

This report was made possible by a grant from the Ford Foundation.

Acknowledgments

Acknowledgments are gratefully extended to the following:
Change magazine, for permission to reprint excerpts from Volume 4, Number 8, October 1972 and Volume 4, Number 9, November 1972, reprinted with permission from *Change* magazine, New Rochelle, New York 10801.
Hawthorn Books, Inc., for permission to reprint an excerpt from *What Black Educators Are Saying* by Nathan Wright, Jr., ed., copyright © 1970 by Hawthorn Books, Inc., with permission of the publisher.
Longman Inc., for permission to quote from *Black Education: Myths and Tragedies* by Thomas Sowell, copyright © 1972 by Thomas Sowell, reprinted by permission of Longman Inc.

Contents

List of Tables   xi

List of Figures   xv

Foreword   xvii

Preface   xxi

Part I

1   Introduction   3

What Is Affirmative Action?   5

Affirmative Action and Other Strategies to Achieve Equal
     Opportunity   7

The Importance of Affirmative Action for Achieving Equal
     Opportunity   8

The Scope of this Study   12

2   Blacks in Higher Education Prior to Affirmative
Action   14

The Status of Black Americans prior to the Civil War   15

"Freedom": The Education of Black People, Past and Present   17

Special Education for Black People   19

Education of Black Americans between the World Wars   22

Education of Blacks in the Postwar Years: Policy of Exclusion
     Yields to Experimentation   27

The *Brown* Decision and the Education of Black People   32

"Good Faith" Efforts and the Higher Education Community   35

Why Affirmative Action for Students   38

The Continuing Controversy over Affirmative Action   44

3   Affirmative Action and the Law   48

The Constitutional Basis for Affirmative Action   48

The Legality of Racial Classifications   51

The Development of Federal Affirmative Action Programs   55

vii

109113

Affirmative Action and the Courts   70
Affirmative Action under Executive Order 11246   74

4   Response to the Critics of Affirmative Action   78
Reaction to the Revised Order   80
Opposition to Affirmative Action: "Unwarranted Federal
      Intervention"   81
Opposition to Affirmative Action: Goals and Quotas   86
The Alleged Assault on Merit   88
The Alleged Effects of Affirmative Action on Minorities
      and on Institutions   93
Alternatives to Affirmative Action: The Ideas of the Critics   98

Part II

5   Affirmative Action and the Federal Government   103
Organization of the Government Enforcement Effort   105
Responsibilities under Executive Order 11246   106
The Government's Affirmative Action Regulations   109
      Personnel Policies and Practices   110
      Method of Implementation of the Plan   112
      Establishment of Goals   113
      The New Format   116
The Establishment and Implementation of Affirmative Action   118
Enforcement of Executive Order 11246   121
      Preaward Compliance Reviews   122
      Postaward Compliance Reviews   124
      Monitoring of Complaints   124
      Sanctions   126
Conclusions   129

6   Affirmative Action in Institutions of Higher
     Education: Four Case Studies   134
Florida State University: A Case Study of a State University   136
      Background   136
      Florida State University Affirmative Action Plan:
        Development and Implementation   136
      Work Force Analysis and Goals   138
      Affirmative Action and the Florida State University
        Community   142
      Progress under Affirmative Action   144

Contents

Affirmative Action and Black Faculty Members 152
Affirmative Action and Black Students 155
Florida State University and the Federal Government 156
Harvard University: A Case Study of a Major Research
    University 158
Background 158
Development of an Affirmative Action Plan 158
Work Force Analysis and Goals 159
Affirmative Action and the Harvard Community 169
Oberlin College: A Case Study of a Private, Liberal Arts College 177
Background 177
The Development of an Affirmative Action Plan 178
Work Force Analysis and Goals 179
Affirmative Action and the Oberlin Community 183
Black Students and Affirmative Action 188
Oberlin and the Federal Government 192
Merritt College: A Case Study of a Community College 192
Background 192
Peralta District Affirmative Action Plan 192
Development of an Affirmative Action Plan 194
Implementation of the Plan 199
Affirmative Action and Students 202
Findings and Conclusions 204

Part III

7

Blacks, Affirmative Action, and the Future 209

Introduction 209
Current Position of Black Faculty in Academic Labor Markets 213
Current Size and Distribution of Black Faculty 213
Current Availability of Qualified Blacks 216
Implications of the Data for Current Utilization
    and Need for Affirmative Action 217
The Academic Labor Market to 1990 222
Recent Labor Market Conditions 222
Projections of Overall Demand for Faculty through 1990 223
Projections of Overall Supply Conditions 226
Implications of the Projections for Labor Market
    Conditions 228
Projections of Conditions in the Academic Labor Market
    for Blacks to 1990 229
Projections of the Availability of Blacks to 1990 230

The Role and Impact of Affirmative Action and the
      Projections of Demand for Blacks to 1990   237
Projections of Black Hiring   241
Projections of Total Black Faculty to 1990   243
The Proportion of Blacks on Faculties to 1990   245
Labor Market Conditions for Black Manpower   248
Implications of Slack Labor Markets for Affirmative Action
      Efforts   250
Slack Labor Markets and Pressure to Upgrade
      Qualifications   250
Slack Labor Markets and Racial Discrimination   252
Slack Labor Markets and the Need for Government Action   253
Public Policies and the Future Prospects for Blacks on the Faculties
      of Higher Educational Institutions   254
The Need for Policies to Increase the Rate of Participation
      of Blacks in Graduate Education   254
The Impact of Temporary Hiring Targets   259
General Public Policies That Could Ease the Disruptions
      in the Academic Labor Market   263
Policies to Improve General Demand for College Faculties   264
Policies to Moderate Rapid Supply Formation   268
Policies Encouraging Alternative Use of Manpower   269
Conclusions   271

Epilogue   272

Appendix A   276
      Historical Documents   276

Appendix B   317
      Executive Orders   317

Appendix C   358
      Format for Development of an Affirmative Action Plan
      by Institutions of Higher Education   358

Appendix D   367
      Basic Model Used in Chapter Seven for Projecting
      Future Supply of Faculty Members   367

Notes   370

Selected Bibliography   393

Index   411

List of Tables

Table 2-1	Rosenwald Fund Survey, 1945–47 and the Southern Education Reporting Service Survey, 1967–68	37
Table 2-2	Percent Distribution of Estimated Graduate Enrollments, Doctorates Awarded, and U.S. Population by Race and Ethnic Identity	41
Table 2-3	Doctorates Awarded (U.S. Citizens) FY 1976	42
Table 3-1	Legal Basis for Affirmative Action	56
Table 5-1	OCR Higher Education Staffing Pattern	108
Table 5-2	Status of Affirmative Action Plans by Regional Office, FY 1976 and 1977	120
Table 5-3	Preaward Reviews by Regional Office, FY 1976	123
Table 5-4	Compliance Reviews by Regional Offices	125
Table 5-5	Status of Complaints Alleging Discrimination Based on Race and Sex for FY 1976	126
Table 5-6	Number of Sanctions Initiated by OCR Regional Offices as of May 1977	128
Table 6-1	Florida State University Employees by Race and Sex, Fall 1972	139
Table 6-2	Florida State University Vacancy Projections, 1973–74	140
Table 6-3	Florida State University Goals	141
Table 6-4	Florida State University Projected Increase in Minority Employment	141
Table 6-5	Florida State University Goals, 1972–73 to 1977–78	142
Table 6-6	Work Force Distribution, Fall Quarters, 1972 and 1974	146
Table 6-7	Florida State University Administrative and Professional Staff by Sex and Race, Fall 1972 and 1974	147
Table 6-8	Florida State University Faculty by Race and Sex, Fall 1972 and 1974	148
Table 6-9	Florida State University Faculty Rank Distribution by Race and Sex, April 1973 and March 1975	149

Table 6-10	Florida State University Average Salary, April 1975	150
Table 6-11	Hiring Goals at FSU, 1973–74 and 1974–75	151
Table 6-12	Utilization of Black Faculty at Harvard as of 30 June 1976	160
Table 6-13	Projected Change in the Number of Minority and Total Faculty at Harvard between 30 June 1976 and 30 June 1978 and Percentage of Minority Faculty, 1976 and 1978	164
Table 6-14	Projected and Actual Number of Minorities at Harvard on University-wide Faculties, Selected Ranks, 1975	166
Table 6-15	University-wide Black Faculty at Harvard, Total and Percentage for 1971, 1973, 1975	166
Table 6-16	Percentage of Blacks among Employees on Harvard Faculties as of June 1976	167
Table 6-17	University-wide Utilization of Nonteaching Personnel at Harvard, 1971–1975	168
Table 6-18	Oberlin Faculty Members by Race and Sex, 1976 (9–10 months)	179
Table 6-19	Oberlin Faculty Members by Race, Sex, and Salary Range (9–10 months)	180
Table 6-20	Oberlin Professional and Administrative Staff by Race and Sex, 1976 (9–10 months)	180
Table 6-21	Oberlin Professional and Administrative Staff by Race, Sex, and Salary Range, 1976 (9–10 months)	181
Table 6-22	Oberlin Professional and Administrative Staff by Race and Sex, 1976 (12 months)	181
Table 6-23	Oberlin Professional and Administrative Staff by Race Sex, and Salary Range, 1976 (12 months)	182
Table 6-24	Representation of Minorities and Women at Oberlin and Affirmative Action Goals for the College of Arts and Sciences	184
Table 6-25	Black Student Enrollment in Major Private Colleges and Universities, 1974–75	190
Table 6-26	Comparison of Situation in 1972–73 to Goals, Peralta College District Overall (Percentage of Certified Contract Personnel)	193
Table 6-27	Ethnic Distribution of Merritt Students, 1967–72	194

Table 6-28	Comparison of Situation in 1972–73 at Merritt to Goals, by Sex and Ethnic Background	197
Table 7-1	Faculty by Type of Institution and Race, 1972–73	214
Table 7-2	Stock of College Teachers, 1970	215
Table 7-3	Field of Employment of Ph.D. Labor Force, 1973	217
Table 7-4	Number and Percentage Receiving Ph.D.'s, 1973, by Field (U.S. Citizens only)	218
Table 7-5	Cartter Enrollment Projections, 1970–1990	225
Table 7-6	Demand for College Faculty, 1961–1974 and Projections of Demand for New College Faculty, 1975–1989	227
Table 7-7	Annual Average Numbers of Master's and Ph.D. Degrees Awarded	228
Table 7-8	Ratio of Demand to New Degrees Conferred, 1961 to 1986	229
Table 7-9	Percentage of Black Enrollment in Graduate Schools, 1968–1974	230
Table 7-10	Proportion of Blacks Ages 18–34 in Undergraduate Enrollment, 1968–1974	231
Table 7-11	Proportion of Students Enrolled in Previous Year through the Next Year	232
Table 7-12	Proportion of Blacks Remaining in Each Year's Class Given the Proportion in the First Year	233
Table 7-13	Proportion of Black Students in Freshmen Enrollment, 1966–1974	235
Table 7-14	Projections of Total Graduates, 1974 to 1990	238
Table 7-15	Projections of Hiring Black Faculty at the Ph.D. Level, 1975–1989	242
Table 7-16	Projections of Hiring Black Faculty at the Non-Ph.D. Level, 1975–1989	243
Table 7-17	Projected Annual Total Hiring of Ph.D. and Non-Ph.D. Faculty, 1975–1989	244
Table 7-18	Estimated Total Black Faculty, 1974, and Projections of Total Black Faculty, 1975–1990	245
Table 7-19	Estimated Black Faculty, 1974 and Projections of Ph.D.-Level Black Faculty, 1975–1990	246

Table 7-20	Estimated Non-Ph.D. Black Faculty, 1974, and Projections of Non-Ph.D. Black Faculty, 1975–1990	247
Table 7-21	Projections of Percentage of Blacks on Faculty at Selected Years	247
Table 7-22	Ratio of Hiring of Black Faculty to New Black Graduates	249
Table 7-23	Projected Change in Total Black Hiring, 1975 to 1990, from an Increase in the Proportion of Ph.D.'s Hired to 44 percent	252
Table 7-24	Projections of Blacks among the New Graduates with Advanced Degrees in 1990 under Different Growth Assumptions	256
Table 7-25	Projections of Blacks on the Faculty with Ph.D.'s in 1990	257
Table 7-26	Projections of Blacks on the Non-Ph.D. Faculty in 1990	257
Table 7-27	Projections of Blacks on Faculty at Selected Years Given a 25 Percent Higher Attrition Rate	259
Table 7-28	Projections of Black Ph.D. Faculty for 1990 Given Equal Opportunity and an 11 Percent Hiring Target	261
Table 7-29	Projections of Black Non-Ph.D. Faculty for 1990 Given Equal Opportunity and an 11 Percent Hiring Target	262
Table 7-30	Blacks on the Ph.D. and Non-Ph.D. Faculties in 1990: Case (1) Base Case Enrollments; Case (2) An Increase to a 10 Percent Higher Enrollment Level; Case (3) An Increase to a 20 Percent Higher Enrollment Level	266
Table 7-31	Percentage Distribution Employment by Employer's Category in the 1973 Roster of Doctoral Scientists and Engineers	269
Table 7-32	Percentage Distribution of Academic Employment by Type of Activity	270

List of Figures

Figure 6-1   Florida State University Affirmative Action Goals for   152
              Minorities

Figure 6-2   Comparison of Historical Ethnicity to Goals for Certi-   195
              fied Contract Personnel (Peralta College District Over-
              all)

Figure 6-3   Comparison of Sex Mix in 1972 to Goal for Black Certi-   196
              fied Contract Personnel (Peralta College District Over-
              all)

Foreword

The Institute for the Study of Educational Policy (ISEP) was established in 1974 with substantial support from the Ford Foundation to act as a national clearinghouse for data and a research center on the issues affecting equal opportunity for blacks in higher education. Through its reports and monographs, through its seminars and workshops, and through its announcements and public testimony, ISEP attempts to fill a vacuum in the organized body of knowledge on minority participation in higher education. One major aim is to make a significant contribution to the formulation and evaluation of contemporary educational policy to assist the public and private sectors in approaching equitable minority representation in professional and academic fields as well as in other areas of employment. Clearly, affirmative action programs are related to this aim.

Although the top priority program objective of the Institute is to issue an annual or biennial report on the status of blacks in higher education, the National Advisory Board of ISEP at its first two meetings advised the staff to monitor and review carefully the climate of opinion toward oppressed racial minorities and the poor in the United States. The Board commissioned a review of the national mood which resulted in the 1977 publication of *The Changing Mood in America: Eroding Commitment?* by Dr. Faustine Jones, for three years a Senior Fellow at the Institute. A shift in opinion from liberalism toward neoconservatism was found, and it expressed itself in a number of ways, one of which was and is an assault on affirmative action. The Board then directed the staff to study the status of affirmative action for blacks in higher education, a project which has been run by Dr. John E. Fleming, a Senior Fellow at the Institute.

When this broad project was undertaken, it was found that it was necessary to place the need for affirmative action programs, especially for blacks, in the appropriate historical context. This resulted in the 1976 publication of *The Lengthening Shadow of Slavery: A Historical Justification for Affirmative Action for Blacks in Higher Education,* by Dr. Fleming. As the study of affirmative action proceeded, it became more and more ambitious, analyzing the legal and governmental aspects of affirmative action, responding to the critics of affirmative action, doing case studies of higher educational institutions, and projecting the future of supply and demand in these programs. This more extensive project has resulted in this publication, *The Case for Affirmative Action for Blacks in Higher Education,* by Dr. Fleming, Mr. Gerald Gill, a Research Fellow, and Dr. David Swinton, an Associate Senior Fellow, all of the Institute. *Affirmative Action for Blacks in Higher Education: A Report,* issued in June 1978, is largely a summary of this study with policy recommendations, developed closely with the advice and direction of the National Advisory Board, for improving affirmative action.

As this volume goes to press, the United States Supreme Court is considering the *Bakke* special minority admissions case. As this study makes clear, special minority admissions programs in graduate and professional schools are essential to increase the pool of minority faculty members and staff for effectively executing affirmative action programs in higher education. Moreover, the underlying principle of affirmative action posits the propriety of providing special assistance and treatment to groups heretofore excluded on the basis of discrimination. The National Advisory Board hopes that this study will illuminate both facts and values pervading this controversial problem.

Currently the Institute is committed to the concept of affirmative action, and sincerely hopes that this study will not only further enlighten the public regarding this issue, but will also provide the basis for improving affirmative action programs in particular and higher education in general.

I should like to, on behalf of the Board, especially acknowledge the critically important role of Dr. John E. Fleming, the Senior Fellow in charge of the Institute's affirmative action project. The fine work of the coauthors of this monograph, Dr. Swinton and Mr. Gill, is also acknowledged. The Board commends all of them on a job well done.

Finally, Howard University and the Institute gratefully acknowledge the substantial and continual support of the Ford Foundation.

KENNETH S. TOLLETT
Chairman
National Advisory Board
Institute for the Study
of Educational Policy

Preface

The Case for Affirmative Action for Blacks in Higher Education is the second of a two-volume work undertaken by staff members of the Institute for the Study of Educational Policy. The first volume, by John E. Fleming, *The Lengthening Shadow of Slavery: A Historical Justification for Affirmative Action for Blacks in Higher Education,* provides the historical background for the present-day efforts to secure equal employment opportunity for blacks in higher education. A forerunner to this volume, the first volume documents the struggle of black people for education under the severely restrictive conditions first of slavery and later of enforced segregation. As this study clearly shows, it was the official policy of the federal, state, and local governments to keep blacks in a state of ignorance during slavery and then ensure that the education finally extended would be of an inferior quality, yet suitable for preserving the second-class status of blacks in American society.

The historical exclusion of blacks from the larger academic community, as outlined in *The Lengthening Shadow of Slavery,* has had a compounding effect that can be overcome only through positive intervention. Affirmative action is one means of intervening. In and of itself it cannot, and is not designed to remedy the suffering and deprivation of generations of black Americans. As defined by Executive Order 11246 and its implementing regulations, affirmative action is designed to rectify existing discrimination by making sure the employment process operates in a way that is fair to all candidates, regardless of race or sex. In the area of higher education, affirmative action can ensure that blacks today have a fair opportunity to compete for all educational benefits.

The National Advisory Board of the Institute for the Study of Educational Policy suggested we entitle this volume *The Case for Affirmative Action* because the members perceived that the commitment to full equality for all citizens has diminished in intensity in recent years, both in institutions of higher education and in the society at large. The Nixon and Ford administrations advocated "benign neglect" as their response to the plight of black Americans, and this policy proved detrimental to the enforcement of affirmative action programs as well as other social programs. The most vehement attacks on affirmative action efforts in higher education, however, have come from within the educational establishment itself. These critics disregard the systemic nature of discrimination and ignore the continued need for positive action. Our study of affirmative action programs in higher education indicates that any civil rights policy which does not address the problem of institutionalized discrimination has a negative impact on black opportunities in the society, especially in employment.

The emphasis on affirmative action for blacks in higher education is important because of the role academia plays in American life. Colleges and universities do more than provide employment opportunities; they are responsible for educating today's youth and tomorrow's leaders. In an ever-shrinking world, education is too important not to reflect the cultural diversity of American society which must exist in the larger pluralistic world. The strategy of affirmative action is one means to achieve fair opportunities for those underrepresented and cultural richness for the larger society, which comes from cultural diversity.

We present the case for affirmative action, but it is up to the nation as a whole and its individual members to make the commitment to equality of opportunity. The Carter administration can establish the moral leadership and encourage vigorous enforcement of the law, but the American people must also act to ensure equality of opportunity. Institutions of higher education, as guardians of knowledge and promoters of values, are invested with a special responsibility in this area. The extent to which they succeed or fail will have a direct bearing on the lives of all Americans.

The authors undertook this volume with a sense of urgency, for it seems that the social commitment to the goal of equal opportunity, and the strategy of affirmative action in particular, is wavering. If this book helps clarify the meaning and significance of affirmative action for blacks in institutions of higher education, the authors will deem their efforts a success.

We are indebted to a number of persons and organizations for making this study possible. First, we thank the entire staff of the Institute for the Study of Educational Policy and the members of the National Advisory Board for their substantial support and criticism as the manuscript moved from the planning stage through numerous drafts to final publication. Our special thanks go to Kenneth S. Tollett, Chairman of the Board and ISEP Director, and to Senior Research staff Faustine Jones, Elizabeth Abramowitz, Michael Olivas, and Lorenzo Morris. We also appreciate the contributions of the following members of the research and editorial staff: Julius Hobson, Jr., Cynthia Smith, Emma Nicholson, Herschelle Reed, and Elaine Cambosos. The secretarial staff provided excellent typing services, and we extend thanks to Teresa Bragg and especially Brenda Knight who worked untiringly on each of the drafts.

Chapter three has been considerably improved through the research efforts of Evelyn Gonzales and Linda Earley who served as legal research assistants at ISEP. Cheryl Smith and Justine Finch, graduate assistants in the W. A. Harriman College of Urban and Policy Science (State University of New York at Stony Brook), provided special assistance to David Swinton. Cheryl Smith assisted in the research and interviews at Harvard University and gave useful criticism of each draft of this section. Justine Finch was of great assistance in programming and running the model for the projections and in reviewing drafts of chapter seven.

We extend our sincere appreciation to Dr. Rayford W. Logan, Professor Emeritus, Howard University, who gave fully of his time in criticizing early drafts of chapter two. We are particularly grateful that he shared with us unpublished manuscripts in his possession on notable American Negroes.

We wish to thank the presidents, affirmative action officers, faculties and staffs of Florida State University, Harvard University, Oberlin College, and Merritt College for their cooperation during our research for the case studies. Their active support and the liberal gift of their time allowed us to obtain a glimpse of how affirmative action is actually working at various types of institutions.

We have received additional support and cooperation from the following institutions: Howard University, the State University of New York at Stony Brook, and the Library of Congress. We extend our special thanks to the staffs of the various federal agencies who contributed much to our knowledge of affirmative action. We are particularly indebted to the national and regional staffs of the Department of Health, Education and Welfare's Office for Civil Rights, Department of Labor, Office of Federal Contract Compliance Programs, the U.S. Commission on Civil Rights, and the Equal Employment Opportunity Commission.

We thank the following people who took time from their busy schedules to read drafts of this report and who, through their criticism, contributed to the quality of the final product: Sharon Bush, Howard Glickstein, Mary Lepper, and Jerome Paige.

No one single person contributed more to the production of this book than our editor, Jane Midgley, who untiringly worked to improve the quality and clarity of the various drafts. In more than one instance, she actually contributed to the research as errors and inconsistencies were discovered. We extend our appreciation for a job well done.

Finally, we thank the Ford Foundation for its moral and financial support. We are particularly grateful to Benjamin Payton for his commitment to the work of ISEP.

The authorship of this document has truly been a joint effort. Initially we each were assigned responsibility for different chapters. However, there was a considerable degree of interaction and reaction to drafts through several successive stages of revisions, so that it is impossible to separate the contribution of each individual. The results reflect a fair degree of consensus of views, often after hours and even days of debate. Thus, all remaining disagreements among the authors are minor.

To our wives and families, we thank you for your patience and endurance. To our readers, we acknowledge our responsibility for any errors which remain.

JOHN E. FLEMING
GERALD R. GILL
DAVID H. SWINTON

March 1978

Part I

Chapter One

Introduction

The public policy of affirmative action is a natural extension of the long struggle for equal rights in this country. The struggle began when the first slaves were imported from Africa. From the birth of the Constitution, blacks have fought for their rightful place as citizens of this country, but in the past American society has offered them justice with one hand while withdrawing it with the other. The Thirteenth Amendment to the Constitution freed blacks from slavery, the Fourteenth Amendment gave them citizenship, and the Fifteenth Amendment gave them the right to vote without which they would not have had the means to protect their rights as citizens. Although Congress recognized the legitimate claim of black people to these basic human rights, it was soon evident that the nation was unwilling to enforce them and thus began the process of reversal. This process culminated in the infamous *Plessy* v. *Ferguson* decision of 1896 which sanctioned the doctrine of separate but equal as public policy.

For nearly sixty years, blacks struggled to progress under such severe legal, economic, and social restrictions as to hinder group advancement to full equality. In 1954, the nation again offered blacks the hope of full citizenship and justice when the Supreme Court in the *Brown* decision held *de jure* segregation unconstitutional. Today legal segregation as public policy is almost nonexistent, but the vestiges of slavery and generations of segregation and deprivation and the continued existence of illegal discrimination have created real barriers to the attainment of full equality. The ghettoes, characterized by vast unemployment, family instability, and delapidated housing, are monuments to America's denial of equal justice and the failure of public policy to eradicate these disadvantages.

But justice cannot be denied even though America has, thus far, partially succeeded in delaying it for black Americans. As President Carter emphasizes the need to honor the human rights of people throughout the world, Americans must realize there cannot be a well-ordered and just society at home when inequality exists to such an extent that it disadvantages a large segment of society. In the past, various branches of government have failed to recognize and protect sufficiently the rights of black citizens to fair and equal treatment. The most significant policy development designed to address past and present discrimination is being challenged before the Supreme Court in the *Allan Bakke* v. *Regents of the University of California*. Regardless of the Court's decision, the foundation for human rights extends beyond Court decrees, congressional legislation, or presidential executive orders. Education is now understood to be fundamental to the advancement of mankind. The right to share in the heritage of civilization through education is so basic that it relates to an objective order of justice and law which transcends governmental bodies. The history of the Afro-American people is one of a continuing struggle to get the government at all levels to recognize such rights and to enforce them equally for all.

Affirmative action is just one strategy designed to provide justice and equality for blacks. It is a peaceful strategy for making the transition to a fair and equitable society. If the American society decides not to support affirmative action programs in the future, such a course will hinder the advancement of justice, but it certainly cannot and will not stop blacks from striving to achieve what is rightfully theirs. There is little question that if affirmative action fails, blacks will seek new strategies, some of which may not permit the nation to move smoothly and peacefully to a more equitable society.

Since its inception as a major part of the strategy for achieving equality of opportunity in employment, affirmative action has been surrounded by controversy. The controversy has been stimulated in part by those who traditionally oppose government intervention on behalf of minorities. Much of the controversy, however, results from misunderstanding affirmative action. This misunderstanding arises from failure to understand the concept of affirmative action, from problems in implementing the strategy, and from unrealistic expectations in terms of the potential of equal opportunity and affirmative action strategies to transform the social structure into one which reflects greater equality. Much of the present controversy will subside when these misunderstandings are corrected.

What Is Affirmative Action?

This study is intended to make a contribution to the task of clarifying the concept of affirmative action embodied in Executive Order 11246, issued by President Lyndon B. Johnson in 1965. The Department of Labor was given overall authority for developing regulations to implement the provisions of the order. The Executive Order and its implementing regulations propose two avenues for eradicating employment discrimination. The first is nondiscrimination. Black Americans have challenged the federal government to end racial discrimination from the beginning of American history. The failure of half-hearted efforts during the Reconstruction period to end discrimination allowed racial discrimination and prejudice to become institutionalized. Therefore, by the time Congress passed the Civil Rights Act of 1964, employment discrimination had become systemic. The federal program of nondiscrimination was ineffective in eradicating systemic discrimination because by its very nature systemic discrimination had become implicitly part of the employment process. Because policies of nondiscrimination are basically neutral, past and present discriminatory treatment places blacks at a disadvantage in seeking educational and job opportunities. In addition to this first requirement of nondiscrimination, the Executive Order and its implementing regulations require affirmative action to make the employment system fair.

Affirmative action is a preventive procedure designed to minimize the probability of discrimination. Affirmative action within the federal program is defined as the deliberate undertaking of positive steps to design and implement employment procedures so as to ensure that the employment system provides equal opportunity to all. Affirmative action implies the deliberate and conscious design of each element in the system for distributing employment opportunities. In such a deliberately designed system, nothing is left to chance which might lead to illegal discrimination. Procedures for recruiting job applicants, evaluating the qualifications of candidates, notifying potential candidates about opportunities for promotion, delegating new assignments, and awarding salary increases and benefits are designed and implemented so as to ensure that the opportunities are made available to all on a fair basis.

By its very nature the practice of affirmative action imposes a constraint on all employers subject to its requirements. The choice of procedures and methods for operating an employment system is limited by the requirement that any procedure selected must meet the prior test of being able to assure the provision of equality of opportunity to all groups. Given this requirement of affirmative action, it will no longer be legal for employers to choose procedures for operating their employment systems that will lead to discrimination either intentionally or unintentionally.

Moreover, employers are required to take positive steps to ensure that they are not discriminating. Most important among these steps is the requirement that employers conduct an analysis of their work force and employment system to determine if they are hiring minorities and women at a rate that would normally be expected by their availability in the general work force. If these analyses indicate that minorities and women are not being hired when they are available for employment, then employers must take additional steps to expand their applicant pool to give minorities and women a fair opportunity for employment. After determining the number of vacancies and projected vacancies, employers are then able to project how many minorities and women they should be hiring over a specified period of time. These projections enable the employer to set goals that are not to be confused with quotas, which by their very nature establish hiring ceilings. Goals are management tools to enable employers to assess their rate of progress in providing equal opportunity. Failure to achieve the projected goals means that employers must reevaluate the employment process to determine if there are any policies and procedures which hinder the rate of progress that would ordinarily occur in the absence of racial or sexual discrimination.

The federal government has tied affirmative action to its contract compliance program. All employers receiving federal contracts of $50,000 or more with a work force of at least fifty employees are required not to discriminate on the basis of race, creed, national origin, or sex and to develop written affirmative action programs to ensure that minorities and women are hired at a rate their availability in the work force would suggest. This study examines how effectively the program is working in institutions of higher education, particularly to what extent black faculty members are attaining employment in these institutions. Blacks were selected because of the peculiar nature and pervasiveness of their exclusion in the past. Blacks in higher educational institutions are concentrated on because the Institute for the Study of Educational Policy (ISEP) is concerned primarily with the status and needs of blacks in higher education and the implications of educational policy for their present and future status.

Affirmative Action and Other Strategies
to Achieve Equal Opportunity

In generic usage, the term *affirmative action* is a rubric for a host of strategies designed to achieve equal opportunity. But affirmative action as spelled out by Executive Order 11246 and its implementing regulations is a defined set of positive steps that are designed to eliminate current discrimination and make the employment process fair. Affirmative action requires that contractors expand their recruitment by making a special effort to see that blacks are notified of employment opportunities, have a fair opportunity to apply and be considered for employment, and, once hired, have a fair opportunity for promotion. Some critics have viewed this effort as preferential treatment, but if these requirements are properly interpreted, it is clear that they are merely steps to make the employment process fair. The ultimate goal of affirmative action and other equal opportunity strategies is the achievement of fair representation of blacks in all areas and at all levels of employment in the higher education sector. A fair representation implies parity between the number of blacks in the national population and their employment at all levels in academia. The assumption is that if all artificial barriers to access to education were lifted and the effects of past discrimination overcome, blacks would gain qualifications for positions in academia that would approximate their proportion in the population at large and under a nondiscriminatory system, would be hired in the same proportions. This does not suggest that every department or even every institution would have 11 percent blacks. In order to avoid a quota system and to allow for group and personal preferences, there may be professional fields in which blacks are "underrepresented" and others where blacks are "overrepresented." But overall, blacks would eventually account for about 11 percent of the positions in academia.

To achieve this goal, there must be equal opportunity. The extent to which past and present discrimination prevent the achievement of equal opportunity will be examined in this volume. Since discrimination has resulted in the lack of educational opportunities for blacks and thus the limited supply of black faculty, affirmative action in academic employment must be tied to affirmative action programs for black students. The very nature of employment discrimination in academia necessitates that the relevancy of extending affirmative action programs to graduate and professional students be examined. Education is too important to individuals and society as a whole to allow for the arbitrary establishment of criteria that exclude whole segments of the populace, an exclusion that will have far-reaching consequences through life. Executive Order 11246 and its implementing regulations establish a strategy for achieving a bias-free employment process, but the concept of affirmative action may be too limited and may not be sufficient. The focus on affirmative action in employment in no way implies that it is and should be the only strategy used to achieve equal opportunity. The research of the authors indicates that other strategies are necessary to overcome the legacy of past and present discrimination.

Such strategies designed to redress the effects of past discrimination are not new to higher education. In the wake of civil rights activities and protests in the 1960s, many colleges and universities began experimenting with special minority admissions programs, special recruitment and training activities and, in some cases, open admissions. The institutions that started such programs recognized that traditional admissions procedures and evaluations of qualifications for college students perpetuated striking inequalities in the society and precluded too many people from competition for positions of influence and leadership. These compensatory efforts directed toward students were effective in increasing the minority enrollment in both undergraduate and graduate institutions in recent years, but they have been vehemently criticized in the 1970s and will be subject to a test of legality by the Supreme Court in 1978. Since the success of affirmative action in the hiring of black faculty partially depends upon a qualified pool of candidates, the loss of these programs would severely limit its effectiveness.

The Importance of Affirmative Action
for Achieving Equal Opportunity

This volume will examine why government-enforced affirmative action is a necessary, appropriate, and efficient strategy for achieving equal employment opportunity in institutions of higher education. The question of necessity can be formed as follows: Can the government fulfill its obligation to *ensure* equal opportunity in employment to all of its citizens without requiring employers to practice affirmative action? It is clear that if the answer to this question is no, the government has no choice but to require that employers observe the practice of affirmative action. Indeed it would seem that the requirement should be extended beyond the present application under the executive orders to cover all institutions subject to the legal requirement of the civil rights laws to provide equal opportunity in employment. Not only should the requirement be imposed on those who receive large government contracts but ideally all institutions of higher education should develop affirmative action plans.

The key word in the above question is *ensure*. The government has a well-recognized obligation to enforce and uphold the laws of the land and the Constitution. It has a well-recognized obligation to ensure the protection of the rights of all of its citizens. Thus it follows that the government is also obligated to uphold equal opportunity laws and to ensure equal employment opportunity for all citizens.

It seems clear that equality of opportunity in employment cannot be ensured without affirmative action, especially in academia. There is ample historical evidence to support this conclusion, as is discussed in chapter two. Moreover, the operations of employment systems in higher education have traditionally barred blacks.

The most salient point about discrimination is that once one gets beyond the point where employers make explicit declarations of their discriminatory intents, it becomes very difficult to detect and prove that discrimination is in fact occurring. The reasons for this are quite evident. First, it is possible to discriminate explicitly and disguise the discrimination behind other smoke screens, such as claiming that the candidate does not meet the qualifications. If the required qualifications are never explicitly declared in advance then it will not be possible to detect this particular transgression. Discrimination can also be implicit; one can design qualifying criteria and recruitment campaigns, for example, so as to reduce the chance of generating any qualified candidates from groups which are targets of discrimination.

Moreover, it is particularly possible to carry on explicit discrimination and implicit discrimination in higher education. This is because within the educational universe the hiring units are small and the volume of hiring done by a particular unit is small. The qualifying criteria are often vague, rely heavily on subjective judgments, and vary widely among the various hiring units. In addition, the decision-making process, especially for hiring faculty and research personnel, tends to be extremely decentralized within higher educational institutions. The conditions exist, therefore, in which a person can make an obviously biased decision that falls within a wide range of what can be viewed as reasonable and this variability makes it practically impossible to prove in any instance that discrimination has in fact occurred.

As long as explicit or implicit discrimination can exist and escape detection in an unregulated employment system, some regulation of the employment process will be required to ensure equal opportunity in employment. This required regulation is part of the affirmative action program, which simply requires employers to declare and make explicit criteria and procedures which on their face and in application will not result in discrimination. In the absence of the affirmative action requirement, the government will have no mechanism to ensure equality of opportunity in employment.

It seems to be clearly appropriate for the government to regulate the employment process to ensure the equal protection of all citizens. Philosophically, the government's basic obligation as guarantor of the social contract and the right of all citizens is to take necessary actions to carry out that obligation. The history of social legislation and government regulations for consumer protection, for instance, is replete with examples of a continuing refinement of the government's role in achieving the public purpose of protecting the rights of consumers in many different respects. In many instances in the protection of consumer rights, the government regulations require positive actions of a preventive nature. The history of governmental regulations demonstrates that the public purpose cannot always be served by simply reacting to violations after they occur but frequently requires positive steps to be taken to minimize the probability that violations will occur.

Affirmative action properly pursued does not violate the legitimate rights of anyone. Neither employers nor employees have a legitimate right to operate or benefit from a discriminatory employment process. It seems to be just as reasonable for the government to require employers to design employment procedures that can be reasonably expected to result in equality of opportunity for all, as it is to require food processors to design food processing systems that give reasonable assurance of producing food that will not endanger a consumer's health. In neither case is there a necessity that any particular establishment be guilty of a prior violation in order to sustain the reasonableness of the preventive actions. In both instances it is reasonable to expect that improperly designed systems will in fact increase to an unacceptable level the probability of violations. The risk of violation and the associated cost to individual citizens and the society are both high enough to justify the undertaking of more positive measures to minimize this risk and lower the cost.

Affirmative action is designed to ensure that the employment distribution system will provide fair opportunities to all without taking into consideration irrelevant personal characteristics. The efficiency of this strategy depends upon how well it achieves this goal. Some estimates of the potential usefulness of this strategy can be obtained by considering what would be required to establish a bias-free employment system and comparing it to what the affirmative action program actually attempts to achieve. A bias-free system ensures that information about opportunities is available without bias, that standards and criteria for distributing opportunities are free from bias, and that the implementation of employment procedures is nondiscriminatory. The federal affirmative action program has the components to achieve a bias-free system. The affirmative action effort has both the means to ensure that the procedures established to eliminate illegal discrimination are actually implemented and the mechanisms to detect and correct deficiencies in implementation.

The affirmative action regulations have established specific procedures for conducting searches, hiring, promoting, and establishing qualifications which will presumably lead to bias-free results. In some cases, such procedures have been devised by government and imposed on various institutions. In other cases, institutions have been given wide latitude in constructing reasonable procedures subject to governmental approval. The former mechanism ensures uniformity and the latter permits diversity which may facilitate adapting the requirement to the diversity of the institutions which make up academia. In any case, however, the procedures incorporated in an affirmative action plan, whether through experience or reasoning, have presumably passed some prior test of potential effectiveness. The procedures appear to be at least potentially effective in promoting fairness in the employment process.

The uncertainties involved in designing procedures suggest that the specific efficiency of any particular implementing procedure can only be established through actual trial. It is to be expected that initial efforts to ensure equal opportunity will require refinement as experience is gained. The willingness to recognize the necessity of learning by doing in the affirmative action area will minimize frustration and permit the development of a truly effective program over time.

Careful attention must also be paid to the implementation of whatever affirmative action steps are taken. Each plan must have a built-in mechanism to ensure continued feedback of information to check the workings of affirmative action and monitoring procedures. Properly designed goals and timetables are an essential management tool at this stage. The government must not only ensure that the designed affirmative action procedures include internal monitoring and control procedures but it must also ensure through its own monitoring program that affirmative action is actually being implemented in good faith by each institution.

The public policy of requiring higher educational institutions to adopt affirmative strategies with respect to the employment of minorities applies to institutions subject to Executive Order 11246. Currently the policy is implemented under Revised Order No. 4, which applies only to a limited class of employers who are government contractors. Affirmative action strategies have been adopted voluntarily, however, by some institutions not subject to Revised Order No. 4. As indicated earlier, the scope of application of affirmative action should be universal, and institutions not subject to its provisions should voluntarily adopt affirmative action plans.

This volume deliberately concentrates on the efforts of the government to bring about equal opportunity in institutions of higher education because of the important and vital role of government and the often excessive and unfair criticism of affirmative action from academia. Nevertheless, it is implicitly recognized that the success of any affirmative action program depends upon individual minority group members and the extent to which they are able to take advantage of opportunities. It is evident from experience that blacks have taken full advantage of the limited opportunities made available to them in the past. If past experience is any guide to future performance, it would appear that blacks will take advantage of all future opportunities.

The Scope of This Study

This report examines the affirmative action effort in higher education systems in three parts. Part 1, consists of the first four chapters and provides essential background information to place affirmative action in context. Chapter two discusses the efforts of blacks to obtain an education and examines the extent to which equal opportunity has existed in the higher education community. This examination of history has made it clear that equal opportunity has not been achieved in the past without government action. Chapter three discusses the legal-constitutional foundations of the public policy of affirmative action. Ample justification exists in the Constitution, laws, and judicial precedents to establish the legality of the affirmative action strategy. Furthermore, equal opportunity is a self-evident, individual requirement of the implicit social contract and that whatever strategies are required to promote this basic right are also consistent with the philosophical foundations of the society. Laws and judicial precedent notwithstanding, affirmative action is justified. If there is any conflict, the laws and judicial rulings must be brought into conformity with the requirements of affirmative action. Chapter four discusses the criticisms of affirmative action. The attempt here is to place these criticisms in proper context and to show that the validity of the strategy in principle survives the various criticisms.

Part 2 includes chapters five and six and is a brief examination of the current practice of affirmative action. Chapter five deals with the government's role in affirmative action. The government has two essential roles to play: the first is to establish the practice of affirmative action throughout institutions of higher education; the second is to enforce the practice of affirmative action once affirmative action systems have been established. Chapter five examines the government's effort in both respects. The intent is to identify strengths and weaknesses in the current government approach and make suggestions for improving the effort.

Chapter six examines the current practice of affirmative action within selected institutions of higher education. The intent of this chapter is to show how certain institutions have responded to the affirmative action requirement, what procedures have been successful, and what procedures have failed. The experiences of these institutions are useful in providing insights for changes in public policy that might lead to greater success in carrying out affirmative action strategies.

Finally, part 3 looks closely at the current positions of blacks in faculty employment in institutions of higher education. This examination is intended to increase the understanding of the necessity of affirmative action and to lay the foundation for anticipating the results of successful affirmative action over the next ten to fifteen years. Using various assumptions, some aggregate projections are made concerning the likely impact of affirmative action on future black participation on the faculties of institutions of higher education. Also discussed are some public policies that could accelerate the process for attaining equal opportunity.

Chapter Two

Blacks in Higher Education
Prior to Affirmative Action

The history of black Americans has a direct relationship to the need for affirmative action for blacks in institutions of higher education in the 1970s.* The neglect of the education of black people as well as the blatant racism in educational policies and practices are scathing indictments of American educational institutions and the society at large. Professor Allen B. Ballard poignantly maintains that:

They [white colleges] could have brought black faculty into their colleges in numbers sufficient to have created the image of integrated faculties at the very center of American civilization. They could have granted DuBois, Woodson, Wesley and Locke the prestige and research facilities that would have kept ill-intentioned and badly informed whites out of the business of defining the black man and his role in this society.[1]

But, unfortunately, this did not happen. White colleges and universities have not been in the vanguard of providing educational and employment opportunities for black students and professors. Black scholars have had to endure a pervasive, continuous pattern of discrimination. To understand the overt, and later covert, forms of discrimination and racism practiced in higher education as public policy, one must understand the history of American society and the black experience within

---

* This chapter is basically a summary of John E. Fleming's *The Lengthening Shadow of Slavery: A Historical Justification for Affirmative Action for Blacks in Higher Education* (Washington, D.C.: Howard University Press, 1976). It is suggested that the reader consult this work. It documents the struggle of blacks for education and the extent to which they have suffered from discrimination fostered by public policy.

that larger history. With the exception of the American Indians, no other group in American history has been so consistently and systematically discriminated against and denied its basic human rights. This process was unusually detrimental to blacks because race prejudice was institutionalized and sanctioned by the force of law. The following brief review of the historical plight of black people illustrates the need for a special effort on the part of American society to eradicate discrimination and its destructive effects on black Americans as a group and as individuals.

The Status of Black Americans Prior to the Civil War

Racism is older than the nation itself. While the early colonists sought freedom for themselves in the New World, vast stretches of land and a shortage of labor created the situation which first encouraged indentured servitude and later chattel slavery. Slavery became the basis for the socioeconomic interdependence between the races in southern society and also defined the nature of that relationship in northern society.

In the South, the policy of enslavement of black people was supported by an elaborate system of laws and controls designed to assure that blacks remained at the bottom of a caste society. These laws and controls circumscribed every aspect of the lives of slaves and prohibited them from learning to read and write. Without prohibitions against literacy, slavery as an institution would have been difficult to maintain. There was also a concerted attempt to remove the history of black people from written records in order to destroy their knowledge of the past and thereby skew their attitudes toward the present and future. This attempt to destroy black culture was reinforced by the slave codes which further regulated the slaves' entire existence.

What was true for the slaves was almost as true for the free Negroes prior to the Civil War. In the South, the slave codes were often used to govern the behavior of free Negroes; they were only quasi-free as a result. The plight of northern blacks did not differ markedly from that of their southern, free brethren. They were discriminated against in all aspects of life, but the most damaging restriction was the denial of the chance for self-improvement through education. It was the official policy at all levels of government to keep blacks illiterate and thus prisoners of a caste system where they would be consigned to the bottom of American society. Throughout American history blacks would be used as the basis for defining the bottom of the socioeconomic system.

Prior to the Civil War, each state had its own special laws to regulate the behavior of its black inhabitants. These laws were sanctioned by the U.S. Constitution, a document paradoxically dedicated to liberty and equality which at the same time protected the right of whites to hold black people in chattel slavery. The Supreme Court, in the now infamous *Dred Scott* decision of 1857, ruled that blacks, slave or free, were not, and could never be, citizens of the United States. American policies during slavery, both official and unofficial, reinforced by northern discrimination, created an atmosphere which continued beyond the slavery period and influenced the course of race relations to the present.

While it was slavery itself which first created insurmountable problems for black people, the issue of what place black Americans would occupy in the larger society transcended slavery. The problem was that racism became systemic in American society to the point where it was officially recognized as the *modus vivendi* for the nation as a whole. But blacks continually demonstrated their desire for education and for advancement above a servile status. Historical records are replete with the efforts of slaves to learn skills and to read and write. In spite of the closed system, a few managed, with encouragement from their masters, to achieve a remarkable degree of education. Free blacks also took advantage of the few opportunities available to them. They organized schools which they supported from their meager resources, and they took advantage of opportunities provided by the abolitionists who aided in the establishment of separate Negro schools and a few colleges for blacks, because they were excluded from white institutions.

Blacks made great strides within the oppressive system, but not enough to have a meaningful impact on their illiteracy rate by the end of the Civil War. Of the four million slaves and five hundred thousand free blacks in 1860, there were only twenty-eight known black college graduates, and not all of them had been educated in American institutions. Blacks had demonstrated their ability to learn, but the issue was whether they would be allowed to learn and improve their status in American society.

Educators, like most Americans, did not escape the overwhelming racism which existed prior to the Civil War. Before the war, it was extremely rare for an American institution of higher education to admit a black student, and almost unheard of for one to employ a black professor. One exception to this pattern was Charles Reason, who served as professor of mathematics and belles lettres at Central College in

McGrawville, New York. Central College, founded by abolitionists, also employed two blacks as instructors.[2]

"Freedom": The Education of Black People, Past and Present

The beginning of the era of Reconstruction was, in many ways, both a positive and negative experience for black people. Since only those slaves who resided in states in rebellion against the federal government were theoretically freed by the Emancipation Proclamation, most slaves gained their independence through the adoption of the Thirteenth Amendment to the Constitution in 1865. Between 1865 and 1875, a number of measures were taken to compensate the freedmen for generations of involuntary servitude. The Fourteenth Amendment, which nullified the *Dred Scott* decision by providing national and state citizenship for the freedmen, was ratified in 1868. With adoption of the Fifteenth Amendment in March 1870, states were prohibited from denying citizens, meaning the freedmen, the right to vote on the basis of their race, color, or previous condition of servitude. Since Congress retained the power to enforce the provisions of the amendments by appropriate legislation, it passed a series of civil rights acts designed to protect the freedmen from their former masters. (*See* chapter three for a detailed discussion of the significance of these Reconstruction amendments.)

The Bureau of Refugees, Freedmen, and Abandoned Land, established in 1865, was the major program established to aid the freedmen. The bureau distributed food, clothing, and other supplies and provided job placements, homestead land, and educational facilities. One of the bureau's major successes was to provide schools and teachers for the freedmen. Thousands of freed blacks of all ages crowded into the small one-room school houses day and night to become literate. But this great humanitarian effort was short-lived. Congress had successfully overridden President Andrew Johnson's veto in 1866 and managed to extend the life of the bureau. Within a few years, however, Congress was unwilling to sustain the cost of aiding the freedmen even at a minimal level.

The bureau ended its activities in the South by 1870; consequently freedmen were forced to rely on their own meager resources as they faced the future. The nation, both North and South, seemed unprepared to extend full equality to black people. The decision to discontinue the bureau was a political one in that the bureau for a time looked as if it

could have made substantive changes in the social order of the South.*
The shift in American policy toward government intervention on behalf
of the freedmen was too brief to have any lasting effect on generations of
deprivation. What followed Reconstruction was basically the continuation of the policy of subjugation and oppression.

After a brief experience with participatory democracy, blacks and
their allies were for all practical purposes eliminated from state governments as conservative whites wrested control of one southern state after
another from so-called radical influence. Federal troops were withdrawn
from the South in exchange for the election of the Republican candidate
for president, Rutherford B. Hayes, in what is known as the Compromise of 1877. The most severe blow of all, however, came through a
series of Supreme Court decisions which virtually nullified the work of
Congress. One by one the various civil rights acts, or sections thereof,
were declared unconstitutional. Then in 1896 in *Plessy* v. *Ferguson* the
highest court of the land gave the federal government's official sanction
to the policy of race segregation. Legally, blacks were "free and equal
citizens" for only thirty-one years between the periods of enforced
slavery and enforced segregation, from 1865 to 1896.

While violence against blacks after the era of Reconstruction ended in
1877, the threat of black political participation arose again with the
emergence of the Populists and their initial desire to unite white and
black people in the South in the interest of political and economic reform. This threat resurrected the ugly face of racism in a form seldom
seen during the years of slavery. Lynchings were rampant; lesser forms
of violence and acts of terror became commonplace. There was a brief
attempt on the part of Congress to interfere with the atrocities occurring
in the South, when Henry Cabot Lodge of Massachusetts introduced a
bill to provide federal supervision of federal elections in 1890. But the
bill was defeated along strict party lines and the constitutional rights of
black people turned into a purely political issue.

Hence, between the last decade of the nineteenth and the first decade
of the twentieth century, southern whites had completely eliminated
blacks from the political process and severely limited their participation
in the economic process. State constitutions were revised to eliminate

---

* Another bureau that, in contrast, survived is the Bureau of Indian Affairs. The
bureau, established in the War Department in 1824 and transferred to the Interior
Department in 1849, became active after 1871, when the status of Indians was changed
to "Wards" of the federal government. At best one could say that the BIA had little
positive influence, which might explain why it is still in existence.

blacks from the polls while allowing illiterate whites to continue to exercise the franchise by virtue of being descendants of persons who voted
prior to 1865 (the "grandfather clause"). What was not achieved by
"legal" means, was accomplished through the violence and intimidation
that went unabated far into the twentieth century. Probably no other
group in American history expected so much from freedom, and received so little. Blacks, ostensibly freed, had indeed been reduced to a
state of peonage if not, in many instances, virtual slavery. Southern
policies toward blacks were particularly devastating to the race because
the vast majority of black people lived in the South. The failure of the
Lodge bill and the *Plessy* decision indicated that the federal government
policy, at best, was one of malignant neglect.

Special Education for Black People

An extremely good case can be made for affirmative action for blacks
in higher education today when one closely examines how educational
policies for black people developed. The initial thrust to aid blacks in
their efforts to obtain a degree of literacy had a positive beginning after
the war with the efforts of the Freedmen's Bureau, and especially as a
result of the work of northern white missionaries who came south to
establish schools and colleges patterned after the best institutions of
New England. The efforts to establish a liberal educational tradition for
blacks soon conflicted with the ideas of those who thought that the best
educational policy was the establishment of vocational-industrial education for the newly emancipated slaves. Many advocates of vocational
education for blacks believed that blacks were inferior beings and thus
incapable of mastering a liberal arts education. Little regard was given
to their previous condition of servitude and the strict prohibitions
against slaves learning to read and write. It was apparent that the nation
was all too willing to accept assumptions about black inferiority without ever extending to them the opportunity to acquire the type of education that would allow them to develop as a group.

While the American Missionary Association and other philanthropic
and humanitarian groups were working to establish such universities
and colleges as Fisk University in Nashville, Tennessee; Shaw University
in Raleigh, North Carolina; and Morehouse College in Atlanta, Georgia;
General S. C. Armstrong was establishing Hampton Normal and Agricultural Institute in 1868 for Negro youth, which would eventually
emerge as the prototype for black education. Armstrong believed that

racial differences in blacks required a special type of education; while blacks could learn, they lacked the ability to assimilate and digest knowledge at a higher level, as well as the capacity for abstract thought. Armstrong's philosophy for educating Negroes was instilled in the young Booker T. Washington when he was a student at Hampton, and Washington later became the leading exponent of vocational education.

The Peabody Fund, established with funds from George Peabody in 1867, did much to influence the general acceptance of special education for Negroes throughout the South. Racial prejudice on the part of southern whites convinced them that little or no effort should be expended on Negro education. In fact, blacks were excluded from or discriminated against in the very school systems the freedmen helped establish during Reconstruction. Dr. Barnas Sears, the Peabody Fund's first general agent, influenced the course of southern educational policies by refusing to allocate grants to the few school systems which maintained integrated education. His successor, J. L. M. Curry, believed in white supremacy and advocated vocational education, especially for blacks.

As more and more philanthropic foundations were established, most in turn accepted the policy that vocational education was best suited for black people. Industrial capitalists also concluded that it was in their best economic interest to promote a compromise between the North and South as well as between white and black southerners. The Republican party no longer needed the Negro vote as southern politicians became less hostile to northern economic interests. With Booker T. Washington's 1895 Atlanta Compromise, in which he tacitly approved segregation, and the Supreme Court's *Plessy* decision the following year, the stage had been set for public policies sanctioning the segregation of blacks, as well as their relegation to the lowest levels in a caste society.

White institutions of higher education continued to ignore the plight of blacks. Only a few were willing to accept even a token number of Negro students, and virtually all refused to hire black faculty members. Two noted exceptions were Georgetown University in Washington, D.C., and the University of South Carolina. Father Patrick Healey, S.J., son of a white father and black mother, moved from the position of instructor at Georgetown University to president of the university in 1873. Richard Greener, the first black graduate of Harvard University, taught physics at the University of South Carolina from 1873 to 1877, when the school was briefly opened to all races.[3]

For the remainder of the nineteenth century, there were few blacks who were permitted to work in a predominantly white academic institution, with the exception of Edward C. Williams. Williams was appointed as the first black assistant librarian of the Adelbert College Library in 1892, but was not given a faculty position. In 1894 he served as the librarian of the Hatch Library and four years later, university librarian of Western Reserve. In 1909, he left Cleveland to accept the position of principal of M Street High School, in Washington, D.C., and remained there until he was appointed librarian of Howard University. Williams, one of the first blacks to receive a major appointment at a white school, left to teach in the black community.[4]

The policy of segregation and exclusion, so firmly grounded in academia, precluded the participation of black scholars even when they proved to be extremely qualified. Although W. E. B. DuBois was one of the most qualified scholars in the nation, he was never accorded in academia the prestige he so richly deserved. DuBois graduated from Fisk University with his A.B. degree in 1888, but was required to enter Harvard as a junior. Still, he graduated *cum laude* in 1890, earning a second bachelor's degree. DuBois continued at Harvard, earning his M.A. degree in 1891 and his Ph.D. in 1895. His dissertation, *The Suppression of the African Slave Trade to the United States of America, 1638–1870,* was published in 1896 as the first book in the Harvard Historical Series.[5]

DuBois studied at the best universities in America, and in Europe at the University of Berlin. Despite his impeccable credentials, he was not offered a teaching job at a white institution. His first academic job was at Wilberforce University in Ohio, where he taught Greek and Latin. In 1896–97, he accepted the position of assistant instructor in sociology at the University of Pennsylvania, where he was hired to study Philadelphia's largely black Seventh Ward. But his year at the university was not a pleasant one. Recalling his appointment and experience, DuBois later wrote:

I was offered a salary of $800 for a period limited to one year. I was given no real academic standing, no office at the University, no official recognition of any kind; my name was even eventually omitted from the catalogue; I had no contact with students, and very little with members of the faculty, even in my department.[6]

Clearly DuBois was ostracized and isolated from the rest of the academic community at the University of Pennsylvania. This isolation did not prevent DuBois from successfully completing the project. After a year of scholarly research, he produced *The Philadelphia Negro* (1899), a study of the conditions under which Negroes were forced to live in the city of "brotherly love." This study was reviewed in a number of periodicals. The *Yale Review* noted that *The Philadelphia Negro* was "a credit to American scholarship and a distinct and valuable addition to the world's stock of knowledge concerning an important and obscure theme." The *Outlook* reported that the study was a balanced account and said of DuBois, "he is less apologetic than a generous-minded white writer might be."[7]

When DuBois completed his study, he was again forced by race prejudice and discrimination to turn to the black academic community for employment. In 1897, he joined the faculty of Atlanta University in Georgia as professor of economics and history. There he continued his brilliant career as a scholar. He was also one of the founders of the Niagara Movement, and later, the National Association for the Advancement of Colored People (NAACP).

DuBois himself was keenly aware that at the turn of the century few blacks were qualified to teach in either black or white colleges. But he placed primary blame on the white colleges' neglect and their indifference to the possibility of employing black scholars. In support of this assertion, DuBois stated that "there were a great many Negroes, who if they knew there was going to be a chance of that sort, would have prepared for it."[8]

W. E. B. DuBois and other enlightened educators knew even then that it would take a massive effort on the part of the federal government to reverse the national policy of segregation and racial discrimination. But instead of providing an affirmative approach, the government itself became part of the problem. After receiving the political support of the journalist William Monroe Trotter, DuBois, and other black leaders, President Woodrow Wilson betrayed that support and gave his sanction to segregation in Washington government offices. During World War I, blacks literally had to fight for the right to die to make the world safe for the democracy from which they were excluded.

Education of Black Americans between the World Wars

The demand for labor during the war years improved the black economic position in relation to the white worker; but, the new economic status of the black worker was very tenuous, and was shattered after the war when white men returned to claim "their jobs." The policy of racism had become so ingrained in American society that these white men naturally assumed that they should receive preference for jobs based upon their race, regardless of their qualifications. The reward black veterans received for having helped make the world safe for democracy was a return to an atmosphere charged with racial prejudice and hostility. Violence against blacks reached its peak during the summer of 1919, described as the "Red Summer" by the author James Weldon Johnson.

Blacks were more and more convinced between the two world wars that the type of vocational-industrial education provided had not prepared them for the realities of the twentieth century. With poor academic and outmoded vocational training, they were ill-prepared for labor unionism, factory systems, mass production, and corporate enterprise. A 1917 survey of Negro education by the U.S. Bureau of Education and the Phelps-Stokes Fund revealed the serious weaknesses of black higher education and simultaneously noted the overwhelming desire of blacks to obtain an education. After the publication of the survey, there were serious attempts on the part of black colleges to improve substantially the quality of their training. Since most of them were located in the South, they could expect little financial assistance from the very state governments whose responsibility it was to provide all their citizens with educational opportunities. Even less aid was forthcoming from the federal government.

Since both state and federal governments sanctioned the policy of separate but equal, it was incumbent upon them to enforce the law as laid down in the *Plessy* decision. The states maintained rigidly enforced educational systems, but made no attempt to provide a semblance of equality in financial support and facilities. The federal government quietly acquiesced in its responsibility to provide blacks with equal protection under the law. Although education was by no means the responsibility of private foundations and funds, they attempted to fill the void left by unresponsive state and federal governments, but they lacked the resources to adequately address the needs of black institutions.

A subsequent survey in 1927 illustrated the amount of progress which had been achieved. The survey had been prompted by the continued failure of blacks to get into medical schools. One result was the publication of a list of thirty-one black colleges capable of offering premedical work. Heretofore, black colleges had been forced to devote a large portion of their resources to providing elementary and secondary education for their students since most southern states, through their educational policies, deliberately did not provide adequate precollege facilities or financial resources for black students. Although most black colleges were able to eliminate their primary and secondary departments by the time the report was published, much remained to be done to bring these schools to collegiate standards. Since southern states maintained a policy of providing inferior education for blacks, institutions continued to suffer from lack of financial support, poor library facilities, inadequate laboratory equipment, poor administration, and insufficient teacher preparation.

The effort to improve the quality of education was a constant, uphill battle. It was not until 1930 that black educators succeeded in getting the Southern Association of Colleges and Secondary Schools to establish a system of inspections, not to qualify black colleges for membership, but to place them on a "special" list of black institutions "approved" by the association. White scholars failed to protest this discriminatory treatment. This continued emphasis on forced segregation and continued low-level funding prevented black educators from experiencing the cross-fertilization with other educators so necessary for the development of good educational programs. White students and faculty members also suffered from being denied the experience of attending classes and working with blacks. Black institutions were not permitted membership in the association until 1957, only twenty years ago.

The inability of black institutions to produce more than a bare minimum of black graduate and professional students puts a severe strain on the black educational system. Xavier, Fisk, Howard, and Atlanta universities, and Hampton Institute were the only black institutions offering adequate graduate and professional education for blacks in the South, but even these had a combined enrollment of only 300 students and graduated only 76 students with the master of arts degree in the 1932–33 school year. Since no black institution awarded the doctorate and few had professional programs, blacks were dependent upon predominantly white institutions for advanced study. The failure of white institutions to respond to the needs of black students is readily apparent when one considers that prior to 1929, there were only 51 blacks awarded the doctorate, the first one in 1876.

As black institutions through their own efforts strengthened the quality of their programs and challenged white colleges to admit more of their black students, the number of blacks who were awarded the doctorate increased to 119, all awarded between 1935 and 1939. Of the 379 blacks who received their Ph.D.'s between 1876 and 1943, 316 had received them between 1930 and 1943. Although there were a total of 38,765 Ph.D.'s awarded between 1926 and 1942, only 335 or substantially less than 1 percent were black Ph.D. recipients. Most of these Ph.D. recipients had been trained as undergraduate students in black institutions before going on for graduate work in the major white universities. While colleges and universities did not require that all or even most of their faculty members possess the doctorate, they continued to ignore capable blacks who, by all objective standards, qualified to teach in academia. There were, however, one or two exceptions. William A. Hinton's appointment as an instructor of bacteriology and immunology at Harvard University was one such anomaly. Dr. Hinton served as instructor from 1921 to 1946, lecturer from 1946 to 1949, and then in 1949 was finally promoted to clinical professor in honor of his achievements. It was the first time in Harvard's 313-year history that a black had been appointed to the rank of professor. In 1950, Dr. Hinton retired as professor emeritus.

Hinton was born in 1883 in Chicago, the son of former slaves. He received his B.S. degree from Harvard College in 1905, but lacked sufficient funds to continue his medical studies. While teaching at a number of black institutions, he continued his studies of bacteriology and physiology during summer sessions at the University of Chicago. He finally entered Harvard's Medical School in 1909, completing his course in three years. He was offered, but refused, a scholarship established for Negro students. In competition with his white fellow students, he won the Wigglesworth Scholarship and Hayden Scholarship. Because race prejudice prevented him from taking his internship at Boston Hospital, he accepted a part-time position at Wasserman Laboratory, then part of Harvard Medical School, where he taught serological techniques. In 1915 Wasserman Laboratory was transferred to the Massachusetts Department of Public Health. Dr. Hinton was then appointed assistant director of the Division of Biologic Laboratories and chief of Wasserman Laboratory. While remaining at Wasserman, he accepted the appointment of instructor of preventive medicine and hygiene at Harvard Medical School in 1918.

Dr. Hinton also published articles in well-known medical journals and became a foremost authority on syphilology. In 1936, he published the classic text on syphilis and its treatment.[9]

But Dr. Hinton's career was a rare exception; restrictive hiring policies literally forced blacks to teach in southern black colleges where they were denied the support necessary for academic advancement. A few black scholars were able to find employment in elite public high schools, such as Dunbar High School in Washington, D.C.

Although discriminatory hiring practices had some salutary effects—the high quality of education offered at such high schools as Dunbar and Frederick Douglass in Baltimore—their overall effects were far more negative. There was a tendency for some Negro scholars teaching in Negro colleges to become isolated and conservative, emphasizing teaching to the exclusion of research. They had to please cautious administrators as well as hostile white communities to keep college funding and to avoid threats to personal security. Describing the plight of black scholars, sociologist E. Franklin Frazier wrote that Negro college teachers were forced to seek employment in black institutions because they could not find employment elsewhere.[10] Echoing the comments of Frazier, Christopher Jencks and David Riesman remarked that black scholars did not enjoy the "safety net" of going North if they lost their jobs. Should such events occur, the only alternative in many cases would be to seek employment in a "poorly paid federal civil service job," such as in the U.S. Post Office.[11] In sum, black scholars were denied opportunities to teach on white campuses, to do scholarly supported research, and to have contact with the larger academic community. To retain their positions in black schools, they were often forced to adopt cautious and conservative attitudes. Thus, during the years 1900 to 1940, black scholars were in an untenable position. Their plight was an indictment against the entire higher education community.

World War II brought an increased awareness on the part of blacks, as well as an increase in their demand for the elimination of legal obstacles and a push for racial equality. The legal foundation for the elimination of segregated education began during the 1930s, when the NAACP developed and implemented a systematic plan for attack on the doctrine of separate but equal. A break in the doctrine of separate but equal occurred when the Supreme Court ordered the admission of Lloyd Gaines to the University of Missouri Law School. But Gaines disappeared "mysteriously" before he could even attempt to enroll, and was never seen again. As a result of the court decision, Missouri opened a separate law school for blacks in order to avoid integration.

As the NAACP launched the attack on segregated education, A. Philip Randolph initiated a major protest against discrimination in the U.S. military and defense industries. Only after he received the threat of a massive march on Washington did President Franklin D. Roosevelt relent and issue Executive Order 8802 in 1941, which was designed to end discrimination in the defense industry and which established the Fair

Employment Practice Committee (FEPC). (*See* chapter three for a detailed discussion of the FEPC and the development of the government contract compliance program.) Although weak, it was the first concrete effort on the part of the federal government since Reconstruction to deal with the systemic nature of prejudice and discrimination. Although totally inadequate for the task at hand, the establishment of the FEPC marked a turning point in federal policy toward black people. Nearly seventy years had elapsed before the federal government attempted in any way to eliminate public practices of inequality. Blacks obtained some jobs in defense industries but segregation, albeit not discrimination, in the armed services did not end until after President Harry Truman issued his Executive Order 9981 in 1948.

Education of Blacks in the Postwar Years: Policy of Exclusion Yields to Experimentation

In institutions of higher education, policies of "exclusion" gradually yielded in a few instances to policies of "experimentation." From 1940 to 1946, approximately twenty-six blacks were appointed to the faculties of northern white universities. Several reasons had been advanced for an interest in hiring black scholars. The Second World War caused a shortage of faculty members in all institutions of higher education. This fact, plus the work of philanthropic boards, served to spearhead the entry of a few black scholars onto white campuses. In 1941, Dr. Allison Davis was appointed to a full-time position at the University of Chicago, breaking the modern racial barrier in higher education. The Julius Rosenwald Fund was instrumental in helping Dr. Davis secure his appointment. Long active in trying to secure appointments of qualified black scholars to white faculties, the foundation provided funds to supplement the salaries of prospective black instructors.[12]

In 1946, the University of Chicago appointed Abram L. Harris, another black scholar, as a member of its faculty. Dr. Harris, the descendant of former slaves, received his B.A. degree from Virginia Union in 1922 and his Ph.D. in economics from Columbia University in 1931. He began his teaching career at West Virginia State College in 1924, and later moved to Howard University in 1927 where he remained until he received a full-time appointment at the University of Chicago in 1946. At Chicago, he engaged in the study of economic philosophy.

In 1931, Dr. Harris published with Sterling D. Spero *The Black*

Worker and the Labor Movement. He published *The Negro as Capitalist* in 1936. He also worked tirelessly for the unification of black and white workers at a time when such sentiments were not popular.[13]

The new phenomenon—the hiring of black instructors—had, according to a most optimistic assessment in the *Negro College Quarterly,* "assumed the proportions of an epidemic; and we hope that it will continue to spread, for its effects can only prove wholesome and salutary to American democracy."[14] This breakthrough in higher education, together with the lifting of racial barriers in professional baseball and the ending of segregation in the armed forces, seemed to indicate to many optimists the coming of a new era in race relations.

But in opposition to this optimism lay the reality that only forty-three northern colleges and universities had black faculty members during the mid-1940s and not all of these black appointments were for permanent positions. A survey of predominantly white institutions toward the end of the decade indicated that approximately 72 of the 1,051 colleges employed black teachers. Some black scholars were hired only as visiting lecturers for a summer, a semester, or for a year. Professor Sterling A. Brown of Howard University, for example, taught at Vassar College during the academic year 1945–46; at the University of Minnesota during the summer of 1946; and at the New School for Social Research in New York City during the spring of 1947.[15] These men increased, usually by 100 percent, the black faculty on white campuses, but only on a temporary basis. White higher education was still closed to black scholars.

For example, an outstanding American scholar, E. Franklin Frazier, was excluded from white academia during the 1940s, but was appointed as Resident Fellow of the Library of Congress. Frazier, the son of a bank messenger, graduated with honors from Howard University in 1916 with an A.B. degree. Frazier studied at the Russell Sage Foundation, the Columbia University School of Social Work, and the University of Chicago, where he received his Ph.D. degree. He also spent a year at the University of Copenhagen. From 1922–27 he was director of the Atlanta University School of Social Work and an instructor of sociology at Morehouse College. His work on race relations forced him to flee Atlanta because whites reacted so strongly against his indictments. He published his classic study, *The Negro Family in the United States,* in 1939, which received the Aimsfield Award for its contribution to race relations, and later the *Black Bourgeoisie* in 1957 (French edition, 1955). Although an outstanding scholar and former Resident Fellow of the Library of Congress, he did not receive a full appointment at a major white institution until 1957 when he joined the faculty of the Johns Hopkins School of International Studies in Washington, D.C.[16] Frazier, despite his preparation and experience, was excluded from mainstream academic institutions for most of his career.

The majority of American colleges and universities did not see the need to reverse their policies of exclusion based upon the irrelevant criteria of race and to appoint qualified blacks to fill even temporary slots or to expose their students to black instructors. In June 1945 Fred G. Wale, of the Julius Rosenwald Fund, brought to the attention of 509 college presidents in the North and West the fact that there were only fifteen Negroes on formerly all-white faculties, up from the two the fund had found in 1941 and who were employed in *non*-teaching positions. Wale had hoped to arouse the interest of college administrators in adding blacks to their faculties. He informed the college presidents that there were over two hundred Negroes with Ph.D. degrees and each year two to three hundred were awarded the master's degree. Wale suggested that the 509 college administrators take advantage of the fund's supply pool in making faculty appointments.[17]

Only 160, or 31 percent, responded to Wale's letters. Of course, half simply replied as did C. B. Hershey, acting president of Colorado College: "We are placing this list in file for future reference." Others expressed sympathy, as did Clarence E. Josephson of Heidelberg College, Tiffin, Ohio, who admitted an interest in integrating his faculty but said that he had his hands full trying to protect the rights of a small group of colored students. He added:

In particular I have run into some difficulty in finding a place for one of these students, who intends to become a public school teacher, to secure her practice teaching. She was refused the privilege by the public schools of our city.[18]

Almost anticipating the current arguments against affirmative action, Herbert G. Espy, president of State Teachers College of Genesee, New York, raised the issue of "whether they [his department chairmen] will feel that the educational needs of our students now warrant our making any special effort to employ Negro teachers or to discriminate against white applicants." Wale's response was that he did not feel the "consideration" of a black applicant constituted discrimination against a white applicant.[19]

Other college administrators who responded to the Rosenwald Fund letter did not indicate a positive attitude toward hiring blacks. Several of the letters cited geographic location as a possible hindrance—too far North or in one case "too close to the Ohio River."[20] Another respondent wrote: "I must confess it seems eminently unwise for a college as small as this in a community of a few thousand with only one Negro family living in it to consider the employment of a Negro staff member."[21] Yet, from a northern city with a sizable black population came this response: "In a city of this size with so large a Negro community it seems best to us that a college for Negro students employing Negro faculty members could and should be supported by the community itself."[22] These responses to the Wale letter clearly indicate the lack of "good faith" efforts to hire black faculty members in the mid-1940s.

Such comments and statements led blacks and some white liberals to question the paucity of black scholars in white institutions. In late 1947 and early 1948, members of the Education Committee of the Cornell University Branch of the NAACP, concerned about the lack of any black faculty members there, questioned the various department chairmen. Seventy-one percent of the department chairmen answered no to the question, "Would you have any hesitation about employing a qualified Negro on your staff?" Seemingly, a major barrier against the hiring of blacks—reluctance by the department chairmen—did not exist throughout most of the university. But the more important question raised by the committee was "Why do you think there are no Negroes on the faculty at Cornell?" A majority of the chairmen claimed that blacks lacked adequate qualifications. Others claimed that black scholars had never applied for positions or were more committed to black institutions. While a majority of chairmen faulted black scholars, directly or indirectly, for the absence of black instructors, several chairmen recognized that the blame lay with the institutions. They cited "discrimination," "tradition," or "other institutions are not doing it" as excuses. Only one chairman acknowledged the situation as it existed. His candid observation was "we haven't been pushed to it. Easiest way out is not to have done it."[23]

This response illustrated that without some form of coercion academic institutions were unwilling to hire blacks who were as qualified and often more qualified than those whites teaching in white colleges and universities. Although there was not an overabundance of outstanding scholars, there were, in the 1940s, a substantial number of blacks who held the Ph.D. While the teaching load in black institutions often precluded research and publication, there were those who could have met the "qualification standards" of some of the best schools in the country during the 1940s.

For example, Rayford W. Logan, the historian, graduated Phi Beta Kappa from Williams College in 1917. After serving in the U.S. Army during World War I, he completed his M.A. in history at Williams. He received another M.A. from Harvard University in 1932 and his Ph.D. in 1936. He served as head of the Department of History, Atlanta University from 1933 to 1938. In 1938, he joined the Department of History at Howard University and assumed the chairmanship in 1942. During the decade of the 1940s he published *The Diplomatic Relations of the United States with Haiti 1776–1891* (1941), *What the Negro Wants* (editor and contributor, 1944), *The Senate and the Versailles System* (1945), *The Negro in the Post War World: A Primer* (1945), and *The African Mandates in World Politics* (1948), in addition to numerous articles in journals.[24]

Another outstanding scholar was Charles R. Drew, a surgeon whose pioneer work in blood research saved innumerable lives during World War II. Dr. Drew graduated from Amherst College in 1926, and received the M.D. degree from McGill Medical College in 1933, at the age of twenty-nine. In 1935, he joined the faculty of Howard University Medical School. While on a General Education Board Fellowship to Columbia University Medical School, he continued his work in blood research. In 1940, he published the result of his research, *Banked Blood: A Study in Blood Preservation,* for which Columbia University awarded him the degree of Doctor of Science. During the war he was selected as director of the American Red Cross Blood Bank. In this capacity, Dr. Drew found he was forced to segregate human blood by race. Because of this controversy and the fact that he held such a high post, he was finally "released" from his duties. He continued his brilliant career at Howard University until his untimely death in 1950.[25]

Percy L. Julian, an internationally known organic chemist, was born in Montgomery, Alabama, the son of a railway clerk. Although he lacked a prestigious educational background when he began college, he graduated from De Pauw University in 1920 as valedictorian and a member of Phi Beta Kappa. He taught chemistry at Fisk University in Nashville, Tennessee, before going to Harvard where he received his master's degree in 1923. He remained at Harvard until 1926, serving as research fellow in biophysics, then as a George and Martha Derby Scholar in chemistry, and finally as University Scholar. As a General Education Fellow, he completed the work for his Ph.D. at the University of Vienna in 1931.

For a short time, he served as head of the chemistry department at Howard University. Between 1932 and 1936, he served as research fellow and teacher of organic chemistry at De Pauw University. In 1936, Dr. Julian became director of research of the Soya products division of the Glidden Company of Chicago. He remained there for seventeen years during which time he made many of his cortisone drugs. Dr. Julian was a primary example of outstanding achievement in spite of inadequate preparation during his early educational career.[26]

In addition to those scholars cited previously, there were many other blacks who qualified by standard criteria to teach in predominantly white institutions prior to 1950. To note a few, there were in history John Hope Franklin, Benjamin Quarles, Carter G. Woodson, Charles H. Wesley, Alrutheus Taylor, Merze Tate, Harold O. Lewis, Chancellor Williams, and many others.

In other fields, briefly, there were: Ambrose Caliver, Dwight Oliver Wendell Holmes, William Allison Davis, Charles Thomas, Benjamin Mays, Horace Mann Bond, John Hope, and John W. Davis in education; Dorothy Porter in library science; James A. Porter in art; Kenneth Clark in psychology; Ralph J. Bunche in political science; W. Montague Cobb in medicine; William H. Hastie and Charles H. Houston in law; Sterling Brown, Alain Locke (the first black Rhodes Scholar), Eva Beatrice Dykes, and Arthur P. Davis in literature; Frank M. Snowden in classics; Ernest E. Just in biology; and Frederick D. Wilkinson in engineering.

This list could go on and on, but from the people cited it is evident that black scholars teaching and researching in the black academic community were a potential source of faculty members for white institutions. But, for the most part, this potential source remained untapped because forced exclusion was institutional policy. It should also be noted that the people named previously were outstanding scholars who were, for all practical purposes, ignored by white institutions that employed substantial numbers of white professors who neither held the doctorate nor excelled in their disciplines. It is clear that race and not scholarship was the overriding consideration in deciding to exclude blacks from predominantly white institutions.

The *Brown* Decision and the Education of Black People

Many blacks hoped that the Supreme Court's 1954 *Brown* decision would encourage all educational institutions to drop their artificial barriers excluding blacks. That decision came some sixteen years after the NAACP had carefully developed its assault on segregation by first attacking the absence of graduate and professional education for blacks in the South. Having experienced substantial success in this respect in the late forties and early fifties, the NAACP, with other organizations and individuals, prepared a direct assault on the doctrine of separate but equal. The suit, in effect, asked the nation to reverse the precedent established by the *Plessy* decision, even though it could not reverse the immeasurable damage suffered under it by generations of black people. For decades black children had been segregated, but at no time had they been provided equal facilities and other forms of educational support. Evidence of this inequality arose as parents in the South sought legal redress. Three cases that arose in Virginia in the 1940s were indicative of the inequality which existed throughout the South. The plaintiffs alleged that "the school boards of the counties have discriminated against the plaintiffs on account of their race and color in that the public schools maintained for the colored children are greatly inferior in construction, equipment and facilities, libraries and transportation service to those provided for the use of white children." The plaintiffs provided evidence to support their allegations: in 1945–46, 52 percent of the black teachers held degrees compared to 27 percent of the white teachers. Yet, white male and female high school teachers earned $2,508.33 and $1,969.92 per year, respectively, while the salaries for black male and female high school teachers were $1,850 and $1,920, respectively.

The same discrepancies existed in facilities. Between 1943 and 1946, there were at least four times as many volumes in white libraries as in black. During the same years, one white high school had laboratory equipment valued at $2,500, while the school for black youths had no equipment of value. In one county during 1943–44, the value of sites and buildings used for white schools was reported at $236,000, while the value of sites and buildings for black children was listed at $18,000. It was clear from this evidence that discrimination based on race existed.[27] It was also clear that case by case litigation would entail large expenditures and take an extraordinarily long time to eliminate segregation in publicly supported schools. The NAACP, therefore, decided to make a frontal attack and take the issue before the Supreme Court.

The Supreme Court agreed to consolidate four other cases with *Brown* v. *Board of Education of Topeka* after a federal district court had ruled against Brown in 1951. The problem posed by the NAACP was that segregation in and of itself was damaging to black children. In its unanimous opinion, the Court found, in all five cases, that school segregation violated the Constitution. Largely bypassing the legal and historical complexities of the case, Chief Justice Earl Warren stated that it was obvious that segregation in the twentieth century imposed an inferior status on the Negro and violated the equal protection clause of the Fourteenth Amendment. This decision also had far-reaching implications for institutions of higher education.

Although the Court found that the black children had a categorical right under the Fourteenth Amendment to attend nonsegregated schools, it did not provide them immediate access to that right. Instead, the Court chose to take into consideration the social revolution involved in the case and ordered desegregation "with all deliberate speed." While ruling unequivocally that segregation in public schools deprived black children of equal protection of the law, the Court provided only a deferred and gradual extension of the rights of black children to desegregated education. In fact, not a single black child involved in the case from Clarendon County, South Carolina, and Prince Edward County, Virginia, ever attended desegregated schools. After the 1954 *Brown* decision, another whole generation of black children was forced to remain in inferior, segregated elementary and secondary schools. These same children were expected to compete with better prepared students in gaining admission to colleges, universities, and professional schools in the 1960s. What minimal efforts were made to compensate them for their inferior education created opposition and allegations of "reverse discrimination" in the 1960s which have continued into the 1970s.

Protracted campaigns in some southern states in the late 1950s were used to nullify the landmark decision through what was termed "massive resistance." The long dormant idea of "interposition" was resurrected. Laws were passed which allowed local school officials to transfer students to maintain segregation; funds were diverted from public schools to segregated private schools; and as a last resort, some public schools were closed, as in Prince Edward County, Virginia. The examples of Governors Orval Faubus in Little Rock, Arkansas, in 1957 and George Wallace at the University of Alabama in 1963 established the pattern followed by whites as they attempted to nullify the *Brown* decision. Charles H. Thompson, writing in the *Journal of Negro Education* in 1956, observed that:

there is something strangely familiar about the way much of the white South is behaving over the U.S. Supreme Court's decision outlawing segregated public schools; even to the truculence, intransigence, demagoguery, and callous disregard for the best interest of the region. Much of the South, as it did during

Reconstruction, continues to look backward to an era that is dead and that is merely awaiting a decent burial; irresponsible attacks are being made upon the Supreme law of the land by many leaders who should set a more sensible and constructive example for their followers; White Citizens Councils—"Uptown Ku Klux Klans," as Hodding Carter so aptly designated them—have sprung up in many areas as did the original Klans under General Forest, and similarly give every indication of getting out of hand; complaints are again being voiced that the South is being misunderstood and maligned and that all that needs to be done is to leave her alone and she will solve the problem, despite 80 years of being "let alone," with the result that the region is no better off, as far as race relations are concerned, than it was in 1877.[28]

"Good Faith" Efforts and the Higher Education Community

Just as the nation was slow in integrating students at all levels, little progress had been achieved by 1958 in integrating college faculties. Approximately 200 Negro teachers were employed in continuing capacities in predominantly white institutions of higher learning. To rectify that scant number, Professor James A. Moss suggested that there should be a "commitment on the part of employing officials in white colleges to translate affirmative, positive attitudes toward nondiscriminatory hiring into broad recruitment practices involving both white and Negro colleges."[29] In bold language, predating that of later executive orders, Professor Moss was calling for white colleges to adopt sincere nondiscriminatory hiring practices and to expand their sources of recruitment. In spite of the Moss suggestion, Theodore Caplow and Reece J. McGee stated that "discrimination on the basis of race appears to be nearly absolute. No major university in the United States has more than a token representation of Negroes on its faculty, and these tend to be rather specialized persons who are fitted in one way or another for such a role."[30]

Few colleges, even in the 1960s, seriously heeded Professor Moss's suggestions about nondiscriminatory hiring and broadening of recruitment practices. The number of black scholars on white campuses had risen to close to three hundred, according to Harold M. Rose in a 1961 study.[31] But Jencks and Riesman concluded that "the men who teach in Negro colleges are less in demand than men who teach in white colleges."[32] Yet, optimism was the general keynote of the early 1960s. One author was confident that the projected boom in college enrollment and the increases in the number of black Ph.D.'s would open up more opportunities for blacks in northern and western colleges and universities.[33]

A follow-up study conducted in 1966 stated that the 1960s so far had been "the period of greatest Negro advance in an unrestricted marketplace." Based on a 20 percent sample, Harold M. Rose asserted that the number of black scholars on white campuses had risen 108 percent. In real numbers, based on a 20 percent sample, over a four-year period this meant an increase from 65 blacks in 1960 to 136 blacks in 1964.[34]

Earlier in this chapter the result of a 1945–47 survey by the Rosenwald Fund was reported; it indicated the paucity of Negroes employed at white institutions. Over two decades later the Southern Education Reporting Service (SERS) conducted a similar survey of the same institutions in 1967–68. In the institutions responding to the survey, there had been some improvements in the number of Negroes employed. It was evident that the percentages had increased ever so slightly from 0.002 percent in 1945–47 to 0.009 percent in 1967–68. Table 2-1 illustrates the extent of "progress" made by the institutions participating in the survey.[35] Although the surveys did not include all institutions and used different populations and did not allow for biased responses, they do, at a minimum, indicate the slow rate of progress up to the 1967–68 academic year.[36]

Critics of affirmative action, most notably Thomas Sowell, would argue that this increase and subsequent increases in the absolute number of black faculty members up to 1971 were the effects of the "straightforward antidiscrimination laws of the 1960s and of the general drive toward racial integration."[37] Yet, in 1960, 5,910 blacks were employed as college and university teachers. This represented slightly more than 3 percent of the total number of college and university teachers.[38] During the academic year 1968–69, blacks composed 2.2 percent of the faculties nationwide, including those working in historically black colleges; in academic year 1972–73, blacks comprised 2.9 percent of college and university faculties.[39] Thus the proportion of blacks on college and university faculties actually declined from 3 percent in 1960.

Prior to 1973, it was evident that predominantly white institutions of higher education had not trained and recruited blacks in large numbers and had not changed their hiring policy of exclusion based upon race. Predominantly white institutions, responding to the civil rights movement of the 1960s, began to recruit more students, but many did not alter their hiring practices to make their faculties more reflective of the society at large. Paul E. Wisdom and Kenneth A. Shaw, in 1970,

TABLE 2-1. Rosenwald Fund Survey, 1945–47 and the Southern
Education Reporting Service Survey, 1967–68

	1945–47	1967–68
Number of institutions contacted	600	179[1]
Number replying	179	138
Percent response	29.8	77.1
Number of respondents supplying complete information	178	130
Number of respondents reporting Negro faculty members	42	79
Percentage reporting Negro faculty members employed	23.6	60.7
Total number of Negro faculty members reported	75	577[2]
Total number of all faculty at institutions supplying information for the survey (approx.)	40,000	60,000
Percentage of Negroes on the faculties of all institutions supplying information for the survey	0.002	0.009[2]
Estimated number of Negroes in the U.S. having completed five or more years of college	3,550[3]	194,000[4]

1. The institutions represented by this number are the same as the ones which replied to the 1945–47 survey.

2. The number listed in the SERS survey was 785 but one institution listed 208 black professionals without differentiating academic from other types. Since the data was so questionable, it was deleted, giving a total of 577 and a percentage of 0.009 instead of 0.013.

3. An estimate made by Fred G. Wale of the Rosenwald Fund in 1947.

4. Estimated by the U.S. Bureau of the Census, March 1966.

Source: Rosenwald Fund Survey and the Southern Education Reporting Service Survey.

suggested that black students came to college "to prepare themselves meaningfully to deal with the problems they faced as black people in a black community. It is only when they arrive on the campus and realize how totally white it is that they become reformists or revolutionists." They further concluded that the reason for this phenomenon was that these black students found all areas of academia controlled by whites to the total exclusion of blacks. Blacks correctly identified the problems: (1) institutional racism, a charge most resented by white administrators; (2) the need for more black students on white campuses; and (3) the need for more black faculty and administrators. These demands, among others, were voiced on campuses across the nation. A response to these

demands was academia's last chance to act in "good faith" to correct
the inequality that was obvious to all, except those who refused to see.[40]

Wisdom and Shaw indicated that it was up to white faculties and
administrators to take positive steps to correct the inequality in academia. They must take steps to determine where the barriers are to
black employment and then eliminate them. Almost anticipating the
application of affirmative action in higher education, they suggested
evaluating the employment process and taking affirmative steps to recruit blacks. Acknowledging the limited number of available blacks,
they further suggested that training programs be established to increase
the available supply. Finally, special tutoring and other compensatory
measures should be expanded to reach those students with college potential who have been severely handicapped by an inferior educational
system and a cultural and economic background.[41]

By the early 1970s, in spite of the increased emphasis on civil rights
and allegedly fair employment practices, the proportion of black
faculty members still had not reached the 1960 level. What this suggests
is a failure of colleges in putting forth a "good faith" effort in training
black graduate students and in recruiting and hiring black faculty members during the 1960s, when the academic market place rapidly expanded
to accommodate increased student enrollment. Further, this lack of
putting forth a "good faith" effort is reminiscent of the reluctance of
state public school systems to integrate after the *Brown* decision. Had
colleges and universities been totally sincere in their "good faith" efforts
as they now profess to have been, they would have initiated programs
to encourage prospective black students to enter graduate school during
the early to mid-1960s. The graduate school enrollments during these
years, therefore, would have contained many more blacks who would
be available for faculty positions in the 1970s.

Why Affirmative Action for Students

Black participation in graduate education has remained severely limited even in the 1970s. Only 3.5 percent of the doctorates awarded to
U.S. citizens in 1974 went to blacks.[42] Although minorities comprise
more than 16 percent of the total population, they comprise less than
6 percent of total graduate enrollments.[43] But even though blacks and
other minorities are still largely excluded from advanced study, many
of the programs designed to promote equal opportunity in higher
education have come under vehement attack in recent years. Since

affirmative action depends on a qualified pool of candidates available for faculty employment, both the continuing inequalities in graduate education and the evident decline in support for special admissions efforts threaten the future success of affirmative action programs.

During the 1960s, under pressure from civil rights groups and activist students, many institutions of higher education that had traditionally excluded minorities established special recruitment and admissions policies.* More than eight hundred undergraduate institutions provided some form of special help for minority and disadvantaged students by 1970, although the scope and degree of formality of these programs differed from institution to institution.[44] Through special recruitment of members of underrepresented groups, special selection measures for admission, and educational programs designed to help students with academic deficiencies, institutions succeeded in increasing the enrollment of minorities in institutions of higher education throughout the last decade. In absolute numbers enrollment of blacks in college increased from 306,000 in 1964 to 814,000 in 1974.[45] It is unlikely that without these efforts at the undergraduate level, as well as similar efforts at the graduate and professional level, black participation in graduate and professional schools would have increased as it has in recent years.

Private foundations have also played an important role in increasing black representation in graduate and professional schools. During the late 1960s and early 1970s, the Ford Foundation, among others, made substantial contributions to Howard and Atlanta universities and several predominantly white institutions in an effort to increase the number of black graduate students. In October 1971, the Ford Foundation initiated a six-year $100 million program to "improve the quality of a limited number of predominantly Negro private colleges and to provide various minority students with individual study awards at most types of institutions."[46] These grants enable minority students to take advantage of opportunities for graduate education in both predominantly black and white institutions.

Because there is no systematic collection of data on degree attainment by race at the associate arts or master's level, it is difficult to know how many blacks receive these advanced degrees. Figures for master's degress awarded in historically black colleges indicate that these schools awarded 2 percent of all master's degrees conferred in 1952–53; by

* See chapter three for a legal discussion of special minority admissions programs and chapter six for an examination of such programs at selected institutions.

1962–63 these schools awarded 1.5 percent of the 91,000 master's degrees earned in the United States. The best estimate of all master's degrees earned by black Americans in the years prior to the civil rights movement of the 1960s is between 2 and 4 percent.[47] In spring 1974, blacks received 5.3 percent of all baccalaureates awarded (half awarded by historically black colleges) and constituted 4.4 percent of graduate enrollments. These figures, though incomplete, do seem to indicate that once black students gain access to four-year institutions and graduate schools, they are likely to persist.[48]

Prior to 1968, as has been explained earlier in this chapter, black students received very few doctoral degrees. Although the data are sparse on the number of doctorates awarded from 1944 to 1968, a Ford Foundation survey indicated that during the period blacks received less than 1 percent of all American-earned doctorates. Since 1968 there have been sharp increases in the number of doctoral degrees awarded to U.S., native-born blacks. By 1972–73, 2.9 percent of doctorates awarded to U.S. native-born citizens went to blacks, and this rose to 3.5 percent in 1973–74.[49] According to the survey of earned doctorates, prepared by the National Research Council and published annually by the National Academy of Sciences, blacks received 5 percent of all doctorates awarded to U.S. native-born citizens in 1976.[50]

Despite these gains, however, it is evident that equal opportunity for blacks and other minorities in graduate education has not been achieved. The proportion of doctorates awarded to blacks still constitutes only a miniscule proportion of all doctorates awarded to Americans. Although blacks comprise approximately 11 percent of the national population, they received only 3.5 percent of doctorates in 1974; whites, comprising 83.1 percent of the population, received 94.5 percent of doctorates in that year. (*See* Table 2-2.) All minorities combined received 5.5 percent of all doctorates awarded. According to a study of the ISEP (1977), black enrollment in graduate and professional schools combined actually declined between 1973 and 1974. U.S. Census figures cited in the report indicate that in 1973, 7 percent of all graduate and professional students under thirty-five years of age were black, but their proportion of graduate/professional enrollment dropped to 6 percent in 1974.[51]

In the important professional fields of business, law, and medicine, minority enrollment has increased in recent years, but there is still a critical need for black lawyers and doctors in particular. Blacks represented 5 percent of the full and part-time students in American Bar

TABLE 2-2. Percentage Distribution of Estimated Graduate Enrollments, Doctorates Awarded, and U.S. Population by Race and Ethnic Identity

Racial/Ethnic Identity	Estimated Graduate Enrollments (%)	Doctorates Awarded to Native-born U.S. Citizens, 1973–74 (%)	Distribution in U.S. Population, 1970 (%)
Total	100.0	100.0	100.0
White	90.8–94.6	94.5	83.1
Total minority	5.4–9.1	5.5	16.9
Black	3.3–5.2	3.5	11.1
American Indian	0.3–0.4	0.5	0.4
Oriental	0.8–2.0	0.6	0.9
Spanish-surnamed	1.0–0.4	0.9	4.6
Mexican American, Chicano, Spanish American	—	(0.6)	(3.9)
Puerto Rican	—	(0.3)	(0.7)

Source: National Board on Graduate Education, *Minority Group Participation in Graduate Education* (Washington, D.C.: National Board on Graduate Education, 1976), p. 45.

Association-approved law schools in fall 1974. But there were fewer first-year black students in law school that year than in 1972.[52] Medical school enrollment for blacks increased substantially between 1969 and 1974, from 3 percent of all medical students to 6 percent. This increase, however, fell short of the goal set by the American Medical Association for 10 percent black enrollment by the mid-1970s.[53] Black doctors represented only 2 percent of all practicing doctors in the United States in 1974, and this shortage of doctors for the black community will continue throughout the decade unless more black students have access to medical school.

These figures, although they indicate the overall participation of blacks in graduate education, do not indicate many important facets of that participation. First, black students tend to cluster in certain areas of study where employment opportunities have been more available and where rigorous academic training, especially in mathematics and science, is not a prerequisite for graduate study. Black students, and minority students in general, tend to major in the social sciences and

TABLE 2-3. Doctorates Awarded (U.S. Citizens) FY 1976

Field	Total	Black	% Black
Physical Sciences (includes mathematics)	3,372	27	0.8
Engineering	1,523	12	0.7
Life Sciences	3,916	63	1.6
Social Sciences	5,684	172	3.0
Arts and Humanities	4,378	91	2.0
Education	7,071	667	9.4
Professions and Others	1,251	53	4.2

Source: Prepared by ISEP from the National Research Council, National Academy of Sciences, *Summary Report 1976 Doctorate Recipients from United States Universities* (Washington, D.C.: National Academy of Sciences, 1977), table 5, p. 24.

humanities, and a large proportion of those who major in the natural sciences in undergraduate school switch to the social sciences when attending graduate school. Education continues to be the most attractive field for black graduate students; in spring 1974, 59.2 percent of the 846 black doctoral recipients earned their degrees in education.[54] The low level of minority participation in graduate programs in such fields as mathematics, engineering, and the physical sciences means that few will be available for employment opportunities in these fields in coming years. The most recent data from the National Research Council indicate that between 1975 and 1976 there was an actual decline in doctorates awarded to blacks in the physical sciences. In 1975, 1.2 percent of Ph.D.'s awarded in the physical sciences went to blacks, but in 1976 only 0.8 percent went to blacks. (*See* Table 2-3.)

Another aspect of black enrollment in graduate programs is the length of time students take to complete doctoral training. In 1976, the median age at time of receipt of doctorate was 31.5 years for whites and 36.2 for blacks. Although black and white doctoral students were registered in graduate school for the same number of years, 6.0, the time lapse between attainment of the B.A. and of the doctorate was more than 12.5 years for blacks, and only 8.7 for whites.[55] These disparities can be explained to some extent by the overrepresentation of black graduate students in certain fields. In education, for instance, the field in which 60 percent of black doctorates are earned, students are usually older upon completion of the Ph.D. program, whereas in many scientific fields students move rapidly through doctoral study.[56] Because of the greater financial need of black graduate students, many of these students find it necessary to drop out periodically to work before continuing advanced study or to work while pursuing an advanced degree.

It is also important to note the continuing role of black colleges in providing opportunities for advanced study for black students. Twenty-eight black graduate schools award the master's degree and in 1972–73 conferred 5,545 M.A. degrees. Three of these institutions, Howard University, Atlanta University, and Meharry Medical College, confer doctoral degrees and awarded 5.7 percent of the doctorates earned by black U.S. citizens in 1972–73.[57] Approximately one-fifth of all black graduate students are enrolled in predominantly black institutions.[58]

Black graduate schools have experienced nearly phenomenal growth in recent years. In 1967, enrollment in black graduate schools was approximately 8,500; by 1973, it had increased to almost 20,000. That there is an obvious need for the continuation and support of these schools was emphasized by the National Board on Graduate Education.[59]

Many of the graduates of black colleges and black graduate schools who are currently making indispensable contributions to the nation in the arts, sciences, business and professions would have been excluded from higher education by the normal admissions policies of the nonminority institutions. If black institutions did not exist, many of the current generations of black applicants to higher education would suffer the same fate.[60]

Although these institutions have attracted large numbers of nonminority students in recent years, they are still in a unique position to contribute to the training of minority graduate students.

The continuing underrepresentation of blacks in higher education is due to many factors, including inadequate academic preparation and the vestiges of discriminatory admissions policies. But at the graduate level especially, financial need is a central obstacle to the completion of programs. As pointed out in a recent ISEP study, "for most blacks, as for low-income groups generally . . . financial aid is a major barrier to persistence in . . . graduate and professional schools. Because of the limited scope of the large federal and state student assistance programs, disadvantaged students wishing to pursue graduate training encounter barriers that their wealthier counterparts may not have to face."[61] The length of doctoral training, along with decreased employment opportunities for doctorate holders may also deter many qualified black students from pursuing advanced degrees.

Any efforts to increase black participation in graduate and professional education must take into account not only the special problems of blacks who do enroll in graduate study, but also the barriers blacks encounter in entering and persisting in undergraduate institutions. In 1974, only 8 percent of all blacks twenty-five to thirty-four years old had completed four or more years of college; of whites in the same age range, 21 percent had completed four or more years of college.[62] Until this gap in college attainment between blacks and whites is closed, graduate and professional enrollment and the number of black doctorate holders will remain low.

It is clear that blacks and other minorities will not receive a bigger share of the opportunities for graduate training and its rewards without a firm commitment on the part of institutions at all levels—secondary, undergraduate and graduate—and on the part of the federal and state governments. But graduate institutions, which have excluded minority students for so long from participation in high-quality graduate programs and from faculties, will bear the greatest responsibility. According to the National Board on Graduate Education study,

> Initiative must derive from the institutions themselves, since they have the fundamental responsibility for selecting those who will receive the benefits of advanced education. . . . While government and other organizations must provide assistance, such support should be viewed as a complement, not a substitute, to existing institutional activities.[63]

As evidenced by the continuing severe underrepresentation of blacks in graduate and professional schools, academic institutions have not yet fully accepted this responsibility.

The Continuing Controversy over Affirmative Action

The academic community was a leader during the 1960s in advocating elimination of discrimination outside the academic marketplace, but it has failed badly in setting its own house in order. The controversy over hiring minorities and women through affirmative action continues. An article by Malcolm J. Sherman in the 1975 winter issue of the *AAUP Bulletin* and letters in response illustrate that affirmative action has not been accepted as a positive means of bringing minorities and women into academia.[64] In his article, Professor Sherman charged that the Department of Health, Education, and Welfare (HEW) efforts at the State University of New York resulted in reverse discrimination against white males. The article illustrated the moral indignation of white males when allegations of reverse discrimination are raised. But even more important, the article brought to light the extent of current discrimination against minorities and women. The following year *AAUP* published letters in response to Sherman's article.[65]

Sandra Rubaii of Tompkins Cortland Community College raised some provocative questions in her letter:

Suddenly Mr. Sherman is concerned with reverse discrimination (which simply means discrimination against himself or those like him). Where was all this concern when the discrimination was against minorities and women?

In her concluding statement, Ms. Rubaii summarized the problem:

The question is no longer the one of uncovering discrimination. The facts are already in. The job is to correct it. . . . We are talking about institutionalized racism and sexism. We need full commitments to institutionalize change. . . . A naive trust in the hiring of the most qualified available persons has resulted in exactly the patterns of discrimination we now have in our institutions. Let us not continue to perpetuate them under the guise of liberal rhetoric.[66]

Other contributors correctly pointed out the restrictive quotas imposed by white institutions to restrict the admission of minorities and women to graduate and professional schools and their deliberate exclusion from faculty ranks. One writer noted that the integrity of academic hiring is no more undermined when emphasis is placed on hiring minorities and women than it was when they were excluded before affirmative action.[67] The truth of the matter is that the integrity of academia was seriously damaged prior to affirmative action and that affirmative action is an attempt to correct past discriminatory acts. Another writer correctly points out that many white males who are currently employed in academia gained their positions because minorities and women were excluded. As long as this system is allowed to continue, discrimination against minorities and women will continue, but to those who are currently in power this seems to be less of an evil than alleged "reverse discrimination."[68]

One cannot change the past, but one can learn from the mistakes of the past. One can readily see that there would have been no need for affirmative action had there been no race prejudice and subsequent black enslavement. Even given the years of enslavement, had the Freedmen's Bureau been adequately funded after the Civil War and allowed to continue its work, many of the practical problems black people now face could have been eliminated. Had not race prejudice and discrimination become institutionalized, there would be little need for special programs to deal with systemic discrimination today. The continuous failure of the nation, both North and South, to face up to its moral and legal obligation regarding blacks, and the extremely slow implementation of the 1954 *Brown* decision, only added more weight and complexity to the need for affirmative action today. If black children had been given an equal opportunity to receive quality education in 1954, by 1966 the number and quality of high school graduates could have been substantially increased and improved, which in turn would have increased the number of black college graduates in 1970 and consequently the number of black scholars available for graduate and professional schools. But these things did not happen.

Most colleges and universities now profess good intentions regarding nondiscriminatory hiring policies and these intentions, in themselves, are some improvement over their past practices. They have been, however, quite slow in translating good faith intentions into actions. Up until the 1940s black scholars for the most part were excluded from most college faculties. The period of experimentation in which black scholars generally taught at white schools on a part-time or temporary basis was replaced in the late 1950s and early 1960s by the beginning of integration where one or two black scholars were hired to teach. Such an attitude, to most of the more enlightened colleges and universities, symbolized good faith. American colleges and universities have always expressed their reluctance to raid the faculties of predominantly black institutions for senior faculty members. Yet they failed to hire new Ph.D.'s also. Indeed, they did not actively recruit black students until societal pressures and federal funds encouraged positive action. They did not urge or foster increased black participation in graduate school, a source of future black scholars. Out of callousness, indifference, or incumbent self-interest they have failed to provide the needed leadership in increasing employment opportunities for blacks and in rooting out discrimination in the academic community until compelled to do so by the federal government or the student body. Thus, the indictment leveled against white colleges and institutions by Professor Harold M. Rose is indeed valid:

The nation's colleges and universities are a product of the social order in which they have evolved. Our academic institutions have not taken a position of leadership in regard to the expansion of employment for Negro educators in the academic marketplace. They have reflected the ills of society rather than assumed a leadership role in attempting to alter the social order.[69]

Through affirmative action programs, institutions of higher education not only have the opportunity to prepare American youth for "life and leadership in a rapidly changing world," but also to vigorously promote equality of opportunity and thus the dignity of all people.

Chapter Three

Affirmative Action and the Law

Affirmative action programs are necessary today because history has taught the difficulty of enforcing civil rights policies from the Reconstruction period to the present without these types of programs. The various amendments to the Constitution, especially the Fourteenth Amendment, and civil rights acts, passed to provide a measure of equality to the freedmen, form the constitutional basis for affirmative action today. This chapter begins, therefore, with a discussion of the implications of these measures for the legality of affirmative action programs.

The Constitutional Basis for Affirmative Action*

Three overlapping and interrelated constitutional arguments can be made in support of affirmative action in general and special minority admissions programs: (1) The Civil War amendments and Reconstruction civil rights acts when construed together lead to the conclusion that they were adopted and enacted for the benefit primarily of blacks and secondarily for other discrete, insular, disadvantaged minorities similarly situated, and formally and incidentally for any group subjected to invidious discrimination. The primary and secondary purposes of these laws not only prohibit discrimination against blacks, but also impose an affirmative duty upon states to establish and secure equity and justice for blacks. The primary and secondary purposes take priority over the formal and incidental purpose of these laws.[1] (2) Although the equal protection clause of the Fourteenth Amendment may

* This section is primarily based upon two papers prepared by Kenneth S. Tollett, Director, Institute for the Study of Educational Policy, Howard University, Washington, D.C.

make a classification based upon race suspect, and thus subject to rigorous critical scrutiny, when a compelling legitimate state interest is secured by the classification, it will be constitutional. (3) The majority may constitutionally discriminate against itself. Professor J. H. Ely has stated this position in the following terms: "Regardless of whether it is wise or unwise, it is not 'suspect' in a constitutional sense for a majority, any majority, to discriminate against itself."[2]

Critics of the Warren Court have argued in the past that all laws should be neutral. But in reality, neutrality is largely an illusion. All laws in a sense discriminate or make distinctions. They create classifications, and classifications, just as conceptions, if they are meaningful and minimally ambiguous and vague, include and exclude something. This is the reason the Constitution condemns invidious discrimination or classifications, but not discrimination or classfications per se. Furthermore, it does not follow that all racial classifications are necessarily invidious. What the drafters of the Thirteenth, Fourteenth, and Fifteenth amendments were primarily concerned with was invidious discrimination against the freedmen or blacks. They were attempting to prevent the enactment and enforcement of laws and practices which would denigrate the position of blacks. The Black Codes and other oppressive activities of the Confederate states after the Civil War not only denigrated the position of blacks but also destroyed the life and property of many blacks, as is evident in the preceding chapter.

The Reconstruction amendments were adopted primarily for the benefit of blacks (freedmen). This does not mean that all Reconstruction laws were only for the benefit of blacks or that specific provisions were not primarily for the benefit of all. What it does mean is that the Reconstruction laws were policies designed to correct the problems and mischief which resulted from the previous policy of enslavement and discrimination. To achieve this goal, Congress passed, and the states adopted, the Thirteenth Amendment which freed the slaves. The Civil Rights Act of 1866[3] extended to blacks citizenship, the right to make contracts, to hold and enjoy property, to serve as witnesses, and to enjoy the equal benefits of all laws. It also provided criminal sanctions for violating these rights.[4] Except for formally freeing blacks, the Thirteenth Amendment and the 1866 Civil Rights Act remained practically dormant, so far as the welfare of blacks was concerned, until 102 years later when the Supreme Court held in *Jones* v. *Alfred H. Mayer Co.* (1968),[5] that the amendment empowered Congress in the 1866 act to prohibit private individuals from discriminating against blacks in the sale of property. The Court maintained that Congress could enact any legislation appropriate for "abolishing all badges and incidents of slavery." Obviously this analysis clearly supports affirmative efforts to reverse the effects of discrimination.

To assure the constitutionality of the 1866 Civil Rights Act, Congress proposed, and the states ratified, the Fourteenth Amendment. The first sentence of this amendment overruled the infamous 1857 *Dred Scott* decision,[6] and made blacks citizens of the United States and of the states wherein they resided. It prohibited abridging the privileges and immunities of citizens of the United States, depriving any person of due process of law, and denying any person the equal protection of the laws. Although the privileges and immunities clause was made practically meaningless in *The Slaughter House Cases* (1873), Justice Miller, in the course of his opinion, stated that he doubted whether any discrimination directed against a group other than "Negroes as a class, or on account of their race, will ever be held to come within the purview of [the equal protection clause]." He further stated that the "pervading purpose" of the Thirteenth, Fourteenth, and Fifteenth amendments was to secure the "freedom of the slave race" and to protect them "from the oppressions of those who have formerly exercised unlimited dominion over *him*."[7]

The Fifteenth Amendment was almost, if not completely, concerned with protecting the rights of blacks to vote. It prohibited abridging the right to vote "on account of race, color, or previous condition of servitude." "Previous condition of servitude" is less general than "race" and "color," and thus for all practical purposes the provision was primarily for the benefit of blacks. At the time of adoption of the Fifteenth Amendment only blacks had experienced a previous condition of servitude.

In addition to the 1866 Civil Rights Act, a series of other acts enacted by Congress between 1866 and 1875 were designed in large measure to protect the freedmen. In 1867 Congress made the reestablishment of government in the Confederate states conditional upon the ratification of new state constitutions written by delegates elected by citizens "of whatever race, color, or previous condition."[8] Two more civil rights acts were enacted in 1866 and 1867 to prevent southerners from reenslaving blacks in different disguises. The 1866 act was passed to prevent kidnapping[9] and to punish those found guilty of the crime; the 1867 act abolished and prohibited forever the system of peonage.[10] In 1870 Congress enacted the Enforcement Act[11] which was amended in 1871.[12] This act provided both civil and criminal relief against those who flouted or circumvented the rights secured by the Fourteenth and Fifteenth amendments. In 1871 Congress enacted another Enforcement Act,[13] or the Anti-Ku Klux Klan Act, in order to deal comprehensively with the violence of the Klan by prohibiting conspiracies to obstruct justice, to interfere with elections, and to deny to any person equal privileges and immunities. The Civil Rights Act of 1875[14] prohibited discrimination on the basis of race or color in inns, public conveyances on land or water, the theater, and other places of amusement.

This brief review of the Reconstruction amendments and civil rights acts is most important to make credible the contention that Congress, in proposing the amendments and in passing the civil rights acts, was preoccupied with the rights and interests of blacks. Structural analysis of these legal materials implies that when they are all considered together they make a strong case that Congress deliberately attempted to reverse the national policy of discrimination and secure a measure of equality for black people.

Thus, this analysis indicated that Congress fully intended to secure justice and freedom for blacks. Through these amendments and laws, a strong constitutional basis for affirmative action programs can be made. This constitutional and legal protection offered blacks can be extended to other minority groups similarly situated. Therefore, such groups as Spanish-speaking Americans and Native Americans logically should be entitled to a reversal of discrimination through affirmative action programs.

The Legality of Racial Classifications

The issue before the United States Supreme Court in the *Bakke* case is whether the equal protection clause of the Fourteenth Amendment permits schools to consider the racial or ethnic background of applicants as one factor in the selection of students. The California Supreme Court answered no. This question raises three major constitutional issues. The first is whether racial classifications are per se invalid. The second is whether they can withstand the strict scrutiny and compelling state interest test which is applied when classifications are based upon suspect classifications, such as race, or touch fundamental rights, such as travel. The third is whether in some special situations, race-conscious classifications need only meet the rational basis test.

Recent court decisions have already established that racial classifica-

tions are not per se invalid. Racial classifications have been used to
remedy racial discrimination in both public school desegregation and
public employment cases. Busing and considerations of racial balance
and proportion were upheld in *Swann* v. *Board of Education* (1971).[15]
Strict numerical quotas and ratios in hiring minorities have been decreed or approved by lower federal courts without the disapproval of
the U.S. Supreme Court.[16] Lower federal courts have invoked racial
distinctions in other areas, such as urban renewal, *Norwalk CORE* v.
Norwalk Redevelopment Agency (1968), and broadcast license renew-
als, *TV9 Inc.* v. *FCC* (1973).[17]

Clearly, where injuries and injustice have been inflicted on the basis
of race, race cannot be totally disregarded in compensating for or correcting them. The U.S. Supreme Court has not held that racial classifications are invalid per se. The Court has simply held that legislation
and state action based upon racial classifications carry a very heavy
burden of justification which must withstand the most rigid scrutiny.[18]
The *Loving* case struck down Virginia's antimiscegenation statute, saying that a valid racial classification must be "necessary to the accomplishment of some permissible state objective, independent of the racial
discrimination which it was the object of the Fourteenth Amendment
to eliminate." This means that the classification must be independent
of invidious racial discrimination and prove "necessary to promote a
compelling governmental interest."[19]

The Supreme Court has not yet clearly articulated what is meant by
a compelling governmental interest. In the educational context, a
strong argument could be made for the proposition that equal opportunity and the reversal of the legacy of discrimination are a compelling
government interest.[20] Thus, affirmative action programs which use
race to promote equal opportunity satisfy a compelling governmental
interest and make legal use of racial classifications. These efforts should
not be characterized as reverse discrimination, but should be recognized
as efforts to bring about the reversal of discrimination, and the legacy
of underrepresentation and the exclusion of minorities from opportunities. In *DeFunis* v. *Odegaard* (1974),[21] the Washington Supreme Court
found that the state had a compelling interest in correcting the underrepresentation of minorities in law schools and thus in the legal profession. Minorities are grossly underrepresented throughout higher education as both employees and students, particularly in graduate and
professional schools, as a result of failure to obtain equal opportunity
in the past.

Benign racial classifications are not always necessarily suspect. Although supporters of special minority affirmative action programs usually believe the "suspect classification" and "compelling state interest" tests apply,[22] two closely related arguments can be made in support of applying the conventional equal protection analysis to benign racial classifications. The conventional test requires only a rational relationship between the classification and a legitimate governmental interest.

First, if blacks and other similarly situated minorities are considered as the primary and secondary beneficiaries of the Reconstruction amendments, including, of course, the equal protection clause, then racial classifications clearly designed to benefit them would not violate the equal protection of the laws. Although on a number of occasions it might be difficult to determine whether a racial classification is clearly designed to benefit a minority, that is not the situation with special minority affirmative action programs. They are designed to expand minority groups' access to opportunities within the higher education sector.

Second, the equal protection requirement obviously is designed to protect discrete, insular, disadvantaged minorities from exploitation and oppression by the majority. Discrete, insular minorities tend to be less protected by the political process, and thus classifications touching them adversely should be rigorously scrutinized. This is not true of the majority group. Therefore, if a majority wished to correct past and present injustices perpetrated against a minority, then the equal protection clause should not require rigorous scrutiny.[23] A decision in favor of the board of regents in the *Bakke* case will not produce the same effect as *Plessy* v. *Ferguson* because blacks do not have the power to inflict the type of injury upon whites that they were authorized to inflict upon blacks by the fraudulent separate but equal doctrine. Special minority admissions programs do not deprive whites of any legitimate benefits. Moreover, even with affirmative action programs, minorities will continue to receive an unfairly small percentage of the opportunities in the higher educational sector for some time. (*See* chapter seven.)

The constitutional-legal discussions also apply to the most controversial aspect of affirmative action, that is, special minority admissions programs. Any substantial progress in increasing black academic employment through affirmative action programs must, of necessity, be tied to special minority admissions programs if more blacks are to be available for future employment. These programs are necessary to correct the underrepresentation of blacks in graduate and professional schools. This correction will assist in accomplishing the compelling state interest of reversing discrimination and the establishing of approximate proportional representation in the professional classes and other employment opportunities. Resistance to these objectives is largely a vestige of racism, as is evident in chapter two. The constitutional barriers to them are more apparent than real. The Reconstruction amendments and civil rights acts were primarily and secondarily for the benefit of blacks and other discrete disadvantaged minorities similarly situated. If race is regarded as a suspect classification requiring rigorous scrutiny in special minority admissions programs, it is necessary to accomplish the compelling state interest of reversal of discrimination and approximately proportional minority participation in graduate education. Once it is determined that the racial classification is benign, it can be argued that the rational basis test of constitutionality under the due process and equal protection clauses is applicable; this test requires a rational relationship between the classification and a legitimate governmental interest or objective.

The historical perspective tells us that blacks suffered in this country for nearly two hundred fifty years of slavery and one hundred years of officially sanctioned segregation, all of which oppressed, dehumanized, and injured blacks as human beings. The country made a positive attempt to correct the history of slavery in the Thirteenth, Fourteenth, and Fifteenth amendments to the Constitution and in the Reconstruction Civil Rights Act, but due, in part, to some of the Supreme Court decisions already mentioned, the attempt was unsuccessful. A decision in the *Bakke* case cannot appropriately be made without taking this history into account.

Whites have been unjustly enriched and advantaged in this society for over three hundred years at the expense, and to the injury, of blacks and other oppressed minorities. Principles of equity, justice, and morality require that when one has been unjustly enriched at the expense and to the injury of another, one should make restitution to the injured party. Providing restitution to those who have been injured by gross deprivations and oppression is not preferential treatment or reverse discrimination but compensatory assistance and the reversal of discrimination.

Blacks' and other minority groups' participation in all aspects of the higher educational sector has been substantially increased or improved by affirmative action programs. If these programs are discontinued the ability of blacks to gain fair participation in employment opportunities and the admission of blacks and other minorities into graduate and professional schools will be greatly curtailed. Blacks' access to and distribution in a broad cross-section of institutions will be impaired by eliminating these programs. The entire affirmative action program will be enshrouded in doubt and uncertainty. No matter how much one may disagree about the proper interpretation and application of the relevant abstract principles to this controversy, if the programs are not upheld, if *Bakke* is not reversed, the forward progress of blacks and other similarly situated minorities may be severely stymied. The affirmance of *Bakke* would be interpreted as the reversal of affirmative action and would be taken as an officially sanctioned signal to turn against blacks in this country. If opposition to special minority admissions programs does not disguise hostility to blacks, then certainly it discloses a lack of seriousness about facilitating a significant increase in blacks' access to opportunities in the higher education sector.[24]

The Development of Federal Affirmative Action Programs

Although the Reconstruction amendments and the civil rights acts following the Civil War were designed to overcome the effects of slavery, the first real administrative effort to tackle the problem of institutionalized racism did not come until the middle of the twentieth century. The New Deal programs of President Franklin Delano Roosevelt did provide a good measure of economic relief to blacks, but these programs were designed to aid poor Americans, not to aid blacks as victims of racial discrimination.[25] It was not until 1941 when veteran labor leader A. Philip Randolph threatened to organize thousands of blacks to "March on Washington" in protest against discriminatory hiring policies in the defense industry, that the federal government responded to the direct demands of blacks for special action to combat racial discrimination. (*See* Table 3-1 for a summary of the executive orders.)

Pressured by the threat of a march on Washington, the president, on 25 June 1941, issued Executive Order No. 8802, designed to end discrimination in the defense industry. This order urged the defense industry to employ workers without regard to their race, creed, color, or national origin. It also established in the Office of Production Management, a committee on fair employment practice (FEPC) to investigate

TABLE 3-1. Legal Basis for Affirmative Action

Document	Issued by Whom	Date	Major Provisions	Enforcement Power
Executive Order 8802	Franklin D. Roosevelt	June 25, 1941	Urged defense industry to hire workers without regard to race, creed, color or national origin; established Committee on Fair Employment Practices to investigate complaints.	None.
Executive Order 9346	Franklin D. Roosevelt	May 27, 1943	Urged government contractors and subcontractors to end discriminatory hiring practices.	None.
Executive Order 9980	Harry S. Truman	July 26, 1948	Ordered hiring in federal government to be done solely on the basis of merit.	None.
Executive Order 10308	Harry S. Truman	December 3, 1951	Established Committee on Government Compliance. Purpose of Committee: (1) to examine and study rules, procedures, and practices of government contractors; (2) to confer and advise with government contracting officials.	None.
Executive Order 10479	Dwight D. Eisenhower	August 13, 1953	Created Government Contract Committee. Purpose of Committee: (1) to make recommendations for improving nondiscrimination provisions; (2) to receive complaints of discrimination.	None.
Executive Order 10557	Dwight D. Eisenhower	September 3, 1954	Required government contractors to include nondiscriminatory provisions in employment, upgrading, demotion,	None.

			or transfers; recruitment or recruitment advertising; layoff or termination.	None.
1957 Civil Rights Act	U.S. Congress	September 9, 1957	Created Commission on Civil Rights to: (1) study and collect information regarding the denial of equal protection of the laws; (2) evaluate laws and policies of federal government in regard to equal protection of the laws.	None.
Executive Order 10925	John F. Kennedy	March 6, 1961	Created President's Committee on Equal Employment Opportunity. Government contractors urged to end racial discrimination in employment.	Limited-committee had the power to impose sanctions and penalties on government contractors who failed to comply with nondiscriminatory provisions.
Title VI of 1964 Civil Rights Act	U.S. Congress	July 2, 1964	Prohibited racial discrimination in any programs or activities receiving federal funds.	Termination of or refusal of funds by federal departments or agencies upon finding of discrimination.
Title VII of 1964 Civil Rights Act	U.S. Congress	July 2, 1964	Prohibited racial discrimination in employment by employers of 25 or more persons.	Limited-EEOC created. Purpose of Commission: (1) To investigate and to resolve complaints of discrimination; (2) to bring suits against those employers found guilty of discrimination.

(Continued)

TABLE 3-1. (Continued)

Document	Issued by Whom	Date	Major Provisions	Enforcement Power
Executive Order 11246	Lyndon B. Johnson	September 24, 1965	Contractor to take affirmative action to ensure that applicants are employed without regard to race, color, religion, or national origin.	Secretary of Labor may investigate complaints and cancel contracts of those contractors who fail to comply.
Executive Order 11375	Lyndon B. Johnson	October 13, 1967	Amended part 1 and part 2 of Executive Order 11246. Added prohibition against sex discrimination.	None.
Executive Order 11478	Richard M. Nixon	August 8, 1969	Amended part 1 of Executive Order 11246. Called for affirmative action programs for the federal government's supervision of Civil Service Commission.	None.
Equal Employment Opportunity Act of 1972	U.S. Congress	March 24, 1972	I. Amended Sections 707 and 709 of the 1964 Civil Rights Act: (A) Effective March 24, 1974 functions of the Attorney General to be transferred to Equal Employment Opportunity Commission which can: (1) bring civil action in district court;	EEOC given power to go directly to court to enforce the law.

(2) request relief-application for a charge for a permanent or temporary injunction, restraining order.

(B) Commission given authority to investigate and act on charges of a pattern or practice of discrimination.

(C) Employers, employment agencies, and labor organizations are to make and preserve records relevant to the determinations of whether unlawful employment practices have been or are being committed.

II. Section 718 added to 1964 Civil Rights Act. No government contract can be denied, withheld, terminated, or suspended in which a contractor had an affirmative action plan unless employer has deviated substantially from that plan. Public and private educational institutions and state and local governments were covered by the act.

complaints received in violation of the order's provisions and to recommend to the executive branch measures to carry out the provisions of
the order. Since a substantial portion of federal funds went to subcontractors, Executive Order 8802's coverage was expanded to include
subcontractors. On 27 May 1943, Executive Order 9346 supplanted the
old order. The new order urged contractors and subcontractors to end
discriminatory hiring practices. The FEPC became an autonomous
agency in the Office of the President.[26]

Thus, for the first time, the federal government officially recognized
a responsibility to take administrative action to combat the extensive
racism and discrimination which existed in hiring. The federal government attempted to provide a partial solution by calling for nondiscriminatory provisions in its contract procurement program. The compliance program was directed at federal contractors for administrative
convenience. In the absence of recognized civil rights laws to prevent
discrimination, the government found the existence of the contract
compliance program gave it a mechanism to impose the nondiscriminatory clause. During World War II many employers were government
contractors or subcontractors, and hence the order had an impact on a
substantial segment of the labor market. The idea was sound, but the
federal effort was pegged to what is now called "good faith" effort on
the part of the contractors not to discriminate and therefore was of
limited effectiveness. This limited effectiveness is clearly evident in the
language used in the original order by which contractors were merely
urged to end discriminatory hiring practices without being required to
take affirmative steps to overcome the effects of discrimination. The
FEPC could investigate complaints, but could only recommend measures to help implement the order. It had no enforcement powers. Almost immediately, it became apparent that racial discrimination would
not be eradicated without some mechanism for enforcement. The failure of President Roosevelt to provide FEPC with enforcement powers
relegated the agency to an investigative and advisory body. But, as
historian Barton J. Bernstein has suggested, the plight of the Negro
"never" received the total support and attention of Roosevelt. Although he did maintain the FEPC, its work could have been more effective if the president had seen to it that more money was allotted to the
committee.[27]

Certain members of Congress, however, were not unmindful of the
seriousness of employment discrimination and the need for strong
federal legislation that would expand and enforce the provisions of the

original executive order. In 1945 alone, there were thirteen bills introduced in the House of Representatives calling for a fair employment
practice act. After generations of employment discrimination, civil
rights leaders were still "asking" that blacks be accorded fair treatment.
From the debates in Congress it was evident that the nation was unwilling to take the step. Southern legislators, who controlled key committees in both houses of Congress, were opposed to any form of civil
rights legislation, while northern legislators debated whether a federal
FEPC should have enforcement powers similar to those of the Interstate Commerce Commission and the Federal Trade Commission. As a
result of the failure to muster sufficient support from the northern
congressmen, the solid opposition of the southern congressmen assured
the repeated defeat of these bills. As a consequence, the administrative
effort initiated by the executive remained the sole federal effort to
eliminate discrimination in employment.

Accomplishments during this period were therefore minimal. The
pattern of discrimination against blacks persisted, despite the work of
the FEPC. Blacks continued to be last hired first fired and excluded
almost entirely from some jobs and industries, including the higher
educational sector, and relegated to the menial and less desirable jobs
in others.

Following World War II, Congress, during January and February
1946, again refused to pass legislation calling for the creation of a
permanent FEPC. Although President Truman publicly appealed for
a permanent FEPC, he never openly criticized the filibusters by southern
congressmen against the bill, nor did he try to rally senators in an
attempt to end the filibustering.[28]

Southerners in Congress, entrenched in seniority positions and un-
accountable to the nation as a whole, continued to block all efforts to
eliminate employment discrimination. President Harry Truman, however, responded to the demands of black Americans. In July 1948, the
president issued Executive Order 9980, entitled "Regulations Governing Fair Employment Practices Within the Federal Establishment."
The order was an attempt to carry out what had, in theory, become
federal policy, that is, nondiscriminatory hiring within federal government departments. The order specified that hiring was to be done solely
on the basis of merit, and federal hiring officials were to take steps to
ensure that all such employment action was carried out in a nondiscriminatory manner.

While reaffirming the spirit of Executive Order No. 8802, President

Truman still called upon Congress for legislation to end discrimination in voting, housing, employment, and education. The orders issued by the president were still confined to areas where the presidential administrative authority was clear: the authority to fix the terms of contract and the authority to determine the hiring practices of the executive branch and the armed forces. Some scholars, such as Howard Zinn, assert that Truman could have issued executive orders in other areas as well.[29] But it is evident that if the president did not recognize clear legislative authority to set up a program to eliminate discrimination in areas not under the administrative control of the executive branch, he would require specific legislation to undertake such activities.

These two new executive orders, like Executive Orders 8802 and 9346 before them, lacked enforcement powers. And, as before, it was evident that the equal opportunity principle was not being applied either inside or outside the government. The pattern of discrimination persisted, as indicated by the employment experiences of blacks. Black leaders and their white supporters recognized this grim reality and continued to call for a permanent FEPC with enforcement powers. With the outbreak of the Korean War in June 1950, they urged the president to establish a wartime FEPC "as an integral factor in mobilization of manpower . . . against . . . aggression."[30] The president was prevented from setting up such an agency by the so-called Russell Amendment which prevented the allotment of any funds for an FEPC without the consent of Congress.[31]

Nevertheless, in December of 1951, President Truman issued Executive Order 10308 which established the Committee on Government Contract Compliance (CGCC). This committee, financed by funds from several federal agencies, was to review the contractors' compliance with the nondiscriminatory provisions required by government contracts.[32] But, like its predecessor, the new committee was "weak and dependent upon persuasion and conciliation."[33] It lacked ample financing and staff and had neither enforcement powers nor the power to hold public hearings. Although virtually powerless, the committee did find that most federal contractors "made little, if any attempt to adhere to its standards" and that the government officials did not possess "the will" to require enforcement.[34] Little change occurred in the practice of racial discrimination in hiring as a result of the committee's activities.

Although President Truman was unable to get Congress to pass a permanent FEPC, he publicly supported such legislation. His Republican successor, Dwight D. Eisenhower, however, did not support a federal FEPC. Repeatedly, Eisenhower stated that such legislation should be left up to the individual states.[35]

During his first year in office, President Eisenhower did issue Executive Order 10479. Implicit in the language of the new executive order was a recognition that stronger measures had to be enacted. It stated that "a review and analysis of existing practices and procedures of government contracting agencies show that the practices and procedures relating to compliance with the nondiscrimination provisions must be revised and strengthened to eliminate discrimination in all aspects of employment."[36]

To revise and strengthen the nondiscrimination provisions, this executive order created the Committee on Government Contracts and abolished the CGCC. This new committee was to make recommendations for improving the nondiscrimination provisions of government contracts and to receive complaints when these provisions were violated. Although the *intent* of the order was to strengthen the already existent nondiscriminatory provisions included in earlier orders, it still lacked enforcement authority which continued to constitute the most serious weakness of the federal contract compliance program. Instead of calling for a strict enforcement of the nondiscriminatory provisions, the committee was to "encourage the furtherance of an educational program by employer, labor, civic, educational, religious, and other voluntary nongovernmental groups in order to eliminate or reduce the basic causes and costs of discrimination in employment."[37]

In September 1954, President Eisenhower, upon the suggestion of the committee, issued Executive Order 10557 which extended the contractor's obligations to include nondiscrimination in "employment, upgrading, demotion, or transfer; recruitment or recruitment advertising; layoff or termination; rates of pay and other forms of compensation and selection for training, including apprenticeship."[38] The committee clearly recognized that discrimination existed not only in hiring but in all facets of employment.

Although the equal opportunity program was becoming more comprehensive, little progress was being made in ending discrimination by federal contractors. The Committee on Government Contracts, like its predecessors in the Roosevelt and Truman administrations, lacked enforcement powers. Without the power to apply punitive sanctions, the committee could not *require* contractors to act in good faith. Part of the blame lay with the Eisenhower administration's lukewarm enforcement of the executive orders and the "go-slow" policy advocated by key members of the administration, which was increasingly evident after *Brown* v. *The Board of Education of Topeka.* Not willing to face intense southern opposition, the administration, by the end of the decade, backed away from an attempt to establish a permanent commission of job equality under government contracts.[39]

Congress did take the first step toward passage of the necessary legislation to eliminate racial discrimination, but the final act was too weak to achieve any meaningful results. The Civil Rights Act of 1957 was the first civil rights legislation passed since 1875. The act elevated the civil rights section of the Department of Justice to division status. The law also created the U.S. Commission on Civil Rights as a temporary, independent, bipartisan agency directed to investigate complaints of discrimination. The commission was also given responsibility to make investigations, conduct studies, and submit reports, findings, and recommendations to the president and Congress, but was not given enforcement powers to implement its recommendations. The other provision of the act was just as weak. It allowed the federal government to bring suits to obtain injunctive relief when a person's right to vote was denied or threatened.[40]

Throughout the decade of the 1950s, the federal effort to end discrimination remained weak because the executive orders lacked enforcement powers. A 1961 report issued by the U.S. Commission on Civil Rights reached this conclusion when, in assessing the various committee's achievements, it concluded that the committees had "little effect on traditional patterns of Negro employment."[41]

The findings of the Commission on Civil Rights were supported by a study of employment discrimination by the Potomac Institute. The institute found that "by 1960, the view was developing that passive nondiscrimination was not enough. Discrimination, it was recognized, could exist and flourish in the simple absence of positive affirmative action."[42] Unemployment figures for minorities continued to increase or remain twice the rate of white employment, and many employed minorities remained, by and large, in low-paying, unskilled occupations. Federal policies remained inadequate and federal enforcement was too irregular and ineffective to adequately correct the situation. Although several northern and western state and municipal governments had established fair employment commissions to curb racial discrimination in employment, their activities did not produce results substantial enough to ease the economic plight of black workers.

In an effort to come to terms with the pervasiveness of the problem, President John F. Kennedy issued Executive Order 10925 on 6 March 1961. The wording of the order showed the administration's awareness of the shortcomings of prior orders. In part, the order stated "a review and analysis of existing Executive Orders, practices, and government employment and compliance with existing nondiscrimination contract provisions reveal an urgent need for expansion and strengthening of efforts. to promote full equality of employment opportunity."[43] The order created the President's Committee on Equal Employment Opportunity (CEEO), composed of the Vice-President, the Secretary of Labor, the chairman of the Atomic Energy Commission, the secretary of commerce, the attorney general, the secretary of defense, the secretaries of the army, navy, and air force, the administrator of General Services, the chairman of the Civil Service Commission, and the administrator of the National Aeronautics and Space Administration. Going beyond the blanket repetitions of the functions of past committees, the order called for all government contractors to take "affirmative action" to end racial discrimination in employment. And if contractors failed to comply with the nondiscrimination clauses, then upon committee review and hearings, the contract could be cancelled.[44] Executive Order 10925 marked the first time an equal employment opportunity agency was given the power to impose sanctions and penalties and the first time an Executive Order required affirmative action.

President Kennedy himself had recognized the importance of the new committee. When he signed the order, he described the committee as "vastly strengthened" over its predecessors because it had been granted sanctions "sweeping enough to ensure compliance."[45] Kennedy's assessment was far too optimistic. A significant turning point, however, had been reached in the effort to end discriminatory hiring. President Kennedy, aware of the problems of lack of personnel and inadequate enforcement, assigned the secretary of labor, "with all the resources of the Department of Labor at his command," to oversee the implementation of equal employment programs.[46]

The institutionalization of racial discrimination was so ingrained that blacks realized there was a need to seek additional remedies rather than to rely solely on executive pronouncements. Such help was not readily available. Although the Kennedy administration was active in attempting to implement the provisions of the executive orders, little was done to encourage Congress to pass civil rights legislation.[47] Like the Truman and Eisenhower administrations, the Kennedy administration faced intense southern recalcitrance. Because of the seniority system, southerners in Congress held power far beyond their numerical strength and consistently tried to use the leadership of key committees to prevent the enactment of civil rights legislation. Furthermore, the Kennedy victory in 1960 was aided immensely by votes of the "Solid South" and the administration was not one to risk losing the support of its white southern allies.

The combined effects of Dr. Martin Luther King's Birmingham campaign and the assassination of President Kennedy finally stimulated the legislative branch to act. In 1964 Congress passed the most comprehensive and far-reaching piece of legislation of this century, the Civil Rights Act of 1964. One of the most important sections of this act is Title VII, which Congress enacted as a comprehensive prohibition against private acts of discrimination in employment. Title VII prohibits discrimination by employers of twenty-five persons or more in labor unions, employment services (public and private), and sponsors of apprenticeship of any other training program. The enforcing mechanism was placed in the Equal Employment Opportunity Commission (EEOC), which was given the authority to investigate complaints, and bring suits against covered employers in federal district courts. Upon a finding of discrimination, the courts could order affirmative relief.[48]

In 1972, Congress amended the act with the Equal Employment Opportunity Act of 1972. This act extended coverage to include federal, state, and local governments and educational institutions. In 1974, the attorney general was granted authority to bring "pattern and practice" discrimination suits concurrently with the EEOC. The act further provided that:

After 1974, EEOC assumed primary governmental authority for enforcement of the law although the Attorney General remains the only government party authorized to sue states and municipalities. Title VII also creates a cause of action enforceable in federal court by aggrieved persons or classes of persons. The law provides for injunctive and affirmative relief including back pay and the grant of attorney's fees to the prevailing party.[49]

Here again, effective sanction power was lacking. Instead of providing EEOC with authority to issue cease and desist orders as recommended by civil rights groups, the EEOC was to rely on tactics of "conference, conciliation, and persuasion." If these methods proved unsuccessful, the EEOC as well as the aggrieved complainant had to seek redress in a federal district court, or request that the Justice Department initiate the litigation in situations where there was found a "pattern or practice" of discrimination. Notwithstanding its complaint-oriented status, the EEOC has developed concern for systemic discrimination and has attempted to combat it by affirmative action.[50]

Previous executive orders were primarily ineffective in that they were aimed at trying to prevent overt forms of discrimination in hiring. While the passage of civil rights legislation aided in reducing the amount of overt discrimination, many employers practiced a more subtle form of racial bias. And even when there was no conscious effort to discriminate, employers' policies and procedures were often designed to inadvertently discriminate against blacks, other minority groups, and white women. In an attempt to eliminate this systemic form of employment discrimination, President Lyndon B. Johnson issued, in 1965, Executive Order 11246. The order mandated further compliance of government contractors by requiring affirmative action in all of the contractor's business, and not just that part of his business covered by government contract. This greatly expanded the number of employees concerned. In addition, the order delegated enforcement responsibility to the secretary of labor, who, in 1966, established the Office of Federal Contract Compliance (OFCC). The OFCC's authority was broadened and strengthened by Executive Order 11375, in 1967, and Executive Order 11478, in 1969.

Not until 1971 was the Executive Order applied to government contractors in the higher education community. The Department of Health, Education, and Welfare (HEW) was designated by the Department of Labor as the compliance agency for institutions of higher education. The HEW guidelines for implementing the executive order indicated that:

affirmative action requires the contractor to do more than ensure employment neutrality with regard to race, color, religion, sex and national origin. As the phrase implies, affirmative action requires the employer to make additional efforts to recruit, employ and promote qualified members of groups formerly excluded, even if that exclusion cannot be traced to particular discriminatory actions on the part of the employer. The premise of the affirmative action concept of the Executive Order is that unless positive action is undertaken to overcome the effects of systematic institutional forms of exclusion and discrimination a benign neutrality in employment practices will tend to perpetuate the *status quo ante* indefinitely.[51]

The HEW guidelines were based on regulations defined and derived by OFCC (later modified by Revised Order No. 4) for implementing affirmative action. The regulations require analysis of "problem areas" and the use of goals and timetables to measure improvement in the employment of minorities, if any, achieved through a "good faith effort." Through the 1960s and into the 1970s, the federal government placed great emphasis on changing hiring practices and policies, but showed extreme reluctance to use its sanction power to coerce, where necessary, those recalcitrant contractors who continued to discriminate while carrying out the "letter" but not the "spirit" of their contractual obligations.

The issuance of Executive Order 11246 and its subsequent amendments indicated that the federal establishment acknowledged that the attack on covert discrimination was insufficient to eradicate a system of race prejudice and employment discrimination. Previous executive orders and state and federal laws were based on the general belief that discrimination was a conscious overt action deliberately taken against individuals: subsequently laws were passed which prohibited discrimination in employment and other areas. The EEOC concluded in 1974:

> Destructive, persistent employment discrimination remains, confirmed by the statistics of unemployment, underemployment and incomes of minorities and women, by the daily experience of agencies administering equal employment laws, and by findings of the courts. Much discrimination, particularly against females, persists through intentional acts. But most pervasive discrimination today results from normal, often unintentional and seemingly neutral practices throughout the employment process. Employment *systems* perpetuate discriminatory effects of past discrimination even when original discriminatory acts have ceased, and, continue to discriminate daily, creating very unequal opportunities for many minorities and women.
>
> Identification and elimination of such systematic discrimination resulting from regular employment practices is the major focus of equal employment efforts today.[52]

An important reason why previous federal executive orders and equal employment opportunity efforts failed to achieve equal opportunity was the lack of sufficient funding and enforcement powers. The committees established were advisory boards which could make recommendations. Even the "vastly strengthened" CEEO relied heavily upon voluntary equal opportunity agreements.[53] But an equally important reason for the failure of these efforts is the very nature of the problem. In the area of employment, discrimination had become part of the *regular* employment policies and practices of employers and thus systemic. With the emphasis on affirmative action, the government sufficiently recognized the problem for the first time and prepared to develop a remedy that would eliminate the problem at its source. (*See* chapter five.)

The affirmative action requirement, as part of the contract compliance program, was designed to make employers reevaluate their employment policies and procedures and correct areas where discrimination existed. The provisions required contractors to evaluate their recruitment practices and change them, if necessary, to assure that blacks, other minorities, and women of all races had a fair opportunity to compete in the employment process. Before the implementation of affirmative action, it was "sufficient," under provisions of executive orders, for a contractor to remain in compliance if he did not overtly and intentionally discriminate against blacks. Under the new requirement, the contractor had to examine his policies and procedures to assure that he did not discriminate inadvertently. Since patterns are difficult to change and often minorities did not seek employment where traditionally they were excluded, it was now incumbent upon the employers to seek out minorities and women.

The history of the government's effort to guarantee the civil rights of blacks illustrates that a sustained affirmative effort backed by the force of the federal government is necessary to end present discrimination. Executive Order 11246, as it applies to institutions of higher education, has been operative since the fall of 1972. The guidelines' have been changed by the Department of Labor a number of times, and HEW's Office for Civil Rights (OCR) has altered its structure and enforcement procedures in an effort to respond to the negative criticism lodged against affirmative action. But considering the relatively short period of time the affirmative action requirements have been in existence, it is too early to determine just how effective these regulations will be in eliminating systemic discrimination. The guidelines, for the most part, have been inadequately enforced by HEW, as is evident from the discussion in chapter five. The other major problem has been and continues to be the opposition of the academic community to affirmative action, as is discussed in detail in chapter four.

Because the current federal affirmative action program for blacks is still implemented through administrative action, those institutions which have little administrative interaction with the government escape the requirement for affirmative action. The Civil Rights Acts of 1964 and 1972, especially in light of the Title IX requirement for affirmative action for women, offer sufficient legislative authority for a universally implemented affirmative action effort. The EEOC's enforcement philosophy seems to be evolving to a recognition of the necessity for affirmative action requirements in order to implement the two civil rights acts.

Affirmative Action and the Courts

Since the passage of the Civil Rights Act of 1964, the federal judiciary has taken an active role in assuring equal employment opportunity. Title VII of the act prohibits discrimination in employment in labor unions, employment referral services, and apprenticeship and training programs. The courts have not only held Title VII constitutional, but have also indicated that employers must take affirmative steps to eliminate vestiges of racial discrimination.

Selected decisions will be examined in which the courts have upheld the use of Title VII as offering "affirmative relief" to end the "pattern and practice" of discrimination. Initially, the courts viewed Title VII as a means of eliminating specific discriminatory practices by employers and labor unions. From approximately 1971 to the present, the courts have expanded both their interpretation and application of Title VII. In several cases the courts have ordered employers and unions to engage in "ratio" hiring[54] or "quota"[55] relief to overcome the effects of past discrimination and to make the employment system fair.

Also examined are selected court decisions in which lower courts have upheld affirmative action programs and plans as mandated by the Executive Order. In most of these cases, involving both Title VII and the Executive Order, the courts have recognized that what appear to be neutral employment policies, practices, and procedures can and do perpetuate the effects of past discrimination. Thus, they have found affirmative action an essential element to eliminate and to correct such policies and practices.

In early cases involving Title VII, such as *Quarles* v. *Philip Morris, Inc.* (1968);[56] *Asbestos Workers* v. *Vogler* (1969);[57] *United Papermakers* v. *United States* (1969);[58] *United States* v. *Sheet Metal Workers, Local No. 36* (1969);[59] and *United States* v. *IBEW, Local No. 38* (1970),[60] the courts have upheld the use of Title VII as a means of eradicating the "present effects of past discrimination." In essence all of these courts have maintained, as did the Fifth Circuit Court of Appeals in *United Papermakers,* that:

when employers or unions discriminate in the past and its present policies renew or exaggerate discriminatory effects, those policies must yield unless there is an overriding legitimate, non-racial business purpose.[51]

Seniority systems have been declared unlawful where they have been based upon past discriminatory hiring practices. Other practices and procedures, including discrimination in pay and exclusion from unions and apprenticeship programs because of race, have been declared unlawful. In place of these practices, the courts have ordered plant-wide seniority, back pay to those discriminated against, and the opening up of unions and apprenticeship programs to minorities.

According to several writers,[62] the most important Title VII case was *Griggs* v. *Duke Power Company* (1971),[63] in which the Supreme Court decided that the use of tests as a prerequisite for either employment or promotion was unconstitutional. Black plaintiffs alleged that the tests were not relevant to the jobs. In his opinion for the Supreme Court, Chief Justice Warren Burger wrote:

The objective of Congress in the enactment of Title VII is plain, from the language of the statute. It was to achieve equality of employment opportunities and remove barriers that have operated in the past to favor an identifiable group of white employees over other employees. Under the Act, practices, procedures, or tests neutral on their face, and even neutral in terms of intent, cannot be maintained if they operate to "freeze" the status quo of prior discriminatory employment practices.[64]

As the language in these cases clearly indicates, Title VII was designed to eliminate those employment policies and practices which have continued the effects of past discrimination.

In more recent years, however, the courts have broadened their interpretation of what is required under Title VII. They have gone beyond ordering an end to specific discriminatory practices and have ordered "affirmative relief" to ensure equal opportunity in employment. In *United States* v. *Ironworkers Local 86* (1971),[65] the Ninth Circuit Court of Appeals upheld an affirmative action program decreed by the district court. Because the union had discriminated against and continued to discriminate against black applicants, the district court ordered the union to offer job referrals to black applicants and ordered apprenticeship and training committees "to select and indenture sufficient black applicants to overcome past discrimination, and to also meet judicially imposed ceiling requirements in apprenticeship program participation."[66]

In cases following *Ironworkers, Griggs,* and *Swann,*[67] the courts have broadened their concept of "affirmative relief" and have even gone beyond the requirements of Executive Order 11246 in fashioning remedies to correct past and present discrimination. They have ordered "ratio hiring,"[68] broad "affirmative relief" requiring the establishing of goals,[69] "hiring quotas,"[70] "affirmative hiring relief,"[71] and "quota relief."[72]

In *Carter* v. *Gallagher* (1971), the Eighth Circuit Court of Appeals concurred with the district court's order that the city of Minneapolis hire at least 20 minority firemen "to eradicate the effects of past discrimination." Because there were no minority firefighters present in a force of 535 men, the circuit court agreed that "some reasonable ratio for hiring" be temporarily implemented to correct this imbalance. The court was also quite careful to point out that such a hiring system was neither a violation of the antipreference section of the 1964 Civil Rights Act nor a quota.[73]

In *Stamps* v. *Detroit Edison Co.* (1973), the District Court for Eastern Michigan interpreted Title VII as providing "the broadest legislative mandate for eliminating racially discriminatory practices in employment." Because the Detroit Edison Company had discriminated against blacks in hiring, job assignments and testing practices, the court ordered the company to engage in a widespread affirmative action program. The company was ordered to upgrade its recruiting and hiring of blacks so that the goal of a 30 percent black work force could be achieved. The company was also ordered to hire three blacks for every two whites hired until one-fourth of the employees in the more skilled jobs were black; and the company was ordered to promote one black employee to supervisor for every white employee so promoted.[74]

The courts in *Carter* and *Stamps* used the remedies of "ratio hiring" and "goals." In more recent years, the courts have gone so far as to order and uphold programs which mandate quotas. They have found that the use of such temporary hiring quotas to correct discriminatory practices do not violate the 1964 Civil Rights Act.

In *United States* v. *Wood, Wire, and Metal Lathers International Union, Local No. 46* (1973), the Second Circuit Court of Appeals upheld a district court order requiring the union to issue work permits to minority workers on a one-to-one basis with white workers. Such an order, the court maintained, did not violate the Civil Rights Act of 1964. For the court said:

. . . the only limitation on the broad powers of affirmative relief is that restricting preferential quota hiring.

However, while quotas merely to attain racial balance are forbidden, quotas to correct past discriminatory practices are not.[75]

In *Morrow* v. *Crisler* (1974) and *NAACP* v. *Allen* (1974), the Fifth Circuit Court of Appeals upheld district court decrees ordering "affirmative hiring relief" or "quota relief." In *Morrow* v. *Crisler*, black plaintiffs brought suit against the Mississippi Highway Patrol for its past and present discriminatory employment practices and procedures. In upholding the district court's decree, the court of appeals stated:

it [the District Court] may, within the bounds of discretion, order *temporary* one-to-one or one-to-two hiring, the creation of hiring pools, or a freeze on white hiring, or any other form of affirmative hiring relief until the Patrol is effectively integrated.[76]

Using *Morrow* as a precedent, the court was more specific in its remedy in *NAACP* v. *Allen*. Like its Mississippi counterpart, the Alabama Department of Public Safety had a history of discriminatory employment practices. To correct this racial imbalance as a result of racial discrimination, the circuit court upheld the district court's order which required that one black state trooper and one black support personnel person be hired for every white hired until blacks comprised 25 percent of the patrol personnel. Such relief, the court contended, was "quota relief" and did not violate the Fifth Amendment, the Fourteenth Amendment, or Title VII. In a lengthy opinion, the circuit court elaborated upon what "quota relief" entailed. According to the court:

. . . it is not the purpose of quota relief to require that anyone who lacks job-related qualifications be employed. However, the "color conscious" relief which we affirm does require that the defendants temporarily institute race as the final determative factor in their appointment of applicants to fill new openings on the patrol and its supporting staff. . . . This utilization of race, although a suspect classification which triggers the most rigorous judicial scrutiny . . . has never been held to be *per se* unconstitutional.[77]

Thus, the circuit court maintained that "quota relief" could be used as a measure of last resort. But, as the court also held:

it is the collective interest, governmental as well as social, in effectively ending unconstitutional racial discrimination, that justifies temporary, carefully circumscribed resort to racial criteria, whenever the chancellor determines that it represents the only rational, nonarbitrary means of eradicating past evils.[78]

In *United States* v. *Elevator Constructors, Local 5* (1976),[79] the Third Circuit Court of Appeals upheld the district court's order requiring the union to establish a goal of 23 percent black membership and to adopt 33 percent black referral quota. This order, the circuit court maintained, violated neither the Fifth nor Fourteenth amendments. Moreover the order did not violate the preferential treatment provisions of Title VII. In perhaps some of the most emphatic language in support of quotas, the court stated:

Nowhere in the enforcement provisions of Title VII is there any prohibition against the imposition of a membership goal or a referral quota to help achieve that goal. Indeed, both remedies would seem to be authorized by the broad language of §706 (g) empowering courts to order "such affirmative action as may be appropriate. . . ."[80]

The courts have seen fit on several occasions to order "ratio hiring" or "quota hiring" as remedies to "eradicate the present effects of past discrimination." These measures, the courts have maintained, are not unconstitutional. Rather, they are to ensure equal opportunity throughout all phases of the employment process.

Affirmative Action under Executive Order 11246

Just as the courts have upheld or have fashioned "affirmative relief" remedies under Title VII, so have the courts, by and large,[81] approved of affirmative action plans and programs as required under Executive Order 11246.

In *Weiner* v. *Cuyahoga Community College District* (1969),[82] for example, the Ohio State Supreme Court upheld a lower court decision allowing the Cuyahoga Community College District to reject a less expensive bid by a contractor for a construction contract because of the contractor's reluctance to assure in its affirmative action plan that blacks would be employed. Citing both Executive Order 11246 and the Ohio Gubernatorial Executive Order of 5 June 1967, the court stated:

A government which has declared discriminatory employment practices unlawful should not then finance them indirectly by binding only its direct contractor, and not the entire contract performance, to a promise of attempted compliance. . . . Accordingly, a bidder for a construction contract to be awarded by a public body of this state may be required to assure, by appropriate promises contained in contract provisions or related instruments, nondiscrimination in employment in the entire performance of the contract.[83]

In *Joyce* v. *McCrane* (1970),[84] the U.S. District Court for New Jersey upheld the validity of the affirmative action plan, as required under the Executive Order, drawn up by the state of New Jersey. This plan, requiring each contractor to set a goal of 30 to 37 percent minority participation, was attacked for setting up "quotas." However, as the court stressed in its opinion, goals are not quotas, but are indicative of "good faith" efforts.[85]

The most important case in which the courts have upheld both the Executive Order and the requiring of affirmative action plans has been *Contractors Association of Eastern Pennsylvania* v. *Secretary of Labor* (1971).[86] In this case the Third Circuit Court of Appeals upheld the validity of the "Philadelphia Plan," an affirmative action plan for construction contractors in the Philadelphia area. This plan, designed to correct the underutilization of minorities in the construction trades, specified that the affirmative action plans of government contractors in the area contain goals for skilled minority trade workers ranging from 19 to 26 percent by 1973. The court rejected the plaintiffs' arguments that the Philadelphia Plan was violative of Title VII, the Executive Order, and the Fifth Amendment. According to the court, neither the language nor the legislative history of Title VII would prevent the enactment of the Philadelphia Plan.[87] More important, the court rejected the plaintiff's charge of an absence of a judicial finding of past discrimination, as required by Title VII. The court held that

while a court must find intentional past discrimination before it can require affirmative action under 42 U.S.C. §2000E-5(g), *that section imposes no restraint upon the measures which the President may require of the beneficiaries of federal assistance.*[88] (emphasis added)

The court also held that the plan did not go beyond the Executive Order. In addition, the court held that the required goals were not racial quotas in violation of the due process clause of the Fifth Amendment.[89]

In *Southern Illinois Builders Association* v. *Ogilvie* (1972),[90] the Seventh Circuit Court of Appeals upheld the affirmative action plan drawn up for the highway construction industry by the state of Illinois. The court in reviewing union training policies, rejected the plaintiff's charge that the plan established hiring quotas in violation of Title VII and the Fifth and Fourteenth amendments. The plan, the court held, "does not impermissibly prefer black persons nor does it discriminate against white persons."[91]

In *Associated General Contractors of Massachusetts, Inc.* v. *Altshuler* (1973),[92] the First Circuit Court of Appeals upheld the affirmative action program of the Commonwealth of Massachusetts. This plan, requiring more of contractors than the federal "Boston Plan," called for at least 20 percent minority representation on the work force of the Commonwealth. Rejecting the plaintiff's argument, the circuit court ruled the state plan was not in conflict with the federal plan.[93] Nor, the court held, did the Commonwealth's plan call for a racial hiring quota in violation of the equal protection clause. Recognizing the present effects of racial discrimination, the court stated:

discrimination has a way of perpetuating itself, albeit unintentionally, because the resulting inequalities make new opportunities less accessible. Preferential treatment is one partial prescription to remedy our society's most intransigent and deeply rooted inequalities.[94]

In a carefully construed defense of the intent of "racial preference" vis-á-vis affirmative action, the court stressed:

equal opportunity . . . carries the simple mandate that opportunities should be open to all on the basis of competence alone. Thus, it would be consistent with the goal of equal opportunity to give first priority to members of a minority that had previously been denied equal opportunity, if those members were otherwise as qualified as were qualified members of the minority population. In order that this special treatment be meaningful, of course, there should be equal opportunity to gain the training necessary to qualify.[95]

This brief examination of challenges to the legality of affirmative action under both the Executive Order and Title VII indicates that the courts have taken the position that affirmative action is a legitimate means for achieving equal opportunity. In fact, under circumstances in which blacks continue to be discriminated against, the courts have gone beyond the requirement of goals and timetables and have actually imposed hiring ratios to overcome the effects of discriminatory treatment.

The legal battle blacks have fought to achieve equal opportunity has been a long and difficult one. With the passage of the Thirteenth, Fourteenth, and Fifteenth amendments, it was evident that the constitutional basis had been established to achieve equal opportunity for black Americans. But the history of race relations during the last quarter of the nineteenth century and well into the twentieth century illustrates the formidable struggle blacks have had in implementing these rights guaranteed by the Constitution. Even with the issuance of Executive Order 8802 in 1941, it has taken over a quarter of a century to establish a moderately effective mechanism for achieving a fair employment system. As soon as that system was in place, it came increasingly under attack in spite of the fact that the federal judiciary has found it an appropriate and necessary means of achieving equal employment opportunity. As affirmative action programs began to have an effect in eliminating discriminatory treatment, especially in institutions of higher education, critics from academia became more vocal in their denunciation of the program. The following chapter will analyze this criticism.

Chapter Four

Response to the Critics
of Affirmative Action

Ever since its application to higher education in 1971, affirmative action has been vehemently criticized by members of the academic community. For the most part, these critics have defined the arguments used in the debate over the concept and the implementation of affirmative action. In many instances they have popularized their opposition by using such code words as "quotas," "reverse discrimination," and "unqualified." These arguments tend to overshadow the real intent of affirmative action programs—to bring about equal employment opportunity in the field of higher education. Thus, this chapter is a response to the arguments of the critics. Briefly, their major contentions are that: affirmative action is unwarranted federal intervention in higher education; goals and timetables are euphemisms for hiring "quotas"; "quotas" violate the merit principle; and finally, no benefit of significance has resulted because of affirmative action.

First, it is obvious from chapter two that federal intervention is essential if higher education is to be opened to all. Historically, predominantly white institutions deliberately denied access to blacks on the basis of race. After segregation was declared unconstitutional and employment discrimination was outlawed, academicians made no serious effort to bring blacks into academe. In fact, data suggest that black faculty members dropped from 3 percent in 1960 to 2.2 percent in 1968 at a time when institutions were rapidly expanding. Further, chapter five illustrates the extent to which OCR has gone to cater to the so-called special needs of academia, while chapter six points out the extent to which many faculty selection committees have been recalcitrant in fulfilling their obligation to follow the spirit of Executive Order 11246.

If federal intervention is warranted in any particular area, it certainly is needed in institutions of higher education.

Goals and timetables are definitely not quotas. The HEW *Higher Education Guidelines* (Executive Order 11246) are clear on this point. In fact, the section on the establishment of hiring goals reads:

> Goals may not be rigid and inflexible quotas which must be met, but must be targets reasonably attainable by means of applying every good faith effort to make all aspects of the entire affirmative action program work.[1]

Nor does affirmative action violate the merit principle, whereby allegedly the most qualified candidate is chosen, irrespective of "irrelevant" criteria, such as race. As chapter two clearly indicates, race was the most obvious criterion in limiting the career opportunities of black scholars. Such exclusion necessarily warrants the consideration of race as a means to rectify this injustice.

Past criteria for hiring have generally limited the supply pool to white males who were a part of the "old boy" network. Affirmative action seeks to correct this exclusionary practice. By expanding the supply pool to include more blacks, affirmative action does not violate the principle of merit. Instead it provides the opportunity for all qualified candidates, regardless of race or sex, to compete on an equal basis.

Affirmative action does bring benefits to blacks. Most important, it has helped to open the door of the academic marketplace to the black scholar. For the first time, black scholars are beginning to make significant inroads into higher education. As the 1973 Bayer study and the 1975 Carnegie Council report indicate, there has been increased hiring of blacks by the more prestigious research universities since the inception of affirmative action.[2] The recently released "Higher Educational Staff Information (EEO-6)" from EEOC shows a marked increase since 1972 in the total number of black faculty members.[3]

The above paragraphs summarize the overall arguments of the critics and offer brief counterarguments. The remainder of the chapter examines in detail the arguments of six critics who are viewed as the most vocal, and perhaps the most representative, of the wide range and diversity among the critics.[4] These critics include George Roche and John Bunzel, presidents of institutions of higher learning. Roche is the president of Hillsdale College, a private, liberal arts college in Michigan, which accepts no federal grants or subsidies. He is the author of *The Balancing Act: Quota Hiring in Higher Education,* a biased and distorted attack on affirmative action. Unlike his fellow critics, Roche attacks *all* forms and types of government regulation. Besides attacking affirmative action, he has been most critical of Title IX of the 1972 Education Amendment which bars sex discrimination at colleges and universities that receive federal funds.[5]

John Bunzel, president of the California State University at San Jose, is one of the most pronounced critics of the use of "goals and timetables" which he, like the other critics, has equated with "quotas." Other critics, Nathan Glazer, Sidney Hook, Paul Seabury and Thomas Sowell, reflect the attitudes of faculty members opposed to affirmative action. Nathan Glazer, professor of education and social structure at Harvard, is one of the most vocal critics of affirmative action. He has achieved notoriety through the recent publication of *Affirmative Discrimination: Ethnic Inequality and Public Policy.* Often quoted by critics, both inside and outside academia, this book is a bitter attack on affirmative action policies and programs in education, employment, and housing.

Sidney Hook, professor emeritus of philosophy at New York University and senior research fellow at the Hoover Institution, Stanford University, and Paul Seabury, professor of political science at the University of California, Berkeley, have opposed the implementation of affirmative action ever since its inception. Their common objections to affirmative action have led them to assume prominent roles in the Committee on Academic Nondiscrimination and Integrity. This committee, composed of over five hundred academicians, has maintained that appointments to college and university faculties should not be based upon race or sex.[6]

Thomas Sowell, professor of economics at UCLA, has been perhaps the most controversial critic of affirmative action. No doubt the novelty of a black academician actively attacking a program designed to benefit blacks has gained him access to the news media. In 1975 and 1976, he wrote several articles attacking affirmative action.[7]

Reaction to the Revised Order

Revised Order No. 4, issued by the Department of Labor in 1971, called for colleges and universities, previously exempt as federal contractors from developing affirmative action plans, to do so. This order, "shook the academic community from its posture of indifference."[8] But opposition to the Revised Order had been raised even before it had been applied to the academic community. Professor Edward Shils of the University of Chicago viewed the Revised Order as requiring colleges and universities to use race and sex as criteria for faculty appointments. The use of such criteria, he argued, would lead to unqualified or, at best, less qualified blacks being appointed to college faculties.[9] Shils intended to rally opposition to the application of the Revised Order to higher education, and he did gain the support of many prominent members of academe.

Sidney Hook adopted and elaborated upon much of the Shils argument. Hook, like Shils, was among the first to advance the argument that the application of affirmative action requirements constituted unwarranted federal intervention in the internal affairs of colleges and universities. According to Hook's argument, the limited presence of minorities and women on college faculties did not necessarily imply discriminatory practices. But Hook was more incensed that OCR would threaten to cut off federal support unless the numerical proportions of minorities and women were increased to reach their proportions in the total population.[10] This view was no less than a deliberate misinterpretation of the regulation. The order clearly stated that hiring goals should be determined by the availability of qualified minorities and women. Yet Hook argued that affirmative action plans would force colleges and universities to hire unqualified blacks and women.[11] Before the universities were covered by Executive Order 11246 and before a single affirmative action plan had been adopted, Sidney Hook had described affirmative action in higher education as "wasting time, effort, and taxpayer's money." He thought there was "sufficient work for the Office for Civil Rights to do in enforcing the Presidential directive in areas where minorities are *obviously qualified* and are *obviously suffering* from unfair discrimination" [emphasis added].[12] Before a single black person or woman had been hired under affirmative action, Hook had labeled them unqualified.

Opposition to Affirmative Action: "Unwarranted Federal Intervention"

For widely variant reasons, the critics of affirmative action characterize the concept and implementation of affirmative action as unwarranted federal intervention into higher education. Some assert, as does George Roche, that the federal presence in higher education is a threat to all colleges and universities.[13] The arguments of some of the other critics are not necessarily based on ideological opposition to the federal presence in higher education. Critics such as Sidney Hook and Thomas Sowell maintain that the program of affirmative action was not and is not needed. Both, particularly Sowell, contend that the 1964 Civil Rights Act and a more enlightened public opinion among Americans led to the breakdown of many racial barriers. Sowell maintains that before the issuance of the Revised Order in 1971, more and more colleges and universities were seeking to hire blacks.[14] While it is true that more colleges and universities were actively seeking black scholars for the first time, they did so in response to the demands of black students and in response to the assassination of Dr. Martin Luther King, Jr.

Sowell's assumption is largely based upon information found in a doctoral dissertation by Kent G. Mommsen entitled, "Career Patterns of Black American Doctorates." Mommsen did find that an "overwhelming" majority of the black doctorates he surveyed in 1970 believed that there was a greater demand for them than there had been twenty years earlier.[15] Sowell, however, fails to mention that Mommsen found that close to 70 percent of the black Ph.D.'s thought racial discrimination was either "prevalent" (49.5 percent) or "extremely prevalent" (18.9 percent) at white institutions. Another 30 percent thought that racial discrimination in hiring "existed somewhat." Thus, of 709 black Ph.D.'s surveyed in 1970, over 98 percent indicated that racial discrimination in hiring existed in white institutions.[16] This evidence clearly refutes Hook's argument that OCR should involve itself in areas other than higher education. Obviously, black Ph.D.'s did not share Professor Hook's optimistic viewpoint of equal opportunity in higher education. Moreover, this survey, conducted in 1970, raises serious questions of Sowell's assertion that a more enlightened attitude towards hiring minorities existed on most college campuses before the issuance of the Revised Order in 1971. For Mommsen, in explaining his data, suggests that "tokenism rather than a true lifting of racial barriers may be in part responsible for the current high demand levels for black American doctorates."[17]

Nor does Sowell discuss the numerical presence or nonpresence of minority academicians on white campuses during the late 1960s. In 1969, Andrew Billingsley, then the assistant chancellor for academic affairs at the University of California, Berkeley, commented on that institution's failure to employ minority scholars. Contending that the situation at Berkeley was neither better nor worse than at other major universities, he stated:

On the Berkeley campus alone over one hundred new faculty members are hired each fall. Certainly one would think that in a reasonably open institution at least ten of these would be black, brown or red. . . . Out of a regular faculty of more than thirteen hundred, the university's Berkeley campus boasts six blacks, two Mexicans, and one American Indian.[18]

Such a scant number of minority faculty, particularly of black faculty, Billingsley felt, was a "rampant racism out of all proportion to the interest or qualifications or availability of black scholars."[19]

While critics such as Hook and Sowell maintain that affirmative action is unnecessary, they overlook the perceptions that black scholars have had of white institutions. Why do black scholars perceive white institutions as being discriminatory? That question neither Hook nor Sowell chooses to address. And, as the figures from Dr. Billingsley indicate, the perceptions of black scholars were not erroneous ones. Thus, even during a period when predominantly white schools were looking for black faculty, it was clear that "good faith" efforts were not enough.

Still, the critics base much of their opposition upon what they consider to be the federal government's involvement in the internal affairs of colleges and universities. One writer has gone as far as to suggest:

Is the affirmative action program as applied to universities the Nixon Administration's humorous way of getting back at the anti-Nixon college community without rallying opposition on the left? One can imagine the outcry among civil libertarians had the administration sought to pry into faculty personnel files under any pretext other than fair hiring.[20]

Paul Seabury and Thomas Sowell do question the motivation of bureaucratic appointees of the Nixon administration in implementing affirmative action.[21] Such an argument is designed to draw suspicion upon an administration that has been viewed by many as both anti-intellectual and antiblack. However, the implementation of affirmative action programs extends from the Kennedy, Johnson, Nixon, and Ford administrations through the Carter administration. Thus, the implementation of affirmative action as decreed by Revised Order No. 4 cannot be seen as an aberration perpetrated by the Nixon administration. For affirmative action continued, although weakly enforced, under the Ford administration, another administration viewed by many as being anti-black. Increased support of affirmative action is apparently being voiced by the Carter administration. Key cabinet members, such as the attorney general, the secretary of HEW, and the secretary of labor, have made favorable comments regarding affirmative action.[22]

Aside from their claims that affirmative action is unnecessary, the critics fear the federal government's involvement in the faculty hiring procedure. Critics such as Sowell, Hook, and Seabury view the federal government's compliance power as posing a grave financial threat to universities receiving federal monies.[23] But these critics ignore the fact that institutional support was never supposed to rest upon the flow of federal money. Only certain institutions of higher education, such as Howard University, were originated with a federal commitment to existence and funding. Although it is highly improbable, any university could voluntarily refuse federal funds and thus avoid this federal intervention in their internal affairs. Since they do accept federal income, they are obligated by their contractual agreement to accept federal regulations on fair hiring practices.

Also, the federal government has been extremely reluctant to use its power to cut off funding for failure to comply with Executive Order 11246 and Revised Order No. 4.* No college or university has ever had its federal funds terminated because of failure to meet the federal regulations governing the contract compliance program. HEW and the Labor Department have consistently failed to implement sanctions when institutions have been in violation of the law.[24] There are approximately thirteen hundred institutions of higher education required to have developed affirmative action plans, but as of October 1977, only 107 plans had been approved.[25]

But the crux of the critics' contention of unwarranted federal intervention lies in their claim that academic freedom is being violated by the implementation of affirmative action. Academic freedom, as traditionally understood, means that professors have the right to teach, to conduct research, and to publish without outside interference.[26] In recent years, however, the concept of academic freedom has been expanded to include the maintenance of "university autonomy" and "faculty self-rule" in the face of government regulations.[27] Yet, this expanded meaning of academic freedom translates largely into a direct attack on only one government regulation: affirmative action. No other type of government regulation or legislation that is applicable to higher education—pension rights and retirement benefits, health and safety regulations, equal pay legislation, age discrimination legislation, student aid and veterans benefits, and student rights legislation—has been or is subjected to the wrath of members of academia as is affirmative action.[28]

* See chapter five for a detailed discussion of federal enforcement of the Executive Order.

For example, compared to their outcries against affirmative action, the critics have been remarkably silent in their public response to the Family Educational Rights and Privacy Act of 1974 or, as it is more widely known, the Buckley Amendment.[29] As applied to higher education, this act prevents the granting of federal funds to any college and university which bars students from inspecting their personal records. The lack of protest by the critics manifests the hypocrisy of their argument of academic freedom. They condemn the federal government's compliance power in enforcing affirmative action but raise no objection to the barring of federal funds to institutions not complying with the Buckley Amendment. They loudly condemn, in the name of confidentiality, attempts by the federal government to ensure fair hiring practices yet offer little protest of "confidentiality" when students are given access to their respective files. They maintain that confidentiality is betrayed when a department has to explain how it arrived at the decision to offer employment to a candidate but make little mention of confidentiality when a student has the right to read a professor's recommendation.[30]

This same self-serving use of the terms *government regulation* and *academic freedom* also marks some of the critics' views of affirmative action vis-á-vis government regulations for the handicapped. They disapprove of federal regulation to aid the victims of racial discrimination, but they approve of federal intervention to aid the victims of physical and mental affliction. This callousness has recently been expressed in the comments of George Will, the nationally syndicated columnist. Will has called affirmative action regulations "the most serious violations of academic freedom in U.S. history."[31] On the other hand, he writes, the new HEW regulations for the handicapped are reflective of a "touch of justice."[32]

Affirmative action, like several of the aforementioned laws and regulations, is an example of intervention into the affairs of higher education. But such governmental intervention is not unwarranted. Note the comments of Alan Pifer, president of the Carnegie Corporation:

. . . I regret that it has become necessary, because of intransigence, or at least a lack of perceptiveness, on the part of higher education, for government to take coercive action (through Executive Order affirmative action requirements). Measures such as these seem to me to constitute an invasion of campus autonomy and an abridgement of academic freedom. On the other hand, government has a basic obligation to protect the rights of its citizens—yes, even women—and without the threat of coercion it seems unlikely higher education would have budged an inch on the issue. Certainly, it had every chance to do so and failed.[33]

It is obvious that institutions of higher education have not taken an active role in recruiting and hiring black faculty. Their lack of positive action more than justifies federal affirmative action policies.

Opposition to Affirmative Action: Goals and Quotas

Although Revised Order No. 4 outlined the procedure under which colleges and universities were to establish goals and timetables to overcome their underutilization of blacks, the critics were quick to equate these efforts with quotas.[34] The word *quota* evokes from many educators bitter memories of religious and ethnic exclusion from colleges and universities in days past. The labeling of goals as quotas today has served only to intensify the emotional level of the debate over affirmative action.

Such reactions were demonstrated in the results of a 1975 survey of faculty attitudes by Everett Carll Ladd, Jr. and Seymour Martin Lipset. Although there were significant differences in opinion on social issues (such as legalization of marijuana) among younger and older faculty members, no such differences existed in regard to "quotas." According to the Ladd-Lipset findings, when asked if "benign quotas" are justified, nearly two-thirds of the professors surveyed did not believe that they were.[35] One can easily argue that this question was biased and designed to bring about the response that it did. Instead of asking the faculty if affirmative action were justified, Ladd and Lipset used the more emotionally laden words "benign quotas."

Supporters of affirmative action have been all too aware of how the critics have freely interjected the word *quota* into the debates. According to J. Stanley Pottinger, the former head of HEW's OCR, the word *quota* has become "a galvanizing symbol, a bogey-man, a rallying cry."[36] Pottinger's sentiments have been echoed by other supporters of affirmative action who view the quota argument as either a "red herring" or as "a phony issue."[37]

Critics such as Roche, Bunzel, and Hook have continually maintained that there is no difference whatsoever between goals and timetables and quotas.[38] But goals and quotas are not the same. Spokespersons from government agencies have repeatedly stressed the differences. Quotas, Pottinger argues, are "rigid numerical ceilings" whose use implies a deliberate attempt to limit or to establish a maximum. On the other hand, goals are "non-rigid" and "flexible" objectives whose use implies a deliberate attempt to include those blacks, other minorities, and women who historically have been excluded from teaching positions, *whereas quotas are exclusive, goals are inclusive*[39] (emphasis added). Peter Holmes, Pottinger's successor at OCR, reaffirmed the distinction between goals and quotas. Goals, he wrote "are not rigid and inflexible quotas which must be met."[40]

As the debate over affirmative action has intensified, officials of the Carter administration have reiterated the distinctions. Attorney General Griffin Bell has stated:

I oppose quotas and favor goals. And I'll tell you the difference. A goal is something you do to alleviate past discrimination and looks to the day when the merit system operates. A quota is a fixed position.[41]

Likewise, HEW Secretary Joseph A. Califano, Jr. has often stated the difference between goals and "rigid, arbitrary, long-term quotas."[42] More recently, the U.S. Commission on Civil Rights has reemphasized the distinction between the two. In endorsing numerically based remedies, the commission stated:

Experience shows that they have not been treated as fixed quotas requiring the hiring of minorities and women regardless of qualifications and circumstances, but rather as tools to remove institutional obstacles to equal employment opportunity.[43]

Yet critics such as Hook and Sowell have called for the elimination of goals and timetables.[44] Their arguments overlook the fact that goals are a mechanism by which institutions can measure their rate of progress and to what extent they are providing equal opportunity. Any retreat from the obligation to establish goals would only maintain the status quo, that is, the predominance of white males. Without the setting of goals, in spite of the critics' arguments otherwise, colleges and universities would once again be totally free to resume their old hiring practices. Such is the argument of Vernon Jordan:

To rely on administrators' good will and self-policing would ensure that no changes are made in the widespread discrimination that exists. Self-styled "color-blind" policies would leave the buddy system intact and continue to freeze minorities out of the job picture.[45]

The critics' constant equating of goals with quotas continues to hamper the full and successful implementation of affirmative action, and they continue to reject any distinction between goals and quotas. To a large extent, the critics' arguments have so poisoned the intellectual atmosphere that affirmative action is immediately likened to "quota hiring." Their continued misuse of the term *quota* has been and is a deliberate attempt to undermine affirmative action by skewing public opinion and the opinions of policy makers. Pottinger convincingly established this point.

Unfortunately, it is my impression that some critics who argue that goals are quotas are really not arguing against quotas at all. They understand the distinction between the two, and they understand that one need not inevitably become the other. Their insistence on crying "quota" to every discussion on affirmative action and their refusal to accompany their arguments with any alternatives that would appear to guarantee affirmative action without goals, lead to the conclusion that their real target is affirmative action itself.[46]

Through juxtaposition and faulty analogy, the critics argue that goals are quotas. Their constant equating of goals with quotas leads one to believe that the quota argument is a deliberate attempt to weaken the entire affirmative action program at a time when it appears that the program was making progress in bringing blacks into academe.

The Alleged Assault on Merit

Critics of affirmative action allege that affirmative action and merit are antithetical. They claim that under affirmative action a certain proportion of available faculty positions *must* be allotted to minorities under a fixed ratio. Furthermore, they argue, because of the limited number of minorities possessing the doctorate degree, these positions will be going to unqualified or lesser qualified minorities.[47] Paul Seabury maintains that such acts are a clear violation of the merit principle which, in theory at least, "advances and rewards according to ability and accomplishment, rather than according to status, preferment, or chance."[48] The defenders of this principle insist that the most qualified individual should be selected for a faculty position without the intervention of such irrelevant criteria as race or sex.

Critics such as Hook and Bunzel have repeatedly expressed their opposition to the use of "scholastically extraneous factors," such as race and sex, as an "exclusive or predominant criterion for faculty hiring."[49] But neither race nor sex is to be an "exclusive or predominant criterion." Nowhere in the Revised Order are such criteria listed. Had the criteria of race, sex, religion, or national origin never entered the hiring process for faculty members in the first place, praise for and strict adherence to the merit principle would be agreed upon by all. Because race has played, and continues to play, an important role in the hiring process, the Bunzel and Hook arguments that race is "irrelevant" or "scholastically extraneous" must be rejected. Professor Robert Staples offers a convincing rebuttal to the Hook and Bunzel statements. He writes:

It is particularly interesting to watch people who have been around for twenty years talk about race as if it were no factor in the election [sic] of personnel. One can only wonder what they said ten years ago, when blacks were systematically excluded from white colleges on the basis of their race. If race were such an irrelevant factor in hiring faculty, I often wondered why so many white candidates bothered to list their race on the vitae I reviewed while serving on personnel committees.[50]

The critics have continually called for a strict adherence to the merit principle, although it is quite obvious that such an ideal was neither consistently nor uniformly practiced. According to the Ladd-Lipset survey, 51 percent of the professors polled believe that universities have not behaved meritocratically.[51] Dr. Mary F. Berry, former chancellor of the University of Colorado and now HEW assistant secretary for education, points out that "at the very least, 20 percent of the mediocre white males now employed on university faculties *initially obtained and now retain their jobs solely because they did not have to compete with minorities and women, or even other men for them.*"[52] Even critics of affirmative action agree that the merit principle is not infallible. Agreeing in part with Dr. Berry, John Bunzel has admitted that some unqualified faculty members have been hired under the guise of the merit principle. Nevertheless, he argued that "failure to act always according to principles does not discredit the principle. Rather than abandoning it, we should concentrate our efforts on making it more consistently honored."[53]

In spite of his awareness of the abuses of the merit principle, Bunzel has called for the maintenance of the merit principle as it has always operated. But as Bernard Rosenberg and Irving Howe have written: "It is the people on top who are most inclined to find the principle of merit a social convenience, for they are persuaded, of course, that their dominance is a consequence of merit."[54] In more terse language, Vernon Jordan has stated: "The academic community appears to have elevated concepts of 'merit' and 'excellence' to the heights of mythology in its efforts to preserve the prerogatives of white males."[55]

These comments do not suggest that supporters of affirmative action are antimerit, as implied by Paul Seabury in "The Idea of Merit."[56] Rather, affirmative action and merit should be seen as copartners. Brewster C. Denny, professor at the Graduate School of Public Affairs, University of Washington, has argued that "merit, equal employment opportunity and affirmative action are all soldiers in the same cause—a just, whole, fair, productive and representative society."[57]

Yet the critics maintain that affirmative action programs violate the merit principle in favor of "reverse discrimination."[58] Although they offer no clear-cut definition of reverse discrimination, it is usually assumed to mean that "more qualified" white males are being, and will be, turned down for faculty positions so that "less qualified" or even "unqualified" minorities or females may be hired.

Critics such as Hook and Seabury allege that "reverse discrimination" permeates academia.[59] Moreover, they equate "reverse discrimination" against individual white males with the systemic discrimination against blacks. But white males, by no stretch of the imagination, are being excluded from college faculties as blacks and women have been for over one hundred years. As journalist Tom Wicker has indicated:

White males once shut out women and minorities from faculties and student bodies in a deliberate, systematic, discriminatory manner. . . . That they must finally share the opportunity of access to those institutions, and compete fairly for that access, is not "racism in reverse" or "sexism in reverse" but simple justice, long overdue.[60]

What evidence of reverse discrimination do the critics offer? They make numerous references to recruiting letters that express a preference for either blacks or females.[61] Yet the critics, particularly Sidney Hook and George Roche, cite these letters as evidence, even after the issuance of the Holmes memorandum to college and university presidents in December 1974.[62] That memorandum, welcomed by the critics, stated in part:

The affirmative action process must not operate to restrict consideration to minorities and women only. . . . Job requirements must be applied uniformly to all candidates without regard to race, color, sex, religion, or national origin.[63]

But Hook and Roche, in 1975, still denounced letters which HEW had already declared to be violations of Executive Order 11246. Several of the critics also refer to a letter, written at least as long ago as 1972, to a rejected white male candidate:

I am sorry to report that although our department saw you as our top candidate we will not be able to make you an offer for our new position. Our university is an affirmative action employer and the department must attempt to fill the new position with an individual from a recognized oppressed minority group.[64]

The critics of affirmative action use these particular letters as a "bloody shirt," designed to inflame the anger of those already opposed to affirmative action. Others have labelled the letters for what they truly are, smoke screens. The particular department in question did not hire a woman or a minority for the vacancy. Instead, it hired a less-qualified white male candidate from the same graduate school attended by the white male chairman of the department.[65] Critics such as Hook have repeatedly stated that they have discovered more than one hundred instances of "racially determined preferential selection."[66] But have the critics relied solely on letters received by rejected candidates in these cases or have they sought to discover who was actually hired? One wonders how many of these other instances of supposed "reverse discrimination" are really instances of administrators and department chairmen playing games with affirmative action for the purpose of disguising the "old boy" system of hiring by personal influence or old school ties.

These letters deserve strong criticism. Not only do they contradict the spirit of the Executive Order 11246, Revised Order No. 4, and the Holmes memorandum, but they smack of both hypocrisy and deceit. It appears, and strongly so, that the letter writers were out to discredit both affirmative action and the persons hired. Moreover, it is astounding to see the new-found "honesty" on the part of college administrators, since college administrators never have been so candid in their comments to rejected black applicants.

Although an ardent critic, Thomas Sowell has not joined the swelling chorus of those who cry reverse discrimination. Sowell has argued that the scarcity of jobs in academia "means that many aspiring academics would necessarily have had their career hopes disappointed, regardless of affirmative action."[67] Furthermore, he has written:

Now, when a hundred white male applicants are rejected, they can all blame it on one or two minority or female academics who were hired—even though 90 percent of the white males could not have been hired anyway, and there are probably 10 or 20 other white males hired for the one or two affirmative action professors. But administrators can, of course, *tell* rejected applicants that they lost out because of affirmative action, whether it is true or not, because that may be easier than telling them the real reason.[68]

Sowell's argument against reverse discrimination has been partially repeated by a white, male letter writer to the *Chronicle of Higher Education*. Like Sowell, he contends that colleges and universities use affirmative action as a scapegoat. He also writes that, "until I see much more evidence that black people are getting such a great shake at the hands of the mostly white male education establishment, I think this kind of racism must be fought against."[69]

The other critics, most notably Hook and Roche, freely cite the arguments of Sowell, but it is most interesting that not one of them cites his argument against reverse discrimination. Moreover, the Sowell argument effectively refutes the Hook and Seabury contention about the pervasiveness of reverse discrimination. It is difficult to comprehend how reverse discrimination against white males could permeate academia when the vast majority of those being hired are white males.

The critics contend that "lesser qualified" or even "unqualified" minorities have been and are being hired.[70] These are highly subjective statements for, as the comments expressed by several respondents from Oberlin College and Florida State University indicate,* in the absence of objective criteria it is difficult to determine who is "qualified" or who is "better qualified." Nor do the critics reveal how blacks are "unqualified." Is their graduate training suspect? Studies indicate that most black Ph.D.'s received their academic training from the most prestigious graduate schools.[71] Such a fact has led William Moore, Jr., and Lonnie H. Wagstaff to suggest that the critics of affirmative action are calling the graduates of their own respective institutions unqualified.[72] Rather than indicting "unqualified" blacks, the critics should be criticized for the unsubstantiated claims they are leveling against graduates of their respective institutions.

While the critics assail affirmative action as a violation of the merit principle, they make no mention of what is to be done in the case of several qualified candidates, one of whom may be black. In a situation where all factors are equal, that is, when the degree obtained and publications are comparable, preference should be given to the black candidate. The results of the Moore-Wagstaff survey support this position.

* *See* case studies in chapter six.

When polled, black educators on predominantly white campuses stated that preference be given only when blacks and whites are "equally qualified."[73]

The Alleged Effects of Affirmative Action on Minorities and on Institutions

Several of the critics of affirmative action argue that not only has affirmative action infringed upon the rights of universities and led to "quota hiring" and "reverse discrimination," but that it benefits neither blacks nor colleges and universities. Thomas Sowell, Nathan Glazer, and Sidney Hook have been, and continue to be, in the forefront of those who maintain these views. Thomas Sowell, in particular, has achieved much of his notoriety as a critic by insisting that affirmative action actually reduces the chances of blacks achieving true equality in academia.[74] Sowell has argued that there is very little evidence that affirmative action benefits blacks in general because the proportion of the labor force that has benefited from affirmative action is very small.[75]

But affirmative action is not limited solely to the higher education universe. As the numerous court cases cited in chapter three indicate, affirmative action, if enforced, brings benefits to black workers in many sectors of the economy. The comments of journalist and commentator Carl Rowan and Stanford law professor William B. Gould support this finding. According to Rowan:

The little progress that has occurred where black jobs are concerned has resulted from bosses spelling out guidelines and goals. Where such goals do not exist, personnel people regard talk of *fair hiring* as just lip service to be ignored.[76]

Echoing Rowan's comments, Gould contends that "results have been far more effective with goals and timetables, even in economic scarcity, than in boom conditions without goals and timetables."[77] While Sowell, Rowan, and Gould would probably agree that the current unemployment statistics for blacks reveal that affirmative action has not been the economic godsend to end black joblessness, Rowan and Gould do view affirmative action as a positive step in that direction.

Nathan Glazer advances an argument similar to Sowell's. Like Sowell, he contends that affirmative action was adopted after "the remarkably rapid improvement" in blacks' economic position during the 1960s. Further, Glazer contends, affirmative action does not benefit all blacks, but only the skilled.[78] But affirmative action was not implemented as a cure for black unemployment. Affirmative action was not designed to create jobs; it was designed to erase the racial barriers that have historically existed to hinder equal employment opportunity in business and industry and in colleges and universities. The regulations do provide that affirmative action programs apply to all levels of a contractor's work force. More importantly, the regulations clearly state that special employment programs for minority youth, such as after-school, work-study, and summer jobs should be set up.[79] In addition, "motivation, training and employment programs" are to be set up for the hard-core unemployed.[80] Thus, the regulations require contractors to provide training and jobs to those, particularly minority teenagers, who comprise a good part of the unemployed. Instead of venting their wrath at a so-called shortcoming of affirmative action, Glazer and Sowell should direct their concern towards the achievement of a full-employment economy.

While Glazer criticizes the concept and implementation of affirmative action in general, Sowell particularly lashes out against the implementation of affirmative action in higher education. In what is perhaps on the surface the most damaging argument against affirmative action, Sowell maintains that affirmative action "amounts to a moratorium on recognition of *achievements* by such groups [minorities and women], or their achievements tend to be subsumed under the notion of conferred benefits." This, he maintains, helps to perpetuate racism rather than to eliminate it.[81] Finally, he asserts, "what all the arguments and campaigns for quotas are really saying, loud and clear, is that black people don't have it, and they will have to be given something in order to have something."[82]

In viewing the Sowell argument, one should ask to whom is it addressed—black academicians or white academicians. His argument only serves to reinforce the preexisting attitudes of many in higher education. This is evident by the number of critics of affirmative action who parrot this particular argument of Sowell's.[83] Moreover, it is reflected in the attitudes of faculty. During the mid-1960s, as even Sowell notes, the appointments of black faculty members were sometimes viewed suspiciously by whites as "tokenism."[84] Less than a decade later, the appointments of blacks are often viewed with the same, if not increased suspicion.[85] One strongly suspects that it is not the procedure by which blacks are appointed, but the actual appointing of blacks that so unnerves many of those in academia.

If, as Sowell suggests, affirmative action is so damaging to blacks, then why have so few blacks been among its critics? This does not imply that blacks are not averse to criticizing the ideas of other blacks. For example, several blacks in academia, most notably W. Arthur Lewis of Princeton and Martin Kilson of Harvard, have been among the staunchest critics of black studies programs.[86] However, aside from Sowell and his disciple, Walter Williams, blacks in academia have not publicly criticized affirmative action. Perhaps, to paraphrase Robert M. O'Neil, support for affirmative action among black scholars comes from many who see the need for the program and who do not feel "stigmatized" by its existence.[87]

Aside from his contention that affirmative action is damaging to blacks, Sowell contends that affirmative action has brought about very little change in academia. In reality, affirmative action has forced institutions of higher eduction to seriously consider blacks for employment, often for the first time. To support his argument, Sowell cites data from the American Council on Education (ACE) which found that blacks made up 2.2 percent of college teachers in 1968–69 and 2.9 percent of college teachers in 1972–73.[88] These findings, he maintains, are "hardly revolutionary changes."[89] What Sowell has done is to compare data from 1968–69, before the implementation of affirmative action in institutions of higher education, with that from 1972–73, *the first full academic year that affimative action regulations had been in effect*. Moreover, Sowell only presents the percentage figures and does not explain what they mean. While the change in percentages over the four-year period was small, Alan E. Bayer, the conductor of the studies, concluded that those universities most dependent upon federal contracts did slightly increase their hiring of blacks.[90] Economist Richard B. Freeman has reviewed the same ACE data as Sowell, yet he reaches a different conclusion. Freeman contends that the increases were "large percentage gains for a four-year span but ones which still left a sizable gap between academic employment" of blacks and whites.[91] The more optimistic assessments of Bayer and Freeman have been substantiated by a 1975 report by the Carnegie Council. Although the report did not provide a comprehensive study of the hiring of minorities, it concluded that the percentage of minorities hired during the academic year 1973–74 "tended to be significantly higher than among total faculty members."[92]

The recently released EEO-6 data collected by EEOC provide a more detailed test of the success of implementation of affirmative action than does the Sowell analysis. Based on figures collected during the academic year 1975–76 from the overwhelming majority of the nation's colleges and universities, blacks composed 4.4 percent of the faculty members.[93] While this percentage remains low in terms of proportionality, it does show a 52 percent increase in the total number of black faculty members in a three-year period. Thus, affirmative action can produce results when colleges and universities make attempts to comply with affirmative action regulations.

In addition to their claim that affirmative action programs do not benefit blacks, the critics contend that affirmative action does not benefit colleges and universities. Among the critics, George Roche is the only one to state that affirmative action is destroying the black college and university. But Roche offers no statements from black scholars and administrators or any other evidence to support his contention that "black schools are losing their most qualified faculty members to those large, prosperous, predominantly white institutions that can afford to pay substantially higher salaries."[94] The Mommsen dissertation, which was designed to measure effects of the "brain drain," reported that the loss of black scholars to white institutions was small in relation to the number of black Ph.D.'s who stay on black campuses.[95] Moreover, several black college and university presidents such as Dr. James Cheek, president of Howard University, Dr. Andrew Billingsley, president of Morgan State University, Dr. Walter J. Leonard, the newly appointed president of Fisk University, and Dr. Hugh Gloster, president of Morehouse College, are on record in support of affirmative action.[96]

The critics also contend that affirmative action has no positive benefits in terms of costs and results for the predominantly white colleges and universities. Several maintain that affirmative action is "too costly" to implement, particularly in an era of retrenchment.[97] They make repeated mention of the fact that the University of Michigan spent $350,000 in developing its affirmative action plan.[98] Yet no similar criticism is raised over the costs involved in the implementing of other government regulations. Ohio State University, for example, has to spend $250,000 a year to comply with the Buckley Amendment; the University of Illinois may have to spend $557,000 to correct a violation of the Occupational Safety and Health Act.[99] And it is estimated that George Washington University may have to spend more than $5.2 million, and the University of Minnesota $7.2 million, to make the necessary physical changes in compliance with the new regulations for the handicapped.[100] Judging from their silence in most other instances, it is not the cost of complying with all federal regulations that so angers the critics, but only the costs of complying with affirmative action.

Moreover, the costs of implementing affirmative action should not be evaluated in a vacuum. A recent ACE study on the costs of implementing federal programs at six institutions indicates that compliance with the regulations cost these institutions beween $9 and $10 million. The equal employment opportunity laws, the affirmative action regulations, and the age discrimination laws combined cost these institutions roughly $1.7 million. That figure looms less and less imposing when one realizes that the same six institutions paid $5 million in increases in social security taxes.[101]

Affirmative action does require that colleges and universities spend money to develop and implement plans. Contrary to the critics' point of view, the costs involved in implementing and developing affirmative action plans and programs are justified in that they broaden the recruiting network.

The critics also contend that affirmative action has no positive educational benefits for the predominantly white colleges and universities. The very presence of minorities brings a much needed racial and ethnic diversity to academia. There minorities can and do serve as effective role models for both black and white students. Nor will the increased presence of minorities on college and university faculties lead, as Hook has implied, to the lowering of standards for both scholarship and teaching.[102] Affirmative action, rather than lowering standards of scholarship will instead broaden them.

Minority scholars bring both expertise, often not readily available, and different perspectives to predominantly white institutions. Many minority scholars are interested in minority problems and solutions. Their work in such diverse fields as history, sociology, anthropology, economics, political science, psychology, foreign languages, literature, art, music, and urban planning reflect both their interest and concern. Their training enables institutions of higher education to offer a broader range of courses to deal with societal problems. Besides expanding academe's search for knowledge, affirmative action poses no threat to classroom teaching since teaching is generally regarded as one of the strengths of black educators.[103]

Affirmative action is not to be seen as the death knell for either black or white institutions. Instead, affirmative action, as it is envisioned here, encompasses the recruiting, training, and hiring of more black graduate students. Such a process helps to ensure that a large pool of qualified candidates exists from which both black and white institutions may choose.*

Alternatives to Affirmative Action:
The Ideas of the Critics

The six critics included within this report have been most critical of either the concept or the implementation of affirmative action programs. Several of them freely condemn affirmative action but offer no suggestions on how to increase the numbers of blacks on college and university faculties. Paul Seabury has frankly admitted that he is "genuinely baffled" when faced with the question of how to achieve "social equity" on college and university faculties.[104] George Roche is not at all baffled. Citing the example of Jews, Roche claims that racial discrimination can be overcome through "ability and effort."[105] One cannot object to the Roche statement. Clearly, blacks who receive the Ph.D. have exhibited both "ability and effort." However, affirmative action ensures that the hiring process is made more fair.

Thomas Sowell offers no real substantive plan on how to increase black faculty members. Sowell does propose that a better matching of institutions and black faculty could come about by the "vigorous enforcement of nondiscriminatory hiring policies." "*Over a period of time,*" (emphasis added) he contends, such policies would lead to the presence of black scholars on campuses where they will be respected.[106] What Sowell has suggested is a gradualistic approach, but black scholars are no longer inclined to wait for higher education to reform itself through "good faith" efforts.

Both Sidney Hook and John Bunzel call for increases in the number of minority graduate students. In vague generalities, Hook has called for the implementing of "all effective measures—financial, psychological, social and pedagogical, that increase the number of minority graduate students."[107] More recently, he has called for improvement in elementary and secondary education, the establishment of remedial educational programs, and "open enrollment and universal access to postsecondary education" so long as standards are maintained.[108] The Hook suggestions provide long-range goals, but in the meantime remedial

* *See* chapter two.

steps such as affirmative action are needed to deal with present discriminatory treatment. One also questions whether Hook's statements are only idle lip service to equal opportunity. Hook has yet to make these statements in a situation in which he is not denouncing affirmative action.

Unlike Hook, John Bunzel has proposed a seemingly sensible plan to increase minority and female candidates on college faculties. In language similar to that of the Revised Order, Bunzel has written:

A serious search must be made for qualified women and minorities when faculty appointments are being made. At the departmental level, where academic recruitment is initiated, procedures should be established to include a current and realistic estimate of the pool of qualified individuals from which candidates will be drawn. Carefully balancing professional interests and priorities as it sets its own programmatic needs, the department must constantly strive to attract the best faculty possible. To this end it should demonstrate that it has reached out in its search for women and minorities.[109]

To increase the number of minority graduate students, Bunzel has called for increased support, financial and other, from federal and state governments, foundations, and business and industry. To expand the ranks of the qualified, Bunzel calls for programs to publicize and to promote graduate students.[110] Bunzel's concrete proposals in essence do not differ in the main from those suggested by Stephen J. Wright, a former vice-president of the College Entrance Examination Board. Earlier in 1972, Wright had proposed that more fellowship programs be set up to aid minority graduate and professional students.[111] If either of these programs had been implemented in 1972 or earlier, then much of the resulting furor over the lack of qualified minorities might have been avoided.

Ever since the application of affirmative action to higher education, the arguments of its critics have dominated most discussions of the concept and implementation of the program. This chapter has demonstrated how the critics' misreading and misinterpretation of Executive Order 11246 and Revised Order No. 4 have lead to unfair and distorted depictions of the program. With their repeated outcries of "violation of academic freedom," "quotas," and "reverse discrimination," the critics have stigmatized all efforts to achieve equal employment opportunity in institutions of higher education. But their charges and labels are largely straw issues, unsupported by solid evidence and designed solely to increase the opposition to affirmative action. They have engaged primarily in distortion, juxtaposition, and inference in presenting their arguments.

Nor have the critics offered much constructive criticism. While all are conscious of past discrimination against blacks, they remain unmindful of its recurring effects. Although the critics pay homage to the goal of equal employment opportunity, they present no viable and immediate alternatives to affirmative action.

Part II

Chapter Five

Affirmative Action
and the Federal Government

Executive Order 11246, along with its implementing regulations, provides the basic conceptual framework for attaining equal employment opportunity in institutions of higher education. The institutions covered by the order are required not only to end present discrimination in the employment process but also to "recruit, employ, and promote qualified members of groups formerly excluded, even if that exclusion cannot be traced to particular discriminatory actions on the part of the employer."[1] The principal role of government in this area, therefore, is to ensure that the law of the land requiring equality of opportunity is carried out.

It is the federal government's responsibility to ensure that all of its citizens have a fair opportunity to gain skills and compete for jobs in general and in higher education in particular. While institutions of higher education are responsible under the law for altering their former discriminatory hiring practices and taking positive steps to promote fair black representation in academia, in the final analysis it is up to the government to ensure that the laws, executive orders, and regulations are obeyed.

In order to carry out its responsibility to promote equal employment opportunity in institutions of higher education, the government has assumed certain regulatory functions. A principal component in the government's effort to regulate the racial practices of higher educational institutions is affirmative action. The effort to promote affirmative action can be divided into two phases. First, as with all policy matters, the government must ensure that institutions in fact adopt the new affirmative action practices, and second, it must ensure that the institutions in fact carry out these practices once they are established.

There are certain steps which are essential if effective affirmative action programs are to be established. The discussion of these steps will provide the framework for the consideration of the government effort. First, the government must issue clear regulations that will, if implemented, result in an effective affirmative action program. This step has been attempted through the issuance of the executive orders and their implementing regulations. Second, the government must provide the necessary direction and assistance to make sure that each institution adopts and implements the practices as spelled out in the guidelines. This step has been attempted through the effort to get institutions to develop and implement satisfactory affirmative action plans. An assessment of the adequacy of the federal guidelines involves evaluating whether they will be sufficient to ensure (1) that all groups have equal access to information about job opportunities; (2) that all groups have a fair opportunity to apply for the positions; (3) that fair consideration be given to all applicants; and (4) that once hired, all employees receive fair treatment. The implementation effort involves the establishment of a strategy to enforce corrections of any deficiencies detected in the monitoring phase.

To examine how effectively the government is carrying out its responsibility to provide equal opportunity, it is necessary to first review the regulations implementing the provisions of Executive Order 11246 to determine their adequacy in achieving equal opportunity. Next it is necessary to examine the government structure established for assuring that colleges and universities end discrimination and develop and carry out affirmative action programs. The compliance program is then examined to determine how well the government has monitored and enforced the affirmative action program. Finally, some alternatives are suggested to make the program more effective.

It is important to maintain a distinction between the concept of affirmative action and the procedures currently used to implement the concept. There are some significant problems in the government's effort to establish and implement affirmative action. These problems have seriously weakened enforcement of the Executive Order. Yet none of these problems should be permitted to distract from the essential soundness of the concept. Moreover, the federal government must have a major role in bringing about fair employment practices in institutions of higher education because of the historical failure of these institutions to implement equal opportunity on their own. Therefore, the weaknesses in the government's program are uncovered in hopes that by doing so these weaknesses will be corrected and the chances for equal opportunity will be improved.

Organization of the Government Enforcement Effort

When Executive Order 11246 was issued in 1965, the secretary of labor was assigned responsibility for supervising and coordinating the federal contract compliance program.[2] The Department of Labor initially designated thirteen (later reduced to eleven) federal agencies to enforce the provisions of the regulations as they applied to specific industries. The overall responsibility for contract compliance, however, remained with the Department of Labor, where it is lodged in the Office of Federal Contract Compliance Programs (OFCCP). OFCCP is supposed to establish policy and program objectives and evaluate the performance of each compliance agency to ensure maximum progress in reaching the objectives of the Executive Order. OFCCP, as well as each compliance agency, has regional offices which also have been delegated responsibility for contract compliance.[3]

The Department of Labor has delegated to each of the compliance agencies responsibility for conducting compliance reviews which include pre- and postaward compliance reviews, desk audits, follow-up reviews, and complaint investigations. The department has also issued regulations which the compliance agencies are responsible for administering. HEW is the compliance agency responsible for enforcing the Executive Order and regulations in the educational universe regardless of which federal agency entered into the contract.[4]

Prior to 1967, HEW's civil rights responsibilities were spread among the department's various subagencies while enforcement responsibility was lodged in the General Counsel's Office. This administrative structure proved unsatisfactory because it created confusion and unnecessary coordination problems by having civil rights responsibilities divided among so many agencies and levels within the department. Further, the structure required complicated funding arrangements which often made it difficult to even know the total amount of funds used for civil rights activities.[5]

In 1967, at the suggestion of the House Appropriations Committee, civil rights activities were centralized in the Office for Civil Rights (OCR) to correct the cumbersome structural arrangements and to handle anticipated increases in its work load. Over the years, OCR has seen its civil rights responsibilities substantially increased. Under the general direction of the secretary of HEW, OCR is the designated authority to direct, coordinate, and enforce the department's nondiscrimination responsibilities regarding federal financial assistance programs pursuant of Title VI of the Civil Rights Act of 1964; Titles VII and IX of the Education Amendments of 1972; Titles VII and VIII of the Public Health Service Act; Section 407 of the Drug Abuse and Treatment Act of 1972; Section 321 of the Comprehensive Alcohol Abuse and Alcoholism Prevention, Treatment, and Rehabilitation Act of 1970, as amended; Section 504 of the Rehabilitation Act of 1973; and Section 7(b) of the Public Law 93-638. OCR is also responsible for enforcing Executive Order 11246's equal employment opportunity requirements for all contracts involving department funds and federal contracts involving insurance; insurance agencies; medical, legal, and education services; museums and art galleries; nonprofit organizations; and certain state and local governments.[6]

Responsibilities under Executive Order 11246

Although President Lyndon B. Johnson issued Executive Order 11246 in 1965, the affirmative action requirement was not spelled out until 1971, when Revised Order No. 4 was issued by the Department of Labor. The Executive Order was not applicable to nonconstruction aspects of employment in institutions of higher education until 1971, and the affirmative action requirement was not applied to institutions supported by state and local governments until 1973. HEW was also designated as the compliance agency for enforcing the Executive Order as it applies to nonconstruction aspects of employment in institutions of higher education.[7]

HEW's civil rights responsibilities are administered by a special assistant to the secretary for civil rights who has the ultimate responsibility for assuring that HEW's programs are operated in a nondiscriminatory manner. The overall operation for civil rights is lodged in OCR with a director and his assistants. OCR's headquarters office has four major operating divisions: Elementary and Secondary, Higher Education, Contract Compliance, and Health and Social Services. There are several administrative and support offices and attorneys assigned from the Office of General Counsel and funded by OCR, who are counted as OCR's authorized staff. OCR has ten regional offices which have the same organizational structure. The ten regional offices are: Region 1

Boston, Massachusetts; Region 2, New York, New York; Region 3, Phila-delphia, Pennsylvania; Region 4, Atlanta, Georgia; Region 5, Chicago, Illinois; Region 6, Dallas, Texas; Region 7, Kansas City, Missouri; Region 8, Denver, Colorado; Region 9, San Francisco, California; and Region 10, Seattle, Washington.[8]

Within OCR, the Higher Education Division is responsible for non-construction contract compliance enforcement at institutions of higher education in addition to its other civil rights responsibilities under Titles VI and VII of the Civil Rights Act of 1964. The Higher Education Division has three functional branches: (1) Policy, Planning, and Program Development, (2) Operations, and (3) Technical Assistance. There are higher education branches in each of the ten regional offices. The regional offices are headed by a director who reports to the director of OCR and receives no program supervision from the regional director of HEW, who reports directly to the Office of the Secretary. Each OCR regional office has branches corresponding to the branches at headquarters. The chief of the regional higher education branch reports to the OCR regional director. There are specialists under the chief who are responsible for conducting compliance reviews, complaint investigations, negotiations and conciliations, and technical assistance.[9]

The Policy, Planning, and Program Development branch develops planning systems and policy guidelines including an annual enforcement plan which specifies the number of compliance reviews and other activities to be performed during the year. The Operations branch monitors the quality and quantity of performance by the higher education regional branch offices. The Technical Assistance branch develops training programs for the division and provides colleges and universities with technical assistance.[10]

With OCR's growing civil rights responsibilities over the years, it has received a corresponding increase in its budget and authorized staff. In 1967, the department's budget for civil rights enforcement totaled $3,434,000 with 278 authorized staff positions. By 1976, the budget had increased to $25,113,000 with an authorized staff of 904. OCR has not fully used its authorized staff positions; 115 vacancies remained unfilled at the end of fiscal year 1976.[11]

OCR's Higher Education Division had an authorized professional staff in fiscal year 1977 of 210, but as of May 1977 had filled only 176 positions. (*See* Table 5-1.) There were 172 positions authorized for fiscal year 1977 but only 154 filled. For fiscal year 1978, the agency has requested a total of 249 professional staff positions for the regional offices.[12]

TABLE 5-1. OCR Higher Education Staffing Pattern

	Head-quar-ters	Re-gional Total	1	2	3	4	5	6	7	8	9	10
Authorized Professionals FY 1977	38	172	12	17	19	19	29	22	9	9	27	9
Current Professionals FY 1977	22	154	11	16	19	19	28	18	8	8	19	8

Source: ISEP Questionnaire, 18 April 1977.

According to OCR officials, there are a number of reasons why so many positions remained vacant. A recent audit by the personnel office of HEW revealed that too many of the professional positions were over-rated and the agency was prevented from hiring at the GS 13 and above levels. OCR has also been on the verge of reorganizing for about two years. Supervisors are reluctant to fill vacancies until the final structure of the agency is worked out. With the change in administration and the pending reorganization, a conscious effort was made not to fill many of the vacancies in spite of the fact that additional staff was needed and requested for fiscal year 1978. To meet the needs of its ever expanding responsibilities, OCR has requested a budget of $36,061,000 for fiscal year 1978, an increase of $4,757,000 over its current budget for fiscal year 1977.[13]

According to a 1974 report by the U.S. Commission on Civil Rights, the authorized staffing levels for the Higher Education Division varied from a high of eighteen positions in the New York, San Francisco, and Chicago regional offices, to a low of nine positions in the Seattle office. Although the sizes of the regional offices were supposed to be determined by the number and size of institutions, the number receiving federal assistance, the number requiring technical assistance, and the number of minority students, OCR did not always take these factors into con-sideration in allocating staff resources. In 1977 there still remained a large disparity in the number of professional staff in the regional offices of the Higher Education Division that cannot be explained by the above factors. (*See* Table 5-1). The Chicago office has an authorized level of twenty-nine professionals while the Kansas City, Denver, and San Francisco offices have only nine professionals despite the fact that the case load in Chicago is not three times those of the other three offices.[14]

The Government's Affirmative Action Regulations

The current basis for the government's affirmative action effort is Executive Order 11246 issued by President Lyndon B. Johnson in 1965. Under this order the secretary of labor was assigned responsibility for supervising and coordinating the federal contract compliance program. The Department of Labor issued regulations for federal contractors in developing programs to ensure that they provide equal employment opportunities for all groups.[15]

The first priority in getting colleges and universities to develop and implement affirmative action plans is to identify all institutions subject to the provisions of the Executive Order. In October 1972, J. Stanley Pottinger, then director of OCR, sent a memorandum to all college and university presidents stating that all institutions including colleges and universities covered by Executive Order 11246, are expected to be in compliance with the order and its implementing regulations. The OCR director attached guidelines for affected institutions to follow which explain in detail the requirements of the regulations for academia. He added: "The Department of Health, Education and Welfare stands ready to assist in every way possible so that all institutions of higher education will be able to meet the requirements of the Executive Order and other federal requirements regarding nondiscriminatory treatment."[16]

The regulations[17] governing the affirmative action program provide that a contractor who receives federal contracts or subcontracts of $10,000 or more must agree not to discriminate against any applicant for employment, or employee, on the basis of race, color, religion, sex, or national origin. A contractor with fifty or more employees and a contract in excess of $50,000 is required to develop and maintain a written affirmative action program within 120 days of receipt of such a contract.

The regulations contain several main components to assure that institutions develop an effective affirmative action program. These provisions relate to the personnel practices of universities, the managerial structure and procedures that a university must establish to implement an affirmative action program, and the goals and timetables that are established as management tools to assist in judging the success of the affirmative action effort. A brief review of each of these principal aspects of the guidelines is presented below.

Personnel Policies and Practices

According to the guidelines issued by HEW, universities and colleges are required to ensure that their employment standards, criteria, and procedures do not have the effect of excluding minorities. They are required to establish in reasonable detail the standards and procedures which govern institutional employment, including criteria for appointment, retention, and promotion. There is some leeway in explicitly articulating the criteria for academic employment, but institutions are required to outline their policies and practices in sufficient detail to eliminate opportunities for arbitrary and discriminatory employment decisions. Although institutions are permitted "discretion" in decisions regarding academic employment, such discretion must be rigorously examined and eliminated when its effects are discriminatory. There is no suggestion in the affirmative action requirement that unqualified candidates should be hired.

Before the implementation of affirmative action procedures, few institutions of higher education had standard criteria for determining qualifications for employing academic and professional staffs. This made it extremely difficult, if not impossible, to detect discrimination. The affirmative action procedures require all institutions to make employment decisions based upon validated standard criteria and thus allow regulatory officials, for the first time, to know in principle just why certain applicants were hired or employees promoted in preference to others. If these provisions are actually carried out they should facilitate the enforcement of equal opportunity laws.

The institution is also required to examine its recruitment policy to assure that it does not discriminate against minorities and women. Specific steps must be outlined to ensure that minorities and women are represented in the applicant pool. Where recruitment activities and policies, at whatever level, have the effect of excluding minorities and women, they must be changed or eliminated. Where underutilization occurs, specific steps are outlined to allow the employer to increase the applicant pool. The regulations further provide suggestions to help avoid major problem areas in developing an adequate recruitment policy program. These recruitment strategies are designed to ensure that all receive fair notification of employment opportunities. The failure to receive job information has been a barrier to minority access in the past. If these programs are actually carried out they should make the attainment of equal opportunity more probable.

Once an applicant pool has been established, selection from that pool must follow procedures to ensure nondiscrimination. Standards for employment in all areas should be explicit and relevant, as discussed above, and should be available for examination by applicants and employees. Nondiscriminatory application of fair standards is, of course, essential for the attainment of equal opportunity.

Further, an institution is required to examine its job category assignments and treatment of individuals within a job classification to ensure that minorities are not clustered in certain areas where there is lower pay and less opportunity for advancement, which has been a principal problem in the past. Where such patterns of assignment are found, job training must be instituted to upgrade skills, especially when the supply of minorities is limited. Where underrepresentation exists, minorities and women should have the opportunity for advancement through specially established training programs or academic classwork, where appropriate, within the university or, where such programs do not exist, in conjunction with other universities.

The regulations also require that policies and practices governing promotion should be "reasonably" explicit and administered in such a way as to ensure that minorities are given equal opportunity for promotion. Institutions of higher education must spell out in detail just what the requirements are for promotions, especially in the faculty tenured ranks.

There are also provisions which require that where terminations adversely affect minorities, the employer must be able to demonstrate that these terminations were not based on race, religion, color, national origin, or sex. If the employer cannot so demonstrate, such actions are to be closely scrutinized by OCR to determine if they are discriminatory. This provision, of course, is designed to prevent a revolving door policy. A university must also examine all terms and conditions of employment to ensure that discrimination against minorities does not exist, and must ensure that employees receive equal pay and other benefits for equal work.

Universities are further required to identify any differentials based exclusively on race or sex and make whatever payments and adjustments are necessary to remove existing differentials. Further, institutions are subject to the provisions of Title VII of the 1964 Civil Rights Act, the Equal Pay Act, and the National Labor Relations Act.

Finally, institutions should develop internal grievance procedures for all employees which provide for the prompt and equitable hearing of employment discrimination grievances. The procedures should be written and available to all present and prospective employees.

These provisions of the regulations are intended to force universities to correct those aspects of personnel practices which have permitted the perpetuation of discrimination in the past. It is not clear, however, how effective these regulations will be. It is clear that if the universities undertake all that is required, a fair employment system will be established. The regulations permit a wide range of discretion in designing employment procedures and this continues to place the major burden on the government's civil rights officers to determine whether specific procedures are in fact fair. This discretion allows each university to adapt the plan to its own particular situation. In practice, however, there is the danger that the lack of precise specification of what constitutes fair personnel procedures may lead to confusion in the universities and difficulties for civil rights enforcement officers.

Method of Implementation of the Plan

The provisions relating to the implementation of the plan require the chief executive of an institution to clearly state or reaffirm the institution's policy on equal employment opportunity and indicate the mechanism for implementation. This policy should govern all personnel actions regarding recruiting, hiring, training, promoting, and other action relating to personnel decisions. An explanation of the policy should be disseminated internally to ensure that all segments of the university community are familiar with the policy, and externally, to ensure that potential recruiting sources are familiar with the policy.

An affirmative action officer must be appointed by the chief executive and given sufficient support to carry out the responsibilities of the office. Depending upon the size of the institution, the office must have a full-time director with adequate staff to carry out the affirmative action requirements.

In implementing the plan, the affirmative action office must undertake several actions. Problem areas must be identified by organizational units and job classifications. This requires the institution to undertake an in-depth analysis which must include an analysis of the composition of the work force, applicant flow, selection process, transfer and promotion practices, facilities, seniority practices (including unions), apprenticeship and other training programs, and work force attitude. Specific corrective actions must follow the identification of problem areas and special employment programs designed to aid in the increase of the affected class should be implemented whenever possible.

Job descriptions must be reviewed to ensure that they accurately reflect the position's function. Selection criteria should be validated to assure that the requirements themselves do not inadvertently discriminate against the affected class. The entire selection process, and especially the persons involved, should be evaluated to assure freedom from bias.

Institutions are also required to monitor the employment process (referrals, placements, transfers, promotions, and terminations) to ensure its equal employment policy is carried out. Reports must be made and reviewed on a regularly scheduled basis and recommendations should be made to improve unsatisfactory performance.

These provisions are designed to ensure that the institution actually carries out its affirmative action plan. However, again there is a lack of specificity in these requirements. The provisions relating to the establishment of the affirmative action office allow the university to select its own staffing pattern, and the actual monitoring and reporting requirements are nonspecific. This lack of specificity also increases the difficulty of enforcement agencies and may cause confusion and uncertainty among the institutions. Clearly it also permits greater leeway for those intent on weakening the affirmative action efforts.

Establishment of Goals

The development and use of goals and timetables are at the heart of the effort to monitor the affirmative action effort. These goals and timetables are to guide the affirmative action management efforts within the university as well as to provide information to government enforcement agencies on how well the effort is proceeding. The proper definition and use of goals are therefore crucial. Unfortunately there is much confusion surrounding the development and use of utilization analyses and goals.

The affirmative action regulations require the goals to be set on the basis of a utilization analysis and the prospects for achievement, given good faith effort. The utilization analysis is in principle crucial. In this analysis, the institution must compare its current utilization with current availability. The existence of underutilization is a signal to management that a problem exists. Such a signal should alert management to monitor more closely developments in the problem areas.

The goals can be set according to the results of department by department and occupation by occupation underutilization analyses. The guidelines suggest that goals are to represent what can be reasonably achieved given good faith efforts. These goals will provide management with criteria to judge the success of the affirmative action effort. The failure to reach the goal requires that the institution investigate very closely the employment process in the area experiencing the failure.

A proper utilization analysis requires the existence of specific availability data which are generally not available. For faculties, it may be appropriate to use national market data. But even this national data may be scarce or nonexistent for particular disciplines.

The problem is that the regulations do not specify what data should be used to define availability. As a result, institutions must create their own, and obviously different institutions will have created different data. Often these data are based on inadequate information concerning the number of blacks available for employment. Since the entire educational system was discriminatory in the past and limited the number presently available for employment, future availability would certainly be more appropriate in view of the link between demand and supply information. (*See* the discussion of future supply and demand in chapter seven.)

Data on the actual employment of blacks are also not available on a uniform basis. The recent EEO-6 survey will resolve this issue once it is processed and released. In any case, it seems clear that the government should specify the appropriate data for use in utilization analysis. If appropriate data are not available, they should be obtained through a special survey.

The linkage between underutilization and the necessity for establishing goals should also be made clearer. Underutilization indicates the failure to hire blacks when available. But the key consideration in defining goals will be the expected hiring and the expected availability. Goals should be adjusted whenever the actual hiring or actual availability is greater than expected.

The role of the goals as a managerial tool should also be emphasized. It should be made clear that goals are not quotas but are just indications of what could be expected from a fair employment system. The failure to meet the established goal is not necessarily an indication that the affirmative action plan is not working. So, too, results may exceed expectations because hiring is greater than expected. In either case bias may continue to exist despite the seemingly positive outcome.

Nonetheless, it is reasonable to require specific explanation when an institution fails to achieve reasonably defined goals. An institution's affirmative action officer as well as OCR should take this failure as a signal of possible trouble and should undertake specific investigatory actions. If the results of investigations reveal a failure to implement a bias-free employment effort, then specific corrective action should be taken by the government and the institution.

The discussion has concentrated on the use of goals and timetables in setting hiring goals. However, goals and timetables should also be established for other aspects of the employment system such as distribution by pay grade, promotions, tenure, recruitment, and so forth. The discussion above concerning the utilization analysis and goals applies to these areas of the employment system as well.

The current guidelines make no mention of time limit for the requirement of extensive analyses. The extensive use of goals and utilization analyses should probably be viewed as a temporary measure. Institutions which currently have black representation at or beyond the potential availability (i.e., the proportion of blacks in the labor force) could probably be exempted from the current requirement to develop extensive goals and utilization analyses. Also, as institutions which currently utilize blacks at rates below their supply potential achieve greater black representation, they could be excused from continuing the development of detailed goals. As the entire set of institutions reach aggregate parity with the supply potential, then the requirement for goals can be drastically reduced. The regulations should specify the temporary nature of extensive analyses, goals, and timetables.

Although the basic structure of the regulations is sound, there are a number of problem areas which have not been resolved by the attempts to clarify the regulations to date. The regulations are unnecessarily complex and often confusing because they lack specificity. It would be appropriate to reexamine the regulations in an effort to simplify and clarify them. In revising the regulations, more emphasis should be placed on the achievement of results. They should also spell out clearly just what the required basic elements in affirmative action plans are and where institutions have discretion in determining what elements should be included.

The permissable discretion in the managerial procedures should be narrowed. More specific instructions for the internal monitoring system ought to be included in the regulations. Moreover, the specifics of the utilization analyses should be detailed and the availability data ought to be mandated and supplied by the federal government. In addition, the instructions for establishing goals and timetables should be more specific. The relationship between utilization analyses and timetables should be spelled out. If these steps are taken, the affirmative action guidelines could be more easily enforced by the government.

The memorandum issued to college presidents in December 1974 by Peter Holmes, then director of OCR, emphasized that institutions should not discriminate against white males in carrying out affirmative action programs.[18] The guidelines had already clearly stated that the most qualified applicant for a job was to receive the position. The memorandum gave the impression by its emphasis on "reverse discrimination," under the guise of affirmative action, that the hiring of less qualified minorities and women was a significant problem. This impression led to greater confusion since there was no clear evidence of widespread reverse discrimination and since institutions had not even been required to spell out just what they meant by "qualifications" for faculty employment in an objective fashion. Thus, many administrators and faculty members assumed that the memorandum was an indication that hiring practices could continue as usual, or at best, that institutions were to assume a posture of benign neutrality. Further, the memorandum suggested that goals simply reflect the employer's estimate of results he expected to achieve under affirmative action without specifying how those expectations were to be formed. Instead of clarifying the issue, the Holmes memorandum weakened the Executive Order's requirements.

The New Format

The regulations provide for agreements between government and industry to adopt national formats to apply basic requirements of Order No. 4 to certain industries or multifacility contractors. In August 1975, HEW developed its "Format for Development of an Affirmative Action Plan by Institutions of Higher Education," as a detailed guideline for implementing the requirements of Order No. 4 in the higher educational sector.[19]

The format purports to clarify the regulations as they relate to institutions of higher education in an effort to reduce the criticism from academia that affirmative action regulations as designed do not apply to academe. The new format basically repeats the requirements of the regulations and illustrates how certain sections should be applied to the particular situation in academia. For example, in conducting utilization analyses, the format proposes that institutions combine various job categories and groupings to reduce the institution's work load and to facilitate data processing. This particular interpretation of the regulations, if followed, would do much to eliminate situations where goals can not be established because the job category is too small.

Even with the new format, a number of problem areas remain. Uniform availability data are still lacking, which means that institutions are now required to depend upon inadequate and diverse sources of data. Such a situation allows for mistakes in analysis and inconsistencies in the way goals are established.

Another problem is that the format continues to allow institutions to use "feeder schools," that is, graduate schools from which the institution normally hires. But the format suggests that these feeder schools are appropriate as long as they do not disproportionately limit their selection of affected class members. Yet there remains the possibility that the use of feeder schools can unduly limit the availability of minorities and women.

Although some institutions do not establish a goal for affected class members until their analysis reveals an underutilization of 1.0 person, it would be preferable if the format required that goals be established when underutilization is 0.5 person or greater. The format suggests that goals be established over a three-year period because of the low turnover and lack of expansion, which often means that annual goals result in smaller numbers. If there are increased opportunities for faculty employment, then shorter interim goals might be more appropriate. The compliance officers are to evaluate the success or failure to meet these goals at the end of each goal period (three years or less where applicable).

A major problem pointed out in the discussion of the regulations was the fact that minorities could be grouped together to establish goals. Although, on the surface such groupings might allow for the establishment of higher goals, it is important to determine what particular minority groups are underrepresented and to design goals to overcome this underutilization.

The new format suggests that where it is evident from the utilization analysis that one minority group is substantially underutilized, then separate goals must be established to overcome the underutilization.

Further, an annual review and an updating of goals and timetables must be done until underutilization is eliminated. (*See* chapter six for a detailed discussion of specific affirmative action plans.)

In summary, the review of the regulations implementing the affirmative action program indicates that they basically have all of the components necessary for the development of a good affirmative action program. They have provisions designed to assure that there is an equal opportunity to obtain employment information, that all applicants have a fair opportunity to apply, that employers provide fair consideration to all applicants, and finally, once hired, all employees receive equal treatment. Moreover, they have provisions to establish a structure within the institution to manage the affirmative action effort. The requirement that goals and timetables be established is a key element of affirmative action. Without this requirement employees would have no basis for determining their rate of progress, and the federal government would lack the means to evaluate the contractor's programs.

The Establishment and Implementation of Affirmative Action

Despite the designation of HEW as the compliance agency in the higher education sector, and despite the growth of staff and resources devoted to the task, the government's effort to establish equal opportunity and implement the affirmative action program in the higher education sector has not soared. This is partially due to shortcomings in the regulations, as were pointed out previously, but, more important, due to shortcomings in the implementation and enforcement efforts and inefficiencies in the existing organizational structure.

As was noted previously, the first step involved in ensuring an effective affirmative action program is to identify all institutions covered and to make sure that they understand the requirements so that they can develop affirmative action plans in a timely fashion. OCR has failed in its responsibility on both counts.

There are approximately three thousand institutions of higher education in the United States and OCR estimates that between eleven hundred and thirteen hundred colleges and universities are covered by the provisions of Executive Order 11246.[20] The total number of institutions covered by Executive Order 11246 varies from year to year, depending upon whether the institutions receive $50,000 or more in federal contracts. Further, the failure of other agencies to keep OCR up-to-date on their awards has contributed to uncertainty over just how many institutions are covered by the order. OCR's failure to develop a comprehensive data system means that it is unable to keep track of those institutions subject to the order and their compliance status. Some institutions are, consequently, uncertain whether they are covered. Those institutions with affirmative action plans, either proposed or undertaken, are not sure whether they comply with the order and its implementing regulations. The regional OCR director in Atlanta estimates that there are 400 institutions of higher education in that region, and of that number approximately 50 are subject to the provisions of Executive Order 11246. In Region 5, a spokesperson in the Chicago office suggested that there were 630 college campuses (some universities have more than one campus) of which 250 are required to develop affirmative action plans. A spokesperson in the San Francisco office suggested that only 34 higher educational institutions were covered in the region.[21] It appears that what constitutes an institution varies from region to region; some list multicampuses as separate institutions, while others treat these separate campuses as one unit for enforcement purposes.

OCR needs to give priority to determining systematically how many institutions are subject to Executive Order 11246. Also, if OCR is to develop a system of priorities in implementing the regulations, it needs to know not only which institutions are covered by the order but also which offer the most potential for improving employment opportunities for minorities and females. It should also require uniform classification to allocate staff resources based upon the actual work requirement in each region.

For affirmative action to work, institutions must develop and implement their affirmative action plans. A major reason for the initial slowness in institutions developing plans has been the lack of understanding by academia of what is actually required and the need for technical assistance from OCR. OCR's record in providing technical assistance has been sporadic and uneven. Although affirmative action plans were to be developed and submitted for approval within 120 days of the award of a contract, few if any institutions were able to fulfill this requirement. Contrary to what the critics say, OCR has diligently tried to accommodate academicians and has been more than fair in taking into consideration problems faced by colleges and universities.

Between July 1972 and 9 December 1974, OCR requested that 137 institutions file affirmative action plans. During that same time period 106 institutions voluntarily submitted plans to OCR. OCR, by 9 Decem-

TABLE 5-2. Status of Affirmative Action Plans by Regional Office, FY 1976 and 1977

Regions	No. of plans received during FY 1976	Plans approved during FY 1976	Plans rejected	Plans approved during FY 1977	Plans rejected
1	6	4	2	3[1]	0
2	59	6	4	2	0
3	14	14	14[1]	1	1[1]
4	3	3	0	0	0
5	3	3	3	0	0
6	0	0	0	0	0
7	12[2]	8	7	0	0
8	2	2	0	0	0
9	7	7	0	0	0
10	1	1	0	0	0

1. Plans received were initially rejected, but are now approved.
2. Four voluntary plans.

Source: ISEP Questionnaire, 18 April 1977.

ber 1974, had reviewed or acted on 88 affirmative action plans, 29 of which had been approved and 59 rejected; 155 were still waiting to be reviewed. As of April 1975, OCR had accepted 33 affirmative action plans as meeting the basic requirements of the regulations. The Seattle and Kansas City regions (Regions 10 and 7) had not accepted any affirmative action plans.[22]

By May 1977, OCR made more progress in approving affirmative action plans. During fiscal year 1976 OCR had received 107 plans, of which 48 were approved and 30 rejected. (*See* Table 5-2.) From 1969 to 31 January 1977, OCR had approved a total of 107 affirmative action plans, all at institutions with a million dollars or more in federal contracts.

Although OCR has made some progress in reviewing and acting on affirmative action plans, serious weaknesses still remain.[23] The Department of Labor's regulations require that when a compliance review is made and deficiencies in the equal employment opportunity program are discovered, reasonable efforts be made to eliminate these deficiencies through conciliation and persuasion. Yet a General Accounting Office (GAO) study found that the Dallas and San Francisco regional offices, for example, were conducting prolonged periods of mediation and conciliation while providing technical assistance to colleges and universities in an effort to get them to develop acceptable affirmative action plans.

The Dallas regional office conducted mediation and conciliation for eleven institutions whose affirmative action plans had been disapproved before May 1974 for an average of ten months before the plans were again disapproved. As of 9 December 1974, none of the plans had been approved but mediation and conciliation continued. Of the four institutions the San Francisco regional office requested to submit affirmative action plans, not one had been approved by 9 December 1974. But the regional office had been mediating and conciliating with them for an average of three years. Further, OCR did not approve or reject affirmative action plans within the specified time period of sixty days. The GAO study concluded that OCR's credibility had been seriously impaired because it did not initiate sanctions, where required, but instead provided mediation, conciliation, and technical assistance over prolonged periods.[24]

It is to be expected that there would be some delays in the development of plans, but one would expect that five years after the guidelines were issued, more than 107 affirmative action plans would have been approved. Some of the problems can be attributed to a lack of OCR staff to provide technical assistance to institutions, but even when technical assistance was provided, the process was protracted. In addition, conciliation often continued beyond the time specified in the regulations when sanctions should have been initiated. And even when plans were submitted, OCR was slow in approving them and getting problems corrected. What is clearly needed is for OCR to take its responsibility under the Executive Order seriously and to establish a date when all institutions subject to the order are expected to submit plans for approval. Institutions must have reasonably satisfactory plans or face the imposition of sanctions.

Enforcement of Executive Order 11246

Once plans have been approved, it is essential that adequate enforcement procedures be established to monitor progress in implementing affirmative action. Compliance reviews are one way the federal government monitors its contractors. Failure to hire on a nondiscriminatory basis and to implement affirmative action procedures subjects the contractor to appropriate sanctions. The compliance review consists of a comprehensive analysis and evaluation of the implementation of each aspect of the employment process specified above. Where the contractor fails to implement these provisions or is deficient in some aspect of his or her program, the compliance officer attempts to bring the contractor into compliance through conciliation and persuasion. The contractor commits himself or herself in writing to make the necessary corrections which specify the nature of the action to be taken and the dates for completion.

There are two types of compliance reviews. The preaward review is to be conducted prior to the government awarding a contract of a million dollars or more to a contractor with fifty or more employees. All other compliance reviews are conducted after the contracts are awarded and are to be done on a regular basis.

Preaward Compliance Reviews

Before any contract of a million dollars or more is awarded, the contracting agency must notify the potential contractor that he or she will be subject to a preaward compliance review to determine whether he or she maintains acceptable nondiscriminatory employment procedures and an affirmative action plan. The compliance agency must then determine the compliance status of the contractor and give him or her clearance before the award can be made. The review must be made within twelve months prior to the award of the contract. OCR must issue a show-cause notice if it finds during the compliance review that the contractor has not prepared an affirmative action plan, has deviated substantially from the written plan as approved by OCR, or has an unacceptable program. The notice gives the contractor thirty days to show why enforcement procedures should not be undertaken. Office of Federal Contract Compliance Programs (OFCCP) can extend the thirty days if the contractor can justify such an extension. When a contractor has been given an opportunity for a formal hearing and is still unwilling to remedy the failure to comply with the guidelines, then sanctions must be initiated. With the approval of OFCCP, a formal hearing is convened to determine whether sanctions (contract cancellation, termination, or suspension in whole/in part or debarment of the contractor from future federal contracts), should be imposed.[25]

The U.S. Commission on Civil Rights found that the Higher Education Division of OCR has failed to follow the prescribed procedures. The commission found that during fiscal year 1973 no preaward reviews were conducted.[26] In mid-1975, OCR made an attempt to follow the

TABLE 5-3. Preaward Reviews by Regional Office, FY 1976

Region	Total No.	On-Site	Desk Audit
1	29	7	22
2	3	0	3
3	33	14	19
4	3	0	3
5	7	1	6
6	19	5	14
7	11	4	7
8	6	2	4
9	7	5	2
10	1	0	1

Source: ISEP Questionnaire, 18 April 1977.

regulations when it was requested to clear twenty-nine colleges for pre-award grants. The contracting agencies were slow in requesting OCR clearance and hence OCR was unable to conduct the necessary reviews before the end of the fiscal year on June 30. Therefore, after initially threatening to withhold contracts for up to sixty-five million dollars, OCR asked the institutions to agree to develop an acceptable affirmative action plan or follow a model plan developed by the agency.[27]

OCR is in the process of establishing a data system which will allow the office to determine the compliance posture of the educational universe, but at this time the system is not operational. OCR estimates that during fiscal year 1976, approximately sixty-four institutions have contracts totaling one million dollars or more. Of that number, OCR indicated that approximately fifty on-site preaward reviews were conducted nationally. No explanation was given as to why compliance reviews of all institutions receiving one million dollars or more in federal funds were not done.[28] Table 5-3 shows the number of on-site reviews and desk audits performed by each regional office.

OCR estimates that it takes the same length of time, fifteen days, to conduct both the on-site review and desk-audit. The regional OCR director in Atlanta has indicated that a major problem with preaward reviews is the lack of time given to actually conduct the review. He said that a time period of thirty days was totally unreasonable, since it takes nearly that long to prepare for the review. He added that even if an institution cooperated fully and supplied the compliance officer with all the data requested, it would take nine days to complete the review and report to the funding agency. An investigation by GAO revealed that HEW generally informs the awarding agency that an institution "appeared" able to comply with the Executive Order and was therefore eligible for the award.[29]

Postaward Compliance Reviews

Postaward or regular compliance reviews consist of an analysis of each aspect of the contractor's employment policies, systems, and practices to determine whether the contractor is adhering to the obligation not to discriminate and is fulfilling the affirmative action requirements. When a contractor deviates from his or her obligation as specified in the regulations, then OCR, as the compliance agency, is required to pursue various enforcement measures. The first of these is written notice giving the contractor thirty days to show cause why sanctions should not be imposed. Failure on the part of the contractor to correct any deficiencies or to show good cause for this failure requires OCR to issue a notice of proposed cancellation or termination and debarment from future contracts. OCR has thirty days to attempt conciliation. If conciliation fails, then OCR is to issue notice of hearing.[30]

During fiscal year 1976, OCR regional offices conducted 38 compliance reviews. (*See* Table 5-4.) Thus far in fiscal year 1977 (as of April 1977), the ten regional offices conducted a total of 50 compliance reviews, an average of 5 per region, or less than 1 a month. Although this figure is low, it is a slight improvement over the fiscal year 1976 average of 3.8 per region, or approximately 1 every three months per region.[31] Since OCR estimates anywhere from eleven hundred to thirteen hundred schools are subject to the provisions of the Executive Order, OCR has been slow, at best, in reviewing institutions covered by the order. This slowness in carrying out its responsibility raises the question of why officials at institutions of higher education claim harassment from federal civil rights officials.

Monitoring of Complaints

Another central element in the enforcement strategy is to monitor the number of complaints to determine the extent and degree of problems in particular institutions and in types of institutions. During fiscal year 1973, the Higher Education Division of OCR received 358 complaints

TABLE 5-4. Compliance Reviews by Regional Offices

Region	No. of Compliance Reviews FY 1976 (Oct.)	No. from 10/76 to 4/77
1	7	4
2	0	7
3	14	10
4	0	4
5	1	2
6	5	7
7	4	4
8	2	4
9	5	6
10	0	2
TOTAL	38	50

Source: ISEP Questionnaire, 18 April 1977.

filed under the provisions of the Executive Order. Twenty were referred to EEOC; 201 were investigated, and of that number, 179 were resolved; and 137 were not investigated. By the end of fiscal year 1973, OCR had resolved 53 percent of the complaints received.[32]

During fiscal year 1976, 408 complaints were received; 13 were referred to EEOC; 121 were resolved, and a total of 274 were added to the backlog. The complaints were almost evenly divided between those alleging discrimination based on race and discrimination based on sex. The Chicago region generated the most complaints—85 or slightly more than 20 percent of the total.[33] (*See* Table 5-5.)

OCR has no way of determining the status of its complaints because, as noted earlier, it has not developed and implemented a national data system. An official at OFCCP indicated that too many cases remain open for years without ever being resolved. In at least one instance a regional director administratively closed complaint cases to get rid of the backlog.[34]

A major problem which now exists at OCR is that the staff is devoting all of its time to complaints of discrimination in response to the *Adams* v. *Califano* case and various suits brought by women's groups under Title IX. The result has been that virtually no work is being done under the Executive Order, in spite of the fact that OFCCP was assured during

TABLE 5-5. Status of Complaints Alleging Discrimination Based on Race and Sex for FY 1976

	No. rec'd FY 1976	No. alleging race dis- crimination	No. alleging sex dis- crimination	No. referred to EEOC	No. resolved	Backlog of complaints
Total Regional Offices	408	206	202	13	121	274
Region 1	25	7	18	0	24	1
2	25	14	11	0	9	16
3	56	33	23	0	10	46
4	51	29	22	5	18	28
5	85	38	47	0	22	63
6	30	20	10	0	7	23
7	34	12	22	4	8	22
8	12	5	7	0	6	6
9	54	30	24	3	14	37
10	36	18	18	1	3	32

Source: ISEP Questionnaire, 18 April 1977.

the budget approval process that a specified number of years would be devoted to enforcement of the Executive Order.[35]

It would appear that OCR has given little consideration to its enforcement strategy. The compliance reviews are not done on a systematic basis and not enough time is allowed to conduct preaward reviews. There seems to have been little thought given to how much effort is to be devoted to each enforcement activity. The picture is further complicated by court-ordered clearance of the backlog which has severely hindered OCR from carrying out its responsibility under Executive Order 11246. Although OCR has sufficient authority to carry out its responsibility, it does lack adequate staff to handle all of its responsibilities. At the same time, OCR could improve its compliance program by better organization of its present resources and better coordination of its activities.

Sanctions

Failure to develop an acceptable affirmative action plan or failure to correct deficiencies within the overall program requires the imposition of sanctions. To correct deficiencies, OCR is charged with the responsibility to conciliate, mediate, and provide technical assistance where necessary within a specific time period. To assure that the contractor has "due process," an elaborate system is established in which the contractor is notified of the necessary corrective actions to be taken, given sufficient time to correct deficiencies, provided with ample opportunities for hearings both informal and formal. If the contractor continues to be non-responsive, he or she is given notice that the contract will be canceled, terminated, and that he or she will be debarred from receiving future contracts. Finally, if the contractor continues to fail to live up to the contract obligations, he or she is given an opportunity to request a hearing before sanctions are applied. The contract compliance program is designed to ensure equal employment opportunity as well as fairness to the government contractors by giving them ample opportunity to comply with the provisions of the Executive Order.

When a contractor fails to correct the deficiencies, then a "show-cause" letter is to be issued. OCR has not consistently issued show-cause letters to institutions which failed to develop acceptable affirmative action plans as required by the guidelines. As of 20 May 1974, 14 institutions nationwide had been notified that their plans were unacceptable because of such factors as failure to perform adequate utilization analyses and inadequate plans to recruit minorities and women. Yet, as of 9 December 1974, these schools had not received show-cause notices. In the Dallas region, over a twenty-three month period, OCR rejected a university's revised affirmative action plan three times, but not once did a show-cause notice go out. In lieu of issuing a show-cause notice, the Dallas office delayed awards of contracts to persuade institutions to comply with the requirements. But then it approved four out of the five contracts which had been delayed because these institutions had not developed approved affirmative action plans.[36] Thus, even persuasion as an enforcement tool is lost as long as contractors are awarded contracts prior to the development of acceptable plans.

The U.S. Commission on Civil Rights found in 1975 that OCR often ignores the requirement that show-cause notices be issued immediately on finding a contractor without an affirmative action plan or with an unacceptable one. OCR has instead developed a protracted procedure, which sometimes takes years between the time a contractor is found to have an unacceptable plan and the time a show-cause notice may be issued. After each on-site compliance review, OCR issues a letter of findings, which gives the contractor thirty days after receipt to comply or

TABLE 5-6. Number of Sanctions Initiated by OCR Regional Offices as of May 1977

Regions	No. of show cause notices	No. of hearings held	No. of cancellations, suspensions, and terminations of contracts
1	2	0	0
2	3	0	0
3	13	0	0
4	0	0	0
5	6	0	0
6	10	1	0
7	5	0	0
8	2	0	0
9	5	0	0
10	1	0	0
TOTAL	47	1	0

Source: ISEP Questionnaire, 18 April 1977.

take issue with OCR requirements. Yet the commission found that instead of issuing a show-cause letter, OCR has frequently permitted contractors to revise their plans, upon which a second letter of findings is issued. In this way numerous submissions of revised plans are allowed and the process can extend over a period of years without one show-cause letter being issued.[37]

Table 5-6 indicates the number of show-cause letters sent by OCR to institutions of higher education. Both GAO and the U.S. Commission on Civil Rights indicated that OCR is reluctant to initiate sanctions, and even when show-cause notices are sent, they have never resulted in the application of sanctions. In fact, only one hearing, in the Dallas region, has ever been held.[38]

The Executive Order requires the application of sanctions and penalties against contractors who fail to comply with the provisions of the order and its implementing regulations. The recalcitrant contractor is subject to having his or her contract cancelled, terminated, and suspended in whole or in part, and to debarment from receiving future contracts.[39] It is obvious from the discussion thus far that OCR, and ultimately HEW, have not only been reluctant to impose sanctions, but also have not lived up to their obligations under Executive Order 11246. Sanctions are a necessary enforcement tool and can serve as an effective mechanism to encourage institutions to fulfill their own affirmative action obligations.

Before HEW can effectively enforce the regulations, it must follow the procedures outlined by OFCCP. OCR should provide technical assistance where needed and in a timely fashion. Affirmative action plans should be approved or disapproved quickly. Negotiations and mediation should not be extended indefinitely. By adhering to the regulations, OCR would be in a much better position to begin the sanction process.

Contrary to what the critics maintain, the process leading to the imposition of sanctions is fair and does not violate the right of due process. Sufficient time is specified for securing compliance through conciliation, mediation, and persuasion. The contractor has an opportunity to request a hearing when efforts to conciliate fail. During the hearing process, the burden of proving a contractor is not in compliance is on the government.[40]

The failure of HEW to impose sanctions in the past has seriously weakened its enforcement arm. Although the present sanctions and penalties should be enforced, OFCCP ought to develop, as the Carnegie Council recommends, "a more flexible set of sanctions for noncompliance with affirmative action requirements."[41] It would be appropriate to establish graduated monetary penalties for noncompliance and if these penalties fail to bring the contractor into compliance, then proceedings leading to cancellation, termination, suspension, and debarment from receiving future contracts should be initiated.

Conclusions

From the preceding discussion, it is clear that HEW, as the compliance agency for higher educational institutions, has not always followed the guidelines issued by OFCCP. It has not consistently adhered to OFCCP standards nor has it used its full authority to ensure that institutions of higher education fulfill their contractual obligations. In a 1975 report, the U.S. Commission on Civil Rights criticized HEW for not revising its *Higher Education Guidelines* to reflect changes in the regulations since 1972. Further, HEW has failed to correct major weaknesses in the guidelines, such as the failure to require institutions to identify and validate all their employment selection standards. There is the implicit suggestion, the commission concluded, that institutions of higher education are exempt from the strict application of the job validation criteria.

Although critics insist that OCR has unnecessarily interfered with faculty selection procedures, the commission found that OCR has unquestioningly accepted the standards used by college and universities in selecting and promoting faculty personnel.[42] Elsewhere in this report, it is indicated that less than 50 percent of all college teachers have the Ph.D. degree. The case studies in the next chapter clearly indicate that criteria for faculty selection vary considerably within each institution and from institution to institution, and that HEW has been reluctant to interfere with promotion and selection standards.

Although this report is concerned with affirmative action in the nonconstruction aspect of contract compliance in higher education, it should be noted, in passing, that on 1 October 1977, the construction aspect was taken from HEW and given to the Department of Housing and Urban Development (HUD). An OFCCP official said that HEW has one of the largest compliance agencies but has developed the worst track record with the possible exception of the Department of Agriculture. Thus, in an attempt to improve the overall operation, OFCCP is giving HUD responsibility for construction because HEW was inactive in this area.[43]

While the senior staff is mindful of the problems facing the agency, they have in the past been unable to effectively eliminate many of these problems. In an effort to improve OCR's operation, Martin Gerry, then acting director of OCR, proposed in December 1975, a reorganization plan designed to increase the managerial efficiency of the office. Gerry proposed dividing OCR's major program responsibilities into two units: (1) the Operations Division, and (2) Planning and Policy Division, each under the supervision of deputy directors.[44]

On 27 February 1976, the OCR acting director submitted to the secretary of HEW a reorganization plan for OCR regional offices to complement the proposed changes in the headquarters. The principal reorganizational change would create the three functional divisions: (1) compliance, (2) technical assistance, and (3) compliance support. The plan would eliminate the present four branches: Elementary and Secondary Education, Higher Education, Contract Compliance, and Health and Social Services. At present, OCR has direct oversight over regional OCR directors, but there is little interaction between regional directors and staff of other units in the headquarters. Although regional directors are members of the executive staff, there is no formal mechanism which brings together branch chiefs.[45]

The reorganization plan spells out the responsibility of the regional directors. In addition, each would have a deputy to act in his/her absence. The deputy would have a clear line of authority and report directly to the directors. The director for compliance would have three branch chiefs responsible for (1) review and investigation, (2) conciliation and enforcement, and (3) monitoring. The technical assistance associate director would be responsible for informing recipients of civil rights policy requirements and aiding them in developing proper compliance procedures. The associate director for compliance has two branch chiefs responsible for technical support and management support of the compliance efforts. The assistant director for program analysis evaluation reevaluates the effectiveness of other units.

It is questionable as to whether the proposed reorganization plan would solve OCR's structural problems. At present, the office is fractured and confused as to what it is supposed to be doing. It is necessary, as OCR seems to recognize in its proposed plan, that it must develop comprehensive policy and long-range planning and program evaluation. Although it is desirable to eliminate duplication between OCR headquarters and regional staff, it is questionable whether the delegation of more authority to the regional offices is the best way to accomplish this goal. As critics in academia state, OCR's compliance personnel are often inadequately trained to administer effectively the compliance program. Given these circumstances, the team approach is not the best method to implement the compliance program. OCR should reevaluate the team approach within the three branches of the Compliance Division. First, there is the danger that nonconstruction contract compliance will not receive the attention this important area needs, considering the total civil rights responsibility of the agency. Since there are differences between construction and nonconstruction, elementary/secondary and higher education, these classifications should be retained within the various branches, and investigators, for example, should be trained to handle the problems of higher education only. The same should be done for the conciliation and monitoring branches. Another alternative would be to retain the higher education unit within each region but include the team approach in which each team would have an investigator, conciliator, and monitor. In this way all members of the team would be familiar with the compliance status of each institution assigned.

Unless OCR undertakes a comprehensive training program, many of the problems faced by the agency will remain regardless of how it is reorganized. OCR had not by the end of 1974 developed a nationwide training program for compliance officers, in spite of the May 1974 Labor Department memorandum directing each compliance agency to institute training programs. Up until the end of 1974, training varied from region to region. The Dallas region has developed an eight-week training program coupled with on-the-job training by an experienced training officer. The San Francisco regional office assigns newly hired compliance officers to work with experienced officers for an indefinite period of time.[46]

OCR began to develop a pilot training program, but has since temporarily halted the effort to give the new director an opportunity to evaluate the overall training effort.[47] It is clear from the discussion of the proposed reorganization that staff training will become extremely important. If OCR becomes more decentralized and regional offices are given more authority, it will be imperative that a comprehensive training program be developed to ensure uniformity of operation among the regions and that the same requirements are systematically applied.

Further, OFCCP established a training program for compliance agencies' staffs. To date, HEW has not participated in the program.[48] In addition to participating in the OFCCP program, OCR should rely on its own expertise in the field in developing a comprehensive training package. The program should be operative before additional authority is given in the regional offices.

Civil rights agencies have been reorganized numerous times, OCR in particular. But civil rights enforcement has become too important to allow it to be done in a haphazard fashion. Any reorganization at OCR must be an interim solution. The Carter administration's efforts to rethink the current pattern of civil rights enforcement should be supported. Civil rights enforcement is scattered among too many agencies. Enforcement under the Executive Order should be more centralized.

OFCCP has also proposed reorganizing its own program. The agency found that the present fragmented structure presents basic problems:

1. The span of control under the structure is so unwieldy as to defy the implementation of any reasonably effective management system.
2. The structure prohibits the development of a system which holds enforcement officials accountable for their performance.

3. The structure precludes the implementation of a rational and efficient system for utilizing compliance and enforcement resources.

Although the basic findings of OFCCP are good, the OFCCP recommendations that "the responsibility and authority, including budget and staff resources of the compliance agencies must be consolidated within the Department of Labor,"[49] are questionable. The department's record in contract compliance enforcement is uneven at best.[50] The entire civil rights enforcement program must be evaluated and reorganized in a comprehensive fashion. Therefore, individual agencies should wait until President Carter's report is published before attempting individual reorganization.

Chapter Six

Affirmative Action in Institutions of Higher Education: Four Case Studies

It was not until 1971, when Executive Order 11246 was applied to academia, that many colleges and universities were required to begin affirmative action programs. Some institutions which were not covered by the provisions of the order have also voluntarily incorporated affirmative action into their employment procedures. These programs are all in their early stages and, as with any innovations, there will naturally be a period of adjustment during which difficulties are encountered and, hopefully, overcome. Although it is too early to judge the effectiveness of affirmative action in higher education, it is important at this stage to examine selected efforts, both to identify problems in design and implementation and to find ways of improving the practice of affirmative action in the future.

The four case studies are presented to show how affirmative action works in different types of institutions and also to pinpoint problems which arise in different educational environments. Although it was not possible to examine all of the voluminous material, the extensive interviews with those responsible for carrying out affirmative action plans revealed how each academic community has contended with the obligation to provide fair employment practices. Hopefully, some of the positive measures employed by these institutions to increase the representation of blacks on faculties may be successfully employed by other similarly situated colleges and universities.

For the purpose of studying affirmative action, four major institutional types are distinguished: the major state university; the major private research university; the small, private, liberal arts college; and the community college. This classification could have been expanded, but these four types provide sufficient insight into the variety of circumstances in which affirmative action has to be implemented. The four institutions chosen for the case studies are Florida State University, a major southern state university; Harvard University, a major private research university located in the northeast; Oberlin College, a private liberal arts college located in the midwest; and Merritt College, a community college located in California.

It was expected that the problems and difficulties encountered at the different types of institutions would vary. For instance, the problem of determining qualifications should be simpler at the community college level, where the possession of an appropriate credential is frequently adequate to prove qualification. At a major research university, however, credentials alone are seldom sufficient, and wide judgments are made on the quality of credentials and accomplishments. The size of faculty and therefore the relative numbers of opportunities will be generally large in a major state university as compared to a small, liberal arts college. This fact should make the definition of goals easier at the larger institutions. State schools will also generally be part of large university systems, which may give them access to greater resources for implementing affirmative action plans than those available to smaller schools.

Although recognizing that details differ from plan to plan, an attempt has been made to discover the general problems in the implementation of affirmative action in institutions of higher education. For each of the four institutions the following facets were examined: the design of the plan; the procedure for implementation; the results, if any, achieved under the plan; and the general attitude toward affirmative action within the institution. Special attention was paid to the work force analysis, the development of goals and timetables, and the establishment of a monitoring system. Also examined were the procedures established for recruitment and how widely blacks are recruited.

The results achieved under each plan were also closely analyzed and evaluated within the constraints of a steady state educational universe and the current economic retrenchment. An attempt was made to determine what role attitudes play in achieving results. It was concluded that next to strong enforcement by the federal government, positive attitudes within institutions toward affirmative action are essential, if the program is to be effective.

Florida State University: A Case Study of a State University

Background

Florida State University (FSU), chartered in 1851 as a school for women, is one of the nine state-supported institutions in the Florida higher education system. The campus itself is located on 332 acres on the edge of Tallahassee, the state capital. FSU became coeducational in 1947 and thereafter experienced a rapid acceleration in growth; enrollment increased from 2,000 women in 1947 to 8,000 men and women in 1957. By 1976, the number had increased to 22,000 students. There is a student to faculty ratio of 13 to 1, and 85 percent of the full-time faculty hold doctorates. Like other southern colleges and universities, FSU was a segregated institution until 1965, when the first black student was allowed to enroll. Within two years approximately 45 blacks were admitted. In 1976 there were 1,453* black students; 240 of these were graduate students and 1,213 undergraduates.

The university has fourteen colleges and schools and a Department of Dance. It offers courses of study in eighteen major disciplines leading to the baccalaureate degree in eighty-one fields of study; to the master's degree in seventy-seven fields; and to the doctorate in fifty-two fields of study. The academic divisions include the College of Arts and Sciences, College of Business, College of Communication, College of Education, College of Law, College of Social Sciences, School of Criminology, College of Home Economics, School of Library Science, School of Music, School of Nursing, School of Social Work, School of Theatre, School of Visual Arts, and the Department of Dance.

Florida State University Affirmative Action Plan: Development and Implementation

Dr. Stanley Marshall was elected president of Florida State University by the board of regents in 1969. Dr. Freddie Groomes was hired as assistant to the president for minority affairs† (affirmative action officer) in 1972. One of her first duties was to provide the president with basic information concerning the university's obligation under Executive Order 11246, and he in turn outlined the university's commitment to equal opportunity and affirmative action.

---

* This figure does not include the 231 nondegree students.
† This title has now been changed to assistant to the president for human affairs.

The president proposed to the board of regents that FSU be designated the pilot institution within the state university system and be responsible for developing a master affirmative action plan for other institutions in the system to follow. This proposal was endorsed by the board of regents. The master plan was never fully implemented throughout the state system, but a modified plan was eventually placed in operation at FSU. President Marshall informed the FSU community in August 1973, of the university's moral and ethical commitment to nondiscrimination and of the comprehensive affirmative action program that had been developed and would be implemented.

Officials at FSU are interested in seeing that its affirmative action program becomes part of the regular employment process. Instead of giving responsibility for the implementation of the plan to a person outside the general line of authority, the program is implemented through administrative channels. Thus, a key element of the plan is the fact that all administrators have responsibility for its implementation. The affirmative action officer views her job as one of educating the community and providing technical assistance where it is needed.

Another feature of the plan is the Human Relations Associates which is a university-wide network of employees who serve as liaisons between divisions, colleges, deans/directors, and the Office of University Human Affairs. The associates work to improve the affirmative action program, serve as troubleshooters in the areas of employment practices for minorities and women, and see that members of such groups are aware of the alternatives available if they have employment grievances. Any complaints which cannot be resolved are brought to the attention of the university's Equal Opportunity Commission, established to resolve internal grievances before formal charges are brought against the university. The commission has broad representation from the university community and is to receive and investigate complaints of discrimination from all areas of the university. It can hold formal hearings when appropriate and must maintain transcripts of all proceedings. The commission recommends to the president of the university that complaints be dismissed, if found invalid, or specifies action to remedy cases of discrimination which violate university policy.

The university counsel indicated that part of his responsibility is to prevent discrimination before it occurs. To this end, he works closely with the affirmative action officer to examine areas where potential problems might exist and to eliminate them. Counsel sees his legal function as one of preventive law and recognizes that often there are valid potential problems which can be solved before they occur.

Work Force Analysis and Goals

The HEW *Higher Education Guidelines* require that each institution perform a work force analysis to determine if underutilization of minorities and women exists within the work force. At the beginning of the affirmative action program in 1972, the FSU analyses indicated a total work force of 3,477 employees, of whom 19.2 percent were minorities, and 44.5 percent were women. Both minorities and women were clustered in the nonacademic career service categories. Blacks comprised 17.4 percent or 605 employees; of these 358 (10.3 percent) were men and 257 (7.1 percent) were women. Table 6-1 illustrates where various groups were located in the three major divisions of the university. While blacks accounted for 17.4 percent of the total employees at FSU in 1972, they represented only 1.6 percent of the faculty and 1.8 percent of administrators and professionals. Other minorities—American Oriental, American Indian, and Spanish surnamed—totaled 2.1 percent or 20 faculty members. Of the other minorities, American Orientals totaled 17, thus considerably inflating the figures when all minorities were combined.*

Although there were some minorities as deans or chairpersons of departments, minorities were not represented at all in the faculty ranks of the schools of Continuing Education, Criminology, and Library Science. Minorities were congregated in the School of Arts and Sciences, where they totaled forty faculty members, twelve of whom were in the College of Education. FSU also found that women were clustered in the lowest faculty ranks. White women tended to be overutilized in the schools of Home Economics, Library Science, and Nursing, fields which traditionally have been reserved for females.

Based on FSU availability data, minority men were underutilized in four units: Home Economics, Law, Library Science, and Social Work; minority women were underutilized in Nursing, Music, Library Science, and Home Economics. White men were overutilized in Arts and Sciences, Education, Music, and Social Welfare.

The university also relied for its availability pool on recent recipients of doctorates and ignored older doctorate holders and those minorities and women currently outside of the academic labor market. Using the base year of 1969–70, FSU found that out of a total of 29,866 doctorates

---

* Although underutilization of minorities exists in the career service area, the primary concern is with professional positions, both faculty and nonfaculty, and the discussion will be limited to these two groups.

Affirmative Action in Higher Education

Affirmative Action in Higher Education   139

TABLE 6-1. Florida State University Employees by Race and Sex, Fall 1972

Employees	Number	Percentage
Faculty	1,170	100
White	1,126	96.2
male	908	77.6
female	218	18.6
Black	19	1.6
male	10	1.1
female	9	0.8
A. & P.[1]	167	100
White	160	95.8
male	91	54.8
female	69	41.3
Black	3	1.8
male	1	0.6
female	2	1.2
C. S. Employees[2]	2,140	100
White	1,525	71.3
male	541	25.3
female	984	46.0
Black	583	27.2
male	347	16.2
female	236	11.0

1. Administrative and Professional.
2. Career Service Employees.

Source: Florida State University Affirmative Action Plan.

awarded nationally, 777 went to minority men and 199 to minority women. The FSU system had awarded 699; 33 to minority men and 7 to minority women. Nationally, 3 to 4 percent of doctorates were awarded to minorities, while the FSU system awarded approximately 6 percent of its doctorates to minorities. It is evident that minorities received substantially fewer doctorates than their ratio in the population suggests they should receive.

Within faculty ranks, minority men and women were underutilized in professor and associate professor ranks. When salaries were com-

TABLE 6-2. Florida State University Vacancy Projections, 1973–74

	Faculty	Administrative and Professional
President's Administration	0	0
Administrative Affairs	0	2
Academic Affairs	72	3
Student Affairs	0	12
Total	72	17

Source: Florida State University.

pared, minorities and women were in the lower salary grades, while the reverse was true for white men. Salary discrepancies were broken down for females but not for minority males. In all salary ranks, men made an average of $15,479 per annum compared to $12,028 for women. The discrepancies were larger in the higher ranks—male professors made $20,706 compared to $17,818 for female professors—although women instructors tended to make more than men, $8,302 compared to $8,022. A study of increments over the last five years indicates that men consistently received higher increments. Finally, males held 53.8 percent of all tenured positions, while women held 38.6 percent. A similar analysis was not done for minorities.

In order to project goals for overcoming this underutilization, FSU had to determine what vacancies would probably occur. Since there were no plans for immediate expansion, vacancies had to be computed on the basis of past turnover through retirement, terminations, and so forth. The university vacancy projections for 1973–74 are summarized in Table 6-2. Anticipated turnover for the academic faculty was seventy-two and seventeen for administrative and professional.

The university proposed to fill the faculty vacancies in the following manner:

Total Vacancies	72
Minority Men	22
Minority Women	9
White Men	18
White Women	23

TABLE 6-3. Florida State University Goals

	Projected goals	Current number of minorities
Arts and Sciences	13	32
Education	5	12
Business	6	2
Home Economics	2	1
Music	1	2
Library Science	1	0
Continuing Education	0	0
Division of Institutional Research Services	0	1
Criminology	1	0
Social Work	2	3

Source: Florida State University.

The thirty-one vacancy projections for minorities are distributed among the various schools as indicated in Table 6-3. There were 1,045 faculty members at FSU, 39 of whom were minority men and 16 minority women. If all goals were achieved, minority men would increase by 22 and minority women by 9.

The five-year projection for faculty and administrative, and professional position is indicated in Table 6-4. The five-year faculty projection broken down by race and sex is listed in Table 6-5.

The projection on the increase in minority employment was based upon the assumption that in ten years faculty and administrative and

TABLE 6-4. Florida State University Projected Increase in Minority Employment

	Number	1972–73 Percent of total univ.	Number	1977–78 Percent of total univ.
Faculty	55	4.8	113	8.9
A. & P.[1]	9.5	6	20	9.5

1. Administrative and Professional.

Source: Florida State University.

TABLE 6-5. Florida State University Goals, 1972–73 to 1977–78

	72–73	73–74	74–75	75–76	76–77	77–78
Faculty						
Minority Men	39	41	46	50	54	60
Minority Women	16	23	30	36	45	53
White Men	861	800	801	772	755	736
White Women	247	266	307	340	379	420
Total	1,163	1,130	1,184	1,198	1,233	1,269

Source: Florida State University.

professional categories at the university should reflect the general population characteristics. FSU officials concluded that their affirmative action plan must be of optional effectiveness and that the availability of "qualified" workers must proceed at a steady pace over a ten-year period if the goals are to be achieved. Further, FSU officials believed that in order to meet commitments and good faith efforts regarding successful recruitment and hiring of minorities, there must be a deliberate effort made to increase the availability of these persons holding the Ph.D. degree. (*See* "Affirmative Action and Black Students.")

Affirmative Action and the Florida State University Community

The plan itself received a mixed review when it was first proposed to the university community. The dean of faculties, a long-term employee of the university, thought that there was a commitment to hiring minorities present before the university developed a written affirmative action plan, but admitted that the plan has helped in their efforts to overcome systemic discrimination. It had been most successful, she felt, in finally convincing people that there are certain standard employment procedures which must be followed in hiring personnel, and that they would no longer be allowed to hire arbitrarily and would be held accountable for their actions.

While this was reflective of the attitude of those in administrative positions, the Faculty Senate attacked the plan as an encroachment on their traditional authority. An official of the university described the senate as one of the less liberal elements, but indicated that once the senate realized that the plan was backed by the administration, most members reluctantly went along with the program.

In an effort to institutionalize the policies outlined in the plan, the president tied salary increases of administrators to their performance in achieving the goals of the plans. A key element in the criteria for promotion was the administrator's record in relation to affirmative action. Where an administrator was weak in providing leadership, his division was also weak. For example, the College of Arts and Sciences, which includes 40 percent of all faculty members, had only two blacks. The College of Law and Social Sciences has been able to attract many more minorities, and this is in part due to the leadership of the provost who held his staff accountable for implementing affirmative action. When various department heads took a laissez-faire attitude in the hiring process, the provost found it necessary to put a freeze on new hires until they took their responsibility seriously. This freeze encouraged them to put pressure on selection committees to expand their availability pools to include more minority members. After he began scrutinizing every appointment, the departments showed improvement in meeting their goals. He contends that he was able to achieve results because members of his division knew that he had the support of the president.

A major problem at FSU was that too many faculty members saw the new procedures as an infringement on their "right" to select new employees. When some department and committee chairmen continued to use the "buddy system" in hiring new employees, a system of monitoring was established in which all decisions on new hires, promotions, and terminations had to be reported to the affirmative action officer with the reasons and justification for the action taken. Further, at a grass roots level, the plan is monitored by the Human Relations Associates, whose job is to help educate the university community as to its affirmative action responsibilities and to identify potential problem areas. They also have the responsibility to refer discrimination complaints to the affirmative action officer.

The major weakness of the system is that much of the monitoring is done after the person is hired. Also, many selection committees are appointed without minority and female representation. It would seem that minorities and women on the Human Affairs Associates could be used to ensure that such groups are represented. Another major problem was the retrenchment in new hires. The plan had a good start in the fall of 1973 because there were new jobs available. But as the uni-

versity cut back hiring in response to recession and a slowed growth
rate, fewer positions became available. The other major problem was
the failure to replace those blacks who left the university's employment.
In an effort to stem what appeared to some as a retrenchment in commitment, the president suggested to the university that a temporary
university-wide goal of 80 percent of all new hires be minorities and
women. Since the university had a vacancy rate of 5 percent or less,
and since the state instituted a hiring and pay freeze in 1975, the president's decision resulted in few new blacks although the employment
picture for women improved slightly.

Progress under Affirmative Action

In October 1973, the FSU affirmative action plan was formally submitted to Region 4 for approval. Although work on the plan was
started as early as July 1969, before Executive Order 11246 applied to
academia, it was not reviewed by OCR for compliance with the Executive Order until March 1971. After over two years of revisions, during
which time FSU developed a master plan for the state university system, OCR continued to provide technical assistance until the submission of the final document. In January 1974, the plan was accepted. In
July 1975, FSU submitted an update of its affirmative action plan to
OCR, as required by the regulations.

In the revised, updated plan, FSU reaffirmed its commitment to equal
employment opportunity. FSU reported that all initial steps to establish the affirmative action program had been accomplished and the
work force had been analyzed in detail. As noted earlier, the analysis
revealed serious underutilization of minorities and women in faculty
and nonfaculty professional ranks. FSU also reported that personnel
policies and practices continue to be reviewed and alterations made
whenever it is evident that such policies and practices adversely affect
the employment opportunities of minorities and women.

Since FSU is one of the few institutions which has an approved
affirmative action plan and has developed an updated plan, it is possible to measure the progress achieved under the plan in recruiting
minority professionals, both academic and nonacademic. In establishing long-range goals for faculty and administrative and professional
positions, FSU wanted to achieve minority representation similar to
the minority representation in the national population. Although the
university has initiated a study to determine the impact of the current

economy on new hires and availability pools, and thus the potential effect on the university's goal attainment, until accurate data are available FSU's goals will remain the same.

In the work force analysis, data comparisons are available for 1972 and 1974. These data suggest that black employees have increased in all categories. Other minorities (Orientals, Indians, and Spanish-surnamed) remained the same, or 1.8 percent of the total work force.

Minorities increased their faculty representation from forty-four, or 4 percent, in 1972 to seventy-three, or 6 percent, in 1974. The number of administrators also increased from seven, or 4 percent, to nineteen, or 12 percent. (*See* Table 6-6.) These data suggest that FSU was able to increase its number of minority professionals (faculty and administrative and professional) by more than 55 percent within a two-year period. Tables 6-7 and 6-8 illustrate the progress of blacks under the FSU plan. Overall black administrators and professionals increased from three, or 1.8 percent, in 1972 to fifteen, or 9.8 percent, in 1974. Black, female, non-academic professionals made the most progress, increasing from two in 1972 to eleven in 1974.

Although substantial progress has been made, FSU continues to have an underrepresentation of black male professionals. It is also evident, in comparing nonfaculty professionals with faculty members, that FSU is making substantial progress in the recruitment of blacks for non-academic positions, while making substantially less progress in the area of faculty employment. Table 6-8 indicates that of the 1,126 faculty members in 1972, only 19, or 1.6 percent, were black. Black faculty increased by 45 percent to 3.8 percent of the total faculty in 1974 and was almost evenly divided between black males (24) and black females (21). The data also indicate that white males continue to be overrepresented on the faculty, since minorities constitute 17 percent of the total population. According to FSU long-range goals, the white male percentage of the faculty will eventually have to decrease from its current (1974) 77 percent to 42 percent, assuming a static ethnic growth rate.

Table 6-9 illustrates the distribution of faculty members by rank, race, and sex for April 1973 and March 1975. According to these percentages, minority faculty representation has increased at the ranks of academic administration (i.e., "other" category) and instructor. The percentages at the ranks of professor remained unchanged while slightly increasing at the associate rank for black males. At the assistant level, the percentages declined for black males and increased slightly for black females.

TABLE 6-6. Work Force Distribution, Fall Quarters 1972 and 1974

Employment Category	Total		Minorities				Nonminorities			
			Fall 1972		Fall 1974		Fall 1972		Fall 1974	
	Fall[1] 1972	Fall[2] 1974	No.	% of Total	No.	% of Total	No.	% of Total	No.	% of Total
Faculty	1,170	1,179	44	4	73	6	1,126	96	1,106	94
Administrative & Professional	167	152	7	4	19	12	160	96	133	88

1. Includes contracts and grants.
2. Contracts and grants not included.

Source: Florida State University.

TABLE 6-7. Florida State University Administrative and Professional Staff by Sex and Race, Fall 1972 and 1974

	Male				Female				Total			
	Fall 1972		*Fall 1974*		*Fall 1972*		*Fall 1974*		*Fall 1972*[2]		*Fall 1974*[3]	
	No.	*% of Men*	*No.*	*% of Men*	*No.*	*% of Women*	*No.*	*% of Women*	*No.*	*% of Total A&P*	*No.*	*% of Total A&P*
Other[1]	91	97.8	80	95	69	93.2	53	78.6	160	95.8	133	87.5
Black	1	1.1	4	5	2	2.7	11	15.7	3	1.8	15	9.8
Oriental	1	1.1	0	0	3	4.1	3	4.3	4	2.4	3	2
Indian	0	0	0	0	0	0	0	0	0	0	0	0
Spanish	0	0	0	0	0	0	1	1.4	0	0	1	0.7
TOTAL	93	100	84	100	74	100	68	100	167	100	152	100

1. Includes Caucasians.
2. Contracts and grants included.
3. Contracts and grants not included.

Source: Florida State University.

TABLE 6-8. Florida State University Faculty by Race and Sex, Fall 1972 and 1974

	Male				Female				Total			
	Fall 1972		Fall 1974		Fall 1972		Fall 1974		Fall 1972[2]		Fall 1974[3]	
	No.	% of Men	No.	% of Men	No.	% of Women	No.	% of Women	No.	% of Total Faculty	No.	% of Total Faculty
Other[1]	908	96.8	871	94.7	218	93.9	235	90.7	1,126	96.2	1,106	93.8
Black	10	1.1	24	2.6	9	3.9	21	8.1	19	1.6	45	3.8
Oriental	17	1.8	8	0.9	2	0.9	0	0	19	1.6	8	0.7
Indian	1	0.1	2	0.2	2	0.9	0	0	3	0.3	2	0.2
Spanish	2	0.2	15	1.6	1	0.4	3	1.2	3	0.3	18	1.5
TOTAL	938	100	920	100	232	100	259	100	1,170	100	1,179	100

1. Includes Caucasians.
2. Contracts and grants included.
3. Contracts and grants not included.

Source: Florida State University.

TABLE 6-9. Florida State University Faculty Rank Distribution by Race and Sex, April 1973 and March 1975

	Total		Minorities				Nonminorities			
			Men		Women		Men		Women	
Faculty	*April 1973 Number*	*March 1975 Number*	*April 1973 %*	*March 1975 %*	*April 1973 %*	*March 1975 %*	*April 1973 %*	*March 1975 %*	*April 1973 %*	*March 1975 %*
Prof.	336	342	1	1	0	0	88	89	11	10
Assoc. Prof.	290	321	3	4	1	1	81	77	15	18
Assist. Prof.	378	329	5	3	3	4	71	67	21	26
Instructor	129	102	3	7	3	5	32	36	62	52
Other	Not Given	44	Not Given	14	Not Given	0	Not Given	74	Not Given	12

Source: Florida State University.

The Case for Affirmative Action

TABLE 6-10. Florida State University Average Salary, April 1975

Category	Minorities		Nonminorities	
	Men	*Women*	*Men*	*Women*
Faculty	$14,984	$13,822	$18,083	$14,294
Administrative and Professional	15,697	13,170	19,979	13,544

Source: Florida State University.

In spite of gains, FSU reported continued underutilization of minorities. It found minority men underutilized in Home Economics, Law, Library Science, and Social Work based on their availability in the work force. Minority women were underutilized in Nursing, Home Economics, Division of Institutional Research Services, Music, and Library Science.

The university still faces the problem of salary differential. Generally all men were paid at a higher level than all women. (*See* Table 6-10.) In the category of faculty members, on the average, white men received more than $3,000 more than black men and over $4,000 more than white women. Black men and white women received salaries that were nearly equal, while all groups were paid higher than black women. The same general pattern existed in the administrative and professional category, but with slightly larger differentials. Much of the discrepancy in salary levels can be explained by the fact that white males hold most of the higher paying positions.

Of the 1,124 faculty members, 548 or slightly more than half were tenured as of January 1975. Of the 548 tenured faculty, only 4 were classified as minority. Only in the College of Education (1) and the College of Arts and Sciences (3) has tenure been achieved for minorities. Part of the differential can be explained by differences in length of service. As of May 1975, the average length of service for blacks in all ranks was one year three months for black men and one year six months for black women. For white men and women, the figures are eight years seven months and six years eleven months, respectively. Yet, when the average length of service by rank for both white males and females is

TABLE 6-11. Hiring Goals at Florida State University, 1973–74 and 1974–75

	Fall, 1973–74				Fall, 1974–75			
	Projected		Actual		Projected		Actual	
Category	No.	%	No.	%	No.	%	No.	%
Faculty								
Minority Men	41	3.6	21	1.8	46	3.9	49	4.2
Minority Women	23	2.0	17	1.5	30	2.5	24	2.0
Administrative and Professional								
Minority Men	3	1.5	3	2.0	4	2.0	4	2.6
Minority Women	10	5.2	11	7.3	10	5.4	15	9.9

Source: Florida State University.

broken down, it can be seen that females consistently have worked longer in all ranks except instructor. White men, however, are consistently paid higher average salaries than white women.

A comparison of the goals established by the university with those actually achieved for the 1973–74 and 1974–75 academic years indicates that FSU made substantial progress in meeting its goals. (*See* Table 6-11.) During the 1973–74 academic year, the university consistently failed to meet its goals, which was partially due to a cutback in hiring. But during 1974–75, in three of the four categories listed in Table 6-11, FSU was able to meet its goal for minority women faculty members; in actual numbers it increased their representation from seventeen in 1973–74 to twenty-four in 1974–75. During the same period the number of minority men faculty members more than doubled, from twenty-one to forty-nine. However, most of this increase was in the non-tenured faculty ranks.

By 1983, FSU projects having an average of 13 percent minorities in faculty and nonfaculty professional positions. Figure 6-1 indicates that the university has now achieved its hiring goal for minority administrators and professionals. As of 1974, there is a lag by 7 percent in achieving its 1983 goals in faculty employment.

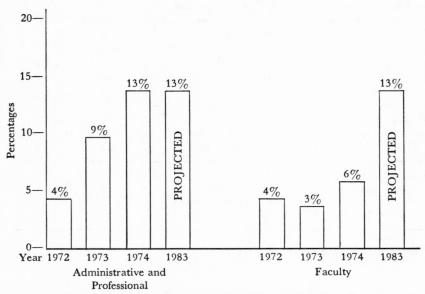

FIGURE 6-1. Florida State University Affirmative Action Goals for Minorities

Affirmative Action and Black Faculty Members

One goal of the FSU plan is to give diversity to the current faculty and to provide role models for the black students enrolled. One dean expressed concern that black faculty members who have the trust of the students should be available to assist minority students when they encounter difficulties at the predominantly white institution. Prior to the affirmative action plan there was an effort to recruit minority faculty members, but the effort failed because the white community of Tallahassee was opposed to the idea of blacks teaching at a white institution. After the plan was developed and another effort was made to recruit black faculty members, opposition arose in the Faculty Senate.

One official suggested that some members of the Faculty Senate opposed affirmative action because of the poorly prepared and biased report of the Faculty Senate subcommittee. Some felt that the plan encroached on the faculty's prerogative to select new members of their own discipline, imposed quotas, and lowered standards. Yet the administration was adamant that employment standards would remain high.

The administration emphasized to all concerned the need to provide diversity and variety among the faculty members and stated that affirmative action was a legitimate goal of any academic institution. The procedure for hiring faculty members was not altered. Faculty selection committees continued to make their recommendations to their respective chairmen after potential employees were screened and ranked. The affirmative action procedure is designed to ensure that minorities and women are adequately represented in the applicant pools.

On the issue of the university hiring less qualified blacks and women, one dean suggested that she did not think that even the white males who raised the issue believed that the university was hiring unqualified faculty members. The university attorney suggested that it was difficult for members of the faculty to stop using the traditional method of hiring in favor of a more fair method. Further, it was difficult for them to acknowledge that women and minorities are as qualified as males and, in some professions, even more qualified. Blacks, for example, can play a very important role in a predominantly white university in exposing white, middle-class students to minorities and to those with different cultural backgrounds.

He emphasized that qualifications are defined by white males and are not necessarily the best criteria just because they happen to fit their own academic interest. The dean of faculties readily admitted that there are numerous fields that don't necessarily require the doctorate degree, although it is unlikely that the university as a whole will drop the Ph.D. for the entry-level positions because of the emphasis placed on graduate education. But although this was generally true for the university, each department still must evaluate this requirement according to its own particular needs.

At FSU there was only one tenured black on the faculty. One official indicated that the explanations given to justify the lack of black faculty are often simply excuses. He maintained that there are no systematic criteria for promotions and tenure. Some departments such as social work, which have graduate programs, do not require the Ph.D. for tenure. Since some departments are research oriented and others are not, the criteria should vary according to the particular need of each department. One provost suggested that the issue of merit is raised primarily in relation to blacks and women. The merit principle is often used to eliminate nonwhite males but still allows incompetents to achieve tenure. He further stated that those objecting to the plan do not fear incompetent blacks, but rather fear competition with competent blacks using the same standards of merit that have not been employed fairly. He suggested that the traditional selection criteria—degrees, recommendations, and research—may or may not determine a person's qualifications.

Black faculty members also echoed this sentiment. Some said that it was difficult to know exactly what the requirements are for promotion and tenure. Although the standards are spelled out in general terms in the faculty handbook, there is a need for more objective criteria in determining the quality of research, teaching, and community service and how each is weighed in determining who is hired and promoted. Blacks, who are usually employed on short-term contracts, need to be informed of the standards soon after they are hired, or, preferably, before. This would help prevent so many from leaving at the end of their contracts.

The black faculty saw a relationship between student pressure and the number of blacks on the faculty. They felt that without some form of pressure, the white faculty members would not be encouraged to seek blacks and to replace those who leave. The problem is severe at the present time because the current generation of students seems to be indifferent to the civil rights gains of the 1960s and are not applying pressure to hire more blacks. Black faculty members hoped that the affirmative action plan would serve the same purpose as student pressure had previously and acknowledged that it was not the black students' job to ensure that blacks are hired.

The problem of hiring blacks is compounded by the cuts in state financial support. Members of the administration are aware of the difficulty they encountered in hiring blacks for the staff and, since most blacks were among the last hired, they are worried that additional cuts in university allocations would require reduction of their numbers. The administration is seeking ways to reduce staff without adversely affecting new hires of blacks and women. As one dean explained, the FSU system is trying to support too many universities, and this places a strain on resources. Since FSU is in a no-growth situation, it is examining ways to retain and somewhat expand its program. The university is interested in becoming primarily a graduate school. The dean also suggested a possibility of providing more public service, especially to government employees who are located in the capital city. In the process, the university must do more not only to recruit blacks but also to see that they have a fair opportunity to obtain tenure. Certainly, since 56 to 60 percent of the total faculty have tenure, blacks should have increased representation in the tenured ranks as more are admitted at the entry level.

Affimative Action and Black Students

Officials at FSU realized that there is a direct relationship between the number of black students and the availability of black faculty members. To correct the relatively slow progress in minority faculty hiring, the university submitted to the state legislature a plan for increasing minority availability in academic as well as administrative and professional areas. The plan was accepted, funded, and implemented through the state university system in September 1974 as Grants-in-Aid for Black Graduate Students and Black Faculty and Administrative and Professional Staff. Initially there were 15 awards made throughout the university system, but in 1977–78, a total of 27 awards were made, 9 for each category. The university made a special effort to increase the number of minority students. In 1973, blacks represented 5 percent of all graduate students; by fall 1974, the percentage had increased to 6.1 percent. Of the 595 full-time graduate assistantships, 7 percent, or 41, were awarded to minorities. Minorities accounted for 7.3 percent of all graduate students. Blacks comprised 5.5 percent of the undergraduate student enrollment of 17,000 students in 1973. This percentage had increased to 6.4 percent by fall of 1974.

The university's effort to increase the number of blacks in graduate and professional schools has been hampered by a shortage of funds for graduate fellowships. The dean of faculty said that attempts are being made to channel grants to minorities. Also, the university can admit 10 percent of its students on a special program, which can be used to increase minority student representation. Although graduate departments tend to give too much weight to the graduate record examination scores, the main problem for black students is lack of financial resources. If the supply plan had been funded, minorities and women would have had their salaries subsidized and would have been able to complete their graduate work without financial worry. As it turned out, FSU received a limited amount, about $4,000 each, for three to five students.

Many blacks at FSU found themselves in a position of having to borrow money and seek loans to remain in school. These students are, therefore, shouldered with heavy debts by the time they complete their undergraduate degree and in many cases are unable to go on to graduate school.

Although financial need was the primary problem of black students, there were many others. Students felt the recruitment program for both black faculty and students was ineffective. The scarcity of black faculty members contributes to the isolation black students already feel. The lack of tutors and counselors, as a result of financial cutbacks, is another major problem facing black students.

When the university reduced the number of counselors from thirteen to three, that left just one black counselor from a high of four. There is only one black counselor in the financial aid office, an area critical for black students, since they often lack the necessary money to complete their education. One black graduate student suggested that the university should evaluate the total needs of its minority students to determine how best they can be served. One area on which she would place more emphasis is tutoring for those with potential for college work but who have inadequate educational backgrounds. Blacks also felt a need for black professors to serve as role models, especially for those black students who go through the system without ever encountering a black instructor. One student said that many of her instructors are unable to understand the particular problems black students face in a white institution.

In 1965, there were only 8 black students in the university. By 1967, the number had increased to 45. In 1976, the total number of black students had increased to 1,684 out of a total of 22,000 students. Although blacks constitute approximately 7 percent of the students, the administration is aware of the need to actively recruit at all levels if the university is to meet its commitment to increase the available supply.

Florida State University and the Federal Government

Although FSU has had a close working relationship with OCR, there have been some problems. For example, the guidelines have not always been clear. Prior to the approval of the FSU plan, OCR Region 4 requested supplemental data. Eighteen items were brought to the attention of FSU for additional data; one question raised was whether the university maternity leave policy of granting no more than four months leave for pregnancy and childbearing was justifiable in light of guidelines which stipulate that leave be of a "reasonable length of time." Yet OCR did not spell out what was meant by "reasonable time."

In another query, OCR Region 4 inquired about the status and/or result of the state employment study and its impact on FSU testing programs. No mention was made of FSU's failure to validate the criteria and selection procedure for academic employees as required by the regulations.

At the same time, OCR was diligent in noting shortcomings of the plan and suggested corrective action. One suggestion was that since no blacks and few females were on the Faculty Senate, steps should be taken to encourage their representation. The same suggestion was made for such committees as promotion and screenings. The suggestions were very timely in light of the paucity of black tenured faculty. OCR also suggested that the guidelines for promotions failed to emphasize the university's affirmative action responsibilities and that steps should be taken to correct this deficiency.

FSU officials were aware that it was up to them to be creative in their program because the Executive Order's regulations are minimal requirements which do not go far enough to solve the problem of systematic discrimination. Goals and timetables are necessary ingredients of affirmative action plans because of the difficulty in evaluating an institution's commitment to equal opportunity. The university's attorney believes that it is incumbent upon institutions of higher education to be the initiators and to create affirmative action plans that meet this particular need. He further believes that the guidelines as written should continue to be applied to nonacademic as well as academic staff.

Some at FSU saw the December 1974 Peter Holmes memorandum to college presidents as confusing or unnecessarily complicating the problem of increasing minority and female representation. Some said that instead of helping, the memorandum actually hurt at FSU. The guidelines were clear in stating that once the standards for selection and promotion were validated, institutions were free to select the most qualified. Yet, the memorandum was viewed by some as a hint that they could return to the "business-as-usual" stance so prevalent before the affirmative action plan. Others said that FSU had done too much, and that the university should slow down its efforts to hire minorities and women. One person indicated that the "most" qualified has always been a nonissue, since hiring is not done on the basis of who is the most qualified. Applicants are screened, a small group is selected as qualified, but the person selected as "most qualified" is usually the person considered to "fit in" with the social order of the department.

The university counsel thinks that HEW should be more precise in its use of the terminology in the *Higher Education Guidelines* and should define what is meant by qualifications and qualifiable. Others see a conflict between federal and state requirements and think that HEW should understand that the university is often caught in the middle. For example, HEW puts pressure on FSU to validate its selection criteria for nonacademic employees, but the university cannot change those standards because they were set by the state. Because FSU is part of the state-wide higher education system, some policy changes cannot be made without approval at the state level. Such obstacles should be taken into consideration in approving affirmative action plans. But for the most part, FSU officials found HEW supportive of their efforts to achieve equal opportunity.

Harvard University: A Case Study of a Major Research University

Background

Harvard University is a major comprehensive teaching and research institution located in the cities of Cambridge and Boston, Massachusetts. The university is large, with ten separate schools or faculties. These ten faculties are: the Faculty of Arts and Sciences (FAS), the Graduate School of Business Administration (GSBA), the School of Dental Medicine (SDM), the Graduate School of Design (GSD), the School of Divinity (SD), the Graduate School of Education (GSEd), the John F. Kennedy School of Government (JFKSG), the Law School (LAW), the School of Medicine (SM) and the School of Public Health (SPH). The university has a current enrollment of over 15,000 students and more than 11,500 employees. The faculty at Harvard has more than 3,900 members and over 2,600 nonteaching professional and managerial employees.

Development of an Affirmative Action Plan

Affirmative action began at Harvard in 1966 when the university first formally announced an equal employment opportunity policy. During the remaining years of the sixties, the university undertook several positive steps to increase opportunities for Afro-Americans. Among these efforts were steps to recruit larger numbers of black students and the establishment of the Afro-American studies department. Throughout this early period there was strong activist pressure from Afro-American students and others from the university to eliminate racial discrimination in employment and elsewhere.

In 1970 Clifford Alexander, Jr., a member of the board of overseers, was appointed to develop an affirmative action plan. As a result of this initiative, an Office of Minority Affairs was created in the Office of the President in June 1970. An affirmative action plan was developed and submitted to HEW in February 1971. This plan was accepted by HEW in 1971. Subsequently, in view of Order Number 4 the plan was revised and resubmitted in 1973. It was accepted by HEW in that year. Thus, Harvard has been operating under an approved affirmative action plan since 1971. The plan was updated and revised again in 1976, and this latest revised plan was approved by HEW in November 1976.

The current plan under which Harvard carries out its affirmative action effort formally contains all of the elements specified by the Executive Order and the HEW guidelines. In fact, the compliance officer in charge of Harvard's case at the regional Office for Civil Rights indicated that Harvard's plan was among the best and has been used as a model plan for other universities in the region.

Work Force Analysis and Goals

The current utilization of blacks on the faculty at Harvard University is very low, as can be seen by the data in Table 6-12, which was extracted from Harvard's revised affirmative action plan. The data in this table cover all of Harvard's schools with the exception of the SDM. For some unexplained reason, data for this school is not included in the published portion of the revised affirmative action plan.

As can be seen in the table, blacks comprised 1.54 percent of Harvard's ladder faculty as of June 1976 and roughly 2.4 percent of the nonladder faculty. Interestingly enough, in 1976 there were proportionately more black full and associate professors than assistant professors. In fact, there were even absolutely more black full professors than black assistant professors in 1976. Ladder faculty is an academic term for those faculty members on a tenured track or who already have tenure. The term nonladder faculty indicates those faculty members who hold faculty positions that do not lead to tenured rank.

The relative utilization of blacks varied across the various faculties. The School of Medicine (HSM) tended to have proportionately fewer black ladder faculty members than the other schools, with the exception of the JFKSG, which had none. Of the other schools the FAS, GSBA and GSD all had roughly 2 percent black ladder faculty. GSEd, with four out of thirty-three ladder positions held by blacks, had the highest pro-

TABLE 6-12. Utilization of Black Faculty at Harvard as of 30 June 1976

		Total Number	Number of Blacks	Percentage of Blacks
University-wide	Professor	840	15	1.79
	Assoc. Professor	479	7	1.63
	Asst. Professor	928	12	1.29
	Total Ladder	2,197	34	1.54
	Total Nonladder	1,747	41	2.35
Faculty of Arts and	Professor	372	5	1.34
Sciences	Assoc. Professor	46	2	4.35
	Asst. Professor	168	5	2.98
	Total Ladder	586	12	2.05
	Total Nonladder	98	11	11.22
Graduate School of	Professor	81	1	1.23
Business Administration	Assoc. Professor	32	0	0
	Asst. Professor	36	2	5.56
	Total Ladder	149	3	2.0
	Total Nonladder	19	0	0
Graduate School of	Professor	24	0	0
Design	Assoc. Professor	11	1	9.09
	Asst. Professor	14	0	0
	Total Ladder	49	1	2.04
	Total Nonladder	47	5	10.63
Divinity School	Professor	20	1	5.0
	Assoc. Professor	3	1	33.3
	Asst. Professor	2	0	0
	Total Ladder	25	2	8.0
	Total Nonladder	16	2	12.5
Graduate School of	Professor	18	1	5.56
Education	Assoc. Professor	10	2	20.0
	Asst. Professor	5	1	20.0
	Total Ladder	33	4	12.12
	Total Nonladder	21	1	4.76
JFK School of	Professor	8	0	0
Government	Assoc. Professor	3	0	0
	Asst. Professor	2	0	0
	Total Ladder	13	0	0
	Total Nonladder	4	0	0
Law School	Professor	55	3	5.45
	Assoc. Professor	—	—	0
	Asst. Professor	9	0	0
	Total Ladder	64	3	4.69
	Total Nonladder	12	1	8.33

(Continued)

TABLE 6-12. (Continued)

		Total Number	Number of Blacks	Percentage of Blacks
School of Medicine	Professor	225	3	1.33
	Assoc. Professor	289	1	0.35
	Asst. Professor	643	3	0.47
	Total Ladder	1,157	7	0.61
	Total Nonladder	1,514	21	1.39
School of Public Health	Professor	37	1	2.7
	Assoc. Professor	35	0	0
	Asst. Professor	49	1	2.04
	Total Ladder	121	2	1.65
	Total Nonladder	16	0	0

Source: Harvard University Affirmative Action Plan.

portion of blacks among their ladder faculty. It was followed by SD and LAW.

With respect to nonladder faculty, SD, FAS, and GSD made the largest use of blacks among their nonladder faculty. The heavy use of nonladder positions for blacks in FAS and GSD must at least raise serious questions when compared with their low utilization among the ladder ranks. This is also true of the relative use of nonladder blacks in the SM. On the other hand, GSEd, SPH, and GSBA use proportionately fewer blacks in the nonladder ranks than in the ladder ranks and thus may be under-utilizing blacks in these ranks.

The data on the utilization of blacks by departments within schools varies greatly from department to department. The twelve ladder black faculty within FAS are all found within seven departments. These departments are: Afro-American studies (5), physics (2), history (1), government (1), sociology (1), psychology (1) and applied sciences (1).

Thus twenty-seven out of thirty-four departments of FAS have no blacks at all. Moreover 41.6 percent of all black faculty in FAS are found within the Afro-American studies department. There are only three departments besides Afro-American studies with black faculty members in the junior ladder ranks, that is, below full professor. They are physics, applied sciences, and psychology. These departments have no black full professors. The other three departments with blacks all have one black full professor each and no blacks at the junior level.

There are no data on the relevant utilization of blacks within departments of SM. However, there is a table in the affirmative action plan showing the total black appointees in clinical departments as of 15 May 1976. These figures show percentages ranging from 0 to 4 percent, but, it is not clear what these numbers mean. They apparently include interns and residents along with faculty members. The reason for including this table rather than a regular utilization analysis is not clear. SM should be of particular importance due to the large size of its faculty, the relatively low utilization of blacks, and the fairly high enrollments of blacks in medical schools in recent years.

SPH does not show separate figures for blacks, but it shows minorities present in only three of ten departments. Moreover, since there are only two blacks among the six minority employees, blacks cannot be included in more than two of the ten departments.

The proper assessment of the utilization of blacks would require good availability data by individual specialty. Unfortunately, there is no such data nor is there data on the size of faculties within individual departments. Harvard's affirmative action plan provides data on availabilities. The sources vary by field, and in some cases the data refer to proportions with Ph.D.'s and in some cases to recent degree data.

Criticism of Harvard's utilization analysis was made by the Task Force on Affirmative Action at Harvard. According to this group, Harvard frequently did not use the most up-to-date data. Nor did the departments make separate availability estimates for each rank. In addition, the affirmative action plan did not provide information concerning turnover by rank and thus the data required to assess the goal or projected hiring are missing. These criticisms all continue to be valid. In addition, a separate utilization analysis for each minority group was not usually prepared.

On the other hand, Harvard's interpretation of underutilization was interesting. Even though twenty-seven out of thirty-four departments in FAS have no blacks, Harvard indicated no underutilization of minorities in any of its FAS departments. In general, Harvard's affirmative action plan did not explicitly recognize underutilization of blacks in any specific area. Ambiguities in the definition of availability pools and generally small numbers in any specific specialty enabled the university to avoid indicating underutilization in the published plan. In addition, the extensiveness and form of the utilization analysis included in the published plan varied from faculty to faculty.

The hiring goals of Harvard University for each of the nine faculties included in the statistical analysis are shown in Table 6-13. There is no indication of departmental goals in this document and no breakdown for indivdual minority groups. This is of particular importance because university-wide blacks currently represent only 27 percent of the minority faculty. Thus the implications of minority hiring goals for the employment of blacks are unclear. The proportion of blacks among the minority faculty is less than half in all of the larger faculties. It is 0.43 in GSBA, 0.32 in FAS, 0.29 in SPH, and 0.22 in SM. Nonetheless, this table can give some indication of prospects.

Overall, the projections call for an increase in the faculty size of fifty full professors and seventy-seven associate and assistant professors through 1978. Of this increase six full professorships would go to minorities and twelve associate and assistant professorships would go to minorities. These changes lead to a very small increase in the proportion of minority candidates within each ladder rank. In nonladder ranks, the university-wide increase in faculty size is projected at seventy individuals of which twenty are projected to be filled by minorities. This projection increases the proportion of minorities in nonladder ranks from 6.4 to 7.2 percent.

As pointed out earlier, the significance of these changes is not clear since figures on turnover or total availabilities of positions are not provided. Nonetheless, it is clear that in the aggregate the projected increase in the minority presence is small.

The situation again varies for each faculty; some faculties actually project declines in the proportion of minorities over the next two years at some ranks. FAS, for instance, projects an increase of only two minority faculty members at the full-professor level although it expects a total increase of twenty-three positions. This faculty projects no increases in the numbers of minority faculty below the full-professor level although fourteen additional positions are expected to be available.

Other faculties projecting declines in the proportions of minority faculty members in specific ranks are: GSBA at the associate level, GSD at the assistant and associate levels, and SD at the associate level. Most of the increases in minority faculty are projected for SM. Here thirteen out of the sixty-three increases in new ladder positions are projected for minorities and fourteen out of seventy-four increases in nonladder positions are projected for minorities.

These planned goals are generally modest at best, and the impact of these goals on blacks may be even smaller. However, as Harvard projects no underutilization, these modest goals cannot surprise anyone.

TABLE 6-13. Projected Change in the Number of Minority and Total Faculty at Harvard between 30 June 1976 and 30 June 1978 and Percentage of Minority Faculty, 1976 and 1978.[1]

		Minority	Total	%1976	%1978
University-wide	Professor	+6	+50	4.9	5.3
	Assoc. Professor	+12	+77	4.7	5.3
	Asst. Professor	+12	+77	4.7	5.3
	Nonladder	+20	+70	6.4	7.2
Faculty of Arts and Sciences	Professor	+2	+23	5.1	5.3
	Assoc. Professor	0	+14	7.0	6.6
	Asst. Professor	0	+14	7.0	6.6
	Nonladder	0	−9	22.4	24.7
Graduate School of Business	Professor	0	−1	3.7	3.8
Administration	Assoc. Professor	−1	−1	6.3	3.2
	Asst. Professor	+3	0	5.6	13.9
	Nonladder	+2	+3	0	11.1
Graduate School of Design	Professor	0	+1	0	0
	Assoc. Professor	−1	+1	18.2	8.3
	Asst. Professor	−1	+5	14.3	5.3
	Nonladder	+2	+4	14.8	15.7
Divinity School	Professor	0	−2	5.0	5.6
	Assoc. Professor	−1	−1	33.3	0
	Asst. Professor	0	0	0	0
	Nonladder	+1	−2	12.5	21.4
Graduate School of Education	Professor	0	0	5.5	5.5
	Assoc. Professor	0	−1	20.0	22.2
	Asst. Professor	0	+3	20.0	12.5
	Nonladder	+1	−5	9.5	12.5
JFK School of Government	Professor	0	0	0	0
	Assoc. Professor	0	+1	0	0
	Asst. Professor	+1	+1	0	33.3
	Nonladder	0	0	0	0
Law School	Professor	+1	+4	5.3	5.8
	Asst. Professor	0	−2	11.1	14.3
	Nonladder	+1	+4	8.3	12.5
School of Medicine	Professor	+2	+20	5.7	6.1
	Assoc. Professor	+4	+21	2.4	3.5
	Asst. Professor	+7	+22	3.6	4.5
	Nonladder	+14	+74	5.1	5.7
School of Public Health	Professor	+1	+5	2.7	4.8
	Assoc. Professor	0	+6	8.6	7.3
	Asst. Professor	+1	+6	6.1	7.3
	Nonladder	0	+4	0	0

1. 1976 is actual percentage and 1978 is projected percentage.

Source: Harvard University Affirmative Action Plan, Revised Plan, 1976.

A 1973 article in the *Harvard Crimson* was titled a "Big Step Nowhere." This article decried the overly modest goals contained in the 1973 Harvard affirmative action plans. Walter J. Leonard, then special assistant to the president who oversaw the Harvard University affirmative action effort, replied to the editorial and noted agreement with the editorial's point concerning the overly modest goals. But Leonard pointed out, however, that his office could only submit the projections submitted to it by the various departments, and that his hands were tied as far as increasing the goals.

In general, the use of goals and timetables does not appear to enjoy wide support within the administration. Harvard develops goals and includes them in its plan because of the requirements of the affirmative action regulations. Some administrative officials interviewed resented the requirement of defining goals and felt that defining goals on the basis of utilization analysis may actually interfere with the achievement of equal opportunity. Goals are not widely viewed as an important management tool, and nowhere in the plan was there a formal integration of the goals into the affirmative action system.

Harvard University has had little difficulty in meeting its overall modest goals for hiring minority faculty. (*See* Table 6-14.) The comparison of projected minority faculty on 30 June 1975 with actual minority faculty on 30 June 1975 shows that the goals established in 1973 were generally met and slightly exceeded for three out of five ranks and missed for two out of three ranks. The total projected minority faculty size for 1975 was 146 and the actual size was 149. The projected increase for minorities was 19 and the actual increase was 22. However, the total number of faculty positions in the ranks was also greater than the projected numbers by 93. The projections called for minority faculties to receive about 10 percent of the projected available positions in these ranks, whereas in fact it is estimated that minority groups received about 7 or 8 percent of the positions which became available in these ranks. But the method utilized for projecting the positions becoming available was not clear. Thus, while minorities accounted for 6.1 percent of the faculties in these ranks in 1971, their proportion increased modestly to 6.6 percent by 1975.

The results of the affirmative action effort for black faculty are shown in Table 6-15. Between 1971 and 1973 there was an increase of twelve ladder faculty positions held by blacks and a decline of eight in nonladder positions. From 1973 to 1975 the rate of increase in ladder positions declined as the number of blacks in these positions increased by one. The number of blacks in nonladder positions increased by four.

TABLE 6-14. Projected and Actual Number of Minorities at Harvard on University-wide Faculties, Selected Ranks, 1975

	Projected Total Minority	Actual Total Minorities	Projected Increase for Minority Faculty	Actual Increase for Minority Faculty	Difference Between Actual Total Faculty and Projected Total Faculty
Professor	37	40	5	8	+18
Associate Professor	18	17	1	0	+1
Assistant Professor	34	38	8	12	+21
Instructor	14	17	2	5	+20
Lecturer	43	37	3	−3	+33
Total of All Ranks	146	149	19	22	93

Source: Harvard University Affirmative Action Plan, Revised Plan, 1976.

In fact, between 1973 and 1975 the number of black faculty in the ranks of assistant professor, associate professor, and instructor actually declined. As a result the proportion of blacks in the ladder ranks actually declined between 1973 and 1975. The decline in the number of blacks holding assistant and associate professorships occurred despite the fact that the total positions at these grades increased by ninety-six between 1973 and 1975.

TABLE 6-15. University-wide Black Faculty at Harvard, Total and Percentage for 1971, 1973, 1975

Faculty	1971	1973	1975	1971	1973	1975
	Total			Percentage		
Professor	6	12	15	0.8	1.6	1.9
Associate Professor	4	6	5	1.5	2.0	1.7
Assistant Professor	5	9	8	0.9	1.9	1.4
Total Ladder	15	27	28	1.0	1.8	1.7
Instructor	5	6	5	2.5	3.1	2.0
Lecturer	23	14	19	7.6	4.6	5.7
Total Nonladder	28	20	24	5.6	4.0	4.1

Source: Harvard University Affirmative Action Plan, Revised Plan, 1976.

TABLE 6-16. Percentage of Blacks among Employees on Harvard Faculties as of June 1976

	Univ.-Wide	FAS	GSBA	GSD	GSEd.	JFK SG	LAW
Professionals	3.6	2.1	4.6	0	3.0	0	4.9
Managers & Officials	5.8	3.3	3.4	0	15.2	0	2.8
Technical/Professionals	8.0	5.5	*	*	0	0	N.E.
Secretarial/Clerical	9.4	5.9	8.2	6.8	12.2	0	10.1
Crafts	9.5	1.7	*	*	N.E.	N.E.	N.E.
Service/Maintenance	16.4	7.7	*	*	N.E.	N.E.	N.E.

	Med. & Dental Schools	SPH	V.P. Admin.	V.P. Alumni Affairs	Finance V.P.	V.P. Govt. & Comm. Aff.	Presi-dent
Professionals	1.8	0.6	9.8	0	1.7	25.0	5.4
Managers & Officials	1.3	3.9	12.1	0	5.2	0	2.3
Technical/Professionals	9.4	9.4	13.3	*	20.0	*	0
Secretarial/Clerical	14.0	21.4	11.4	6.2	11.9	18.2	10.4
Crafts	0	0	11.3	*	N.E.	N.E.	N.E.
Service/Maintenance	27.2	23.1	15.8	*	*	N.E.	31.3

* No proportion shown because total number of employees is too small; generally 1 or 2.

N.E. No estimate provided in the affirmative action plan.

Source: Harvard University Affirmative Action Plan, Revised Plan, 1976.

Table 6-16 gives a summary of statistics concerning Harvard's utilization of blacks among its nonteaching personnel as of June 1976. As can be seen from this table, the largest concentration of blacks is in the less desirable positions, and the proportionate utilization in general declines as the desirability of the position increases. Where there are exceptions in the table, they are usually because of the utilization of one or two blacks on a small total staff.

The next point of note is that there is considerable variation across faculties in their utilization of black personnel. This utilization varies from the zero utilization at all levels in the JFKSG and the low utilization on the GSD, and vice-president for alumni affairs staffs, to the relatively high overall utilization by the offices under the vice-president for administration. Even across a relatively homogeneous occupational

TABLE 6-17. University-wide Utilization of Nonteaching Personnel at Harvard, 1971–1975

	1971	*1973*	*1975*
Professional	3.1%	3.6%	3.9%
Technicians	9.8%	7.0%	8.9%
Clerical	7.8%	9.5%	9.2%
Skilled	8.3%	7.0%	9.1%
Semiskilled	32.7%	26.3%	N.A.
Laborers	12.7%	13.5%	14.7%
Service	10.6%	15.4%	15.9%

Source: Harvard University Affirmative Action Plan, Revised Plan, 1976.

group, like secretarial and clerical workers, there is widespread variation in individual faculty utilization of blacks.

Harvard does not indicate any underutilization of blacks among non-faculty employees university-wide. Its utilization analysis is based on the proportion of blacks in the relevant occupational groupings in the cities of Boston or Cambridge, or in the Boston Standard Metropolitan Statistical Area (SMSA). The data are taken from the 1970 census.

The wide disparities that exist between the various staffs in the utilization of black employees should also be a cause of concern. It would appear that where there is a will, availability cannot be a constraint in the case of nonteaching employees. Considerable additional thought is required to correctly evaluate the performance of the various staffs with respect to hiring nonteaching personnel.

Table 6-17 shows the progress made in hiring nonteaching personnel from 1971 through 1975 university-wide. As can be seen, the progress has been modest and it has not been smooth. Between 1971 and 1973 the relative utilization of blacks decreased in the technical, skilled, and semiskilled categories. Although these proportions recovered somewhat by 1975, the utilization of black technicians was still lower in 1975 than it had been in 1971. Moreover, utilization of clerical personnel also showed a small decline between 1973 and 1975. Overall, the largest increases in utilization occurred in the nonskilled categories.

The goals and projections for utilization of black nonteaching staff are included with the overall projections for minority staff. In general, the projections call for small increases in the utilization of minority staff at all levels in most faculties. These small increases occur even where blacks are currently well utilized. In only a few cases are there projections of declines in the proportions of blacks in specific job categories. The basis for the projections of goals in the case of nonteaching faculty is also not clearly stated in the plan.

Affirmative Action and the Harvard Community

Despite the existence of this approved plan there is not general agreement within the university community that affirmative action is working well to produce equal opportunity in employment for Afro-Americans at Harvard University. The results in terms of increased employment of faculty so far have been modest and in some cases nil. Moreover, there is suspicion among some in the university community that race is still important in determining the outcomes of the employment decision-making process at Harvard. Few observers, even those who think that affirmative action is working, expect there to be any dramatic change in the racial composition of Harvard's faculty in the near future.

There are two important reasons for the difficulties and suspicion in implementing affirmative action at Harvard. The first of these is that the university has a very complex organization with much decentralization in decision-making and autonomy among the component faculties. The second is that the university has a well-known reputation of being among the top quality institutions in the world. As a consequence, there is widespread concern for securing the highest quality faculty and other employees. Yet the very concept of quality is largely subjective and judgmental, leaving wide scope for the practice of racial discrimination in employment.

The corporation, which consists of the president, the treasurer and the five fellows of the university, is the principal governing board of the university. The board of overseers reviews certain corporation actions and oversees the academic affairs and conduct of the university. The central administrative unit of the university is the Office of the President. The president is said to have limited centralized power with which to carry out the executive function. He therefore administers the university through exercising leadership and gaining the cooperation of the ten faculties, the deans, and the department heads.

Each of the ten faculties is headed by a dean who has direct charge of the administrative and academic affairs of the school or faculty. Each faculty is said to have a considerable degree of autonomy in terms of academic purposes and administrative functions.

The affirmative action plan and other university publications in the area of affirmative action, emphasize the decentralized nature of the university. This characteristic of the university was also repeatedly mentioned during interviews with officials of the central administration and the several faculties. Under Harvard's structure most of the initiative and responsibility for hiring professional teaching and nonteaching staff utilized within the various schools rests within these schools. And within the schools the initiative in the hiring process generally rests at the departmental level, although the degree of decentralization and involvement of the Dean's Office varies from school to school.

In FAS almost all hiring initiatives originate at the departmental level. In addition, the departments determine what types of expertise are required, conduct the search, and assess the relative qualifications of the various candidates. In these processes the central FAS administration takes a very limited active role.

On the other hand, in some of the smaller faculties, such as the JFKSG, the Dean's Office appears to play a larger role throughout the hiring process. Even in these cases, however, search is generally conducted by faculty from within the appropriate fields. The Dean's Office at GSBA also appears to play a more active role in search although here, too, out of necessity, the dean must rely heavily on area and program chairpersons.

Thus, the faculty hiring process university-wide is extremely decentralized. Higher levels of the university enter the process in reviewing and approving lower-level decisions and determining overall resource availabilities. Even these decisions, however, are to some degree made below the university-wide administration level, since each school frequently has independent funding sources and, as noted, a high degree of autonomy.

The decentralized character of the university is reflected in the structure for implementing and monitoring the affirmative action effort. The university's affirmative action officer is a special assistant to the president. He is charged with coordinating and overseeing the implementation of the affirmative action process. He plays no direct role in the hiring process and has no authority to independently intervene in the employment process. He does become involved if a complaint is raised or if other actions reveal that the employment procedures did not comply with affirmative action requirements. He also serves in an advisory capacity and uses his office to attempt to persuade the various faculties to carry out their affirmative action commitments.

Each faculty has a designated affirmative action officer. This person is generally an assistant or associate dean and in most cases has other duties and responsibilities besides affirmative action. While these individuals are generally charged with ensuring that the employment process conforms to the affirmative action plan, the university-wide affirmative action officer has no direct authority over these individuals, who report to the chief administrative officer of their respective faculties. However, there is interaction between the university-wide officer and the faculty officers; advice, reports, and information are exchanged among these individuals.

In most cases these officers have direct review authority over hiring, promotion, or other employment decisions. In some cases they can deny or hold up a request if they are not satisfied with the affirmative action aspects of the decision. In others they can only make recommendations to their dean. In the interviews, however, it was clear that most of these individuals exercised their function principally by ensuring that the documentation of the hiring procedure was in order. They seldom participated in the actual decision making or questioned the actions and judgments of the department. As long as the paperwork was in order, most of these individuals were satisfied.

The degree of involvement of the affirmative action officer in the hiring process varied widely among the faculties. Some of the officers took more initiative in monitoring and advising in the hiring process, and designed more elaborate procedural safeguards to ensure the fairness of the process. But even these more active individuals had to rely heavily on departmental committees and expertise.

The secretary to the corporation also has a role in the affirmative action process. The secretary's office is charged with detecting violations of the affirmative action requirements in documentation submitted to the corporation for final approval of employment-related decisions such as hire and tenure. If such a discrepancy is found the secretary reports it to the president and the special assistant for affirmative action. The personnel office also plays a role in the process, having principal responsibility for data collection and for employment of nonexempt personnel.

In short, the authority and responsibility for implementing and monitoring affirmative action efforts is widely dispersed throughout the university. At the central administrative level it is split among the personnel office, the office of the special assistant, and the secretary's office. There is also a university-wide equal opportunity committee. This committee is very large and includes all of the affirmative action officers.

It has no clear line of responsibility or authority and serves mainly to disseminate information.

Even though the special assistant is the nominal officer in charge at the university-wide level, he has little formal role in the actual hiring or monitoring process. He has a very limited staff and is kept extremely busy attending meetings throughout the university. This office also appears to have limited authority over the affirmative action process within the university.

Harvard University prides itself on being one of the best teaching and research universities in the country. It therefore puts strong emphasis on attracting the highest quality faculty as well as student body. As stated in the affirmative action plan, "Harvard, as a great teaching and research university with extremely able students and a position of academic leadership to maintain, seeks its faculty from among the most gifted and accomplished individuals the academic world can supply." The emphasis on the "quality" of faculty and on the necessity of attracting the highest quality faculty and student body were repeatedly emphasized in talks with university officials. This emphasis most certainly affects the conduct of affirmative action, since the definition of quality is judgmental, and the implementation of quality control rests exclusively in the hands of the existing faculty, the very practitioners of exclusion in the past.

The heart of Harvard's affirmative action effort in terms of expansion of opportunities for blacks centers on their recruitment efforts. Recruitment is particularly important at Harvard, since not only entry level positions but also higher level positions are generally filled from the outside. The affirmative action effort takes the form of more extensive searches for faculty and research personnel and the form of longer posting of positions for nonfaculty, nonprofessional employees. The Harvard plan lays out specific guidelines and suggestions for searches for faculty employment. But it is important to note that Harvard's plan specifically recognizes the relative autonomy of each department. Therefore, much of what is in the overall affirmative action plan with respect to recruitment and searches are suggestions rather than requirements.

In addition to the general proviso that search should be within the "widest possible sphere," there are five specific suggestions which "each faculty is encouraged to adopt." These are: (1) maintain "an up-to-date list of potential women and minority candidates for appointment at each level of instruction"; (2) "women *or* minority faculty members should be included, whenever possible, on search committees" or consulted where inclusion is not possible; (3) "efforts should be made to contact minority or female professors elsewhere for suggestions of candidates"; (4) positions should be advertised in professional journals, placement offices, or other professionally relevant media *best recognized by the specific faculty or department involved*; (5) schools or departments should seek to increase their own numbers of minority and women graduate students and use them as another future source of candidates.

There are a number of points to be made about these procedures. First, as noted, no department or faculty is actually required to adopt these practices. As far as could be determined from interviews, no department has in fact formally implemented all of these suggestions. In particular, little evidence was found that suggestions (1) or (5) were actually being followed by any of the faculties whose procedures were reviewed for this study. Moreover, in the case of the only department-level search committee contacted in FAS, a general ignorance was found of the guidelines concerning conduct of the search and a general lack of compliance with any of the suggestions of the affirmative action plan.

The extensiveness and form of searches appeared to vary widely from faculty to faculty and from department to department within each faculty as did the degree of compliance with the suggestions of the affirmative action plan with respect to minority recruitment. This variation appeared to hinge on two factors. The first is the extent to which minorities are present in the school or department, either within the student bodies or within the faculty. The second factor is the personal involvement and authority of the department's or faculty's affirmative action officer.

Nonetheless, despite the variation in the extent of search there was general agreement on all faculties that affirmative action had led to wider and more extensive searches. Candidates were discovered by those who searched hard, and these candidates probably would not have been discovered otherwise. More effort was put into designing and carrying out searches, and some efforts were specifically put into discovering minority candidates. All those spoken with fully admit that these efforts probably would not have been undertaken, if not for the requirements of affirmative action.

While there is no clear numerical evidence on this question there is rather widespread agreement that the expanded search has produced a larger number of applicants. Some individuals indicated that the greatest impact of a general widening of the search patterns has been to increase the pool of white, male applicants. Yet, the numbers of minority and female candidates have also increased. In the search conducted by the Department of Urban and Regional Planning in 1976, for example, 302 applications were received for five positions. Of this number 18 were from minority candidates and 42 were from female candidates. These figures were said to represent a significant increase over the previous year's applications from minority and female candidates. A similar increase in the numbers of proportions of minority candidates also appears to have occurred in other departments and faculties conducting wide-ranging searches.

The other important aspect to recognize about faculty recruitment is that the search takes place strictly within the parameters specified by the hiring units. The hiring units specify the nature of the openings and the qualifications required for potential applicants. These specifications can be drawn very broadly or very narrowly with the obvious consequences for minority recruitment.

The university's plan specifically let the departments determine the appropriate places for advertising positions. As a result, few departments or faculties advertise in nontraditional or minority journals. In many cases the searches are restricted to a select list of graduate departments for nontenured positions. Tenured searches may be even more restrictive in practice. However, the impact of these quality controls in the search process on the generation of minority candidates is not clear.

An increase in the number of applicants from minority groups, however, does not necessarily lead to increased hiring of minorities. In the case of the Urban and Regional Planning Department, for example, only one offer was made to a minority candidate and this offer was not accepted. A further indication of the lack of relationship between generating applications and an increase in job offers was the failure of the special student recruitment effort undertaken by the Graduate School of Arts and Sciences (GSAS) in 1976.

In that year Harvard GSAS undertook several recruitment efforts. Plan 1 involved an exchange of potential minority applicants with Princeton and Yale. Under this plan there were 11 applicants, but none was admitted. Plan 2 involved an exchange with a coalition of eight other schools. Here 47 applications were received and one was admitted. Under Plan 3 Harvard subscribed to the minority locator service of the Educational Teaching Service. This plan resulted in 21 applications, and all of the applicants were denied admission. In a fourth effort a committee of students wrote over four hundred letters to colleges throughout the country. This effort resulted in 12 applications, and all applicants were denied admission. Finally, letters were written to the deans of black colleges. This effort resulted in 12 applications, and 2 applicants were admitted. In total, the special recruitment effort generated 103 applications, and only 3 of those who applied were offered admittance.

Although the above relates specifically to graduate students and not employment, it does illustrate the results of Harvard's expanded search on increased opportunities for minorities. The fact of the matter is that the actual results in terms of hiring may be even worse for black employment than indicated here for students. The weak connection between expanded recruitment and actual black employment increases is widely recognized by the administrators and others involved in the affirmative action effort. This fact is also specifically recognized by the regional Office for Civil Rights.

The failure of the expanded faculty searches to produce dramatic increases in black hiring does not indicate that Harvard is not in compliance with the affirmative action laws. The implications of the slow pace of hiring blacks are interpreted differently by different observers. Dean Keller, the equal opportunity officer for FAS, interprets the results on the FAS faculty as encouraging. In her view a slow rate of increase should be expected in the progress of blacks and females, given the low rate of hiring and the low availabilities of blacks and women. She feels that the hiring of women and minorities since the inception of the affirmative action plan has proceeded at a rate at or above their respective availabilities and thus that progress has been made. On the other hand, Walter J. Leonard, the university-wide affirmative action officer, found the university's progress slow and discouraging. He felt availabilities at the junior level were not the principal problem and that more blacks could have been hired if the departments had the commitment. Leonard emphasizes a disaggregated view of performance at the university, whereas Keller emphasizes a view based on aggregate results.

The affirmative action plan has no specific provisions governing the deliberations in which the preferred candidate is selected from among the various candidates for the position. Presumably the job is supposed to go to the best candidate. In all instances it is recognized that it is within the prerogative of the department to assess the relative merits of various candidates.

In some cases procedural safeguards are introduced into the selection process to ensure that minorities receive a fair hearing. The most extensive safeguards were those used by the Graduate School of Education. Here, at each stage of the selection process, the proportion of minorities remaining as the pool of candidates was narrowed is compared with the proportion in the initial pool. If the proportion advancing in the selection process is less than the proportion at the start, an explanation is required. This procedure generally results in a larger number of minority candidates advancing through the selection process. It is also the case that any single individual on the search committee can cause any particular applicant to be considered by the entire committee. The Graduate School of Education also generally requires a specific explanation as to why the leading minority candidate is not chosen and always places a woman and/or a minority individual on the search committee.

No other school reviewed at Harvard utilized such extensive checks on the selection process. In general, the search committee made its own decisions in cutting down the initial list. Explicit explanation as to why the candidate selected was chosen, when it was not a woman or a minority, was generally required, however.

Nonetheless, safeguards or not, the criteria and their application lie in the exclusive domain of the departments or hiring units. The necessity of leaving quality judgments up to the hiring units was explicitly accepted by most university administrators interviewed, as long as hiring units' choice could be supported. This position was also supported by OCR which considered itself not competent to second guess Harvard's quality decisions.

It is also generally the case that the quality criteria are not well-articulated or specific. Qualifications tend to be general and qualitative. The application of the criteria requires considerable judgment on the part of selection committees. This reliance on judgment is especially the case at Harvard because of its heavy emphasis on high quality. Standard credentials are not sufficient to qualify an individual. Judgment based on references, quality of publications, graduate school, recommendations, interviews, and so forth, are all somehow made and weighted to produce a final ranking of candidates.

It also is clear that in general the university, the separate faculties, and the departments do not bend with respect to quality of candidates in order to hire minorities. Almost everyone spoken to agreed that the minority candidate would have to be the most qualified among the pool of available candidates to be hired. The biggest concession to a minority candidate was that some indicated that in the event that two candidates were equally qualified, the position would be awarded to the minority candidate. Moreover, it was also the case that no one, either from higher levels in the university or from OCR, apparently felt any pressure to abandon or modify Harvard's quality standards. In general, most felt that as long as they could provide an explanation of their choice, it would be accepted and would comply with the affirmative action requirement.

Oberlin College: A Case Study
of a Private, Liberal Arts College

Background

In 1833 two young missionaries, the Reverends John J. Shipherd and Philo Stewart, met in Lorain County, Ohio, to discuss ways to bring spiritual uplift to a "perishing world." The result of that meeting was the establishment of Oberlin College. In a natural extension of its Christian activities, Oberlin became the first college in the United States to adopt as its policy a ban against racial discrimination, and the first institution to grant the Bachelor of Arts degree to women on an equal basis with men. Prior to 1865 Oberlin did more to educate free blacks than any other predominantly white institution in the nation and has consistently, over the years, maintained an integrated student body.

Today Oberlin consists of a College of Arts and Sciences and a Conservatory of Music. Oberlin is consistently rated among the best colleges in the country for its faculty, student body, and facilities, and is rated by the Barron's Profile as highly competitive. Seventy percent of all Oberlin graduates eventually do further study in graduate and professional schools. Oberlin has a student enrollment of approximately 2,640 students; approximately 12 percent are Afro-Americans. The median test scores of men and women on the scholastic aptitude test (SAT) exceed 600 on both verbal and mathematics. The total expenses per year at Oberlin exceed $5,000, but approximately 44 percent of all students receive financial aid. The college offers the Bachelor of Arts degree and has a limited master's degree program, primarily in music. The college itself is located in the small town of Oberlin (pop. 9,200), some thirty-four miles southwest of Cleveland. The college is governed by a board of trustees consisting of twenty-eight members.

The Development of an Affirmative Action Plan

Oberlin College does not receive $50,000 or more in federal contracts and therefore is not subject to the provisions of Executive Order 11246. Nevertheless, in keeping with the spirit of the college and its founders, the board of trustees decided in 1973 that the college should have an affirmative aciton plan, and that the plan should follow the guidelines published by HEW. The administration was also instructed to seek federal approval of its plan once it had been developed.

In late 1974, the acting president of Oberlin College appointed a committee to draft an affirmative action plan. The Affirmative Action Policy Committee, with the aid of an outside consultant, prepared a plan and submitted it in the spring of 1975 to the General Faculty Council for its endorsement. It was apparent that the plan needed further work and the committee continued to work on it during the fall and winter of 1975–76.

The redraft of the affirmative action plan was presented to the General Faculty Council and then to the general faculty for its approval in May 1976. Some faculty members felt that there was not enough flexibility in the plan and others were critical of several sections. The general faculty, after some discussion, approved parts of the plan and referred back to the Affirmative Action Policy Committee the sections on general policy and employment policies and practices.*

The most controversial section under general policy was item 6 which read:

Hiring groups are encouraged to place a positive value on potential diversification of the workforce when considering the qualifications presented by individual candidates.

The chairman of the committee suggested that many faculty members disliked this aspect of the plan because they thought it would result in reverse discrimination. This was partially the fault of the Affirmative Action Committee because it had not adequately done its job of educating the college community on what the new procedures entailed.

---

* Since the interviews were conducted at Oberlin, the Affirmative Action Policy Committee again reworked these sections and presented them to the general faculty in February 1977. The general faculty amended the two sections and they were approved as amended. As yet no goals and time-tables have been established for any departments. A new committee, established by the general faculty as part of the affirmative action plan, and the affirmative action officer are working with departments to develop this aspect of the plan.

TABLE 6-18. Oberlin Faculty Members by Race and Sex, 1976 (9–10 months)

Total Faculty	Male				Female			
	Total	*Black*	*White*	*Others*	*Total*	*Black*	*White*	*Others*
218	178	8	165	5	40	0	39	1

Source: Oberlin College Affirmative Action Plan.

Yet even after the education process was completed, some confusion remained over whether blacks and other minorities would actually receive preferential treatment because of the emphasis in the plan on seeking diversity within the college. The statement concerning faculty diversity was the most controversial, and when it was referred back to the committee for reworking, it was subsequently omitted. College administrators stressed that Oberlin would in all circumstances seek to hire the most qualified candidates to fill faculty vacancies.

The committee also encountered difficulty in finding an affirmative action officer within the limited budget of the college. After months of searching, the committee finally hired a Cleveland lawyer who serves in the position on a part-time basis.* The affirmative action officer is directly responsible to the president of the college. The committee decided that the plan should be implemented prior to its completion and approval by HEW. Although Oberlin's employment policies and procedures have been altered according to the new plan, goals and time-tables have not been developed. As of summer 1976, the committee and the affirmative action officer had drafted projected goals, but these were to be used only as a guide for department heads in establishing their own goals. The committee continued to encourage the faculty and staff to seek minority candidates in their applicant pools, even without specific numerical guidelines.

Work Force Analysis and Goals

Table 6-18 gives the utilizations analysis of faculty members at Oberlin as of 1976. Blacks constituted 3.6 percent of the faculty, or 8 of the

---

* The affirmative action officer resigned in September 1976.

TABLE 6-19. Oberlin Faculty Members by Race, Sex, and Salary Range (9–10 months)

Salary Range	Total	Male				Female			
		Total	Black	White	Other	Total	Black	White	Other
$10,000–12,999	26	19	1	17	1	7	0	7	0
$13,000–15,999	68	48	1	45	2	20	0	19	1
$16,000–18,999	50	43	4	39	0	7	0	7	0
$19,000–24,999	62	57	2	53	2	5	0	5	0
$25,000–29,999	10	9	0	9	0	1	0	1	0
$30,000 & above	2	2	0	2	0	0	0	0	0

Source: Oberlin College Affirmative Action Plan.

218 faculty members. There were no black female faculty members. Table 6-19 gives the breakdown of faculty members by race, sex, and salary range. At this time, however, none were represented at the two highest levels. Females were generally concentrated at the lower salary levels.

For professional and administrative staff (9–10 months), there were two black females and no black males. In this category, blacks accounted for 17 percent of the total. In the salary range, the numbers were too small to have any statistical significance. (*See* Tables 6-20 and 6-21.)

There were ninety-eight members of the professional and administrative staff in the twelve-month category. Blacks held seven of the professional and administrative positions and represented approximately 7 percent of the total. Blacks, both male and female, were lo-

TABLE 6-20. Oberlin Professional and Administrative Staff by Race and Sex, 1976 (9–10 months)

Total A&P	Male				Female			
	Total	Black	White	Other	Total	Black	White	Other
12	6	0	6	0	6	2	4	0

Source: Oberlin College Affirmative Action Plan.

TABLE 6-21. Oberlin Professional and Administrative Staff by Race, Sex, and Salary Range, 1976 (9–10 months)

Salary Range	Total	Male				Female			
		Total	Black	White	Others	Total	Black	White	Others
$7,500–9,999	2	1	0	1	0	1	0	1	0
$10,000–12,999	2	0	0	0	0	2	1	1	0
$13,000–15,999	4	3	0	3	0	1	0	1	0
$16,000–18,999	3	2	0	2	0	1	0	1	0
$19,000–24,999	1	0	0	0	0	1	1	0	0
$25,000–29,999	0	0	0	0	0	0	0	0	0
$30,000 & above	0	0	0	0	0	0	0	0	0

Source: Oberlin College Affirmative Action Plan.

cated in the middle salary range. Females were generally located in the lower levels. (*See* Tables 6-22 and 6-23.)

Oberlin is in the process of establishing goals and timetables based on its utilization analysis. The establishment of goals is far from complete, but Oberlin has set up preliminary goals in its College of Arts and Sciences. Within the College of Arts and Sciences' twenty departments and seven programs, there were 160 faculty members in 1975–76. Minorities accounted for 6.8 percent of the total arts and sciences faculty (10 minority men and 1 minority woman). Within the College of Arts and Sciences there were 116 tenured faculty members. Of these, 99 were white males, 12 women (1 minority woman) and 6 minority males. A breakdown by percentages reveals that 84.5 percent of the

TABLE 6-22. Oberlin Professional and Administrative Staff by Race and Sex, 1976 (12 months)

Total A&P	Male				Female			
	Total	Black	White	Others	Total	Black	White	Others
98	71	5	64	2	27	2	21	4

Source: Oberlin College Affirmative Action Plan.

TABLE 6-23. Oberlin Professional and Administrative Staff by Race, Sex, and Salary Range, 1976 (12 months)

Salary Range	Total	Male				Female			
		Total	Black	White	Others	Total	Black	White	Others
Below $7,500	4	2	0	2	0	2	0	2	0
$7,500–9,999	7	3	0	2	1	4	0	3	1
$10,000–12,999	24	14	1	12	1	10	1	6	3
$12,000–15,999	21	14	1	13	0	7	0	7	0
$16,000–18,999	16	12	1	11	0	4	1	3	0
$19,000–24,999	18	18	2	16	0	0	0	0	0
$25,000–29,999	2	2	0	2	0	0	0	0	0
$30,000 & above	6	6	0	6	0	0	0	0	0

Source: Oberlin College Affirmative Action Plan.

tenured positions in the College of Arts and Sciences were held by whites, 10.3 percent by women and 5.2 percent by minorities. The white male to white female ratio was 8 to 1.

When Oberlin established the goals and timetables for the College of Arts and Sciences, the goals and timetables were to be used as an example of what might be done. In determining the sample goals the college anticipated a vacancy rate per year of 7.15 positions due to resignations and retirements. However, 12.47 vacancies were projected as replacements for faculty members on sabbatical and unpaid leaves.

Oberlin initially projected its preliminary goals over a three-year period for women and yearly for minorities. A goal is established for women when their representation in availability pools exceeds that of each department by 0.64 person; for minorities it is 0.30 person. The major problem, as can be seen in Table 6-24, is the low rate of new hires at Oberlin. At the same time, minorities were found to be under-represented in eighteen of the twenty-seven departments and programs. Preliminary hiring goals were established for minorities in six departments. It must also be emphasized that these were preliminary goals and were not prepared college-wide.*

The new hiring procedures developed as part of Oberlin's plan re-

* Since the completion of the interviews, these figures were dropped from the plan. Oberlin is in the process of developing a new method for assessing availability pools and establishing goals and timetables.

quire that all jobs be posted when vacancies occur to ensure that the recruitment process will be fair. Applicants for employment are then sent to the hiring authority for consideration. When there is an indication that a particular department has not been hiring minorities at a rate that would ordinarily be expected from their availability in the labor force, the affirmative action officer might suggest that the applicant pools be expanded to increase the number of minorities. In such situations, the affirmative action officer must certify that the procedure for hiring was fair before a person can be hired. If the officer gives the process a negative review in situations involving faculty members, the dean of the college reviews the procedures. He then either approves the procedure or suggests that the search be extended.*

Affirmative Action and the Oberlin Community

The response from the college community to the plan was generally favorable. Most people agreed that Oberlin should hire more minority faculty members. Many faculty members, however, questioned the procedure for accomplishing this goal and felt the plan was too rigid. Although they realized that many of the "details" were still being ironed out, they definitely thought the plan should be flexible enough to allow for personnel action in emergency situations. The special assistant to the president pointed out that problems are caused when a person resigns or dies unexpectedly just prior to a new academic year, and that it would be literally impossible to follow the entire procedure and expect to be able to hire someone before the college opens. The college would like to begin the hiring process as early as January, but, as the president indicated, this approach is not always possible because of budgets being formulated.

Most of the criticisms of the plan were based on the extra costs and time required for implementing the procedures. The heads of departments were concerned about the cost, but since the college does not separate affirmative action costs from the regular recruitment budget, it is difficult to know what the expenditure for the plan actually is. Many thought that advertisements in various journals were too expensive for the results they obtained. One vice-president, whose sentiments

---

* This procedure is no longer practiced by the college. There is more contact at the beginning of the recruitment process between the department chairperson and the affirmative action officer. The affirmative action officer may still write a negative review, but the Divisional Council determines the viability of the search process.

TABLE 6-24. Representation of Minorities and Women at Oberlin and Affirmative Action Goals for the College of Arts and Sciences

Program or Department	Mean Hiring Rate Per Year	Percentage Available in Work Force		Percentage of Current Staff		Net Difference in F.T.E.[3],[7]		Affirmative Action Goals[8]	
		Minorities	Women	Minorities	Women	Minorities	Women	Minorities[5]	Women[6]
Art									
History	0.66	3.0	53.0	—	69.0	−0.16	+0.86	—	—
Studio	0.50	5.0	25.0	—	25.0	−0.20	—	A. A. Goal	A. A. Goal
Biology	1.13	5.0	20.0	—	11.0	−0.45	−0.80	A. A. Goal	A. A. Goal
Chemistry	0.88	5.0	11.0	—	—	−0.35	−0.77	A. A. Goal	A. A. Goal
Classics	0.38	1.3	28.0	—	—	−0.04	−0.84	A. A. Goal	A. A. Goal
Communications	0.50	9.6	20.0	—	25.0	−0.40	−0.33	A. A. Goal	—
Economics	0.69	3.0	8.0	—	—	−0.17	−0.44	—	—
Education	0.37	8.0	28.0	33.0	—	+0.76	−0.84	—	—
English	1.88	2.5	34.0	—	23.0	−0.38	−1.60	A. A. Goal	A. A. Goal
Geology	0.50	1.2	4.0	—	—	−0.05	−0.16	—	—
German/Russian									
German	0.60	1.1	40.0	—	21.0	−0.09	−2.20	—	A. A. Goal
Russian	0.40	0.0	24.0	—	—	—	−1.93	—	A. A. Goal
Government	0.94	4.0	16.0	—	13.0	−0.30	−0.20	A. A. Goal	—
History	1.17	3.0	18.0	—	11.0	−0.28	−0.68	—	A. A. Goal
Mathematics	1.00	2.8	8.0	13.0	—	+0.78	−0.64	—	A. A. Goal
Philosophy	0.63	5.0	15.0	—	—	−0.25	−0.75	—	A. A. Goal
Physical Education	1.38	N.A.	N.A.	18.0	45.0	N.A.	N.A.	N.A.	A. A. Goal
Physics	0.75	2.2	3.0	—	—	−0.13	−0.18	—	—

								A. A. Goal	A. A. Goal
Psychology	1.06	4.0	33.0	—	12.0	-0.34	-1.81	—	—
Religion	0.71	1.6	8.0	11.0	—	+0.57	-0.45	—	—
Romance Languages	1.08								
French	0.75	11.0	46.0	12.0	46.0	—	—	—	—
Spanish	0.33								
Sociology/Anthropology	1.13								
Sociology	0.75	6.0	27.0	33.0	—	+1.64	-1.62	A. A. Goal	A. A. Goal
Anthropology	0.38	7.6	32.0	—	33.0	-0.24	-0.14	—	—
Programs									
Black Studies	[3]	[3]	[3]	100.0	—	[3]	[3]	[3]	[3]
Creative Writing	0.12	N.A.	N.A.	—	—	N.A.	N.A.	N.A.	N.A.
East Asian Studies	0.42	40.0[1]	10.0[1]	40.0[4]	10.0	—	—	—	—
Human Development	0.12	[2]	[2]	—	100.0	-0.06	+0.70	N.A.	N.A.
Humanities	0.04	N.A.	N.A.	—	—	N.A.	N.A.	N.A.	N.A.
Interarts	0.63	N.A.	N.A.	—	40.0	N.A.	N.A.	N.A.	N.A.
JNES	0.12	12.5	14.6	—	—	-0.13	-0.15	—	—

1. Approximate.
2. See Education and Psychology.
3. Undeterminable at this time.
4. Includes one female minority.
5. Represents a goal over a three-year period.
6. Represents a yearly goal.
7. Full-time Equivalence.
8. These affirmative action goals have been reevaluated.

Source: Oberlin College Affirmative Action Plan.

were echoed throughout the college community, indicated that there was too much paper work generated by the plan. No one, however, seemed to have a clear idea of what they could do to reduce the amount of time necessary to carry out the procedures.

The dean of the conservatory suggested that the procedures have resulted in some resentment, but that they had improved the employment process and made it much more democratic. He emphasized that much of the time originally involved in developing the plan has been reduced because the data have now been placed on a computer. He also pointed out that such innovative employment procedures would not have been created without the push from the affirmative action program.

The personnel officer indicated that because the plan was implemented before its component parts were completed, much of the criticism was premature. He stressed the considerable amount of time involved in implementing any affirmative action plan.

The general consensus of the faculty interviewed was that the plan should be rigorously enforced and that no preferential hiring be done at all. The chairman of the affirmative action committee also shares that view, but believes that when two people are equally qualified, blacks should be selected as long as they continue to be underutilized on the faculty due to past discriminatory practices. One central problem is that no one seems to know just what constitutes qualifications. The chairman believes that race and/or sex might be a valid personnel qualification when all else is equal and when few or no minorities and women are on the faculty. This view was also shared by other faculty members and administrators. An associate dean expressed the view that diversity is a valid consideration for employment. The college does not want to draw all of its faculty members from institutions such as Harvard, and actively seeks to hire a variety of professors from different schools. If a particular department, for example, seeks a non-Harvard graduate, no one questions that decision. Only when the issue of race is added is there controversy.

The associate dean, who is also an assistant professor of sociology and anthropology, pointed out that racism affects a person's decisions, often in very subtle ways. A person's background colors his decision and judgments in ways in which the person cannot always be conscious. When one approaches a person of different race or ethnic background, one often cannot appreciate differences. She pointed out that since Oberlin does not have the data to evaluate what constitutes a good teacher and what adequately defines qualifications, the hiring process reverts to subjectivism.

The president of the college was emphatic in his statement that the board of trustees was strongly committed to hiring minorities on the faculty. The president said that this commitment was made during his predecessor's administration and that he would continue the policy under his administration. He frankly admitted that before affirmative action, recruitment of minorities was left to those who were willing to make the effort.

Even though there is a commitment to recruit black faculty members, there is uncertainty over just what their larger role at Oberlin should be. An associate dean observed that since there were so few blacks on campus, the same ones had many demands placed on them and were constantly being selected to serve on committees. A black faculty member pointed out that affirmative action should be a two-way street and that part of the program should prepare whites to accept others who come with different perspectives.

Initially, blacks were brought into only the physical education and Afro-American studies departments. Eventually they were employed in other departments as well and a few were selected as chairmen. Most are on the tenured track, but only three blacks had received tenure as of 1976. The dean of the music conservatory said that his faculty had a fairly good representation of blacks; in 1975–76 there were three black faculty members in the conservatory. He pointed out he was not limited to hiring only candidates who held the doctorate. Except for music education, music history, and theory, most departments in the conservatory do not require the Ph.D.* In fact, only one out of the forty faculty members in the applied music area has the Ph.D. in the conservatory. The dean said that he looks for equivalents: outstanding artistic achievement, broad experience, and the overall quality of the candidate's career. As for the entry-level positions, the National Association for Schools of Music, which keeps track of minorities doing graduate work, indicates that there is a great number of talented candidates available to teach jazz and Afro-American music. The conservatory, however, by no means limits black faculty to these areas.

The college has been most successful in recruiting professional blacks

---

* There were sixty-one members of the 1976–77 conservatory faculty. Of these, nine had Ph.D.'s, two had Ed.D.'s, one a D.M., and one a D.M.A. Using only Ph.D.'s, three out of every twenty had a Ph.D.; using all of the degrees, approximately one out of five had a doctorate.

for nonacademic positions. The hiring of blacks for faculty positions is complicated by the fact that there are fewer and fewer faculty positions open and hence no large turnover. The major area of hiring is for part-time slots to replace persons on sabbatical, but blacks are naturally reluctant to leave a full-time job to accept a temporary appointment. Blacks generally can demand a higher salary than whites because they are in such short supply in all fields which, according to the law of supply and demand, accelerates their salaries. The college has a general policy that all faculty members of the same rank receive approximately the same compensation, regardless of field.

Nearly everyone agrees that standards should not be lowered for anyone, but there was no consensus as to what constituted the "most qualified." One associate dean did suggest that many faculty members wanted to define standards too narrowly without looking at the total contribution nonwhites and nonmales can make to the college community. He said that a major problem was that selection committees start recruiting too late in the year and do not get adequate representation of minorities in their recruitment pools. The dean thought that just because results were meager, however, the process was far from a waste of time because affirmative action does make the entire selection process more fair. Because women are much more available, their representation on the faculty has increased.

The president indicated that the major obstacle to increasing the black faculty was the no-growth situation at the college, which limits the number of available positions. He said that for the first time Oberlin was operating on a deficit, which exceeded $250,000 last year. He also suggested that salaries were not always competitive and that they were forced, like other institutions, to compete for the few available blacks.

Black Students and Affimative Action

Oberlin has been more successful in recruiting black and other minority students than in recruiting minority faculty. The college has made a conscious decision to diversify the student body. Just as some institutions want a balanced geographical distribution or a fairly even distribution between the sexes, Oberlin wants a fair representation of minority students.

The president indicated that there has always been at Oberlin a certain nucleus of minority students, including Asian Americans. As former dean of the conservatory, he remembers that during the 1940s the school had a strong representation of blacks. In 1971 the college decided to actively recruit minorities and established a goal of 110 freshmen; this total was to be composed of blacks with some increased representation of Latinos. The president thought this goal had been achieved only once, and felt the expense of attending Oberlin may be one reason for it. The college continues to attract what is called the "no-need" student, that is, the black student who can afford to pay his own way and who will, because of his socioeconomic and educational background, do well at Oberlin.

But the president emphasized that Oberlin has a reputation to uphold and that the college would not sacrifice quality. He also pointed out that even maintaining high standards, minority representation increased from 2 to 3 percent in the 1960s to 6 or 7 percent in the 1970s. The president said that Oberlin has the second highest black representation for a private, liberal arts college. (*See* Table 6-25.) He placed the percentage at 11.8 and indicated that only Antioch College, with more liberal admission standards, exceeds Oberlin's percentage with 15.2 percent minority students. He was proud to note that Oberlin does better in recruiting minority students than the top rated Ivy League schools. The president thought that Oberlin, as a liberal arts college, was best suited for providing a first-rate education for blacks and other groups and emphasized that this is where the school is placing its limited resources. He thought that in the long run this would make a substantial contribution to the overall affirmative action program since Oberlin has the highest number of its graduates obtaining the doctorate than any other private, four-year college.

Oberlin, over a five-year period, successfully moved towards its goal of increasing minority representation on campus to 15 percent, with blacks accounting for 11 to 12 percent of the total student population. In 1976, a study of student attainment* found that blacks constituted 14 percent of the graduating class, an all-time high. Prior to the initiation of the program, Oberlin generally accepted students with high SAT scores, high class rank, and middle-to-upper income backgrounds. The director of admissions said that to accelerate admission of low-income black students, less emphasis was placed on high SAT scores and greater emphasis was placed on the student profile, motivation, and high achievement.

---

* Oberlin College, "Report on Cost and Returns to Investment in Form of Student Attainments and Institutional Development of the 1971 Commitment," mimeographed, 1976.

TABLE 6-25. Black Student Enrollment in Major Private Colleges and Universities, 1974–75*

	Black			Total	
School	Men	Women	Total	Undergraduate	% Black
1. Antioch	226	108	334	2,192	15.2
2. Oberlin	159	155	314	2,667	11.8
3. Wesleyan (CT)	88	92	180	1,947	9.2
4. Dartmouth	203	61	264	3,152	8.4
5. Brown	220	198	418	5,050	8.3
6. Amherst	106	—	106	1,299	8.2
7. Wellesley	—	155	155	1,905	8.1
8. Carleton	72	54	126	1,640	7.7
9. Pomona	43	57	100	1,323	7.6
Princeton	180	149	329	4,336	7.6
10. Swarthmore	41	48	89	1,241	7.2
Williams	79	53	132	1,829	7.2
11. Harvard	293	156	449	6,287	7.1
12. Vassar	30	110	140	2,163	6.5
13. Yale	169	95	264	4,723	5.6
14. Wooster	54	47	101	1,974	5.1
15. Smith	—	128	128	2,609	4.9
16. Grinnell	23	32	55	1,168	4.7
17. Bowdoin	34	25	59	1,284	4.6
Bryn Mawr	—	39	39	850	4.6
18. Haverford	25	—	25	775	3.2
19. Middlebury	30	25	55	1,871	2.9
20. Denison	27	25	52	2,131	2.4
21. Reed	7	3	10	1,114	0.9
22. Kenyon	4	5	9	1,451	0.6

* As of September 1974.

Source: Office for Civil Rights, HEW.

As a result of these innovations, Oberlin found that minority students were able to successfully complete its academic program without the lowering of standards or quality of instruction. The study found that black students scored lower than other students in an analysis of grade-point averages, but on a semester-by-semester basis these scores paralleled and converged slightly with the scores of other students over a period of time. Further, Oberlin found that rank in class or grade-point average was a stronger predictor of college performance than SAT scores. A higher percentage of minority students completed their degrees than other nonminority students at Oberlin, than students in selective institutions, and than the national norm. They were able to complete enough hours each semester for advancement toward graduation and were more inclined to take advanced courses than were white students. Finally, the study found that black students who had a high need for financial assistance, sought out "many opportunities for completion of degree work and beyond."

The admissions director emphasized that although the figure of 110 was the target, he recruits as many black students as possible. He felt the biggest obstacle was the fact that most low-income students needed financial aid. It was uncertain just how many black students received aid, but roughly 35 percent of all financial aid goes to black and Latino students. The director was quick to add that all students admitted are capable of work at Oberlin and that therefore standards are not lowered. The director added that there is no valid reason for saying that only those with the top scores on the SAT will be admitted to any institution. He saw no reason why preference should be given to a person who makes a high SAT score and underachieves in other areas while denying admission to a person with low SAT scores but who is a high achiever otherwise.

Once students are admitted, according to an associate dean, all face the same rigorous program that is sufficient to train students for graduate school. Another dean maintains standards are not lowered for minority students because Oberlin wants to provide them, as others, with a first-rate education which will allow them to go on for an advanced degree. He added that Oberlin has special tutoring programs for students who need them. The black Oberlin student retention rate is as high as the college average. Many of the black low-income students have average test scores somewhat lower than whites, but Oberlin tries to identify deficiencies early and provide students with special attention when needed, so these students can keep up with other students.

A member of the Affirmative Action Committee also said that although 50 percent of the students who use the special services are minorities, the program was designed to aid all students with deficiencies in reading, writing, math, and courses in which they are having particular difficulty. The philosophy behind the special services is not to lower standards, but to bring deficient students up to the average. One teacher suggested that the difference in test scores between low-income blacks and upper-income whites does not generally increase over four years. This difference indicates that although black students are at a disadvantage, they do not fall further behind. In fact, overall they may have learned more after four years. One does not have to push these low-income students, many of whom are moving into the hard sciences and doing well.

The president concluded that Oberlin could make greater strides in educating minority students if more federal assistance were provided. He emphasized that the resources at private, liberal arts colleges are limited.

Oberlin and the Federal Government

Since Oberlin does not come under the Federal Contract Compliance Program, its contact with the federal government has been limited. From time to time, guidance has been sought from HEW's Chicago Regional Office for Civil Rights, but the chairman of Oberlin's Affirmative Action Committee thought that little was accomplished from this contact. He found it difficult to pin down the requirements and felt that the school has to be careful in following the federal guidelines not to violate Ohio state fair employment practices and procedures. One major criticism was that there are too many federal regulations. The college was also unsure just what added responsibility would result from the new regulations governing nondiscrimination against the handicapped.

Merritt College: A Case Study of a Community College

Background

Merritt College, located in Oakland, California, is a two-year community college maintained by the Peralta Community College District of Northern Alameda County. It includes a comprehensive technical education complex as well as a liberal arts program. Merritt has a total day enrollment of 6,500 students in addition to 3,500 part-time evening students. The college is a free public institution, open to any resident of the district who has either reached the age of eighteen or graduated from high school.

Peralta District Affimative Action Plan

On 4 June 1973, the Board of Trustees of the Peralta District adopted an affirmative action plan for its certified contract (faculty) and classified

TABLE 6-26. Comparison of Situation in 1972–73 to Goals

Peralta College District Overall
(Percentage of Certified Contract Personnel)

	1972–73 Situation	1978–79 Goal	Necessary Change in Five Years
Asian			
Total	3.69%	6.20%	+2.60%
Female	1.48%	3.10%	+1.62%
Male	2.21%	3.10%	+0.98%
Black			
Total	18.40%	38.70%	+20.30%
Female	6.90%	19.35%	+12.45%
Male	11.50%	19.35%	+7.85%
Caucasian			
Total	72.40%	45.80%	−26.36%
Female	22.66%	22.90%	+0.24%
Male	49.74%	22.90%	−26.60%
Chicano			
Total	5.40%	7.90%	+2.50%
Female	1.48%	3.95%	+2.47%
Male	3.92%	3.95%	+0.03%
Other			
Total	0.16%	1.40%	+1.20%
Female	0.00%	0.70%	+0.70%
Male	0.16%	0.70%	+0.54%
Total	100.00%	100.00%	—
Female	32.52%	50.00%	+17.48%
Male	67.48%	50.00%	−17.48%

Source: Basic Affirmative Action Plan, Section 3.03, Peralta Community College District Board Policy Manual and Appendix, Table A-14-A-20.

(nonfaculty) employees throughout the district for a five-year period. In developing the goals, the board assumed that the total number of certified contract employees would not increase and that women would constitute 50 percent of all employees in each ethnic group. Table 6-26 gives the overall employment status of faculty members in the district by race and sex in 1972–73 and the goals to be achieved by 1978–79.

TABLE 6-27. Ethnic Distribution of Merritt Students,[1] 1967–72

Year	Blacks %	Whites %	(Lang./Sur.) Spanish %	Other	Total Number
1972	34.8	52.7	4.0	8.5	8,881
1971	38.6	48.1	6.9	6.4	9,041
1970	33.5	48.7	10.5	7.3	3,444
1969	32.0	49.0	12.4	6.6	4,498
1968[2]	—	—	—	—	—
1967	29.7	56.4	7.4	6.5	7,554

1. Full and part-time students.
2. Figures not gathered.

Source: Basic Affirmative Action Plan, Peralta Community College District, Table A-4.

If the goals are achieved, the percentage of black faculty members will increase from 18.56 percent in 1972–73 to 38.70 percent in 1978–79. Since white males are overrepresented on the faculty, their percentages would decrease from 49.74 percent to 22.9 percent during the same time period. (*See* Figs. 6-2 and 6-3.)

The current president of Merritt College is the institution's second black president. Soon after his arrival in October 1973, he was informed by the district office that the board of trustees had developed a district-wide affirmative action plan and that each college was to develop its own plan. The board indicated that the racial, ethnic, and sexual makeup of the faculty and staff of each institution should generally reflect the composition of the community served by the college. Merritt has approximately 50 percent minorities, with blacks comprising 35 percent of the school's population.

Development of an Affirmative Action Plan

The goals for Merritt College were to reflect the general population (weighted 40 percent) and the student population (weighted 60 percent). In 1967, blacks represented 29.7 percent of the total student body, but by 1972 the percentage had increased to 34.8 percent (*See* Table 6-27). The goals at Merritt, as well as those within the Peralta District, were rather ambitious because they were to reflect the characteristics of the

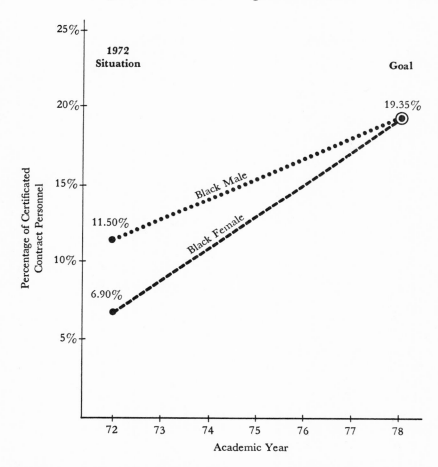

FIGURE 6-2. Comparison of Historical Ethnicity to Goals for Certified Contract Personnel (Peralta College District Overall)

population which it served. Because they were not based either on the availability of minorities and women or the projected turnover in faculty members, the goals were problematical from the beginning.

Table 6-28 gives the ethnic and sexual breakdown at Merritt. In 1972–73, blacks represented 16.4 percent of the faculty. The goals for 1978–79 projected the percentage of blacks to increase to 38.8 percent

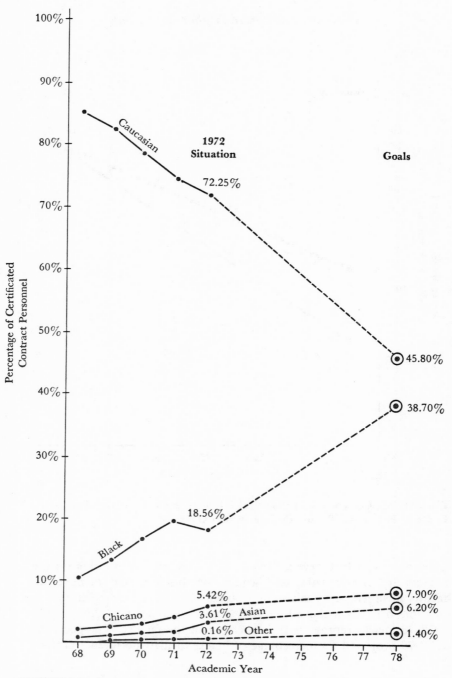

FIGURE 6-3. Comparison of Sex Mix in 1972 to Goal for Black Certified Contract Personnel (Peralta College District Overall)

196

TABLE 6-28. Comparison of Situation in 1972–73 at Merritt to Goals, by Sex and Ethnic Background

	1972–73 Situation (head count)	1978–79 Goal (head count)	Necessary Change in Five Years (head count)	Necessary Annual Rate of Change Over Five Years (head count)
Total	188	188	—	—
Female	62	94	+32	+6.4
Male	126	94	−32	−6.4
Black				
Total	31	73	+42	+8.4
Female	11	36	+25	+5.0
Male	20	37	+17	+3.4
White				
Total	141	86	−55	−11.0
Female	47	43	−4	−0.8
Male	94	43	−51	−10.2
Chicano				
Total	10	14	+4.0	+0.8
Female	2	7	+5.0	+1.0
Male	8	7	−1.0	+0.2
Asian				
Total	6	12	+6.0	+1.2
Female	2	6	+4.0	+0.8
Male	4	6	+2.0	+0.4
Other				
Total	0	3	+3.0	+0.6
Female	0	2	+2.0	+0.4
Male	0	1	+1.0	+0.2

Source: Basic Affirmative Action Plan, Section 3.03, Peralta Community College District Table A-18.

of the faculty, while the percentage of white faculty members would be reduced from 75 percent to 45.7 percent. These figures illustrate the problem very graphically. Most of the increase in minority group hiring would occur as a result of a corresponding decrease in majority group employment. At the same time, since no one was to be dismissed, the goals were to be achieved as whites died, retired, or resigned. Further, the goals did not take into consideration the areas to be replaced and, as noted above, the availability of minorities in those areas.

In the contract certified faculty in the fall of 1973, there was a total of 175 positions. Males held 67.8 percent of the positions compared to 32.2 percent held by females. White males held 52.5 percent and white females held 26.0 percent for a combined total of 78.5 percent. Blacks held a combined total of 14.2 percent: 9.7 percent males and 4.5 percent females. In 1973, the percentage of black faculty members exceeded the percentage of blacks nationally. Merritt's goals, as indicated, were not based on the characteristics of the national population, but were to reflect the racial and sexual ratio of the district as well as the student population.

After a little over two years, Merritt College had made little progress toward reaching its goals in the area of faculty employment. During the spring of 1976, there were a total of 174 faculty members (certified contract). Of that number, 26 or 14.9 percent were black: 15 or 8.6 percent males and 11 or 6.3 percent females. While the overall percentage of blacks had increased by 0.7 percent there was a slight reduction in the percentage of black males, and a 1.8 percent increase in the number of black females. White males actually increased their representation from 52.5 percent to 53.4 percent; white females decreased from 26 percent to 23.6 percent.

During this period there was an actual reduction in the number of authorized faculty members (contract). The number declined from 188 in 1972–73 to 174 in the spring of 1976, a reduction of 14 faculty members. Although the percentage of white men increased, their actual numbers declined by 1; the number of white women declined by 6. The number of blacks declined from 31 to 26; black men declined by 5 and black women remained constant. The combined total for other minority groups declined by 2.

The above results occurred because of a reduction in the number of students attending Merritt in comparison with the number attending other colleges within the system. At the time Merritt College was experiencing a steady state condition, other colleges within the system were experiencing substantial growth. The process resulted in an actual decline in the number of faculty members. The Merritt officials anticipate an increased rate of retirement in the future which will give the college additional vacancies. If approved by the district office, Merritt plans to increase their minority representation. In all likelihood, the lack of available minorities will continue to make their goal attainment less than that projected, but improvement in search techniques and widening of availability pools should have some impact on the college's ability to hire minorities.

Implementation of the Plan

Merritt College, according to the HEW San Francisco Regional Office, is not subject to the provisions of Executive Order 11246 because the college does not have $50,000 in government contracts. Nevertheless, Merritt selected to follow the federal guidelines in developing its procedures for implementing its affirmative action plan. An Affirmative Action Committee was established to develop the plan. After a draft plan was completed, the committee initiated a program to educate members of the college community on what the plan entailed and their responsibilities under the plan.

Prior to the development of new hiring procedures, the chairman of each department received job applications, and with the assistance of other staff, recommended his choice to the dean. Two or three candidates were generally interviewed before the final selection was made. According to a member of the Affirmative Action Committee, the procedure is now more formalized with clearer lines of accountability. Job opportunity announcements are screened at various levels to determine if the job descriptions are related to the job requirements. A screening committee is then established and after interviewing all applicants, it sends the top three choices to the president for his selection. The applicants are not rated, so that the final selection process will not be influenced by the committee. The most unique aspect of the plan is that for each new position, the screening committee is required to review all applicants who meet the basic requirements for the job, which essentially is the holding of a credential. A credential is certification from the state that an individual has the basic qualifications to teach a particular course or in a field. Once a person has the credential, he or she is qualified to teach in any community college in the state.

In screening all applicants, Merritt's aim is to provide each person with a fair opportunity to obtain employment while trying to achieve a diversified environment. Both faculty and administrators emphasized that Merritt's policy was to employ the most qualified candidate, but few saw the need or desirability of employing overqualified faculty members who, in all probability, would remain at the college just long enough to find employment in a four-year institution.

One department chairman described how the college seeks to obtain the most qualified candidate within the framework of the affirmative action procedures. In seeking a replacement for a Chinese-language instructor, the chairman indicated that after interviewing numerous applicants, the best person for the job was a black woman who had the enthusiastic endorsement of the Chinese instructor she was to replace. She was selected because of her fluency in the language. A Spanish-speaking instructor indicated that affirmative action procedures were eliminating much of the discrimination he faced when he came to the college in the mid-1950s. He was quick to emphasize, however, that discrimination remains and that affirmative action is still necessary.

The plan is implemented at three levels. First, when a vacancy occurs and the slot is advertised, the screening committee interviews all applicants, and finally the entire process is reviewed by the Affirmative Action Committee which receives a full report after the person has been hired. This particular aspect of the monitoring process should occur before the person is hired to insure that the affirmative action procedures have been followed. The committee also receives semiannual statistical reports on vacancies and new hires.

A major problem is that Merritt has, on the average, a faculty with the longest service in the district and over the last few years, a static or contracting student body. There have, therefore, been few vacancies. In fact, for the academic year 1976–77, the college anticipates being able to fill only 4½ slots, and even these must be approved by the district office. One hopeful sign is that within the next five years, five to ten faculty members will retire. These slots will be available for new hires, if the district allows Merritt to keep and fill the positions.

Another problem is that there is no full-time affirmative action officer, and those staff with affirmative action responsibility are not entirely sure where their responsibility ends and where that of others begins. Some interviewed thought that the president, in the final analysis, was the affirmative action officer. Others thought that it was the dean, who agreed. Some thought that it was not necessary to have a full-time officer. It is evident that an affirmative action officer is necessary and should devote at least 50 percent of his or her time to coordinating an effective affirmative action program. One additional weakness in the plan was that it lacked a grievance procedure.

Merritt is in a somewhat better position for evaluating qualifications than most institutions, because they accept the idea that any person with a credential automatically meets the minimum qualifications. In addition, the selection committees look at such things as a person's experience in teaching in community colleges, recommendations, desire to work with comunity college students, and, of course, they take into consideration the college's goals to bring in more minorities and women. There seems to be no question that weight is given to sex and race in considering applicants, but neither are overriding issues in the final selection process. It was emphasized by one official that the selection committees' first and foremost concern in selecting the final three applicants is whether they can do the job. One staff person pointed out that the best qualified on paper might not be the best qualified to do the job; this can be especially important if the person will not make a good teacher, which is the best way a faculty member on a community college can serve the students. One person emphasized that even so, there still remains a degree of subjectivity in the selection process. The president, in consultation with the appropriate dean, makes the final selection after reviewing the applicant pools to assure that minorities and women have had a fair opportunity to be considered. If he is satisfied, then the final selection is made. If he is not, then the applicant pool must be expanded.

Some faculty viewed the plan as too complex and felt it involved too much paper work. Some thought that the emphasis should be placed on results as opposed to complex procedures. Others thought that the procedures were just too time consuming. But not one person interviewed, even those who were highly critical, felt that the plan should be eliminated because of the procedures and everyone felt that affirmative action was necessary to eliminate past and present inequality. One administrator thought the best way to achieve results was to give preference to minorities if they have the credential or minimum qualifications. He also emphasized that all employees have the responsibility to ensure that new employees succeed in their jobs. Too many people, he felt, will hire minorities and women but do nothing to aid them in adjusting. He thought that not only was this unfair to the employees, but that it was actually a poor reflection on the employer.

One dean suggested that the plan is good because it opens up the employment process and forces the college, for the first time, to keep all decisions open and to justify why one person is hired over another.

An assistant dean suggested that only through pressure from the federal government has change occurred and that this pressure is still necessary. He added that federal pressure is beginning to make it possible for minorities to enter the trades. Since it is a slow process to move from an apprentice to a journeyman, they still have trouble getting black craftsmen to teach in the college.

Affirmative Action and Students

Any person can be admitted to Merritt if he or she is eighteen years old and a high school graduate or its equivalent, or sixteen years old and has passed the high school proficiency examination, and can profit by the experience. The use of a two dollar fee, which is required of all students, has been approved for purposes of meeting payment on a HUD loan for the student center. The president, faculty, and staff emphasized that the student at community colleges is the central focus, although one or two faculty members suggested that this is changing as more college officials view education as a form of business. The president indicated that graduation from a community college is not the determining factor as to whether or not a student has successfully completed his or her goal. He emphasized that not all students are degree oriented; many come to the college seeking to upgrade their skills or looking for a particular course to take. Their success is viewed in terms of whether they obtained what they came to get, and one of the college's functions is to see that they achieve their goals. Merritt students range in age from twenty to thirty years old. Emphasis is placed on having unprepared students compete with themselves so that they aren't overwhelmed by competition with others.

One dean suggested that the role of the college is changing. The student body consists of older students, more part-time, and fewer day students. The needs of the students are therefore changing, and the college is trying to respond to these needs in various ways. First, there are fewer students who are interested in transferring to four-year colleges because many students feel the B.A. degree is not as valuable as it used to be. The college also has to compete with four-year colleges for students because these institutions have lowered their enrollment requirements as they compete for new students. Some faculty members believe that two-year colleges serve a need because they are able to give attention to the inadequately prepared student. Also, students are attracted to the trades because they realize that they can be assured of jobs once they complete their training.

To meet the needs of all the students, especially low-income students, a career Guidance Center was established during the spring semester, 1976. The center combines the services of the college placement office, the Cooperative Education Program, and Career Counseling Services. The purposes of the center are: to provide in one central location related services and information; to allow joint approaches to career education which eliminate the duplication of efforts and gain the benefits of shared ideas; and finally, to strengthen and broaden the career education section of the college.

The center assists students in developing their career goals and has 2,200 active files. There are 600 students participating in the Cooperative Education Program. The program is an effort to make the students' education more relevant to the world of work. With counseling, the students set up their own learning objectives and are placed part-time into various businesses and industries. This placement allows the students to gain the work experience needed to break into the job market and at the same time provides employers with potential full-time employees. The program is flexible and adjusts to the needs of individual students. Some four-year colleges are now adopting this innovative program.

One official indicated that a major problem for the students is transportation. Bus service is provided but, ideally, students should have their own cars now that the college has moved from the flatland of Oakland to Oakland Hills. The move did not change the ethnic ratio of students. According to one dean, with federal assistance for tuition and with grants the college provides, students can manage financially. There are still a few who drop out because of financial need, lack of interest, or motivation. Each student who formally drops out is supposed to have an extensive interview to discuss why he or she is leaving the college, but often this interview does not happen. Therefore, it is difficult for the college to assess the needs of these students.

Under the former president, a transfer program was developed with four-year colleges. Students enrolled at Merritt were later allowed to take a limited number of courses at a four-year college at the same time. This program allowed certain students to gradually adjust to a new and strange situation. Eighty percent of the students who transferred to four-year colleges successfully completed their remaining two years.

During 1975–76, 278 students participated in the program, 43 percent of whom were black.

Many of the students who first enter Merritt are tested to determine if they have difficulties that they need to overcome. If they do, they are referred to the learning assistance laboratory where they receive special, personalized assistance. There is a day-care center on campus for parents with children. Officials recognize the need to place more emphasis on math and science at the college level and encourage it at the high school level. The president thought this was a service the college could perform to prepare students for college. Students should be informed as to what they need to do to prepare themselves and what Merritt has to offer them once they enroll. In view of the large Spanish population the college serves, bilingual classes are also necessary to aid Spanish-speaking students to adjust. The president felt that even though there were various support services available, he saw the need for more to assure that fewer black students drop out.

Thus students at Merritt, especially minority and low-income students, are provided with a full range of support programs which begin in high school before their admission and continue throughout their tenure at the college. The concurrent programs allow the student to prepare educationally and psychologically for advanced work in four-year institutions.

Findings and Conclusions

Examining the implementation of affirmative action at four different types of higher educational institutions revealed a great complexity in the affirmative action structures. This complexity is the result of a strong attempt to implement affirmative action without disturbing the existing institutional arrangements. In three of the four institutions examined, the administrative structure is unduly complex and results in nonuniformity of the affirmative action effort throughout each institution. The community college had streamlined its hiring structure by establishing uniform hiring procedures for all units of the college.

Not all institutions examined have an affirmative action officer whose responsibilities were centralized in one office directly under the president or administrative head. It was found that a strong centralized office is essential for effective enforcement of affirmative action procedures. Affirmative action by its very nature must interrupt business as usual, if it is to succeed. Because of the difficulty of altering procedures in such a decentralized environment, it might be useful if the implementing regulations explicitly required the establishment of a centralized, affirmative action office in all institutions. It was found that the size of the affirmative action office should correspond to the size of the institution. While the larger institutions maintained full-time affirmative action officers, the smaller colleges relegated this responsibility to persons on a part-time basis which seriously hampered the effectiveness of the program.

The extensiveness of searches varied widely not only from institution to institution but also within each institution, and no uniform procedures were utilized from department to department. Uniform search procedures would remove much of the confusion in faculty and professional searches. Prior determination of the appropriate places for advertising ought to be established in each discipline and the places selected should ensure fair notification of universities. In this connection, OCR might develop more specific and detailed directions for conducting searches.

Although faculty selection is of crucial importance to departments, more attention should be paid to how these parameters are drawn. The specifications should be reviewed, at minimum, by the affirmative action officer for possible discriminatory impact. Too often quality judgments were left exclusively in the domain of the departments. Other universities and colleges undoubtedly use the same methods. Since weighing the qualifications is central to the selection process, this state of affairs makes it difficult to assess the extent of discrimination.

It was found that not enough attention was paid to making the hiring criteria explicit before the search began. The relative weights to be placed on different criteria should also be explicitly determined. All subjective judgments probably cannot be eliminated, but the basis for the judgments can and should be made more explicit. In this regard, since ad hoc selection procedures are so rooted in academic practice, it may be important for OCR to take a more active role in encouraging more objective procedures and standards.

Searches and recruitment are the most expensive items in both time and money involved in affirmative action. In many instances greatly expanded searches produced meager results in terms of increases in the number of qualified black applicants. Because each university department is probably hiring a very small number of professionals in each specialty in any given year, the cost per hiring could become high.

The purpose of affirmative action search procedures is not to add expenses but to assure a fair search. National skill banks and national job listings might facilitate and reduce the cost for searches and, if properly developed, could also advance equal opportunity.

In all the institutions examined there was a need for the development of solid availability data for each discipline. The utilization analyses used by institutions vary widely and leave much to be desired. The sources and types of data utilized to determine availability vary not only from institution to institution but also within the disciplines, and often are not broken down by racial groups.

At one of the institutions there was little support for goals, timetables, or utilization analyses. It is believed that this was due to a failure to understand the function of these elements as tools to assist in the management of the affirmative action effort. Too often goals were seen as backdoor attempts at establishing quotas. Findings of under-utilization were resisted as accusations of intentional bias. These tools were misunderstood by enthusiastic supporters as well as detractors from affirmative action.

In one instance, little use was made of these analyses in implementing and guiding the affirmative action effort. There remains controversy in all institutions over whether or not affirmative action is working effectively. If more explicit guidelines are given on how to establish goals and assess the accomplishments of affirmative action, part of this problem would be resolved. Also, the utilization of black faculty varied in the ladder and nonladder ranks. More attention ought to be paid to the utilization of blacks within the university community when conducting the utilization analyses and fixing goals.

At the beginning of this chapter it was indicated that affirmative action has been required of institutions of higher education for too short a time to make any value judgment. Yet overall it was found that if there is a commitment to implement the procedures at all levels, affirmative action can be an effective mechanism for bringing blacks into the academic marketplace. Further, it can aid institutions in developing sound management policies and procedures. While many problems remain, the review of how affirmative action is working in four institutions reveals that it can be an effective policy for altering a biased employment system.

Part III

Chapter Seven

Blacks, Affirmative Action, and the Future

Introduction

This chapter estimates the impact of affirmative action in institutions of higher education on the future employment opportunities for blacks on the faculties of institutions of higher education through 1990. It is important to be able to anticipate the results of a policy to determine if the policy will adequately achieve its goals and to avoid unrealistic expectations concerning the anticipated results of the policy. This chapter attempts the following: (1) to estimate the number of blacks on the faculties of higher educational institutions as a result of implementing affirmative action; (2) to determine the factors which influenced the results; (3) to identify policies that might alter the outcomes.

It is clear that blacks are not currently represented on the faculties of institutions of higher education at anything near their faculty potential. It is also clear that what representation there is, is not evenly distributed across fields or institutional types. The current situation results from the denial of equal opportunities in the past at all levels of the educational system. (*See* discussion in chapter two.) This situation will not be improved in the future if the inequality of opportunity which has existed within the educational sector in the past is allowed to persist. As was stated previously, affirmative action is the strategy designed to prevent the continuation of discrimination. It is therefore essential to have some estimate of the likely impacts of affirmative action on the limited black presence.

Analyses of the current utilization of blacks do not produce clear-cut evidence for an overall supply-demand gap. As noted in chapter four, many of the critics of affirmative action seem to imply that the lack of clear evidence of a visible surplus of qualified blacks can be taken as evidence for a reduced need for affirmative action enforcement efforts. Even if it were true that there were few blacks with the qualifications and inclination to teach on college faculties who were being denied the opportunity through discrimination, and evidence on this matter is not clear, this would not imply that there is no need for continued affirmative action enforcement efforts. As indicated by the projections, even with equality of opportunity it will be a long time before the vestiges of past discrimination, which are reflected in the small pools of qualified blacks, the skewed distribution of these qualifications, the particular distribution of blacks among the various classes of institutions, and the overall low participation of blacks in the labor market, will be eliminated.

From the discussion in previous chapters, it is clear that where there have been recent gains in employment for blacks they have come under the pressure of the demands for equal opportunity and as a result of the undertaking of affirmative action efforts. It is necessary to continue the enforcement of affirmative action efforts at least until equality of opportunity is built into the practice and fabric of the system and affirmative action is a natural part of the employment process. This day may be approached when the vestiges of past discrimination begin to vanish, when the black presence in academia approaches its faculty potential, when the distortion in the distribution of blacks by institutional type and discipline can be explained by variances in taste and propensities, and when the supplies of blacks have approached their supply potential. The projections indicate that these events will not take place in the next ten or fifteen years even with strict enforcement of the present requirement of affirmative action.

Affirmative action, of course, is only one of several factors which will affect the future employment opportunities of blacks; the general demand for faculty at higher educational institutions and the general supply of faculty also play crucial roles. In the analysis presented in this chapter the impact of affirmative action on opportunities for blacks has been examined, given projections of the future supply and demand conditions in academic labor markets in general. The basic projections presented here are estimates of the future employment of blacks in higher education, assuming that affirmative action results in equal opportunity as defined below, and assuming a continuation of the present policies and trends which are determining the future labor market conditions for higher educational institutions.

These estimates represent the base case projections and are not to be considered predictions about the future. At best they are conditional predictions. Whether or not they come to pass depends essentially upon how affirmative action in fact affects future opportunities, and whether or not future policies and trends continue the present course. These projections indicate that if current policies are continued the actual gains in black faculty presence will not be dramatic. The vestiges of past and present discrimination will gradually recede but at a very slow pace. Hopefully, this slow attainment of a fair presence will not detract from the value of affirmative action. The validity of the affirmative action strategy was discussed in the introductory chapter. The appropriateness of the affirmative action strategy cannot be based on the absolute employment gains which follow the implementation of the strategy, because they depend also on labor market conditions. Rather, it must be based on the effectiveness of the strategy in achieving its expressed goal, namely, assuring equality of opportunity for minorities and others. Throughout the base case projections of this chapter it has been assumed that this goal is achieved and thus, by assumption, that affirmative action is successful.

If equality of opportunity were not achieved, the future situation for blacks in higher education would be even worse than the projected outcomes of the base case. Not only would there be no additional gains but it is probable that the current small presence would be dramatically reduced. Thus, the relative gains in employment because of equal opportunity are likely to be significant.

Moreover, as indicated in the discussion of the effects of the future labor market conditions on the prospects for equal opportunity, it seems clear that affirmative action enforcement efforts will be necessary to ensure equality of opportunities, given the tight labor market conditions projected for the future. Further, as also indicated in the discussion of public policies affecting higher education labor markets, there is the possibility of implementing policies which will improve the absolute gains for blacks during the projection period. If any of these policies are pursued, the absolute gains in employment from the attainment of equal opportunity through affirmative action will be greater.

Finally, in the projections which follow it has been assumed implicitly that blacks will take advantage fully of the opportunities opened through affirmative action programs. This assumption implies that blacks will take advantage of opportunities to enroll in graduate programs and will also succeed in these programs at rates comparable to whites. The validity of this assumption obviously depends upon the ability of the black community, the family, and other institutions to provide the motivation for the pursuit of opportunities. Although this question has not been dealt with, it should be clear that if blacks fail to take advantage of affirmative action programs, the projected results will not be attained.

Projecting anything about the future is difficult under the best circumstances, but the task is made exceptionally difficult by a substantial lack of solid data to reveal current and past trends of demand and supply of black faculty. As a result, the actual procedures rely on educated guesses based on the few available data points and general understanding of the operation of the higher education sector.*

The actual magnitudes projected here should not be taken as precise estimates of the future situation. The accuracy of the numbers cannot be any greater than the accuracy of the underlying data, and much of the data are not of the finest quality. In the absence of reliable data to identify certain key relationships, it was necessary to rely on ad hoc techniques and expert judgment to establish these relationships. It was felt, however, that the projections reported herein are sufficiently accurate to establish the likely order of magnitude and the direction of change in the key variables concerning the impact of affirmative action programs on the future employment of blacks.

In addition to the introduction, this chapter contains five other major parts. They include: (1) the current position of blacks in the academic market place; (2) the general conditions that will exist in the academic labor market during the projection period; (3) the projections of the supply and demand for black faculty given successful affirmative action; (4) the probability of attaining equal opportunity without effective affirmative action; and (5) some public policies which might improve the prospects for blacks in academic labor markets during the projection period.

---

* After this chapter had been prepared, EEOC released preliminary data from EEO-6. These data indicate that the proportion of blacks currently on faculties may be higher than all previous estimates and the data on which this chapter is based. However, in view of the preliminary nature of the EEO-6 data, no attempt was made to reconcile these data with previous estimates, or to revise the estimates in this chapter. If the EEO-6 data should prove right this would result in an upward shift in all of the faculty stock estimates, but would not affect the hiring estimates.

Current Position of Black Faculty in Academic Labor Markets

In assessing the current position of blacks in the labor markets of institutions of higher education, two concepts are important. The first is the supply potential and the extent to which blacks have realized their supply potential. The supply potential refers to the number of blacks that would be present on the faculties of higher educational institutions if the employment and qualifications systems in these institutions had been fair in the past. (*See* the discussion of fairness in chapter one.) A refined concept of supply potential would take into account, among other factors, the relative interest as well as financial and intellectual means. However, in the absence of an ability to create a refined measure of potential, the proportion of blacks in the labor force is used as a measure of their supply potential. Therefore, the question of how close blacks are to their supply potential is evaluated by how near the proportion of blacks on the faculty is to the proportion of blacks in the labor force.

The other important concept needed to assess the current status of blacks in the academic marketplace is the utilization rate. This concept refers to the rate at which blacks are employed relative to their availability of supply. Utilization rates may be taken in the aggregate and they may also be disaggregated. Ideally, a measure of availability should be developed which reflects the various types and degrees of qualification including degree level, quality of education, experience, and publications. But because of the limited data available, it has not been possible. Only gross measures of qualification, such as possession of a Ph.D. or master's degree, are available to measure availability.

Currently, there are very sparse data on the position of blacks and other minorities in the labor force of institutions of higher education. It is clear, however, from the limited data that are available, that blacks are significantly underrepresented in the labor force of higher educational institutions, relative to their potential representation.

Current Size and Distribution of Black Faculty

Data reported by Alan Bayer indicated that in 1972, about 2.9 percent of the total faculty in institutions of higher education were black, whereas about 11 percent of the overall labor force were black.[1] (*See* Table 7-1.) It is estimated that the current full-time equivalent faculty

TABLE 7-1. Faculty by Type of Institution and Race, 1972–73

	All Institutions	*Two-Year Colleges*	*Four-Year Colleges*	*Universities*
Total	518,849	94,475	202,719	221,655
Black	15,046	1,988	11,068	1,995
Percent Black	2.9	2.1	5.4	0.9

Source: ISEP calculations based on data included in *Teaching Faculty in Academe 1972–73* by Alan Bayer. (Washington, D.C.: American Council on Education, 1973), p. 27.

in institutions of higher education is roughly 500,000. Since black faculty comprise close to 3 percent of this number, there are approximately 15,000 black faculty. If they had reached their faculty potential, based on their presence in the labor force at large, there would be approximately 55,000 black faculty in institutions of higher education. The current number of black faculty, therefore, is roughly 40,000 below the faculty potential.

The presence of blacks on the faculties in 1972 varied by type of institution from 0.9 percent of the faculty at universities to 5.4 percent of the faculty at four-year colleges. The percentage in four-year colleges is distorted by the fact that this category includes almost all predominantly black colleges. If these colleges were eliminated, it is very unlikely that the faculties of four-year colleges other than the predominantly black colleges would contain any more than 2 percent blacks. In 1972, for instance, if only 60 percent of the faculty in predominantly black colleges were black, and most of these were in four-year colleges, then the proportion of blacks on the faculties of other four-year colleges would be about 1.8 percent.*

Data from the 1970 census indicate that blacks comprised about 3.3 percent of the college teachers in 1970.[2] (*See* Table 7-2.) The census figures also suggest that there is a wide variation by teaching fields in

* According to Bayer, predominantly black colleges had 12,609 faculty members in 1972–73. The total faculties on other four-year colleges were 190,110, of which 5.4 percent, or 10,946, were black. Assuming that 60 percent of the predominantly black college faculty are black, and that they are all four-year colleges, yields 7,765 blacks on predominantly black college faculties and 3,381 on other four-year faculties. Blacks represent 1.78 percent of these latter faculties.

TABLE 7-2. Stock of College Teachers, 1970

Type	Total	Non-Black	Black	% Non-Black	% Black
Agriculture	5,157	5,070	87	98.3	1.7
Atmosphere, earth, marine, space science	4,782	4,782	0	100.0	0.0
Biology	20,398	19,920	478	97.7	2.3
Chemistry	15,382	15,092	290	98.1	1.9
Physics	14,212	14,066	146	99.0	1.0
Engineering	26,474	26,236	238	99.1	0.9
Mathematics	25,641	24,814	827	96.8	3.2
Health	28,178	26,966	1,212	95.7	4.3
Psychology	12,908	12,595	313	97.6	2.4
Business & Commerce	13,915	13,296	619	95.6	4.4
Economics	10,183	10,055	128	98.7	1.3
History	17,092	16,589	503	97.1	2.9
Sociology	6,918	6,573	345	95.0	5.0
Social Science	12,732	12,345	387	97.0	3.0
Art, Drama, & Music	30,654	29,599	1,055	96.6	3.4
Physical Education	17,023	16,375	648	96.2	3.8
Education	7,552	7,226	326	95.7	4.3
English	39,412	38,302	1,110	97.2	2.8
Foreign Language	21,256	20,910	346	98.4	1.6
Home Economics	4,285	4,010	275	93.6	6.4
Law	3,005	2,943	62	97.9	2.1
Theology	5,189	5,119	70	98.7	1.3
Trade, industrial & technical	3,433	3,122	311	90.9	9.1
Miscellaneous	19,393	19,109	284	98.5	1.5
Not specified	140,538	134,015	6,523	95.4	4.6
Total	496,412	479,830	16,582	96.7	3.3

Source: U.S. Bureau of the Census, *Detailed Characteristics of the Population—1970.*

the proportion of blacks employed in institutions of higher education. The variation is from none in atmosphere, earth, and space science, to 9.1 percent in trade, and industrial and technical science.

There are no good data concerning the distribution of black academicians by academic rank. Excluding the four-year predominantly black colleges, one would suspect that a relatively higher proportion of blacks would be found in the lower academic ranks. Although blacks are found at all academic ranks, Moore and Wagstaff indicate that they are con-

centrated in the lower ranks.[3] They also suggest that blacks disproportionately occupy the ranks of the nontenured, the part-timers, the temporarily appointed, and those who have additional administrative
responsibilities.[4] This point would suggest that any data on the absolute numbers of blacks in universities must be interpreted with great
caution.

In summary, the data suggest that in 1970, between 2.5 percent and
3.5 percent of the faculty in higher educational institutions were black,
most were concentrated in the predominantly black colleges, and there
were wide variations in the proportion of blacks across fields of specialization, type of institution, and type of appointment.

Current Availability of Qualified Blacks

In order to determine the extent of utilization of available black
manpower, one has to compare the current employment with the current supply. Again, the information available to describe the supply is
limited. There is practically no information on the proportion of blacks
among those people who already possess master's degrees or on the
number of blacks among those who have recently attained master's
degrees. There is, however, limited information on the numbers of
blacks among those recently receiving the Ph.D. degree and some information on the numbers of blacks among those who possess a Ph.D. degree in a scientific field. Throughout this report the terms *Ph.D.* and
doctorate are used interchangeably to name all doctorate degrees except
the professional degrees.

According to a recent study by the National Academy of Sciences,
blacks comprised 0.8 percent of the Ph.D. scientists with U.S. citizenship
in 1973.[5] These data include only those with Ph.D.'s in scientific fields;
they exclude those with Ph.D.'s in the humanities, arts, and education.
(*See* Table 7-3.) These data reveal that the proportion of blacks with
a scientific Ph.D. varies significantly by field, with the lowest representation in the natural sciences and the highest in the social sciences.

According to a widely cited Ford Foundation study, the proportion
of all doctorates held by blacks was, at most, 1 percent in 1968.[6] There
are no data at all on the stocks of blacks with master's degrees or other
degrees which qualify them for employment on college faculties.

The National Academy of Sciences has recently begun making available annual estimates on the ethnic and racial classification of persons
who earned the Ph.D. in the previous years. The data for 1973 indicate

TABLE 7-3. Field of Employment of Ph.D. Labor Force, 1973

Field of Employment	Total[1]	White	Black	% White	% Black
Mathematics	13,811	12,797	132	92.7	1.0
Physics	15,610	14,534	31	93.1	0.2
Chemistry	26,224	24,411	313	93.1	1.0
Earth Science	9,528	9,174	23	96.3	0.2
Engineering	32,592	29,295	87	89.9	0.3
Bioscience	52,982	49,475	486	93.4	0.9
Psychology	22,501	21,913	182	97.4	0.8
Social Science	24,122	22,627	281	93.8	1.2
Other Fields	10,184	9,725	121	95.5	1.2
Total	207,554	193,951	1,656	93.4	0.8

1. Includes other minorities.

Source: Commission on Human Resources, National Research Council, *Minority Groups among U.S. Doctorate Level Scientists, Engineers, and Scholars*, 1973. (Washington, D.C.: National Academy of Sciences), p. 27.

that roughly 2.7 percent of Ph.D. recipients with American citizenship were black. This proportion varied by field from 1.10 percent in engineering and physical science, to 6.7 percent in education.[7] (*See* Table 7-4.) There are no long-time series data to indicate the trends in the proportion of blacks receiving the Ph.D. degree. However, since the proportion of blacks receiving the doctorate in 1973 was probably larger than the proportion of blacks among those who already possessed the Ph.D. degree, it would suggest that the proportion receiving the Ph.D. may be slowly increasing. But this trend is not certain. Calculations based on data contained in the National Academy of Sciences reports on the Ph.D. scientist stock, indicate that the growth rate of the black stock in the narrowly defined Ph.D. scientist category, over the period from 1930 to 1972, was lower than the white growth rate and was only equal to the overall growth rate from 1960 to 1972.[8] This calculation suggests a shrinking or at best a constant proportion of blacks among the Ph.D. scientists.

Implications of the Data for Current Utilization and Need for Affirmative Action

This limited data on supply suggest that there are relatively few blacks who possess the Ph.D. degree. It would also appear that the pro-

TABLE 7-4. Number and Percentage Receiving Ph.D.'s, 1973, by Field (U.S. Citizens only)

Field of Employment	White	Black	Total[1]	% White	% Black
Engineering, Physical Sciences	6,019	65	6,159	97.7	1.1
Life Sciences	3,722	68	3,957	94.1	1.7
Social Sciences	2,640	49	2,731	96.7	1.8
Humanities & Arts	4,673	71	4,765	98.1	1.5
Professions	1,135	24	1,198	94.7	2.0
Education	6,019	452	6,744	89.2	6.7
Total[2]	24,208	729	25,554	94.7	2.7

1. Including other minorities.
2. Small errors due to rounding.

Source: ISEP calculations based upon data in National Academy of Sciences, *Summary Report 1973: Doctorate Recipients From United States Universities* (Washington, D.C.: National Academy of Sciences, 1974), p. 4.

portion of blacks currently employed in institutions of higher education exceeds the number of blacks with the Ph.D. degree. Moreover, the pattern of distribution of black employment by field roughly approximates the pattern of distribution of black doctorates by field. Thus, it might appear that overall the current utilization of blacks is fair, and the principal problem for the future is one of realizing the supply potential.

It is not possible, however, to draw such a definitive conclusion on the fairness of the current overall utilization of blacks by institutions of higher education on the basis of the available data. For one thing, a large proportion of faculty members in these institutions do not have doctorate degrees (many do not even have a master's degree), and therefore information on the proportion of blacks among those with the doctoral degree is of limited value in assessing the utilization of blacks. Yet there are no good data on the proportions with master's degrees, or other non-Ph.D. degrees which qualify them for college teaching, or on the proportions of blacks among those with doctorate degrees other than scientific doctorates.

Other investigators have concluded from these meager data that there is no overall supply and demand gap and seem to imply from this conclusion that affirmative action in employment is not of pressing importance (*See* discussion in chapter four.) The problem in the future, it is suggested, will be principally one of ensuring adequate supplies. But the paucity of good data cannot give one high confidence in such a conclusion. There may be many blacks at or below the Ph.D. level who already qualify for college teaching. This is especially important in the two-year colleges, where, according to Bayer, only 6.9 percent of the faculty held doctorate degrees in 1972–1973. Overall only 34.7 percent of the faculty held doctorates and even at university levels fewer than half of the present faculty held doctorate degrees.[9]

The Bayer study also indicated that prior experience in academia may not be as important as generally believed. Bayer found that only about 45 percent of the faculty come to their jobs, either with immediate prior teaching experience at the college level, or immediately from a school background. Most of those in the Bayer study reported that their experience was in precollege teaching, administration, research, development, or other nonteaching positions.[11] This evidence suggests that there should be opportunities for qualified blacks who do not currently have academic experience, and who do not have a Ph.D. to enter academe.

This impression takes on added significance in view of the results of the Wagstaff and Moore study cited earlier. They surveyed black faculty at predominantly white institutions and found that only 18.4 percent of those who responded possessed the doctorate degree.[12] They also found that more than 30 percent of all recent community college teachers had come from the secondary school system.[13] And their analyses of the stock of black Ph.D.'s suggest that, at most, only 40 percent of the blacks with doctorates are currently teaching in predominantly white institutions.[14] These results, if valid, suggest that there may be a current supply of qualified blacks in the public school system, government, and private industry who would be available for hire if the opportunities existed. This conclusion is perhaps especially applicable to the community college faculties.

Moreover, even if there is no overall gap between the supply of blacks qualified and available for faculty positions at white institutions and the rate of utilization or demand for them, there may not be equal opportunity. It is not clear that, in the aggregate, one should expect to find underutilization relative to the existing supply because of the linkages between supply and demand. (*See* discussion below.) Evidence that the legacy of discrimination has not been overcome must be sought by examining the distribution of black employment in institutions of higher learning, and also in the overall gap between the actual utilization of blacks and their supply potential. Such an examination would reveal that the current distribution of blacks across fields of specialization is still significantly different from the distribution of the academic population at large. This variance is a result of employment and training opportunities in various fields being denied as a result of past discrimination. For instance, a much larger proportion of black doctorates are concentrated in the field of education. This concentration can be explained by the fact that significant numbers of opportunities were available for blacks at all levels of the educational system in all-black schools under the segregated system.

Further evidence of equal opportunity problems is provided by the fact that the distribution of black employees is skewed by the type of institution. In particular, a large proportion of black educators are still employed by the historically black institutions. This pattern is partially because opportunities have been denied by most nonblack universities in the past. The particular pattern of field specialization mentioned above reinforces the evidence that limited opportunities existed in all traditionally white institutions in the past. The field distribution of black academicians mirrors strongly the teaching curriculums of historically black institutions, which have always been their principal source of employment.

Evidence on the relative pay of blacks is also relevant in assessing their current position in the academic labor market. Some analyses of the limited data available on pay suggest that once one adjusts for field concentration, rank, years of service, and other factors, blacks currently are paid at least as much and perhaps slightly more than their white counterparts. Mommsen has also suggested that blacks are not available for hire away from their current jobs at existing market prices.[15] This evidence is offered as further proof of the lack of current discrimination in higher education.

Wagstaff and Moore, however, suggest that their analysis of the data produced in their survey indicates that "blacks actually earn less than has often been reported."[16] But, even if there is no wage discrimination against those who receive appointments, it would not be relevant to the question of occupational discrimination through the denial of opportunities. Further, it should not be expected that entrenched blacks would be attracted to other opportunities offering equivalent salaries. Clearly, relocating to a new situation from a secure position, establishing oneself in a new area, and giving up social investments all involve significant costs. The more established an individual is, the higher the cost. Discrimination prevented the many blacks who are currently employed by black institutions from entering the nonblack academic market in the past, thus they have become entrenched in the black academic market.

Differential advantages would therefore need to be offered by nonblack institutions to attract entrenched blacks from black institutions. While this may indicate a limited ability to attract entrenched blacks, it provides no evidence at all as to whether or not the nonblack institutions continue to discriminate against blacks. This evidence must be sought in the treatment of nonentrenched blacks, blacks from outside academia, and blacks who have recently attained qualifications. There is little or no evidence that nonentrenched blacks are requiring significantly higher salary offers, or that they are being hired at rates significantly above the rate of nonblacks. Moreover, as Wagstaff and Moore point out, "it is significant that in 1972 the 100 black colleges still hire more of the available black Ph.D.'s than the approximately 2,000 colleges which are predominantly white."[17] If this statement actually refers to hiring rather than current faculty levels, it is indeed suggestive of a lack of equal opportunity in the nonblack sector.

The lack of an overall supply-demand gap, considering the entire market for qualified blacks, should come as no particular surprise, because there are linkages between demand and supply. It would indeed be inconsistent with economic logic for there to be significant pools of qualified blacks in excess of those in demand, in view of the exclusion practiced by most universities in the past. Gaining the doctorate degree, or other qualifications to be employed as a faculty member, is a long, expensive, and arduous process. It is unlikely that many black individuals would continue to go through the considerable hardship of gaining qualifications in the face of the almost certain failure to gain employment because of the racial practices of educational institutions. If the attainment of higher education credentials is viewed as an investment, supply and demand would probably have remained in good balance with relatively few blacks possessing the appropriate qualifications, precisely because of their rational adjustment to the long-established practice of racial exclusion.

The principal effect of this long-term discrimination was to discourage the formation of larger supplies of qualified manpower rather than to create large supply-demand gaps. Moreover, this outcome was doubly assured by the historical discrimination of most universities against black students.

The strongest evidence of discrimination is provided by the very lack of supply itself. The supply of qualified blacks, in general, and for the white controlled sector, in particular, can be expected to increase only insofar as demand increases. The existence of vigorously enforced affirmative action plans within the white-controlled sector provides evidence of continuing fair access. Thus, fair access may reduce some of the uncertainty and fears about the continuance of discrimination, which otherwise might prevent many qualified blacks from seeking qualifications for employment, or even employment opportunities in the predominantly white sector. Affirmative action in employment by these institutions, which have traditionally denied opportunity to blacks, is an important and necessary step in ensuring increases in the supply of qualified black manpower.

There is also some limited evidence of rapid adjustment in black supply when demand changes.[18] The rapid expansion in black enrollments at all levels of the higher education sector since the 1960s is further evidence of the willingness and ability of blacks to take advantage of improved opportunities. With the removal of financial and racial barriers to graduate education, vigorous enforcement of affirmative action in employment plans will have a substantial impact on the effort to increase the supply of blacks qualified for faculty positions.

During the recent period of very rapid increases in the size of university faculties, blacks were not generally hired in significant numbers by institutions of higher education that traditionally excluded blacks. Nor did institutions voluntarily give blacks greater access to graduate education. The experience of the 1960s and early 1970s, therefore, further reinforces the necessity for affirmative action to ensure fair treament.

The Academic Labor Market to 1990

Recent Labor Market Conditions

Throughout the 1960s enrollments in institutions of higher education grew rapidly because of changing demographic patterns and increasing college attendance within each college-age group. During this decade college enrollments more than doubled. According to the National Center for Education Statistics (NCES), the full-time equivalent enrollment in institutions of higher education increased from 3,200,000 in 1961 to 7,003,000 in 1971.[19] In absolute terms, 3,803,000 students were added to college enrollments during the period. The total graduate enrollment increased by 135 percent during the period. The enrollment in two-year colleges increased by 233 percent, and the enrollment in four-year colleges and professional programs increased by 85 percent.

The result of this growth in enrollment was a rapid increase in the demand for college-level manpower. The estimated full-time equivalent instructional staff increased from 214,000 in 1961 to 479,000 in 1971.[20] This represents a net gain over the decade of 265,000 in the number of full-time equivalent faculty. Total hiring in the five-year period from 1966 to 1971 was 251,000, representing 128,000 for increased enrollments and 123,000 for replacement demand. This represents an average demand for new faculty of over 50,000 per year during this time period.

But college enrollments are projected to decline over the next few years. These projected declines are based on changing demographic trends resulting in smaller numbers of individuals in each college cohort. The peak declines will occur somewhere in the mid-1980s. This decline implies that the demand for faculty will decline and, consequently, the aggregate demand for academic personnel will shrink during this period.

Projections of Overall Demand for Faculty through 1990

The principal factor governing the overall level of demand for faculty in institutions of higher education is the need of these institutions for teachers. This need may be roughly related to the level and composition of student enrollments. Given stable, desired, faculty-student ratios for each type of institution and level of teaching, the future enrollment patterns will fix the future patterns of demand for faculty. Technically, the aggregate demand will be determined by the desired student-teacher ratios, the aggregate enrollment rates, and the aggregate faculty exit rate.*

These considerations lead to a model of faculty hiring in which, given the desired faculty-student ratios, demand is determined by enrollments, the previous stock of faculty, and the faculty exit rate. As enrollments expand, all other things equal, faculty demand will increase. On the other hand, as enrollments decline, all other things equal, demand for

---

* Faculty exit rate is the rate at which faculty leave university teaching. This is determined by the rate of retirements, deaths, and resignations.

faculty will decline. Similarly, when the faculty exit rate is high and the stock of old faculty is low, demand will be high.

Given the model of faculty demand outlined above, the demand for total faculty and for black faculty have been projected from 1975 to 1990. The model of demand outlined above has been incorporated into a simple recursive stock adjustment model to make the projections discussed in this chapter. The aggregate demand projections are first developed and then used to determine the demand for blacks. The aggregate demand is determined recursively using enrollment projections and assumptions about faculty exit rates, faculty at the beginning of the projection period, and student-faculty ratios.*

In order to project demand with the model, it is necessary to have college enrollment projections. The enrollment projections are taken from a recent study by Radner and Miller, et al.[21] Radner and Miller used two alternative enrollment projections to predict faculty demand, the Cartter projections and the Haggstrom projections. The Cartter enrollment projections indicate that enrollment levels will continue to increase throughout the 1970s into the early 1980s, but the rate of increase in enrollment will decline during the latter years of the period. By 1982 enrollments growth will have stopped and the level of enrollments will subsequently decline through 1989. The same basic pattern of enrollment growth is indicated by the Haggstrom projections, except that Haggstrom projects a higher level of enrollment than Cartter. Haggstrom's projections also do not show as sharp a decline during the period of declining enrollments. Cartter's projections, however, are closer to the NCES projections discussed earlier and appear more realistic. In fact the enrollments projected by Cartter from 1970 through 1976 are very close to the actual enrollments for this period. Therefore, the Cartter enrollment projections have been used throughout this study.

According to the Cartter projections, enrollment between 1972 and 1982 will grow from 7,115,000 to 9,834,000, which is an increase of 2,719,000, or 38 percent. From 1982 to 1988 enrollments are projected to decline by 1,293,000 students, or to 8,541,000; after 1988 the series shows a slight increase again. (*See* Table 7-5.)

Given the enrollment projections, the faculty demand for any given year can be determined by the model, if one knows the faculty in the previous year, the faculty/student ratio, and the faculty exit rate. It was

---

* The model used to make the projections reported on here is discussed in Appendix D.

TABLE 7-5. Cartter Enrollment Projections, 1970–1990 (in thousands)

Year	Enrollment
1970	6,303
1971	6,755
1972	7,115
1973	7,489
1974	7,831
1975	8,197
1976	8,525
1977	8,799
1978	9,050
1979	9,324
1980	9,537
1981	9,705
1982	9,834
1983	9,746
1984	9,514
1985	9,228
1986	8,862
1987	8,639
1988	8,541
1989	8,545
1990	8,674

Source: Radner and Miller, et al., *Demand and Supply in U.S. Higher Education: A Report Prepared for the Carnegie Commission on Higher Education*, New York: McGraw-Hill, 1975, p. 324.

assumed that the faculty was in equilibrium at the beginning of the projection period. It was also assumed that the adjustments made from period to period could only come about through hirings or retirements. This assumption means that layoffs in periods of drastic decline in need were not considered. Thus, starting with the initial faculty, the faculty in each subsequent period was determined by adding new hires and subtracting exits.

In the projections of aggregate demand two different assumptions were used about the rate of faculty exits. Projections labeled A assume a normal faculty exit rate of 2 percent ($q = 0.02$). The projections labeled B are based on an exit rate of 5 percent or $q = 0.05$. The faculty exit rate of 0.02 per year, used in the A projections, is the assumption employed by Radner and Miller in their recent projections of demand for Ph.D. faculty. However, this exit rate seems low since the statistics provided by NCES indicate a much higher rate of exit during the 1960s. In the NCES projections a demand exit rate of 0.06 was assumed.[22] But given the rapid expansion of the faculty over the last decade, the average age of faculty is probably lower than it has been historically. Therefore, the rate of exit over the next fifteen years is likely to be somewhat lower than the historic rate. Therefore, NCES's rate was reduced slightly to devise the rate of 5 percent annual exit used in the B projections.

It also was assumed that the average student-faculty ratio would be 17.43 at the beginning of the period and would remain constant at 17.43 throughout the period. This student-faculty ratio was the average in 1967, and the assumption of a constant ratio is carried forward from the Radner and Miller "no change" projection.

Once the total demand for faculty has been estimated, it is necessary to allocate the demand among Ph.D.- and non-Ph.D.-level faculty. To do this it has been assumed that the proportion of Ph.D. faculty will remain constant at 35.8 percent of the total faculty throughout the period. This percentage was the proportion of faculty with Ph.D.'s according to the Bayer study cited earlier. The proportion was 35.7 percent in 1967 according to the Miller and Radner study. Thus, the proportion has been nearly constant in recent years. This assumption presumes that the proportion of students going to each type of higher educational institution will not vary very much, and further assumes that the proportions of faculty possessing each type of degree in each of these institutions will remain constant.

The results of the projections are presented in Table 7-6. Both projections A and B indicate a sizable decline in the demand for new faculty throughout the 1970s and 1980s. Naturally the decline under the projection B will be less. The most dramatic decline will occur during the five-year period from 1982 through 1986, where demand has declined from the high of 251,000 in the 1966–71 period in both projection A and B, to 67,000 by projection B or 6,000 by projection A.

Projections of Overall Supply Conditions

At the same time it is likely that supply will continue to grow during this period. In the short run, the proportion of the eligible population going on to any level of training is probably fairly insensitive to labor market conditions. This insensitivity is partly because of the long lag

TABLE 7-6. Demand for College Faculty, 1961 to 1974[1], and Projections of Demand for New College Faculty, 1975 to 1989[2] (in thousands)

	A			B		
	DPh.D.	*DM*	*DT*	*DPh.D.*	*DM*	*DT*
1961–1965	79.6	101.4	181	79.6	101.4	181
1966–1971	110.4	140.6	251	110.4	140.6	251
1972–1976	58.0	84.0	142	85.1	123.9	209
1977–1981	40.0	72.0	112	69.0	124.0	193
1982–1986	2.0	4.0	6	24.0	43.0	67
1987–1989	4.0	8.0	12	27.0	49.0	76

DPh.D. = Demand for Ph.D.-level faculty.
DM = Demand for master's-level faculty.
DT = Demand for Total faculty.

1. Based on National Center for Education Statistics, *Projections of Education Statistics to 1981–1982* (Washington, D.C.: Government Printing Office, 1973), Table 34.
2. 1975–1982 based on *Projections of Education Statistics* and 1983–1989 projected by ISEP.

between the initial decision to attain an advanced degree and the completion of the degree program. Moreover, it is also the case that the short-run information flows are less than perfect. Recent work by Freeman suggests that there is a lagged feedback relationship between labor market conditions and educational decisions.* [23] However, it is likely that supply will continue to grow in the near future, in any event, because of the large number currently enrolled. But to the extent that the adjustment is rapid, the estimates of future supply will be too large.

The aggregate potential supply is the numbers graduating with Ph.D. and master's degrees. These projections of graduates through 1983 are taken from NCES. Using a relationship between NCES's enrollment data and the Cartter "no change" total enrollment figures, the total graduate enrollment projections were extended through 1990. The relationships were estimated by simple, least squares, regression techniques. In the case of the master's relationship, the independent vari-

* The "feedback effect" refers to the incentive created for students to pursue advanced degrees as a result of the success of previous graduates in attaining employment. "Lagged" means that current labor market conditions do not affect the current year's educational decision but affect the decisions in future years.

TABLE 7-7. Annual Average Numbers of Master's and Ph.D. Degrees Awarded (in thousands)

	Master's Degrees	Ph.D. Degrees
1961–62—1965–66	96.5	13.0
1966–67—1970–71	168.8	23.2
1971–72—1975–76	236.4	30.1
1976–77—1980–81	268.5	35.3
1981–82—1984–85	279.2	38.0
1985–86—1989–90	263.6	28.9

Source: National Center for Educational Statistics, *Projections of Educational Statistics to 1983–84*, (Washington, D.C.: Government Printing Office, 1975), Tables 24 and 25; 1983–1990 projected by ISEP.

able was a two-year moving average from the Cartter total enrollment data; in the case of the Ph.D. relationship, the independent variable was a four-year moving average based on the Cartter data. Both relationships exhibited good fits.

The resulting graduate projections are presented in Table 7-7. The table shows the projected average number of master's and Ph.D. degrees awarded in five-year intervals to 1990. It also shows the actual data back to 1961. The average number of both types of degree is expected to grow considerably throughout this entire period, except for moderate declines in the last five-year period.

Implications of the Projections for Labor Market Conditions

In Table 7-8 the ratio of new graduates to demand for college faculty has been calculated over the projection period. Although graduates obtain other jobs besides faculty jobs, especially those below the Ph.D. level, changes in these ratios are rough indicators of changes in the state of the academic labor market for those attaining advanced degrees, all other things remaining equal. As can be seen from the table, the ratios decline throughout the projection period. The large declines in the ratios indicate the magnitude of decline in demand relative to the supply. These numbers indicate fairly tight labor markets, especially for Ph.D. graduates during the 1970s, and more dramatic declines in demand afterwards. There will be a small recovery in the last period,

TABLE 7-8. Ratio of Demand to New Degrees Conferred 1961 to 1989 (in percents)

	Ph.D.		Below Ph.D.	
	A	B	A	B
1961–1965	122	122	21	21
1966–1971	75	75	8	8
1972–1976	37	55	7	10
1977–1981	22	39	5	9
1982–1986	1	13	0.2	3
1987–1989	5	31	1	6

Source: ISEP calculations based on data contained in Tables 7-6 and 7-7.

reflecting both the declining supply of new graduates and the stabilizing enrollments.

These projections indicate that surpluses of qualified faculty-level personnel will exist in the future. This surplus contrasts with the situation of relative shortages throughout the 1960s and early 1970s, when affirmative action and equal opportunity programs were initiated. The projections of overall demand for faculty and the overall supply of new graduates discussed above constitute the base case projections of future labor market conditions. These projections in effect assume that current trends in the enrollment propensities of the population and current staffing propensities of universities will continue into the future. The continuances, of course, will partially depend upon the types of public policies pursued in the future. The current projections essentially assume a continuation of current policies. In a later section policy changes that could improve conditions in the academic labor market will be discussed.

Projections of Conditions in the Academic Labor Market for Blacks to 1990

Given the projections of the general state of the academic labor market in the future, it is possible to consider how blacks will fare during this period. Projections will be developed for the following: the annual demand for blacks, the annual supply of blacks, and the annual stock

TABLE 7-9. Percentage of Black Enrollment in Graduate Schools, 1968–1974

1968	1970	1972	1974
3.4	4.1	5.1	5.3

Source: Frank Brown and Madelon Stent, *Minorities in U.S. Institutions of Higher Education* (New York: Praeger Publishers, 1977), p. 83. Quoted from HEW data.

of black faculty. The change in the relative presence of blacks during this period will also be discussed.

In order to make these projections it is necessary first to estimate the change in black availabilities and then to estimate the impact of affirmative action on the demand for blacks. In the next section the estimates of the availabilities will be developed. They will be followed by a discussion of the impact of affirmative action and finally the projections of demand for black faculty.

Projections of the Availability of Blacks to 1990

The estimate of black supply requires an estimate of the likely trends in the attainment of advanced degrees. This obviously depends upon trends in enrollment and graduations. Data on black graduation for advanced degree programs, as mentioned earlier in this chapter, are sparse. There is some indication, however, that the proportions enrolled in advanced degree programs are increasing. According to HEW data, blacks made up 1.72 percent of graduate school enrollment in 1967 and 5.1 percent in 1972.[24] The available data are not complete but it does suggest that there will be increasing black proportions in availability pools. These increases would also be expected in theory from the feedback effect of affirmative action employment programs in higher education. It is clear that the total proportion of new doctorate degrees being awarded to U.S. blacks is still small—only about 2.7 percent in 1974—but nonetheless it is probably larger than in the past.[25]

Data on black graduate school enrollment have been collected by HEW since 1968. These data have been compiled by Brown and Stent.[26] (*See* Table 7-9.) As can be seen, the estimated percentage of black graduate enrollment was 5.3 percent in 1974. This table also shows a slow increasing trend in the proportion of graduate enrollments that is black. However, the absolute numbers shown in this table are of

TABLE 7-10. Proportion of Blacks Ages 18–34 in Undergraduate Enrollment, 1968–1974

1968	1969	1970	1971	1972	1973	1974
6.4	6.6	7.0	8.4	8.7	8.4	9.2

Source: Brown and Stent, *Minorities in U.S. Institutions of Higher Education*, p. 37. Quoted from U.S. Bureau of the Census data.

unknown validity. Different sources show different proportions of blacks among graduate student bodies, and the HEW data give the highest estimate. In 1970, for instance, HEW estimated a total black graduate enrollment of 4.2 percent; ACE estimated 2.3 percent; the Educational Testing Service estimated 3.3 percent; and the U.S. Census estimated 3.1 percent.[27] The HEW estimate seems high in view of the fact that the 1974 graduate enrollment exceeds the 1974 undergraduate proportion of 5.1 percent.[28] A black graduate school enrollment proportion as high as 5 percent can only imply that blacks who previously graduated are returning in greater proportions than nonblacks who previously graduated. This return is suggested by data on black Ph.D. graduates in 1974, which indicate a mean time elapse between the B.A. and Ph.D. of 12.4 years for blacks compared to 8.5 years overall.[29]

Ultimately, the proportion of blacks going on to graduate training depends on the proportion enrolled in undergraduate school who complete their undergraduate training and decide to enter graduate training. This proportion may well be influenced by the state of the economy and other short-term phenomena, but is probably best considered a socioeconomic constant. Thus, one would expect the proportion going on to graduate school to remain roughly constant given the other socioeconomic parameters. This constant would suggest that trends in undergraduate enrollments would be a good predictor of trends in graduate enrollments. The relationship between undergraduate and graduate enrollments was therefore examined further.

The proportion of blacks in undergraduate enrollment from 1968 to 1974 is shown in Table 7-10. These data also present a number of difficulties, and the proportions given by various sources differ.[30] All the numbers do show, however, increasing black proportions in undergraduate enrollments over the past several years.

A regression equation was estimated relating graduate enrollment to

TABLE 7-11. Proportion of Students Enrolled in Previous Year Through the Next Year

Year	1 Blacks	2 All	Ratio	Cumulative Proportion
2	73.6	75.6	0.97	0.97
3	73.0	77.0	0.95	0.92
4	77.2	87.0	0.89	0.82
5	21.3	35.4	0.60	0.50
6	50.0	71.3	0.70	0.34

Source: Institute for the Study of Educational Policy, *Equal Educational Opportunity: More Promise than Progress* (Washington, D.C.: Howard University Press, forthcoming), Table 4-1.

the four-year moving average of undergraduate enrollments. This regression explained about 35 percent of the variation. However, the coefficients were sensitive to the data points included in the regression equation. The equation fitted to data from 1968 to 1974 also overestimates the end points. Thus this estimation equation was not used.

Further insight into the possibilities for black graduate enrollments can be gained by studying the relative persistence of blacks. The analysis relies on determining the proportion of blacks remaining in school at each level, relative to the proportion of all students remaining in school. If blacks returned for each year at the same rate as nonblacks, then the proportion entering graduate school without interrupting their education would equal the proportion entering as freshmen four years earlier. If the retention rate for blacks were lower (greater), then the proportion from any freshmen class entering graduate school four years later would be less (more).

Data on black college retention rates are available from ISEP and are shown in Table 7-11. Also shown is the ratio of black retention to white retention in each succeeding year. The last column of the table shows the cumulative proportion of blacks remaining in each year, relative to the proportion starting in the freshman year.

As can be seen from these data, blacks tend to return to college at a lower rate than whites in each year. This results in a cumulative shrinking of the proportion of blacks in each higher level class. Table 7-12 shows the proportion of blacks that would remain at each year of college given two different entering freshmen proportions and the reten-

TABLE 7-12. Proportion of Blacks Remaining in Each Year's Class Given the Proportion in the First Year

		Year			
1	*2*	*3*	*4*	*5*	*6*
9.2	8.92	8.46	7.50	4.52	3.16
8.4	8.14	7.72	6.85	4.12	2.89

Source: Institute for the Study of Educational Policy, *Equal Educational Opportunity: More Promise than Progress* (Washington, D.C.: Howard University Press, forthcoming), Table 7-11.

tion rates indicated in Table 7-11. As can be seen, starting with a freshman class which contains 9.2 percent blacks, the first year graduate class would contain only 4.5 percent black students and the second year and above graduate classes would contain only 3.16 percent black students.

The influence of the proportion enrolled in the immediately lower grade level in the prior year is partially offset by the return of students who have completed the next lower level grade but who dropped out of school for some time. The exact magnitude of this phenomenon is unknown but, according to the ISEP report, blacks in general are more likely to drop out and later return to school than other students. In addition, it appears that generally the education of blacks is stretched out over a much longer period of time than for others. Indeed, in view of the above retention rates, there is no other way to explain HEW's high estimates of the proportion of blacks in current graduate school enrollments.

Increases in any of three aspects of the black undergraduate picture could lead to increases in the proportion of blacks going to graduate schools. These aspects are: (1) increases in the proportion of blacks enrolling in undergraduate schools; (2) increases in the rate of persistence in school; and (3) increases in the relative rate of return to school of blacks who have dropped out. Therefore it is necessary to examine the determinants of the proportion of blacks enrolling, the persistence of these students, and the rate of return of dropouts in order to determine if there are likely to be increasing proportions of blacks in graduate schools during our projection period.

Significant increases in the undergraduate enrollments of blacks could result from two factors. First, the proportion of blacks among the college-age population could grow. Second, the proportion of blacks from each cohort attending college could increase.

The first factor is not likely to account for a very dramatic gain. The population projections of the U.S. Bureau of the Census through 1990 indicate that blacks will comprise about 1 percent more of the college-age group by then.[31] Thus, even if all of these additional blacks go to college, it could account for no more than an extra 1 percent in the proportion of blacks in undergraduate enrollment by the end of the period. Moreover, if the present tendency of blacks to enroll in school continues, the increase in enrollments would be less than 1 percent. When this is combined with the much lower relative persistence of blacks through to graduate school, one could expect, at best, another 0.3 percent of blacks among the graduate enrollments by the end of this period from this increase in their relative presence among school-aged groups.

The proportion of blacks in each cohort attending college will increase only if the educational, financial, and racial barriers confronting black youth continue to decline. The rapid increase in enrollment over the last decade resulted from a lessening of all three barriers. It seems very unlikely, however, that the next decade could see further gains of the same relative magnitude. Public programs of financial assistance have probably reached their zenith. Blacks still derive substantial academic disadvantages from their precollege educational experiences and there is no obvious reason for expecting a dramatic change in the future. Finally, purely racial barriers may already have dropped as much as they can be expected regarding access to college.

These considerations would lead one to the conclusion that the proportions of blacks in each cohort attending undergraduate school has probably reached a peak and may even decline. A hint of the possibility of declining black enrollments is seen from a review of the proportions of blacks in freshmen classes. The proportions of blacks in freshman enrollments peaked in 1972 and declined for two successive years in 1973 and 1974. (*See* Table 7-13).

It is not clear why these declines occurred. There is some impressionistic evidence that financial and academic barriers to education may have increased over the past several years as the level of support and commitment for many special admissions and financial assistance programs has declined. Because blacks are disproportionately among the financially and educationally disadvantaged, they would have been dis-

TABLE 7-13. Proportion of Black Students in Freshmen Enrollment, Selected Years, 1966–1974

Year	1966	1971	1972	1973	1974
Proportion	5.0	6.3	8.7	7.8	7.4

Source: Brown and Stent, *Minorities in U.S. Institutions of Higher Education,* p. 29. Quoted from American Council on Education data.

proportionately affected by such cutbacks. In any case, the data concerning freshmen reinforce the conclusion that one cannot expect dramatic increases in the relative black presence in undergraduate enrollments if current policies continue.

The high dropout rates for black students also tend to be related to their inability to overcome financial, educational, and social barriers. The relatively higher black dropout rates appear to be related to the relatively higher disadvantage of black students. There is also little reason to expect this situation to improve.

The larger proportionate presence of blacks in pools of returning students probably reflects, to some extent, their larger presence in the dropout pools. Cumulated savings and experience may make it possible for many of the educationally disadvantaged to return to school after a brief hiatus. This may currently offset a good portion of the higher dropout rates. But there is little reason to expect a greatly increased rate of return to school by black dropouts. This factor may account, at most, for a modest increase in the proportion of blacks in graduate schools in the future.

If the preceding analysis is correct, one can expect trends in all three aspects of the black undergraduate presence to have a small impact on increasing the proportions of blacks in graduate enrollments as long as there is a continuation of present policies. Any gains in graduate education must come as a result of increasing the proportion of each undergraduate class going on to graduate school. The same trends affecting barriers to black undergraduate education are probably operating in graduate education. There is already some evidence that blacks are going on to graduate school at about the rate of other undergraduates. Moreover, the recent significant increases in black enrollments in professional schools probably indicate that enrollments in nonprofessional graduate programs will increase at a slower rate in the future. Thus, at best, one can expect modest increases in the black presence in the graduate schools over the projection period given the continuation of present trends and policies.

Therefore, in the base case projections of black supply, a moderate range of increase for the black proportion in graduate enrollments has been allowed. It has been assumed that the proportion of blacks in graduate enrollments will increase anywhere from 0 to 2 percentage points per year over the next fifteen years. The projections labeled with numbers 1, 2, and 3 (*see* Table 7-14) assume annual percentage point additions to the proportion of blacks in the graduate programs of 0, 0.1, and 0.2, respectively. On the low side, the current proportion of blacks in graduate enrollments, estimated at 5.3 percent, will remain constant over the projection period. In the high projections, the proportion of blacks in the graduate enrollments will increase to 8.3 percent by the end of the fifteen-year projection period.

Given these assumptions about the annual rate of change in the black presence in graduate school enrollments, it is possible to estimate the proportion of blacks in graduate school enrollments annually throughout the projection period, once there are initial starting points. For the Ph.D.* degree, the 1974 estimated Ph.D. enrollment of 2.7 percent was used as the starting point. The overall enrollment estimate of 5.3 percent was used for the overall initial point. Both of these numbers were used to estimate the proportion of black students enrolled in non-Ph.D. (mainly master's) programs in 1974. Given the fact that roughly 12 percent of the graduate degrees awarded are Ph.D. degrees, it is assumed that the proportion of graduate students enrolled in such programs is also 12 percent. This assumption yields an estimate of 5.7 percent black enrollment in non-Ph.D. graduate programs in 1974.

The assumptions about the growth in the proportions of blacks in graduate school enrollments have been used to project the supply of blacks. This projection is accomplished simply by applying the estimated proportions of blacks in the graduate enrollments to the overall graduate degree projections derived earlier in the chapter. This procedure assumes that blacks will graduate in the same proportions as they are enrolled in graduate school. This assumption certainly may produce an optimistic bias in the projections of the rate of black supply. Later on the effect of varying this assumption will be considered.

* Throughout this report, the terms Ph.D. and doctorate are used interchangeably to refer to all doctorate degrees except the professional degrees.

The complete projections of total and black graduates through 1990 are shown in Table 7-14. As can be seen, under the assumption of small to moderate improvement in the representation of blacks in graduate schools, the growth in the black graduates will be continuous throughout the period. According to projection 2, the number of blacks graduating with the Ph.D. degree will increase from 818 in 1974 to 1,505 by 1990, while the number graduating with master's degrees will increase from 13,043 in 1974 to 18,030 by 1990. Under the faster-paced projection 3, the increase by 1990 will be to 2,065 for Ph.D.'s and 22,210 for master's. Under the "no change" projection, the number of blacks graduating will increase through 1983 and decline over the rest of the period, reflecting the movement of the total graduate series. Under the "no change" assumption there will be only 945 blacks graduating with the Ph.D. degree and 13,849 with the master's degree by 1990. These numbers are projected for 1978 for the number of master's degrees, but are the same for the number of Ph.D. degrees.

*The Role and Impact of Affirmative Action and the Projections
of Demand for Blacks to 1990*

Given the availability projections, it is possible to use the model of the academic labor market to project black hiring and black faculty through 1990. These projections can be made by allocating the total hiring between black and nonblack and applying the faculty exit rates to each year's stock. Separate projections are made for Ph.D. faculty and for master's faculty. These projections are then recombined into a total faculty number.

In order to allocate total hiring among blacks and nonblacks, some assumption must be made about the impact of successful affirmative action. The role of affirmative action is to help ensure equal opportunity in the future. If affirmative action is successful, it will result in the attainment of equal opportunity for all in promotions to all ranks, tenure decisions, pay decisions, new hiring decisions, and work assignments. True equal opportunity implies that the probability of attaining any benefit is equal for all people of equal productivity, regardless of race, sex, or any other productively irrelevant factor. It also means that each individual has a chance to gain qualifications that do not depend on productively irrelevant factors.

The long-run implication of successful affirmative action is that each population subgroup will participate in the benefits of employment

TABLE 7-14. Projections of Total Graduates, 1974 to 1990 (in thousands)

	GPh.D.	GBPh.D.			GM	GBM		
		1	2	3		1	2	3
1974	30.3	0.818	0.818	0.818	246.1	13.043	13.043	13.043
1975	32.1	0.867	0.894	0.931	250.5	13.276	13.527	13.777
1976	34.1	0.921	0.989	1.057	257.0	13.621	14.135	14.649
1977	34.9	0.942	1.041	1.152	263.9	13.981	14.778	15.570
1978	35.0	0.945	1.085	1.225	269.9	14.305	15.384	16.464
1979	35.9	0.969	1.149	1.328	274.2	14.533	15.904	17.275
1980	36.6	0.988	1.208	1.427	277.4	14.702	16.367	18.031
1981	37.1	1.002	1.261	1.521	280.4	14.861	16.824	18.787
1982	37.8	1.021	1.323	1.625	281.0	14.893	17.141	19.389
1983	38.7	1.045	1.393	1.741	278.8	14.776	17.286	19.795
1984	38.4	1.037	1.421	1.805	280.4	14.861	17.665	20.469
1985	38.1	1.029	1.448	1.867	275.6	14.607	17.638	20.670
1986	37.3	1.007	1.455	1.902	269.5	14.283	17.516	20.751
1987	36.4	0.983	1.456	1.929	263.9	13.987	17.417	20.848
1988	35.7	0.964	1.464	1.963	260.9	13.828	17.480	21.133
1989	35.1	0.948	1.474	2.001	260.1	13.785	17.687	21.588
1990	35.0	0.945	1.505	2.065	261.3	13.849	18.030	22.210

Key: GPh.D.—Total Ph.D. Graduates.
GM—Total Master's Graduates.
GBPh.D.—Total Black Ph.D. Graduates.
GBM—Total Black Master's Graduates.

Source: 1974 through 1983 based on Projections of Education Statistics to 1981–1982: (Washington, D.C.: Government Printing Office, 1973), 1984–1990 estimated by ISEP.

provided by institutions of higher education to the degree implied by their supply potential. In view of their limited wealth and limited opportunities elsewhere, one would probably expect blacks to eventually have a supply potential which exceeds their proportion in the labor force.* Therefore, the black faculty now numbering roughly 15,000 would probably be 55,000, at a minimum, if what existed were a long-run equilibrium in a fair system of employment in higher education.

In the short run, the possible achievements are constrained by the number of new openings, tenure decisions, promotions, and the number of qualified blacks available for teaching. The implication of effective affirmative action in the short run is that all groups will be represented among newly hired, newly tenured, and newly promoted faculty and staffs in proportion to their numbers in the qualified availability pools. The existing overall patterns in the faculty stocks, which are the results of past discrimination, imply that the groups which have been discriminated against in the past will remain underrepresented in the faculty stock, relative to their potential, for some time.

Effective affirmative action, however, will lead to ultimate convergence between the proportions in the stocks and the supply potential. The rapidity of convergence depends upon: (1) the size of the initial disparities; (2) the way in which affirmative action programs are implemented; (3) the aggregate rate of new hires and promotions; and (4) the trends in the relative supply of blacks. All of these considerations have been incorporated already into the analysis except point (2), which is considered now. A good understanding of this point is essential for working out the implications of affirmative action for the future employment of blacks.

Affirmative action programs may be implemented either through emphasis on the attainment of goals, or through emphasis on the attainment of procedurally fair processes. If goals are used, the way in which they are determined and the way in which they are used in implementing affirmative action could affect the outcome of the affirmative action program.

There are a number of possible bases for defining the goals of affirmative action programs which were discussed in earlier chapters. Goals

---

* The limited wealth of blacks implies that there will be fewer opportunities for blacks in areas where the access to opportunity depends upon wealth. Moreover, as a minority, blacks may continue to have limited access to opportunities in other areas such as politics. As a result, the desirability of positions in higher education will probably be even greater for blacks than it is for nonblacks.

define the objectives and the expectations of accomplishment of the affirmative action program. The goals thus provide management guides for organizing, monitoring, and evaluating the program. Goals are not quotas, but they can be expected to strongly influence the motivation of the institution. An institution is likely to pursue affirmative action more aggressively if it is underachieving with respect to reasonably defined goals than if it is overachieving. On the other hand, goals that are clearly impossible to attain within the given time frame create frustrations and are likely to be eventually rejected.

Goals and timetables are merely management tools. They function as guides for judging whether or not an institution is achieving equal opportunity. If affirmative action is actually fully implemented and successful regardless of how goals are defined, it should result in the attainment of equality of opportunity.

There is no legal requirement which would suggest that affirmative action programs will utilize goals higher than those which can be derived from fairly defined availability pools. It is also clear that institutions themselves would have little internal incentive to overdefine their goals. There seems little reason to expect the use of goals and quotas to establish two hiring systems, since it is not a part of the affirmative action requirement and is, in fact, against the law. Goals and timetables might well be misused by individual institutions, but this situation is likely to be more the exception than the rule.

The implementation of the requirements of Executive Order 11246 and the regulations should ensure equal opportunity in current labor market activities. This is accomplished through the utilization of racially unbiased procedures and numerical goals which are established in accordance with current utilization gaps and availabilities. If these projections of the law are both fully and correctly implemented, and if they are in fact successful, the distribution of opportunities will reflect relative availabilities irrespective of the extent of unemployment.

The affirmative action effort, which currently has many shortcomings in design and implementation, is continuing to evolve. It is not possible to know how affirmative action programs will be designed in the future. It is also impossible to know how fully they will be implemented or how successful they will be. It seems reasonable, however, in projecting the potential impact of affirmative action of the black faculty to assume that affirmative action will be successfully implemented. Thus, it has been assumed for the base case projections that affirmative action will be successful and will *result in the hiring of blacks in proportion to their relative availability.*

Thus, the base case assumption about the effect of successful affirmative action on black employment is that the proportion of blacks hired at a point in time will be equal to their proportion in the availability pools. The proportion among the current graduates has been used as a rough estimate of the availability. This assumption may underestimate black availability if there is a current, relatively large supply-demand gap for blacks, since the use of this assumption also implies that there is no supply and demand gap at the beginning of the period for blacks which is greater than that for nonblacks.

Projections of Black Hiring

Given the above discussion of the rate of growth of black availability and the effect of affirmative action, one can easily project new black hiring. This projection is done by applying the estimates of the relative black presence among recent graduate pools to the estimates derived earlier for aggregate demand.*

The use of three different rates of increase of the proportion in the graduate pools implies three different rates of hiring. The present projections, therefore, take a pessimistic, a moderate, and a fairly optimistic view of the rate of hire, according to whether the proportion of blacks among new graduates remains constant (A1 and B1), increases by 0.1 percent a year (A2 and B2), or increases by 0.2 percent a year (A3 and B3).

The projections of hiring of black faculty from 1975 through 1989 are shown in Table 7-15 for Ph.D. faculty and in Table 7-16 for non-Ph.D. faculty. Except for the dip between 1975–76 for B series projections, all six projections show that the general trend in hiring will be increasing through 1978. After this point, however, all of the projections show that there will be declines. In the A series projections, for both Ph.D. and non-Ph.D. hiring, demand will decline at a moderate pace through 1982, vanish altogether from 1983 through 1988, and pick up at a modest pace again in 1989. In the B series projections, demand will decline at a modest pace through 1981 and will continue to decline

* This procedure will overestimate black hiring as long as the proportion in the graduate pools is growing, if those who were not hired in the previous years are still in the availability pools. This factor, however, should not be too important.

TABLE 7-15. Projections of Hiring Black Faculty at the Ph.D. Level, 1975–1989

	Exit 2%			Exit 5%		
	Constant A1	0.1 yearly A2	0.2 yearly A3	Constant B1	0.1 yearly B2	0.2 yearly B3
1975	209	217	224	471	489	506
1976	247	265	283	388	417	446
1977	237	263	289	383	426	468
1978	252	290	327	403	463	522
1979	222	263	304	377	446	516
1980	199	243	287	358	437	517
1981	179	226	272	341	429	517
1982	60	78	96	224	290	357
1983	0	0	0	142	189	236
1984	0	0	0	105	144	183
1985	0	0	0	53	74	96
1986	0	0	0	122	176	231
1987	0	0	0	185	274	364
1988	0	0	0	239	363	487
1989	118	184	250	308	480	651

Source: Institute for the Study of Educational Policy.

at a faster pace through 1985, after which there will be a recovery. However, by the end of the projection period, annual hiring will have completely recovered in absolute terms under the B3 projection only. As would be expected, the drop in demand is especially severe in the A1 series projections and grows progressively less severe through the B3 projection.

The wide difference in demand under the A and B assumptions is worthy of note. Obviously, the ultimate demand is highly sensitive to assumptions about faculty retirement rates. It would be very important to have additional research directed at establishing the rate of retirement on a firmer basis. For now, these projections should be taken as indicators of the range of reasonable possibilities. It should also be noted that the same exit rate assumptions were used for black and white faculty. This probably overstates black exits, since the black faculty may be comprised of younger entrants. But this factor should not have a major impact on the conclusions about demand.

TABLE 7-16. Projections of Hiring Black Faculty at the Non-Ph.D. Level, 1975–1989

	A1	A2	A3	B1	B2	B3
1975	791	805	819	1,783	1,815	1,846
1976	933	966	999	1,470	1,522	1,573
1977	896	944	991	1,451	1,527	1,603
1978	955	1,022	1,089	1,525	1,632	1,739
1979	839	912	986	1,426	1,551	1,676
1980	753	832	912	1,354	1,496	1,639
1981	678	762	845	1,290	1,448	1,606
1982	228	260	292	848	967	1,085
1983	0	0	0	536	621	705
1984	0	0	0	398	468	538
1985	0	0	0	200	239	278
1986	0	0	0	462	559	657
1987	0	0	0	701	861	1,021
1988	0	0	0	905	1,127	1,350
1989	448	566	683	1,168	1,475	1,782

Source: Institute for the Study of Educational Policy.

It is also important to recognize that black hiring accounts for a relatively small proportion of total hiring under all projections. The projected total hiring of Ph.D. and master's faculty on an annual basis is shown in Table 7-17. The proportion of total Ph.D. hiring which was black in 1975 was 2.7 percent for projection 1, 2.8 percent for 2, and 2.9 percent for 3. At the end of the period the proportions will have increased to 2.7 percent, 4.2 percent, and 5.7 percent for projections 1 through 3, respectively. The proportion of hiring of non-Ph.D. blacks was 5.7 percent, 5.8 percent, and 5.9 percent in 1975, and 5.7 percent, 7.2 percent, and 8.1 percent for projections 1, 2, and 3, in that order, by 1989. Clearly, then, in all the base case projections black hiring will remain a small part of total hiring.

Projections of Total Black Faculty to 1990

The projections of the stock of black faculty are based upon the assumed retirement rates and the faculty hiring projections. These projections are shown in Tables 7-18, 7-19, and 7-20 for total Ph.D. and non-Ph.D. black faculties, respectively.

TABLE 7-17. Projected Annual Total Hiring of Ph.D. and Non-Ph.D. Faculty, 1975–1989

	Ph.D.		Non-Ph.D.	
	A	*B*	*A*	*B*
1975	7,239	17,447	13,879	31,287
1976	9,130	14,383	16,372	25,792
1977	8,170	14,191	15,727	25,450
1978	9,345	14,922	16,759	26,759
1979	8,205	13,950	14,714	25,017
1980	7,368	13,245	13,213	23,752
1981	6,636	12,616	11,980	22,625
1982	2,232	8,292	4,003	14,869
1983	0	5,244	0	9,403
1984	0	3,896	0	6,988
1985	0	1,959	0	2,514
1986	0	4,521	0	8,107
1987	0	6,859	0	12,000
1988	0	8,853	0	15,877
1989	4,380	11,425	7,855	20,488

Source: Institute for the Study of Educational Policy.

The total number of blacks in college faculties will grow continuously in projections A1, A2, A3, and B1 until 1982, and in projections B2 and B3 until 1983. After 1982 or 1983, in all six projections, the stock of black faculty will decline as retirements outpace hirings. The declines will continue through 1989 for projections A1, A2, and A3, through 1988 for projection B1, and through 1987 for B2 and B3. After these dates absolute faculty growth will resume. The increases in the stock which will occur are fairly modest in all projections. Naturally, the overall increases under projections B2 and B3 will be the greatest. By 1990, however, the black faculty will have increased from its estimated 1974 level of 15,698 by a low amount of 3,642 in the A1 projection, and by the high amount of 9,417 in the B3 projection. Similar patterns of growth are exhibited by the Ph.D. and the non-Ph.D. faculty stocks. The Ph.D. stocks are projected to increase between 1974 and 1990, by a maximum of 2,594 and a minimum of 751. The non-Ph.D. stocks will show a maximum increase over the period of 6,823 and a minimum increase of 2,891.

TABLE 7-18. Estimated Total Black Faculty, 1974 and Projections of Total Black Faculty, 1975–1990

	A1	*A2*	*A3*	*B1*	*B2*	*B3*
1974	15,698	15,698	15,698	15,698	15,698	15,698
1975	17,083	17,083	17,083	16,612	16,612	16,612
1976	17,742	17,763	17,785	18,036	18,085	18,133
1977	18,566	18,639	18,711	18,993	19,119	19,246
1978	19,328	19,473	19,617	19,877	20,116	20,355
1979	20,149	20,395	20,641	20,811	21,205	21,599
1980	20,807	21,162	21,518	21,573	22,142	22,712
1981	21,343	21,814	22,286	22,206	22,969	23,731
1982	21,773	22,365	22,958	22,726	23,697	24,668
1983	21,626	22,256	22,887	22,661	23,769	24,877
1984	21,194	21,811	22,429	22,206	23,390	24,574
1985	20,770	21,375	21,980	21,599	22,833	24,067
1986	20,354	20,948	21,541	20,772	22,005	23,237
1987	19,947	20,529	21,110	20,318	21,640	22,962
1988	19,548	20,118	20,688	20,188	21,693	23,199
1989	19,157	19,716	20,274	20,323	22,099	23,875
1990	19,340	20,071	20,801	20,783	22,949	25,115

Source: Institute for the Study of Educational Policy.

As might be expected, the growth in the black faculty stocks also mirrors the pattern of demand. During the period of weakest demand the black faculty declines in all projections. During the periods of highest demand, the black faculty growth is greatest.

The Proportion of Blacks on Faculties to 1990

For purposes of this study, it was assumed that the proportion of blacks with Ph.D.'s on faculties in 1970 was 2.0 percent. Based on this assumption, the census information that 3.2 percent of the college faculties were black, and the assumption that 35.8 percent of the total faculty had Ph.D.'s, the initial proportion of blacks with master's degrees (which is assumed to be all of those without Ph.D. degrees)* was fixed

* It is recognized that all non-Ph.D. faculty do not have master's degrees. For purposes of the projections, however, and in view of the fact that this is the major degree held by non-Ph.D. level faculty, it seems to be a reasonable assumption. Since the supply of those without master's or Ph.D. degrees who are eligible for teaching is not accounted for, the projections understate the supply. On the other hand, it is also clear that all master's degree recipients may not be suitable for college teaching, and this undoubtedly more than offsets the other bias.

TABLE 7-19. Estimated Black Faculty, 1974 and Projections of Ph.D.-Level Black Faculty 1975–1990

	A1	A2	A3	B1	B2	B3
1974	3,315	3,315	3,315	3,315	3,315	3,315
1975	3,604	3,604	3,604	3,504	3,504	3,504
1976	3,741	3,748	3,756	3,800	3,817	3,835
1977	3,912	3,938	3,964	3,998	4,044	4,089
1978	4,071	4,122	4,174	4,182	4,267	4,353
1979	4,242	4,330	4,418	4,375	4,516	4,658
1980	4,378	4,506	4,633	4,533	4,737	4,941
1981	4,490	4,659	4,828	4,664	4,937	5,210
1982	4,579	4,791	5,003	4,772	4,119	5,467
1983	4,548	4,773	4,999	4,757	5,154	5,550
1984	4,457	4,678	4,899	4,661	5,085	5,509
1985	4,368	4,584	4,801	4,533	4,975	5,416
1986	4,280	4,493	4,705	4,357	4,800	5,242
1987	4,195	4,403	4,611	4,263	4,737	5,210
1988	4,111	4,315	4,519	4,235	4,774	5,313
1989	4,029	4,228	4,428	4,263	4,898	5,535
1990	4,066	4,328	4,589	4,358	5,133	5,909

Source: Institute for the Study of Educational Policy.

at 3.9 percent. The proportions were then assumed to grow as determined by the annual rate of hires and exits.

The effect of the projected faculty growth patterns on the proportion of blacks on college faculties is shown in Table 7-21. In general, the proportion of blacks on the faculty will be increasing in all of the projections throughout the period. Also, as expected, the A projections show uniformly lower proportions of blacks on the faculty than the B projections. The proportion of blacks on the faculty overall and at each level will increase most rapidly up to 1982. After 1982 the proportions generally stagnate in all of the A projections and also the B1 projection. They will increase modestly in the B2 projection and most rapidly in the B3 projection.

The difference in the behavior of the proportions between the B and A projections indicates the importance of demand factors, and the differences among the 1, 2, and 3 projections illustrate the importance of supply considerations. The relationships between the A projections indicate that in periods of very slack demand increased supply has very little impact on the growth of the proportion of blacks. Comparison of

TABLE 7-20. Estimated Non-Ph.D. Black Faculty, 1974 and Projections of Non-Ph.D. Black Faculty, 1975–1990

	A1	A2	A3	B1	B2	B3
1974	12,383	12,383	12,383	12,383	12,383	12,383
1975	13,479	13,479	13,479	13,108	13,108	13,108
1976	14,001	14,015	14,029	14,236	14,267	14,299
1977	14,654	14,701	14,747	14,994	15,076	15,157
1978	15,258	15,360	15,443	15,695	15,849	16,002
1979	15,908	16,065	16,220	16,436	16,689	16,942
1980	16,428	16,656	16,885	17,040	17,405	17,771
1981	16,853	17,156	17,459	17,542	18,031	18,521
1982	17,194	17,575	17,954	17,954	18,578	19,201
1983	17,078	17,483	17,888	17,904	18,615	19,327
1984	16,737	17,133	17,530	17,545	18,305	19,066
1985	16,402	16,791	17,179	17,066	17,858	18,650
1986	16,074	16,455	16,836	16,413	17,204	17,996
1987	15,753	16,126	16,499	16,054	16,703	17,752
1988	15,438	15,803	16,169	15,953	16,919	17,886
1989	15,129	15,487	15,846	16,060	17,201	18,341
1990	15,274	15,743	16,212	16,425	17,816	19,206

Source: Institute for the Study of Educational Policy.

TABLE 7-21. Projections of Percentage of Blacks on Faculty at Selected Years

	A1	A2	A3	B1	B2	B3
Total Faculty						
1974	3.5	3.5	3.5	3.5	3.5	3.5
1982	3.9	4.0	4.1	4.0	4.2	4.4
1990	3.9	4.0	4.2	4.2	4.6	5.0
Non-Ph.D. Faculty						
1974	4.3	4.3	4.3	4.3	4.3	4.3
1982	4.7	4.9	5.0	5.0	5.1	5.3
1990	4.8	4.9	5.1	5.1	5.6	6.0
Ph.D. Faculty						
1974	2.1	2.1	2.1	2.1	2.1	2.1
1982	2.3	2.4	2.5	2.4	2.5	2.7
1990	2.3	2.4	2.6	2.4	2.9	3.3

Source: Institute for the Study of Educational Policy.

the B projections indicate that at higher levels of demand, fairly modest improvements in supply can make a significant difference. But comparisons between A and B projections illustrate that, for any given level of supply, the increases in demand cause the largest increases in the proportion of blacks on the faculty.

In the present case, however, the overall improvement in the period from 1970 to 1990 will be modest in even the best case. Especially in comparison with the labor force potential of about 11 percent, the total proportion of blacks on college faculties will increase from the estimated 1974 level of 3.5 percent to 5.0 percent in 1990 in the best case. This proportion is made up of an increase from the estimated 1974 level of 4.3 percent to a 1990 level of 6.0 percent for non-Ph.D. faculties and an increase from the estimated 1974 level of 2.1 percent to 3.3 percent in Ph.D.-level faculties. In the low projections, the increase of the proportion of blacks in the overall faculty will be to 3.9 percent, while the non-Ph.D. faculty will grow to 4.8 percent and the Ph.D. faculty to 2.3 percent.

In fact, with the kind of growth in black supply represented in the projections even under the most optimistic of the cases, it will take at least another thirty-five years after 1990 before 11 percent representation will be reached in the Ph.D. stocks, assuming that the overall faculty stocks stabilize at 500,000. Under the most pessimistic black supply considerations, the supply potential will never be reached and it takes at least twenty more years under the best circumstances to even reach the 2.7 percent level of representation among Ph.D. faculties.

Labor Market Conditions for Black Manpower

Even though the above results are, at best, modest achievements from affirmative action, the rate of demand is still less than the rate of supply throughout the projection period. Consequently, there will be qualified blacks who will be unable to attain employment in the academic labor market. The phenomenon can be seen clearly in the projected ratio of new entrants to the ratio of new hiring. These data are displayed in Table 7-22.

In both the A and B projections, the ratio of hiring to new graduates at both the Ph.D. and non-Ph.D. level fluctuates around a stable level until 1978. Subsequent to 1978, both series show that there will be a steady decline in demand relative to supply through 1982. After 1982, the ratio will drop to zero for the A projections at both levels, and

TABLE 7-22. Ratio of Hiring of Black Faculty to New Black Graduates

	Ph.D. Level		Non-Ph.D. Level	
	A	B	A	B
1975	0.241	0.544	0.055	0.125
1976	0.268	0.422	0.064	0.100
1977	0.251	0.407	0.060	0.096
1978	0.267	0.426	0.062	0.099
1979	0.229	0.389	0.054	0.091
1980	0.201	0.362	0.048	0.086
1981	0.179	0.340	0.042	0.081
1982	0.059	0.219	0.014	0.053
1983	0	0.135	0	0.034
1984	0	0.101	0	0.025
1985	0	0.051	0	0.013
1986	0	0.121	0	0.030
1987	0	0.188	0	0.047
1988	0	0.248	0	0.061
1989	0.125	0.325	0.030	0.079

Source: Institute for the Study of Educational Policy.

return to a level greater than zero only in 1989. In the B projections, at both levels the decline in the ratio will stop at 1985 and rise subsequent to that date.

The ratio is a rough measure of the proportion of graduates in each year that should find jobs in the academic labor market. As can be seen, the prospects of finding academic employment are projected to deteriorate in all of the base case projections through 1985. The probability of a new graduate finding employment on the faculties of academic institutions will decline dramatically from the high probabilities that existed in the early 1970s. By 1985, in the best case, the probability of a new black Ph.D. finding employment in academic institutions is projected to be only between six and seven chances out of a hundred. This is roughly down from the 60 percent to 70 percent chances of finding such employment during the early 1970s. The same phenomena are observed among the non-Ph.D.-level graduates.

It is important to note, however, that the probability of a black graduate finding a job under the assumption of equal opportunity is not lessened by increasing the black representation in the graduating pools. This is because the relative demand or hiring increases in proportion to relative availabilities. Thus, the probability of being hired under equal opportunity assumptions is the same under all of the three supply growth assumptions. Given the assumption of successful affirmative action, the probability of finding academic employment for a new black graduate is influenced only by the overall demand-supply gap. The relative proportion of blacks within the supply pools determines the absolute level of black employment but not the rate of employment under the equal opportunity assumptions.

The projections of low overall demand relative to overall availability are the cause of the high unemployment projections. These high unemployment projections have important implications for the effectiveness of affirmative action in bringing about parity on the faculties of higher educational institutions. These results, however, are projections of what could be expected under the given assumptions and are at best conditional predictions. The projections are accurate only as far as the assumptions on which they are based are accurate.

In particular, should any of the projected outcomes, such as the high unemployment rates for such highly trained manpower or the slow pace of progress toward achieving higher representation of blacks among academic faculties be deemed undesirable, public policies must be formulated to modify them. Before considering such policies, however, it is necessary to explore briefly the implications of the very slack labor markets for achieving affirmative action. Then, the possible public policy responses to the slack demand and the slow pace of achieving black faculty parity with their supply potential will be examined.

Implications of Slack Labor Markets
for Affirmative Action Efforts

How well will equal opportunity or affirmative action commitments withstand times of surplus labor? There obviously is no easy answer to this speculative question. In the past there has been a clearly observable tendency for blacks to be especially hurt in adverse labor markets. The phrase, "last hired-first fired," describes the labor market situation traditionally faced by blacks.

Slack Labor Markets and Pressure to Upgrade Qualifications

The existence of surplus labor makes it easy for institutions to satisfy their demands for labor. It also enables each institution to be more selective in the hiring process. In tight labor markets this flexibility does not exist as widely; only the top institutions are in a position to be selective in hiring. Most of those who are qualified can find employment in some institution.

This flexibility in hiring, which permits a higher degree of selectivity, also permits wider scope for discrimination. This opportunity for discrimination is especially true in labor markets like the academic labor markets, where the evaluation of relative qualifications is a complex process involving many subjective considerations. With an ample supply of qualified whites, it would be comparatively easy to avoid hiring blacks and to justify this avoidance on the grounds that the new black Ph.D.'s have alleged inferior qualifications.

The large surpluses expected in the 1980s will also give institutions an opportunity to increase their required qualifications to unnecessarily high levels. Higher qualifications may also have a negative impact on affirmative action, because blacks would not have had the opportunity to gain experience and publish and thus would tend to be distributed more heavily towards the lower end of the "qualifications" spectrum. There are also already some suggestions for increasing the utilization of Ph.D.-level manpower on college facilities, that would have a detrimental effect on the employment of blacks. Radner and Miller[32] suggest that the qualifications for faculties of community colleges might be "upgraded" to Ph.D. requirements. Moreover, all colleges might use the excess supplies of Ph.D.'s to upgrade the requirement for faculty hiring. However, this clearly would imply lessened opportunities for those potential faculty with less than the Ph.D. As we have seen, the available data on the degree composition of the black faculty stock indicates that it is weighted towards the lower degree levels. The projections indicate that blacks can be expected to remain a much higher proportion of those with non-Ph.D.-level qualifications throughout the period than those with Ph.D.-level qualifications. Consequently, such a strategy would have a disproportionate impact on potential black faculty job seekers.

Table 7-23 shows an example of the impact of an increase in the proportion of Ph.D.'s on the faculty. In this projection it was assumed that the proportion of Ph.D.'s hired is increased to 44 percent, instead of the 35.8 percent assumed in the base case projections. The result is to increase the hiring of black Ph.D.'s and reduce the hiring of non-Ph.D.'s. However, in all cases the reduction in the hiring of black non-Ph.D. faculty is projected to be greater than the increase in hiring of Ph.D. faculty. The result is that over the projection period about 390 fewer

TABLE 7-23. Projected Change in Total Black Hiring, 1975 to 1990, from an Increase in the Proportion of Ph.D.s Hired to 44 Percent

	A1	A2	A3	B1	B2	B3
Ph.D.	+410	+478	+550	+925	+1,157	+1,380
Non-Ph.D.	−803	−874	−943	−1,814	−2,044	−2,272
Total	−393	−396	−393	−889	−887	−892

Source: Institute for the Study of Educational Policy.

black faculty are projected to be hired under projections A, and about 890 fewer under projection B. Thus, the impact of this policy on the overall level of black participation is negative, as suggested.

Indeed, upgrading requirements which have a racially biased impact to unnecessary levels will violate directly one of the major tenets of affirmative action, namely, that qualifications must be certified as necessary for performance of the job. It seems clear, at least from an affirmative action perspective, that upgrading the required qualifications of faculties just to solve the employment problems of Ph.D.'s would be undesirable.

Slack Labor Markets and Racial Discrimination

Unfortunately, there is no way to be certain about the impact of excess supply on the racial practices of institutions of higher education. It would be comforting to believe that commitments to equal opportunity and affirmative action in employment would remain during good times and bad. Whether or not the commitment remains depends essentially upon the racial practices of those who make and/or influence university employment decisions.

The higher educational institution is a complex organization, and its decisions are influenced by the interest groups which make up the university community. These interest groups are faculty and staff, administration, students, alumni, and governing bodies. As in all complex organizations, the objectives of each group will influence the final outcome of the decision-making process to varying degrees, depending upon their respective roles and power. Moreover, higher education institutions are generally nonprofit making and operate in general, noncompetitive environments. These features give these institutions wider scope to satisfy the nonpecuniary objectives of the various interest groups without sacrificing general administrative objectives or risking institutional survival. This will be especially true for employment decisions, given excess supplies of qualified manpower. If any of the various interest groups are dominated by those with white racist objectives, the employment policies will be slanted against blacks.

In most institutions other than the traditionally black institutions, whites are still the dominant groups in university decision-making processes. Their degree of dominance varies within types of institutions and within the particular internal interest groups that comprise the university. White dominance of administrations and faculties is very great. Their dominance of graduate student bodies, alumni groups, and university trustees is also close to complete. Undergraduate student bodies are becoming increasingly integrated, especially on urban campuses, but the white student is still the dominant student group by far on most of the campuses.

The overwhelming dominance by whites of all of the interest groups that comprise the university does not necessarily imply that the institution will behave in a discriminatory manner. What is unknown is whether the various white interest groups within the university will encourage the perpetuation of racism in the future. Certainly, white-dominated universities have behaved in a racist fashion in the past. It is also clear that the benefits to whites from racism increase in times of surplus labor supplies. The answer to the question of the future impact of racism, however, lies in the sociology of racism, a subject which is not well understood. It is not clear how much racism was reduced during the civil rights period of the 1960s and early 1970s. That there is much racism remaining is evidenced by the continuing fight over busing and the conservative drift of politics in general and, of course, by the very intensity of the fight against affirmative action itself.[33] There is certainly, at minimum, great uncertainty over the degree of reduction in racism and racial prejudices among the various white groups which dominate university decision-making.

Slack Labor Markets and the Need for Government Action

If racism is still prevalent at universities, it will be more important than ever to have vigorous governmental efforts to enforce equal opportunity over the next ten to fifteen years. Affirmative action programs have not yet been put to as serious a test as they will experience in the near future in light of the general high demand for college manpower in the recent past. The future era of labor surpluses will generate large internal incentives to discontinue equal opportunity efforts, if the whites within the university choose to behave in a racist fashion. Thus, larger external incentives to continue affirmative action will be required just to maintain the same level of effort. Governmental efforts should not be decreased during this critical future period. On the contrary, governmental efforts to enforce affirmative action should be increased.

The need for government efforts to enforce affirmative action will continue as long as affirmative action is not a routine part of the personnel practices of higher educational institutions, because the lack of routinized affirmative action implies that institutional employment decisions are made in either an implicitly or explicitly racial fashion. This implies that racism could continue to be reflected in the procedures or processes of recruitment, hiring, promotion, and tenure. An active government effort to enforce affirmative action will no longer be required when explicit and implicit racism are no longer incorporated in the practices of institutions of higher education and when the effects of past discrimination have been eliminated. Since neither condition can currently be shown to exist with any degree of certainty in institutions of higher education, it would be foolish to take the risk of discontinuing government incentives. The existence of well-designed governmental enforcement efforts will not cause any significant disruption to anything but the racist practices of higher educational institutions.

Public Policies and the Future Prospects for Blacks
on the Faculties of Higher Educational Institutions

The Need for Policies to Increase the Rate of Participation of Blacks in Graduate Education

As has been shown in the previous projections, one implication of carefully designed and effectively enforced affirmative action is that the proportion of blacks employed on the faculties of institutions of higher education will increase, in the near future, if the relative availability or supply of blacks increases. For, as indicated earlier, under the present guidelines, successful affirmative action implies that black job seekers will receive equal opportunity in employment. The proportion of blacks employed each year should approximate their proportions in the job availability pools. In the aggregate it can be approximated by the proportion of blacks graduating with the appropriate degrees.

Therefore, the rate of increase in the numbers of blacks on the faculties of institutions of higher education is partially determined by the rate of increase in the participation of blacks in the graduate schools of the country. As the analysis of the projections showed, at both demand levels more rapid increases in the participation of blacks in graduate schools can lead to more rapid expansion of their participation on faculties.

As already indicated, blacks are still represented in very small numbers on graduate student bodies. Moreover, the higher the degree program, for any specialty, the smaller the number of blacks. Blacks are also generally concentrated in a few specialties. Moreover, there also seems to be little reason to expect the current low rates of participation in graduate education to increase very rapidly given current policies and trends. Expanded growth in participation of blacks in graduate schools will require not only expanded efforts to increase access at the graduate school level, but also efforts to increase the persistence of black students and improve the quality of education they receive at all levels of the educational system.

To the extent that the current low rates of participation in graduate education result from the lack of perceived opportunities, effective affirmative action may partially correct the supply problem. However, to the extent that other factors are responsible for the enrollment patterns, special efforts to increase the enrollment in graduate education will be required. Certainly affirmative action in graduate school placement is a minimum requirement to ensure effective access of potential black enrollees. Whether or not affirmative action for graduate students is coupled with affirmative action in employment, there clearly must be efforts to provide equal participation in graduate education to ensure the ultimate success of affirmative action, equal employment programs. Without significant increases in the relative supply of blacks, equal opportunity secured through affirmative action programs will be unable to achieve the objective of ensuring participation equal to the supply potential any time in the near future.

By increased participation of blacks as students in graduate schools, it should be understood to mean increased relative participation,

TABLE 7-24. Projections of Blacks among the New Graduates with Advanced Degrees in 1990 under Different Growth Assumptions

Annual Change	% Ph.D.	% Non-Ph.D.
0.000	2.7	5.7
0.001	4.3	7.3
0.002	5.9	8.9
0.003	7.5	10.0
0.004	9.1	11.0
0.005	10.7	11.0

Source: Institute for the Study of Educational Policy.

not merely increased absolute participation. Increased absolute participation results from equal expansion of enrollment for all groups. This type of increase does not lead to higher relative employment of blacks under a regime of equal opportunity to job seekers. In fact, in a situation of surplus labor and equal opportunity, absolute increases in supply merely result in increased unemployment if there is no relative increase in supply. It is important to emphasize that the increased participation of blacks should not be tied to an overall expansion of the system of higher education. What is required is for the black share of any given level of enrollment to increase.

The impact of varying the rate of supply formation on the outcomes of affirmative action programs with respect to black employment has already been discussed. To give further indication of the importance of supply, the impact has been estimated of three higher rates of growth of black participation in graduate schools on the projected levels of black faculty in 1990. In these simulations it was assumed that the annual increase in the proportion of blacks among new graduates would be 0.003, 0.004, and 0.005 percent annually until it reached 11 percent, at which point it would stabilize. Table 7-24 shows the proportion that blacks would form of graduate pools by 1990, under the various rates of change of graduate school participation assumed in this study. As can be seen, with the master's degree the 11 percent participation level would be reached by the two highest growth rates prior to 1990. Only in the case of the assumption of 0.005 annual increases will the Ph.D. participation reach 10.7 percent

TABLE 7-25. Projections of Blacks on the Faculty with Ph.D.'s in 1990

Annual Increase	Number		Percentage	
	A	B	A	B
0	4,066	4,358	2.3	2.4
0.001	4,328	5,133	2.4	2.9
0.002	4,589	5,909	2.6	3.3
0.003	4,851	6,684	2.7	3.8
0.004	5,113	7,460	2.9	4.2
0.005	5,374	8,235	3.0	4.6

Source: Institute for the Study of Educational Policy.

before 1990; and 10.7 percent is still 0.3 percent less than 11 percent reached at the master's level. It seems almost certain, however, that something other than a continuation of present policies would be required to achieve these higher rates of increase for supply.

The impact of the more rapid supply growth assumptions on the size of the black faculty and the proportion of blacks on the faculty are shown in Table 7-25 for Ph.D.-level faculty and in Table 7-26 for non-Ph.D.-level faculty. As expected these increases in supply have a significant effect on both the proportion and the absolute numbers of black faculty. For Ph.D.-level faculty each 0.001 increase in the

TABLE 7-26. Projections of Blacks on the Non-Ph.D. Faculty in 1990

Annual Increase	Number		Percentage	
	A	B	A	B
0	15,274	16,425	4.8	5.1
0.001	15,743	17,816	4.9	5.6
0.002	16,212	19,206	5.1	6.0
0.003	16,681	20,597	5.2	6.4
0.004	17,095	21,799	5.4	6.8
0.005	17,446	22,484	5.5	7.0

Source: Institute for the Study of Educational Policy.

annual additions to black participation in graduate school results in about an additional 262 black Ph.D.-level faculty each in 1990 under the A projections and an additional 775 under the B projections. The percentage of black Ph.D.-level faculty increases by about 0.15 percent for each 0.001 increase in the annual participation for A projections and about 0.45 under B projections. Similarly, the projected numbers of non-Ph.D.-level faculty in 1990 increase by 469 and 1,390 for every 0.001 increase up to 0.003 for projections A and B, respectively. For A projections another 414 is added as the annual increment increases to 0.004 and another 351 as it increases to 0.005; for projection B the additional increases are 1,202 and 685 respectively.

Thus, one can see by these results that public policies to increase the relative rate of participation of blacks in graduate schools could have a relatively large impact on the rate of increase of black faculty participation that would result from effective affirmative action over the projection period.

The projections presented earlier assumed that during the projection period the relative attrition rate for blacks would be no higher than that for nonblacks. As was indicated, an equal rate would depend upon the success of policies aimed at improving the persistence of blacks. Historically, blacks have apparently not stayed to complete their degrees at the same rate as others. Although estimating the magnitudes of the difference in attrition rate is confounded by the lack of data and the propensity of blacks to take longer to complete their degrees, blacks might easily have a rate of attrition at least 25 percent higher than nonblacks.

An idea of the importance of this matter can be gained by reviewing the data in Table 7-27. This table presents one set of results from the simulation of the effect of a 25 percent higher attrition rate. (The top panel of this table shows the projected proportion of blacks on the faculty in 1974, 1982, and 1990 under the assumption of a 25 percent higher attrition rate; the bottom panel duplicates part of Table 7-21, which contains the equivalent base case results.)

As can be readily seen, the higher attrition rate significantly affects affirmative action results. For the non-Ph.D. projections for 1990, the proportion of the faculty range from 4.8 percent to 4.4 percent, a 0.4 percent decrease, and from 6.0 percent to 5.0 percent, a 1 percent decrease. This represents a reduction in the gain of 50 percent and 37 percent, respectively. In the case of Ph.D.-level faculty, the pro-

TABLE 7-27. Projections of Blacks on Faculty at Selected Years Given a 25 Percent Higher Attrition Rate

	A1	A2	A3	B1	B2	B3
Percentage Non-Ph.D. Faculty						
1974	4.3	4.3	4.3	4.3	4.3	4.3
1982	4.4	4.4	4.5	4.3	4.5	4.6
1990	4.4	4.5	4.6	4.3	4.7	5.0
Percentage Ph.D. Faculty						
1974	2.1	2.1	2.1	2.1	2.1	2.1
1982	2.1	2.2	2.2	2.1	2.1	2.3
1990	2.1	2.2	2.3	2.1	2.4	2.7
Non-Ph.D. Faculty						
1974	4.3	4.3	4.3	4.3	4.3	4.3
1982	4.7	4.9	5.0	5.0	5.1	5.3
1990	4.8	4.9	5.1	5.1	5.6	6.0
Ph.D. Faculty						
1974	2.1	2.1	2.1	2.1	2.1	2.1
1982	2.3	2.4	2.5	2.4	2.5	2.7
1990	2.3	2.4	2.6	2.4	2.9	3.3

Source: Institute for the Study of Educational Policy.

jected absolute proportions show reductions ranging from 2.3 percent to 2.1 percent, a 0.2 percent decrease, and from 3.3 percent to 2.7 percent, a 0.6 percent decrease, representing elimination of all of the gains in the first case and a 50 percent reduction in the last. It is clear that the matter of persistence is crucial. The black community must take whatever steps it can to assure that the potential gains from affirmative action are not lost unnecessarily, by failure to remain in school through graduation.

The Impact of Temporary Hiring Targets

Whatever the level of relative supply, affirmative action in the sense of equal opportunity for new graduates will not generally imply that there will be no unemployment for new black graduates. Given the low levels of demand relative to supply, equal opportunity merely assures no disproportionate unemployment for blacks. As we have seen, the projections indicate that just assuring equal opportunity will result in significant unemployment for blacks if present supply and demand expectations are realized. The existence of high rates of unemployment might be expected to have a negative feedback effect on the decisions of potential graduate students, if these students are enrolling to qualify themselves for positions on college faculties. The impact of unemployment on the enrollment decisions of black students can be expected to be higher than the impact on the enrollment decisions of white students, since black students in general make higher sacrifices, in view of their lower incomes, limited access to financial aid, and poorer preparation. This would mean that the already low rate of growth in the relative supply of qualified blacks will be slowed, and thus the growth in the proportions of blacks in college will be even further retarded.

In view of the great disparity between the potential proportion of black faculty and the actual proportions of black faculty already existing, such a result would be undesirable. As a policy matter it would be desirable to ensure that the rates of black unemployment do not increase enought to discourage the increase in relative black supplies, if the desired increase in the rate of attainment of the black faculty potential is to be achieved in a reasonable time period. The struggles to achieve expanded enrollments have just begun to pay off. To permit the high unemployment rates to jeopardize the small gains already made in developing a black supply would, at a minimum, be regrettable.

One obvious way to reduce the expected high level of black unemployment is to increase the relative hiring of blacks. This can be done by explicit recognition of the necessity to go beyond the simple, current, equal employment opportunity concept implied by affirmative action, in order to eliminate past disparities. Thus, temporary hiring targets could be established for the period of demand shortages in order to eliminate the disparities between the actual presence of blacks and their potential presence. There are at least two possibilities which would relate the hiring of blacks to their potential. The first would establish targets based on the potential presence in the labor force. When this target is accomplished, blacks will not experience any unemployment (assuming affirmative action is effective) despite the overall labor surpluses, as long as the actual proportion of blacks on the faculties is below the potential proportion. As long as blacks were below 11 percent of college faculties, all available, qualified blacks would be hired. An alternative procedure that would lower un-

TABLE 7-28. Projections of Black Ph.D. Faculty for 1990 Given Equal Opportunity and an 11 Percent Hiring Target

	A1	*A2*	*A3*	*B1*	*B2*	*B3*
			Absolute Faculty Size			
Equal Opportunity	4,066	4,328	4,589	4,358	5,133	5,909
11% Target	9,574	9,710	9,722	10,792	11,715	12,232
			Percentage on Faculty			
Equal Opportunity	2.3	2.4	2.6	2.4	2.9	3.3
11% Target	5.4	5.5	5.5	6.1	6.6	6.9

Source: Institute for the Study of Educational Policy.

employment of blacks is to relate the demand for blacks to their supply potential. In this case 11 percent of the jobs would go to blacks as long as there are enough blacks available.

In the presence of adequate or excess demand these two procedures would not be necessary, and in any case would have no effect, since all of the available blacks would presumably be employed under an equal opportunity rule. However, in periods of short demand, providing equal opportunity to current job seekers perpetuates the disparities created through past discrimination. These exceptional employment rules could be justified during periods of short demand in order to overcome the effects of the legacy of racism.

The impact of using the 11 percent hiring target instead of the equal opportunity assumption was simulated, and it was found that it makes a significant difference to the absolute hiring of blacks and the rate of progress towards black representation on the labor force in academia, in accordance with the supply potential. These results are shown in Table 7-28 for Ph.D.'s and Table 7-29 for non-Ph.D.'s. As can be seen from comparing the previous projections of black Ph.D. faculty, these temporary hiring targets result in a substantial increase in the level of the black Ph.D. faculty projected for 1990. Under all of the projections the projected number of blacks among the Ph.D. faculty is more than double the base case level. The range, which varies from 9,574 to 12,232, compares to the range of from 4,066 to 5,909 in the base case projections. Naturally this also results in more than a doubling in the projected proportion of blacks on the faculty. Under

TABLE 7-29. Projections of Black Non-Ph.D. Faculty for 1990 Given Equal Opportunity and an 11 Percent Hiring Target

	A1	A2	A3	B1	B2	B3
			Absolute Faculty Size			
Equal Opportunity	15,274	15,743	16,212	16,425	17,816	19,206
11% Target	24,798	25,798	24,798	28,853	28,853	28,853
			Percentage on Faculty			
Equal Opportunity	4.8	4.9	5.1	5.1	5.6	6.0
11% Target	7.8	7.8	7.8	9.0	9.0	9.0

Source: Institute for the Study of Educational Policy.

the sample, equal opportunity assumption the projected proportion in 1990 was the range of from 2.3 percent to 3.3 percent, whereas under the temporary 11 percent hiring target the projected range in 1990 is from 5.4 percent to 5.9 percent. The proportionate increases in non-Ph.D. hiring, though not as dramatic, are also substantial. Each projection of the 1990 black faculty increases by more than 50 percent. The gains range from 53 percent to 62 percent for the A projections and from 50 percent to 75 percent for the B projections, and the presence of blacks on the non-Ph.D. faculty in 1990 rises correspondingly. Thus, for the non-Ph.D. faculty, the 1990 proportion would now be projected to range from 7.8 percent to 9.0 percent, as opposed to the base case range from 4.8 percent to 6.0 percent. It is therefore clear that substantially more could be accomplished under an affirmative action program with temporary hiring targets than under an affirmative action program which merely emphasized fair employment practices.

It seems clear that the adoption of such temporary hiring targets should not be anticipated under existing guidelines and court decisions. Procedurally their implementation would require the temporary use of a hiring quota system. A quota system would undoubtedly produce an outcry from the academic institutions. Nonetheless, such a procedure may be required in order to erase the legacy of racism within a reasonable period of time, in view of the projected slack demand, and thus new temporary guidelines might be required. The short-run cost imposed by these temporary guidelines could be absorbed until the consequences of past racism have been erased. There is no reason to expect the elimination of racism to be without cost.

Affirmative action probably will not lead to blacks being represented in equal proportions in every college's labor force. One would expect black representation to be higher in schools with the high proportions of black students located in communities with large black populations. This obviously is because blacks will be attracted to these schools for a great variety of sociological reasons, and also because the residential patterns will ensure a large concentration of black applicants in the urban locations. As the proportion of blacks increases in some of these institutions, the need for outside enforcement of affirmative action will diminish. This process of concentration should not be discouraged under the guise of equal opportunity. Nor should the presence of a relatively large ratio of black to white faculty be used as an excuse to refuse opportunities to additional blacks. On the contrary, since this process will facilitate the provision of equal opportunity to students as well as employees, the process should receive support.

General Public Policies That Could Ease the Disruption in the Academic Labor Market

It has been suggested that there will be a surplus of trained manpower in the next decade when the increased supplies of trained blacks will start appearing. These surpluses translate into increased unemployment for this high-level manpower. Of course this prediction is based upon existing trends in the overall enrollments and staffing of higher education institutions, the rate of enrollment of students in graduate programs which prepare them for academic careers, and in the utilization of this manpower by employers outside of academia. If any of the trends change, these projections will not be valid. In particular, public policy regarding higher education, the training of higher level manpower, and the utilization of this manpower by nonacademic institutions will help determine the level of surplus manpower and thus of unemployment.

There are three general ways in which public policy can influence the situation in the academic market place: (1) by affecting the academic demand; (2) by affecting the supply of trained manpower; and (3) by affecting the nonacademic demand for highly trained manpower. In the discussion below, public policies are considered that could have a beneficial effect on the outcomes of affirmative action efforts. It is not implied that all, or even most, of these policies should be pursued for the sole purpose of achieving higher levels of black participation in the academic labor forces. However, where these policies may be desirable for other reasons, their beneficial effect for black participation should add additional weight. In any case, understanding the impact of various policy possibilities on the achievement of the goals of affirmative action is important for those most concerned with the outcomes of affirmative action as well as those making the policies.

Policies to Improve General Demand for College Faculties

In view of the projections of declining enrollments, demand declines can be offset either by increasing the faculty-student ratios or by increasing enrollments. Public policies which result in higher faculty-student ratios or in increased proportions of the population enrolling in college could reduce the demand and supply gaps. There appears to be little current public support for generally expanding educational opportunities. In fact, the pressures may be in just the opposite direction. If so, the future gaps in demand and supply may be even worse than previously anticipated.

There are a variety of reasons for the declining public support for generally expanding higher education. Chief among them is the widespread belief that college education has been oversold and the returns are declining.[34] Indeed, there has been an apparent slackening of the growth in demand for college-trained manpower. This decreased demand coupled with increased enrollments has led to higher relative unemployment rates and lower salary advantages for college-trained individuals. Moreover, many of the states and localities which are heavy supporters of higher educational institutions are facing increasing fiscal difficulties and are looking for ways to reduce budgetary expenditures. Consequently, it would appear that any expansion of the higher education universe in the near future will be difficult.

Nonetheless, the higher education community might take the opportunity created by declining demand from the traditional youth market to expand their services into nontraditional markets. Offering increased educational opportunities to older age groups may be a place for future expansion. Demand from older workers, returning female workers, the retired communities, and the educationally disadvantaged could add significantly to the demand for educational services. In general, expansion of services to the nonfull-time adult community may have the potential of offsetting much of the decline in demand.

However, colleges must clearly recognize and actively pursue these opportunities, as some appear to be doing already. The services offered must be of clear value, and marketing is required. Public officials would have to be convinced of the utility of such programs in order to secure general public support. The benefits to be derived from such expansion of educational opportunities deserve close study. But if such increases in nontraditional demand can be secured, it will increase the demand for faculties and thus offset in part the supply-demand gap. This demand will clearly facilitate affirmative action efforts as well as increase the results attained from such efforts.

In order to have some idea of the impact of increased enrollments, the effect of two different cases of enrollment increase in addition to the base case (Case 1) were simulated. In the first simulation (Case 2) it was assumed that starting in 1978 enrollment would increase to higher levels for four years and then remain at the higher level throughout the period. In 1978, the new enrollment was assumed to be 2.5 percent higher than in the base case projections. In the next year 5 percent higher, in the third 7.5 percent higher, and in 1981 and subsequent years it was assumed that the enrollment levels would be 10 percent higher than in the base case. In the second simulation (Case 3), it was assumed that enrollment levels would be increased by 5 percent each year from 1978 until 1981, resulting in enrollments in 1981 and subsequent years which are 20 percent higher than in the base case projections. These enrollment increases could result from public policies or actions by higher educational institutions which expand the enrollment from nontraditional age groups or from policies or actions which increase the rate of participation among the usual college-aged groups.

The impact of the increases is shown in Table 7-30 for both Ph.D.- and master's-level faculties. As can be seen the absolute impacts are approximately the same for the A and B projections. The range of the increase over base case projections for Case 2 is from 481 to 741 persons for Ph.D.-level faculties and from 1,821 to 2,289 persons for the non-Ph.D.-level faculties.

The Case 3 projections result in gains in faculty size that are exactly double the Case 2 gains over the base case faculty size for all of the projections. Thus, policies that would increase enrollments could

TABLE 7-30. The Number and Percentage of Blacks on the Ph.D. and Non-Ph.D. Faculties in 1990: Case (1); Case (2); Case (3)

	A1	A2	A3	B1	B2	B3
			Ph.D. Level Faculty			
			Number			
Case 1	4,066	4,328	4,589	4,358	5,133	5,909
Case 2	4,547	4,913	5,279	4,839	5,745	6,650
Case 3	5,028	5,498	5,968	5,320	6,356	7,392
			Percentage			
Case 1	2.3	2.4	2.6	2.4	2.9	3.3
Case 2	2.3	2.5	2.7	2.5	2.9	3.4
Case 3	2.4	2.6	2.8	2.5	3.0	3.5
			Non-Ph.D. Level Faculty			
	A1	A2	A3	B1	B2	B3
			Number			
Case 1	15,274	15,743	16,212	16,425	17,816	19,206
Case 2	17,095	17,751	18,407	18,246	19,870	21,495
Case 3	18,916	19,749	20,601	20,067	21,925	23,783
			Percentage			
Case 1	4.8	4.9	5.1	5.1	5.6	6.0
Case 2	4.9	5.1	5.2	5.2	5.7	6.1
Case 3	4.9	5.2	5.4	5.2	5.7	6.2

Source: Institute for the Study of Educational Policy.

have a significant impact on the level of black faculty by the end of the period. Every 10 percent increase in enrollment over the base case level results in an increase ranging from 11 percent to 12 percent in the size of the black Ph.D.-level faculty and in similar increases in the size of the non-Ph.D.-level black faculty.

The impact of these enrollment increases on the proportion of blacks on the faculty is small for both Ph.D. and non-Ph.D.-level faculty. The maximum effect of a 10 percent increase in enrollment levels on the proportion of blacks in the faculty by 1990 is 0.1 percent. This obviously is because the rate of blacks hired relative to nonblacks hired is not increased by this general rise in demand. While these increases in enrollments can have a significant impact on improving general labor market conditions and reducing unemployment, they have a less dramatic impact on the rate of black participation on the faculties. This rate requires increases in the relative rate of black hiring which could result from the supply increases or the temporary hiring targets discussed above.

Policies which permit increases in faculty-student ratios could also offset part of the projected decline in demand. Faculty-student ratios have been declining throughout the period of increasing enrollments. The enrollment declines can be taken as an opportunity to restore previous faculty-student ratios. If this reversal should develop, the shortages in demand will be lessened.

The projected enrollment declines will be seized upon by some as an opportunity to reduce absolute faculty sizes and thus the absolute budget levels. However, it can also be seized as an opportunity to increase faculty-student ratios without increases in the absolute level of the budget. Of course the cost per pupil will increase but the aboslute aggregate budget size could remain steady.

Universities should examine carefully the desirability of increasing the faculty-student ratios. Quality may be related to the relative faculty-student ratios. The fact that they have currently decreased below historical levels[35] may also provide support for maintaining budget levels and permitting faculty-student ratios to rise. Finally, it would seem that, at minimum, some fluctuations of the faculty-student ratios must be permitted to avoid severe and sudden disruptions in the academic labor markets.

A specific simulation of the impact of increased faculty-student ratios has not been done. However, it should be apparent that a 10 percent increase in the faculty-student ratio has exactly the same impact on demand for faculty as a 10 percent increase in enrollments.*

---

* A proof of the observation follows.

If Faculty size F is given by

$F = \dfrac{E}{s}$ where E is enrollment and s is the faculty student ratio then the impact of a 10 percent increase in s would be given by

$\Delta F = \dfrac{E}{1.10s} - \dfrac{E}{s}$ and multiplying the first part of the right hand side by $\dfrac{1.10}{1.10}$ yields

$\Delta F = \dfrac{1.10E}{s} - \dfrac{E}{s}$ (Q.E.D.)

Thus the impact of increased faculty-student ratios would be the same as the impact of enrollment increases with a constant faculty-student ratio discussed above.

In summary, public policy encouragement of the full utilization of the available trained manpower to expand educational opportunity and to increase the quality of education should make it easier for institutions to maintain a commitment to affirmative action and thus lessen the need for enforcement agencies to provide negative incentives for affirmative action.

Policies to Moderate Rapid Supply Formation

At the same time, it may be necessary for public policy to slow the rate of growth of overall supply. It might even be desirable to stimulate a reduction in overall supply in order to avoid the excessive unemployment of this highly trained manpower. However it is done, it will be important to ensure that at minimum the supply reduction does not come at the expense of potential black enrollees. At minimum, the growth in relative black participation should be maintained.

Even more, a reduction in the absolute enrollments in graduate schools could be seized as an opportunity to increase relative black participation. In which case, the reduction in the absolute enrollments could have a favorable impact on black employment in institutions of higher education. It would result because the reduced supply-demand gap will make it easier to enforce equal opportunity. Employment of blacks will also be increased if the participation of blacks in the graduate pools is allowed to grow.

The growth of blacks participating in graduate schools will be hard to achieve, given declining overall enrollments. Clearly the availability will be there. However, current methods of screening and ranking for entry probably would not increase the black participation. In fact, the probable tendency would be a reduction in black participation. This reduction would result both because blacks fare worse on the usual admissions criteria and also because the existence of surplus applicants would permit graduate schools wider latitude in forming their entering classes and thus a greater possibility to discriminate.

It will be doubly important to enforce affirmative action in graduate school admissions if the number of places are reduced. If it can

TABLE 7-31. Percentage Distribution Employment by Employer's Category in the 1973 Roster of Doctoral Scientists and Engineers

The Name of Employer	Blacks	Whites	Total
Educational Institutions	63.7	54.1	54.1
Federal Government	7.8	8.4	8.2
Business and Industry	13.4	20.7	20.9
Other Employers	7.1	9.9	9.9
Not Employed[1]	7.8	6.9	6.9

1. Includes retired, unemployed, and nonresponse.

Source: Commission on Human Resources, National Research Council, National Academy of Sciences, *Minority Groups among United States Doctorate Level Scientists, Engineers and Scholars, 1973* (Washington, D.C.: National Academy of Sciences, 1974), p. 30.

be achieved, then such a public policy strategy to deal with the expected unemployment will not hurt blacks and may help.

The impact of this strategy depends strictly on the effect it has on the ratio of blacks in the graduating schools. The effect of varying rates of growth of the black presence has already been discussed. That discussion should give some indication of the numerical impact of supply restriction policies.

Policies Encouraging Alternative Use of Manpower

Finally, public policy might encourage the utilization of highly trained manpower by other nonacademic employers. Currently only a fraction of those persons attaining advanced degrees work for academic institutions. At the master's level, graduate college teaching is apparently not the major source of employment while the reverse is true for Ph.D.-level graduates.

Table 7-31 shows the distribution by category of employers of the Ph.D.-level scientific manpower. As can be seen, 54 percent of the total stock works for academic institutions. For blacks, however, a larger percentage, almost 64 percent, depend on educational institutions for employment. These figures show that part of the increasing stocks of manpower could be absorbed in nonacademic uses. Moreover, in view of the relative underrepresentation of blacks in the stocks of those

TABLE 7-32. Percentage Distribution of Academic Employment by Type of Activity[1]

	Black	White	Total
Teaching	61.9	60.7	60.4
Administration	15.5	8.9	8.6
Research	8.1	20.5	20.8
Other	14.4	9.9	10.1

1. May not add to 100% due to rounding.

Source: ISEP calculations based on Commission on Human Resources, National Research Council, National Academy of Sciences, *Minority Groups among United States Doctorate Level Scientists, Engineers, and Scholars, 1973* (Washington, D.C.: National Academy of Sciences), p. 30.

employed in nonacademic pursuits, it should prove a more important potential source of black employment.

Even within academic employment there are other uses for high-level personnel than teaching. Table 7-32 shows the distributions of employment in the different areas of academic institutions. As can be seen, overall only 60.4 percent reported teaching and administrative positions, whereas almost 21 percent indicated research as their principal work activity. Note again that blacks are relatively over-represented in the teaching and administration categories and under-represented in the research category. It again indicates that if past patterns persist, blacks will suffer most from the reductions in enrollment. On the other hand, the low current representation in the research area would suggest it as a potential source of demand for blacks in the future.

Increases in the use of highly trained manpower in nonacademic and nonteaching pursuits could partially offset the declining demand for college teachers. Public policy could encourage the use of the excess availability of this highly trained manpower to expand research and other activities to deal with the many pressing problems facing society. Business and industry might seize this opportunity to increase the human capital input into their activities. However, prospects for expansion in demand from the alternative sources are not clear. Further study is necessary in this regard.

These policies will have no direct impact on the presence of blacks on university faculties. Nonetheless, they could ease the unemployment situation. This would be important as it would reduce the impact of the slack academic market on the formation of black supply and ease the enforcement of affirmative action.

Conclusions

The projections which are presented previously clearly show that prospects for overcoming the current low participation of blacks on the faculties of higher educational institutions could be bright despite current trends in enrollment, staffing, and graduation rates, if the affirmative action effort is successful and if policies are adopted to ease the difficult labor market situation. It has been shown that the validity of the base case projections will depend to a great extent on the types of public policies pursued over the next fifteen years. There is the possibility for policies which could offset many of the unfavorable outcomes of the base case projections. These policies would result in increased participation of blacks in employment opportunities of higher educational institutions. In the absence of appropriate policies and vigorous enforcement of affirmative action efforts, the base case projections clearly indicate that the pace of attainment of eventual parity will be slow. And, in any case, if much is to be achieved, actions which go significantly beyond the assurance of equality of opportunity are clearly required.

Epilogue

The Case for Affimative Action for Blacks in Higher Education originated out of a sense of urgency. By 1974-75, it was clear that affirmative action was increasingly under attack. This monograph grew out of the conviction that the strategy of affirmative action needed support. To strengthen the affirmative action effort, an analysis and evaluation of the program within the higher education community was conducted. While we have not exhausted a very complex subject, nothing that we have uncovered has caused us to depart from our original belief that affirmative action is a useful and necessary strategy, if equal employment opportunity is to be achieved in institutions of higher education.

Our historical and theoretical analyses, literature review, and discussions with numerous government officials, faculty members, administrators, researchers and other interested parties indicate that affirmative action has had an effect on academia's traditional hiring practices. Also our examination of constitutional amendments, civil rights laws, court cases and executive orders clearly illustrates that the legal foundations of affirmative action are indeed sound.

Our analysis of the affirmative action effort makes it clear that the actions required by the government's programs are designed to eliminate invidious racial discrimination in employment. Critics, however, view such requirements as validation of hiring standards, which may have a racially biased impact, as a violation of "academic freedom." Again critics have charged that the establishment and use of numerical goals amounts to "reverse discrimination." Our study of these issues has left us thoroughly convinced that such charges are a complete misunderstanding of affirmative action requirements. Rather, these practices are intended to ensure that the system is racially unbiased. We con-

272

clude that an institution should not be permitted to make hiring decisions based on irrelevant job criteria which have a racially biased impact, if the employment system is to provide equal opportunity. Hence, a major objective of the study has been to clarify some of the issues involved in the affirmative action effort.

We further conclude that if affirmative action is to work for blacks, it must include concrete efforts to erase the effects of past racist practices; such efforts must include special admissions programs for minority students. It seems clear to us that these practices are also valid. One needs only to recognize that discrimination produces effects that are long lasting and that handicap individuals long after the initial discriminatory acts have been ended. When one also recognizes that disparities can be transmitted intergenerationally, the case for special minority admissions programs is even stronger. While members of a discriminated class can ultimately overcome the effects of past discrimination, it certainly has not been established that this is a necessary outcome. Moreover, it is clear that it would take a considerable amount of time, perhaps generations, to overcome such disparities.

As long as the state has a legitimate interest in establishing a just and fair society, it would follow that the state also has a legitimate interest in undertaking and encouraging such remedial efforts to ensure justice and fairness. There can be no legitimate claim of "reverse discrimination" in these efforts since they are remedial in nature and are intended solely to overturn the effects of past discrimination.

It is important that any remedial efforts be well constructed and implemented so as to avoid unnecessary misunderstandings. Although these efforts are difficult to implement, it is possible, and is important enough, that more thought should be given to ways of eliminating the effects of past discrimination while minimizing undesirable side effects.

While we have in general found that much of the critical literature in this area is overly harsh and often deliberately misleading, we also have found that the current effort to provide affirmative action is not without flaws. We have found problems in both the design and implementation of the affirmative action strategy. Where we had positive suggestions, we have made them. Nonetheless, we find the concept sound despite all of the legitimate complaints which might be lodged against the efforts to implement affirmative action. However, these problems are immediately correctable. On balance, affirmative action is so vitally important as a strategy to promote equal opportunity that its benefits outweigh the cost associated with its current weaknesses. The concept of affirmative action is simple. It places the responsibility on the employer to undertake positive actions to ensure that the employment system is fair. It also implies that the government ought to undertake positive actions to eliminate the effects of past discrimination. Without these requirements, attempts to bring about equal opportunity within a reasonable period of time would be difficult to achieve.

Our analysis of the current situation for blacks in academe makes it clear that a fair system has not been established. Our projections reveal that the rate of progress towards eliminating the disparities through the achievement of nondiscriminatory employment practices will be slow. Twenty years from now the proportion of blacks among both Ph.D. and non-Ph.D. faculties will still be far below parity, even if the requirements of affirmative action are aggressively implemented. We think that both policymakers and critics of affirmative action are not sufficiently aware of the inherent limitations of this effort. Nonetheless, ensuring the fairness of current practices is of paramount importance. Fairness is a legitimate social goal in and of itself.

Finally it is clear to us that equal opportunity cannot be ensured without disrupting business as usual. Almost everybody is willing to undertake equal opportunity if it involves no cost. However, by definition affirmative action will require most institutions to alter their traditional practices that produce discriminatory outcomes. It is also the case that affirmative action programs designed to increase the supply require, by definition, the expenditure of extra resources. This requires by necessity that blacks be treated differently than whites. In short, the effort to correct the results of past discrimination and to prevent the occurrence of current discrimination requires action which interrupt the status quo.

After this manuscript went to press, the Supreme Court ruled in the controversial case, *Bakke* v. *The Regents of the University of California.* By a five-to-four margin the Court, on June 28, 1978, upheld the California Supreme Court decision striking down the special minority admissions program at the University of California, Davis Medical School and ordered Allan Bakke admitted. The Court also ruled by a five-to-four vote that race may be taken into consideration in developing future admissions programs, reversing the California Supreme Court in ruling that race could not be used as a factor in admissions. Justice Lewis Powell stated that where racial ratios are based upon past discrimination, there must be a previous finding of the past discrimination by an authoritative and competent entity. However, student diversity is a compelling state interest which permits race to be taken into account in a properly constructed admissions program. Four Justices thought the affirmative action program at the Davis Medical School violated Title VI of the 1964 Civil Rights Act, but they did not discuss the constitutional question. Four other Justices thought the program was consistent with the Equal Protection Clause. After the Supreme Court ruling in the *Bakke* case, a shroud of uncertainty remains over those programs not well devised.

Justice Powell used the Harvard Special Minority Admissions program as an example of how race could be taken into consideration. Those institutions genuinely interested in increasing minority representation in college and university student bodies will be able to do so. Further, affirmative action in employment, as defined in this study, remains a viable program for achieving equal employment opportunity. As this study indicates, continued advancement in this area is dependent directly upon how vigorously these admissions policies are implemented. Consequently, blacks and other minority groups will have to remain vigilant to avoid a retrenchment in the area of special admissions.

This study has convinced us of the importance of affirmative action. We hope that it contributes to a strengthening of these undertakings by helping to create a better understanding of affirmative action and by contributing to the reduction of flaws in the existing program. The urgency of the matter of achieving equal opportunity still remains. What is required is a redoubling and renewing of the commitment, if this social goal is to be achieved during this century.

Appendix A

Historical Documents

Dred Scott v. *Sanford,* Supreme Court of the United States,
19 How. 60 U.S. 393 (1857).

MR. CHIEF JUSTICE TANEY delivered the opinion of the Court.

This case has been twice argued. After the argument at the last term, differences of opinion were found to exist among the members of the court; and as the questions in controversy are of the highest importance, and the court was at that time much pressed by the ordinary business of the term, it was deemed advisable to continue the case, and direct a re-argument on some of the points, in order that we might have an opportunity of giving to the whole subject a more deliberate consideration. It has accordingly been again argued by counsel, and considered by the court; and I now proceed to deliver its opinion. . . .

The plaintiff was a negro slave, belonging to Dr. Emerson, who was a surgeon in the army of the United States. In the year 1834, he took the plaintiff from the State of Missouri to the military post at Rock Island, in the State of Illinois, and held him there as a slave until the month of April or May, 1836. At the time last mentioned, said Dr. Emerson removed the plaintiff from said military post at Rock Island to the military post at Fort Snelling, situated on the west bank of the Mississippi River, in the Territory known as Upper Louisiana, acquired by the United States of France, and situated north of the latitude of thirty-six degrees thirty minutes north, and north of the State of Missouri. Said Dr. Emerson held the plaintiff in slavery at said Fort Snelling, from said last-mentioned date until the year 1838.

In the year 1835, Harriet, who is named in the second court of the plaintiff's declaration, was the negro slave of Major Taliaferro, who belonged to the army of the United States. In that year, 1835, said Major Taliaferro took said Harriet to said Fort Snelling, a military post, situated as hereinbefore stated, and kept her there as a slave until the year 1836, and then sold and delivered her as a slave, at said Fort Snelling, unto the said Dr.

Emerson hereinbefore named. Said Dr. Emerson held said Harriet in slavery at said Fort Snelling until the year 1838.

In the year 1836, the plaintiff and Harriet intermarried, at Fort Snelling, with the consent of Dr. Emerson, who then claimed to be their master and owner. Eliza and Lizzie, named in the third count of the plaintiff's declaration, are the fruit of that marriage. Eliza is about fourteen years old, and was born on board the steamboat *Gipsey*, north of the north line of the State of Missouri, and upon the river Mississippi. Lizzie is about seven years old, and was born in the State of Missouri, at the military post called Jefferson Barracks.

In the year 1838, said Dr. Emerson removed the plaintiff and said Harriet, and their said daughter Eliza, from said Fort Snelling to the State of Missouri, where they have ever since resided.

Before the commencement of this suit, said Dr. Emerson sold and conveyed the plaintiff, and Harriet, Eliza, and Lizzie, to the defendant, as slaves, and the defendant has ever since claimed to hold them, and each of them, as slaves. . . .

There are two leading questions presented by the record:

1. Had the Circuit Court of the United States jurisdiction to hear and determine the case between these parties? And

2. If it had jurisdiction, is the judgment it has given erroneous or not?

The plaintiff in error, who was also the plaintiff in the court below, was, with his wife and children, held as slaves by the defendant, in the State of Missouri; and he brought this action in the Circuit Court of the United States for that district, to assert the title of himself and his family to freedom.

The declaration is in the form usually adopted in that State to try questions of this description, and contains the averment necessary to give the court jurisdiction; that he and the defendant are citizens of different States; that is, that he is a citizen of Missouri, and the defendant a citizen of New York.

The defendant pleaded in abatement to the jurisdiction of the court, that the plaintiff was not a citizen of the State of Missouri, as alleged in his declaration, being a negro of African descent, whose ancestors were of pure African blood, and who were brought into this country and sold as slaves. . . .

The question is simply this: Can a negro, whose ancestors were imported into this country, and sold as slaves, become a member of the political community formed and brought into existence by the Constitution of the United States, and as such become entitled to all the rights, and privileges, and immunities, guaranteed by that instrument to the citizen? One of which rights is the privilege of suing in a court of the United States in the cases specified in the Constitution. . . .

We proceed to examine the case as presented by the pleadings.

The words "people of the United States" and "citizens" are synonymous terms, and mean the same thing. They both describe the political body who, according to our republican institutions, form the sovereignty, and who hold the power and conduct the Government through their representatives. They are what we familiarly call the "sovereign people," and every citizen is one of this people, and a constituent member of this sovereignty. The question before us is, whether the class of persons described in the plea in abatement compose a portion of this people, and are contituent members of this sovereignty? We think they are not, and they are not included, and were not intended to be included, under the word "citizens" in the Constitution, and can therefore claim none of the rights and privileges which that instrument provides for and secures to citizens of the United States. On the contrary, they were at that time considered as a subordinate and inferior class of beings, who had been subjugated by the dominant race, and, whether emancipated or not, yet remained subject to their authority, and had no rights or privileges but such as those who held the power and the Government might choose to grant them. . . .

In discussing this question, we must not confound the rights of citizenship which a State may confer within its own limits, and the rights of citizenship as a member of the Union. It does not by any means follow, because he has all the rights and privileges of a citizen of a State, that he must be a citizen of the United States. He may have all of the rights and privileges of the citizen of the State, and yet not be entitled to the rights and privileges of a citizen in any other State. For, previous to the adoption of the Constitution of the United States, every State had the undoubted right to confer on whomsoever it pleased the character of citizen, and to endow him with all its rights. But this character of course was confined to the boundaries of the State, and gave him no rights or privileges in other States beyond those secured to him by the law of nations and the comity of States. Nor have the several States surrendered the power of conferring these rights and privileges by adopting the Constitution of the United States. Each State may still confer them upon an alien, or any one it thinks proper, or upon any class or description of persons; yet he would not be a citizen in the sense in which that word is used in the Constitution of the United States, nor entitled to sue as such in one of its courts, nor to the privileges and immunities of a citizen in the other States. The rights which he would acquire would be restricted to the State which gave them. The Constitution has conferred on Congress the right to establish a uniform rule of naturalization, and this right is evidently exclusive, and has always been held by this court to be so. Consequently, no State, since the adoption of the Constitution, can by naturalizing an alien invest him with the rights and privileges secured to a citizen of a State under the Federal Government, although, so far as the State alone was concerned, he would undoubtedly be entitled to the rights of a citizen, and clothed with all the rights and immunities which the Constitution and laws of the State attached to that character. . . .

It becomes necessary, therefore, to determine who were citizens of the several States when the Constitution was adopted. And in order to do this, we must recur to the Governments and institutions of the thirteen colonies, when they separated from Great Britain and formed new sovereignties, and took their places in the family of independent nations. We must inquire who, at that time, were recognised as the people or citizens of a State, whose rights and liberties had been outraged by the English Government; and who declared their independence, and assumed the powers of Government to defend their rights by force of arms.

In the opinion of the court, the legislation and histories of the times, and the language used in the Declaration of Independence, show, that neither the class of persons who had been imported as slaves, nor their descendants, whether they had become free or not, were then acknowledged as a part of the people, nor intended to be included in the general words used in that memorable instrument.

It is difficult at this day to realize the state of public opinion in relation to that unfortunate race, which prevailed in the civilized and enlightened portions of the world at the time of the Declaration of Independence, and when the Constitution of the United States was framed and adopted. But the public history of every European nation displays it in a manner too plain to be mistaken.

They had for more than a century before been regarded as beings of an inferior order, and altogether unfit to associate with the white race, either in social or political relations; and so far inferior, that they had no rights which the white man was bound to respect; and that the negro might justly and lawfully be reduced to slavery for his benefit. He was bought and sold, and treated as an ordinary article of merchandise and traffic, whenever a profit could be made by it. This opinion was at that time fixed and universal in the civilized portion of the white race. It was regarded as an axiom in morals as well as in politics, which no one thought of disputing, or supposed to be open to dispute; and men in every grade and position in society daily and habitually acted upon it in their private pursuits, as well as in matters of public concern, without doubting for a moment the correctness of this opinion.

And in no nation was this opinion more firmly fixed or more uniformly acted upon than by the English Government and English people. They not only seized them on the coast of Africa, and sold them or held them in slavery for their own use; but they took them as ordinary articles of merchandise to every country where they could make a profit on them, and were far more extensively engaged in this commerce than any other nation in the world.

The opinion thus entertained and acted upon in England was naturally impressed upon the colonies they founded on this side of the Atlantic. And, accordingly, a negro of the African race was regarded by them as an article of property, and held, and bought and sold as such, in every one of the thirteen colonies which united in the Declaration of Independence, and afterwards formed the Constitution of the United States. The slaves were more or less numerous in the different colonies, as slave labor was found more or less profitable. But no one seems to have doubted the correctness of the prevailing opinion of the time.

The legislation of the different colonies furnishes positive and indisputable proof of this fact. . . .

The language of the Declaration of Independence is equally conclusive: . . . .

This state of public opinion had undergone no change when the Constitution was adopted, as is equally evident from its provisions and language. . . .

Indeed, when we look to the condition of this race in the several States at the time, it is impossible to believe that these rights and privileges were intended to be extended to them.

It is very true, that in that portion of the Union where the labor of the negro race was found to be unsuited to the climate and unprofitable to the master, but few slaves were held at the time of the Declaration of Independence; and when the Constitution was adopted, it had entirely worn out in one of them, and measures had been taken for its gradual abolition in several others. But this change had not been produced by any change of opinion in relation to this race; but because it was discovered, from experience, that slave labor was unsuited to the climate and production of these States: for some of the States, where it had ceased or nearly ceased to exist, were actively engaged in the slave trade, procuring cargoes on the coast of Africa, and transporting them for sale to those parts of the Union where their labor was found to be profitable, and suited to the climate and productions. And this traffic was openly carried on, and fortunes accumulated by it, without reproach from the people of the States where they resided. And it can hardly be supposed that, in the States where it was then countenanced in its worst form—that is, in the seizure and transportation—the people could have regarded those who were emancipated as entitled to equal rights with themselves. . . .

The legislation of the States therefore shows, in a manner not to be mistaken, the inferior and subject condition of that race at the time the Constitution was adopted, and long afterwards, throughout the thirteen States by which that instrument was framed; and it is hardly consistent with the respect due to these States, to suppose that they regarded at that time, as fellow-citizens and members of the sovereignty, a class of beings whom they had thus stigmatized; whom, as we are bound, out of respect to the State sovereignties, to assume that had deemed it just and necessary thus to stigmatize, and upon whom they had impressed such deep and enduring marks of inferiority and degradation; or, that when they met in convention to form the Constitution, they looked upon them as a portion of their constituents, or designed to include them in the provisions so carefully inserted for the security and protection of the liberties and rights of their citizens. It cannot be supposed that they intended to secure to them rights, and privileges, and rank, in the new political body throughout the Union, which every one of them denied within the limits of its own dominion. More especially, it cannot be believed that the large slaveholding States regarded them as included in the word citizens, or would have consented to a Constitution which might compel them to receive them in that character from another State. For if they were so received, and entitled to the privileges and immunities of citizens, it would exempt them from the operation of the special laws and from the police regulations which they considered to be necessary for their own safety. It would give to persons of the negro race, who were recognized as citizens in any one State of the Union, the right to enter every other State whenever they pleased, singly or in companies, without pass or passport, and without obstruction, to sojourn there as long as they pleased, to go where they pleased at every hour of the day or night without molestation, unless they committed some violation of law for which white man would be punished; and it would give them the full liberty of speech in public and in private upon all subjects upon which its own citizens might speak; to hold public meetings upon political affairs, and to keep and carry arms wherever they went. And all of this would be done in the face of the subject race of the same color, both free and slaves, and inevitably producing discontent and insubordination among them, and endangering the peace and safety of the State. . . .

No one, we presume, supposes that any change in public opinion or feeling, in relation to this unfortunate race, in the civilized nations of Europe or in this country, should induce the court to give to the words of the Constitution a more liberal construction in their favor than they were intended to bear when the instrument was framed and adopted. Such an argument would be altogether inadmissible in any tribunal called on to interpret it. If any of its provisions are deemed unjust, there is a mode prescribed in the instrument itself by which it may be amended; but while it remains unaltered, it must be construed now as it was understood at the time of its adoption. It is not only the same in words, but the same in meaning, and delegates the same powers to the Government, and reserves and secures the same rights and privileges to the citizen; and as long as it continues to exist in its present form it speaks not only in the same words, but with the same meaning and intent with which it spoke when it came from the hands of its framers, and was voted on and adopted by the people of the United States. Any other rule of construction would abrogate the judicial character of this court, and make it the mere reflex of the popular opinion or passion of the day. This court was not created by the Constitution for such purposes. Higher and graver trusts have been confided to it, and it must not falter in the path of duty. . . .

And upon a full and careful consideration of the subject, the court is of opinion, that, upon the facts stated in the plea in abatement, Dred Scott was not a citizen of Missouri within the meaning of the Constitution of the United States, and not entitled as such to sue in its courts; and, consequently, that the Circuit Court had no jurisdiction of the case, and that the judgment on the plea in abatement is erroneous.

We are aware that doubts are entertained by some of the members of the court, whether the plea in abatement is legally before the court upon this writ of error; but if that plea is regarded as waived, or out of the case upon any other ground, yet the question as to the jurisdiction of the Circuit Court is presented on the face of the bill of exception itself, taken by the plaintiff at the trial; for he admits that he and his wife were born slaves, but endeavors to make out his title to freedom and citizenship by showing that they were taken by their owner to certain places, hereinafter mentioned, where slavery could not by law exist, and that they thereby became free, and upon their return to Missouri became citizens of that State.

Now, if the removal of which he speaks did not give them their freedom, then by his own admission he is still a slave; and whatever opinions may be entertained in favor of the citizenship of a free person of the African race, no one supposes that a slave is a citizen of the State of the United States. If, therefore, the acts done by his owner did not make them free persons, he is still a slave, and certainly incapable of suing in the character of a citizen.

The principle of law is too well settled to be disputed, that a court can give no judgment for either party, where it has no jurisdiction; and if, upon the showing of Scott himself, it appeared that he was still a slave, the case ought to have been dismissed, and the judgment against him and in favor of the defendant for costs, is, like that on the plea in abatement, erroneous, and the suit ought to have been dismissed by the Circuit Court for want of jurisdiction in that court.

But, before we proceed to examine this part of the case, it may be proper to notice an objection taken to the judicial authority of this court to decide it; and it has been said, that as this court has decided against the jurisdiction of the Circuit Court on the plea in abatement, it has no right to examine any question presented by the exception; and that anything it may say upon that part of the case will be extra-judicial, and mere obiter dicta.

This is a manifest mistake; there can be no doubt as to the jurisdiction of this court to revise the judgment of a Circuit Court, and to reverse if for any error apparent on the record, whether it be the error of giving judgment in a case over which it had no jurisdiction, or any other material error; and this, too, whether there is a plea in abatement or not. . . .

We proceed, therefore, to inquire whether the facts relied on by the plaintiff entitled him to his freedom. . . .

In considering this part of the controversy, two questions arise:

1. Was he, together with his family, free in Missouri by reason of the stay in the territory of the United States hereinbefore mentioned?

2. If they were not, is Scott himself free by reason of his removal to Rock Island, in the State of Illinois, as stated in the above admissions?

We proceed to examine the first question.

The act of Congress, upon which the plaintiff relies, declares that slavery and involuntary servitude, except as a punishment for crime, shall be forever prohibited in all parts of the territory ceded by France, under the name of Louisiana, which lies north of thirty-six degrees thirty minutes north latitude and not included within the limits of Missouri. And the difficulty which meets us at the threshold of this part of the inquiry is, whether Congress was authorized to pass this law under any of the powers granted to it by the Constitution; for if the authority is not given by that instrument, it is the duty of this court to declare it void and inoperative, and incapable of conferring freedom upon any one who is held as a slave under the laws of any one of the States.

The counsel for the plaintiff has laid much stress upon that article in the Constitution which confers on Congress the power "to dispose of and make all needful rules and regulations respecting the territory or other property belonging to the United States"; but, in the judgment of the court, that provision has no bearing on the present controversy, and the power there given, whatever it may be, is confined, and was intended to be confined, to the territory which at that time belonged to, or was claimed by, the United States, and was within their boundaries as settled by the treaty with Great Britain, and can have no influence upon a territory afterwards acquired from a foreign Government. It was a special provision for a known and particular territory, and to meet a present emergency and nothing more. . . .

But the power of Congress over the person or property of a citizen can never be a mere discretionary power under our Constitution and form of Government. The powers of the Government and the rights and privileges of the citizen are regulated and plainly defined by the Constitution itself. And when the territory becomes a part of the United States, the Federal Government enters into possession in the character impressed upon it by those who created it. It enters upon it with its powers over the citizen strictly defined, and limited by the Constitution, from which it derives its own existence, and by virtue of which alone it continues to exist and act as a Government and sovereignty. It has no power of any kind beyond it; and it cannot, when it enters a Territory of the United States, put off its character, and assume discretionary or despotic powers which the Constitution has denied to it. It cannot create for itself a new character separated from the citizens of the United States, and the duties it owes them under the provisions of the Constitution. The Territory being a part of the United States, the Government and the citizen both enter it under the authority of the Constitution, with their respective rights defined and marked out; and the Federal Government can exercise no power over his person or property, beyond what that instrument confers, nor lawfully deny any right which it has reserved. . . .

Now, as we have already said in an earlier part of this opinion, upon a different point, the right of property in a slave is distinctly and expressly affirmed in the Constitution. The right to traffic in it, like an ordinary article of merchandise and property, was guaranteed to the citizens of the United States, in every State that might desire it, for twenty years. And the Government in express terms is pledged to protect it in all future time, if the slave escapes from his owner. This is done in plain words—too plain to be misunderstood. And no word can be found in the Constitution which gives Congress a greater power over slave property, or which entitles property of that kind to less protection than property of any other description. The only power conferred is the power coupled with the duty of guarding and protecting the owner in his rights.

Upon these considerations, it is the opinion of the court that the act of Congress which prohibited a citizen from holding and owning property of this kind in the territory of the United States north of the line therein mentioned, is not warranted by the Constitution, and is therefore void; and that neither Dred Scott himself, nor any of his family, were made free by being carried into this Territory; even if they had been carried there by the owner, with the intention of becoming a permanent resident.

We have so far examined the case, as it stands under the Constitution of the United States, and the powers thereby delegated to the Federal Government.

But there is another point in the case which depends on State power and State Law. And it is contended, on the part of the plaintiff, that he is made free by being taken to Rock Island, in the State of Illinois independently of his residence in the territory of the United States; and being so made free, he was not again reduced to a state of slavery by being brought back to Missouri. . . .

The plaintiff, it appears, brought a similar action against the defendant in the State court of Missouri claiming the freedom of himself and his family upon the same grounds and the same evidence upon which he relies in the case before the court. The case was carried before the Supreme Court of the State; was fully argued there; and that court decided that neither the plaintiff nor his family were entitled to freedom, and were still the slaves of the defendant; and reversed the judgment of the inferior State court, which had given a different decision. If the plaintiff supposed that this judgment of the Supreme Court of the State was erroneous, and that this court had jurisdiction to revise and reverse it, the only mode by which he could legally bring it before this court was by writ of error directed to the Supreme Court of the State, requiring it to transmit the record to this court. If this had been done, it is too plain for argument that the writ must have been dismissed for want of jurisdiction in this court. . . .

Upon the whole, therefore, it is the judgment of this court, that it appears by the record before us that the plaintiff in error is not a citizen of Missouri, in the sense in which that word is used in the Constitution; and that the Circuit Court of the United States, for that reason, had no jurisdiction in the case, and could give no judgment in it. Its judgment for the defendant must, consequently, be reversed, and a mandate issued, directing the suit to be dismissed for want of jurisdiction.

Lincoln's Preliminary Emancipation Proclamation (September 22, 1862)

I, Abraham Lincoln, President of the United States of America, and commander-in-chief of the army and navy thereof, do hereby proclaim and declare that hereafter, as heretofore, the war will be prosecuted for the object of practically restoring the constitutional relation between the United States and each of the States, and the people thereof, in which States that relation is or may be suspended or disturbed.

That is my purpose, upon the next meeting of Congress, to again recommend the adoption of a practical measure tendering pecuniary aid to the free acceptance or rejection of all slave States, so called, the people whereof may not then be in rebellion against the United States, and which States may then have voluntarily adopted, or thereafter may voluntarily adopt, immediate or gradual abolishment of slavery within their respective limits; and that the effort to colonize persons of African descent with their consent upon this continent or elsewhere, with the previously obtained consent of the governments existing there, will be continued.

That on the first day of January, in the year of our Lord one thousand eight hundred and sixty-three, all persons held as slaves within any State or designated part of a State the people whereof shall then be in rebellion against the United States, shall be then, thenceforward, and forever free; and the Executive Government of the United States, including the military and naval authority thereof, will recognize and maintain the freedom of such persons, and will do no act or acts to repress such persons, or any of them, in any efforts they may make for their actual freedom.

That the Executive will, on the first day of January aforesaid, by proclamation designate the States and parts of States, if any, in which the people thereof, respectively, shall then be in rebellion against the United States; and the fact that any State, or the people thereof, shall on that day be in good faith represented in the Congress, of the United States by members chosen thereto at elections wherein a majority of the qualified voters of such State shall have participated, shall, in the absence of strong countervailing testimony, be deemed conclusive evidence that such State, and the people thereof, are not then in rebellion against the United States.

That attention is hereby called to an Act of Congress entitled "An Act to make an additional article of war," approved 13 March 1862, and which Act is in the words and figures following:

> Be it enacted by the Senate and House of Representatives of the United States of America in Congress assembled, That hereafter the following shall be promulgated as an additional article of war, for the government of the army of the United States, and shall be obeyed and observed as such:
>
> ARTICLE: All officers or persons in the military or naval service of the United States are prohibited from employing any of the forces under their respective commands for the purpose of returning fugitives from service or labor who may have escaped from any person to whom such service or labor is claimed to be due; and any officer who shall be found guilty by a court martial of violating this article shall be dismissed from the service.
>
> SEC. 2. And be it further enacted, That this Act shall take effect from and after its passage.

Also to the ninth and tenth sections of an Act entitled "An Act to suppress insurrection, to punish treason and rebellion, to seize and confiscate property of rebels, and for other purposes," approved 17 July 1862, and which sections are in the words and figures following:

> SEC. 9. And be it further enacted, That all slaves of persons who shall hereafter be engaged in rebellion against the Government of the United States, or who shall in any way give aid or comfort thereto, escaping from such persons and taking refuge within the lines of the army; and all slaves captured from such persons or deserted by them and coming under the control of the Government of the United States; and all slaves of such persons found *on* [or] being within any place occupied by rebel forces and afterwards occupied by the forces of the United States, shall be deemed captives of war, and shall be forever free of their servitude, and not again held as slaves.
>
> SEC. 10. And be it further enacted, That no slave escaping into any State, Territory, or the District of Columbia, from any other State, shall be delivered up, or in any way impeded or hindered of his liberty, except for crime, or some offense against the laws, unless the person claiming said fugitive shall first make oath that the person to whom the labor or service of such fugitive is alleged to be due is his lawful owner, and has not borne arms against the United States in the present rebellion, nor in any way given aid and comfort thereto; and no person engaged in the military or

naval service of the United States shall, under any pretense whatever, assume to decide on the validity of the claim of any person to the service or labor of any other person, or surrender up any such person to the claimant, on pain of being dismissed from the service.

And I do hereby enjoin upon and order all persons engaged in the military and naval service of the United States to observe, obey, and enforce, within their respective spheres of service, the Act and sections above recited.

And the Executive will in due time recommend that all citizens of the United States who shall have remained loyal thereto throughout the rebellion shall (upon the restoration of the constitutional relation between the United States and their respective States and people, if that relation shall have been suspended or disturbed) be compensated for all losses by Acts of the United States, including the loss of slaves.

In witness whereof, I have hereunto set my hand and caused the seal of the United States to be affixed.

Done at the city of Washington, this twenty-second day of September, in the year of our Lord one thousand [L.S.] eight hundred and sixty-two and of the independence of the United States the eighty-seventh.

ABRAHAM LINCOLN

The Emancipation Proclamation
(January 1, 1863)

Whereas, on the twenty-second day of September, in the year of our Lord one thousand eight hundred and sixty-two, a Proclamation was issued by the President of the United States, containing among other things the following, to wit:

"That on the First Day of January, in the Year of our Lord One Thousand Eight Hundred and Sixty-three, all persons held as Slaves within any State, or designated part of a State, the people whereof shall there be in rebellion against the United States, shall be then thenceforth and FOREVER FREE, and the Executive Government of the United States, including the Military and Naval authority thereof, will recognize and maintain the freedom of such persons, and will do no act or acts to repress such persons, or any of them, in any effort they may make for their actual freedom.

"That the Executive will, on the first day of January aforesaid, by Proclamation, designate the States and parts of the States, if any, in which the people therein respectively shall then be in Rebellion against the United States, and the fact that any State, or the people thereof, shall on that day be in good faith represented in the Congress of the United States by Members chosen thereto at elections wherein a majority of the qualified voters of such State shall have participated, shall, in the absence of strong countervailing testimony, be deemed conclusive evidence that such State and the people thereof are not then in Rebellion against the United States."

Now, therefore, I, Abraham Lincoln, President of the United States, by virtue of the power vested in me as Commander-in-Chief of the Army and Navy of the United States, in time of actual armed rebellion against the authority and Government of the United States, and as a fit and necessary war measure for suppressing said Rebellion, do, on this first day of January, in the year of our Lord one thousand eight hundred and sixty-three, and in accordance with my purpose so to do, publicly proclaim for the full period of one hundred days from the date of the first above-mentioned order, and designate, as the States and parts of States wherein the people thereof, respectively, are this day in rebellion against the United States, the following, to wit: Arkansas, Texas, Louisiana—except the Parishes of St. Bernard, Plaquemines, Jefferson, St. John, St. Charles, St. James, Ascension, Assumption, Terre Bonne, La-fourch, St. Mary, St. Martin and Orleans, including the City of New-Orleans—Mississippi, Alabama, Florida, Georgia, South Carolina, North Carolina, and Virginia, and also the counties of Berkley, Accomac, Northampton, Elizabeth City, York, Princess Ann, and Norfolk, including the cities of Norfolk and Portsmouth—and which excepted parts are, for the present, left precisely as if this Proclamation were not issued.

And by virtue of the power and for the purpose aforesaid, I do order and declare that ALL PERSONS HELD AS SLAVES within said designated States and parts of States ARE, AND HENCEFORWARD SHALL BE FREE! and that the Executive Government of the United States, including the Military and Naval Authorities thereof, will recognize and maintain the freedom of said persons.

And I hereby enjoin upon the people so declared to be free, to abstain from all violence, unless in necessary self-defense; and I recommend to them that in all cases, when allowed, they labor faithfully for reasonable wages.

And I further declare and make known, that such persons, of suitable condition, will be received into the armed service of the United States, to garrison forts, positions, stations, and other places, and to man vessels of all sorts in said service.

And, upon this, sincerely believed to be an act of justice, warranted by the Constitution, upon military necessity, I invoke the considerate judgment of mankind and the gracious favor of Almighty God. . . .

Thirteenth Amendment (1865)

SEC. 1. Neither slavery nor involuntary servitude, except as a punishment for crime whereof the part shall have been duly convicted, shall exist within the United States, or any place subject to their jurisdiction.

SEC. 2. Congress shall have power to enforce this article by appropriate legislation.

Fourteenth Amendment (1868)

SEC. 1. All persons born or naturalized in the United States, and subject to the jurisdiction thereof, are citizens of the United States and of the State wherein they reside. No State shall make or enforce any law which shall abridge the privileges or immunities of citizens of the United States; nor shall any State deprive any person of life, liberty, or property, without due process of law; nor deny to any person within its jurisdiction the equal protection of the laws.

SEC. 2. Representatives shall be apportioned among the several States according to their respective numbers, counting the whole number of persons in each State, excluding Indians not taxed. But when the right to vote at any election for the choice of electors for President and Vice President of the United States, Representatives in Congress, the Executive and Judicial officers of a State, or the members of the Legislature thereof, is denied to any of the male inhabitants of such State, being twenty-one years of age, and citizens of the United States, or in any way abridged, except for participation in rebellion, or other crime, the basis of representation therein shall be reduced in the proportion which the number of such male citizens shall bear to the whole number of male citizens twenty-one years of age in such State.

SEC. 3. No person shall be a Senator or Representative in Congress, or elector of President and Vice President, or hold any office, civil or military, under the United States, or under any State, who, having previously taken an oath, as a member of Congress, or as an officer of the United States, or as a member of any State legislature, or as an executive or judicial officer of any State, to support the Constitution of the United States, shall have engaged in insurrection or rebellion against the same, or given aid or comfort to the enemies thereof. But Congress may by a vote of two-thirds of each House, remove such disability.

SEC. 4. The validity of the public debt of the United States, authorized by law, including debts incurred for payment of pensions and bounties for services in suppressing insurrection or rebellion, shall not be questioned. But neither the United States nor any State shall assume or pay any debt or obligation incurred in aid of insurrection or rebellion against the United States, or any claim for the loss or emancipation of any slave; but all such debts, obligations and claims shall be held illegal and void.

SEC. 5. The Congress shall have power to enforce, by appropriate legislation, the provisions of this article.

Fifteenth Amendment (1870)

SEC. 1. The right of citizens of the United States to vote shall not be denied or abridged by the United States or by any State on account of race, color, or previous condition of servitude.

SEC. 2. The Congress shall have power to enforce this article by appropriate legislation.

Plessy v. *Ferguson,* Supreme Court of the United States, 163 U.S. 537 (1896)

MR. JUSTICE BROWN, after stating the case, delivered the opinion of the court.

This case turns upon the constitutionality of an act of the General Assembly of the State of Louisiana, passed in 1890, providing for separate railway carriages for the white and colored races. Acts 1890, No. 111, p. 152. . . .

The information filed in the criminal District Court charged in substance that Plessy, being a passenger between two stations within the State of Louisiana, was assigned by officers of the company to the coach used for the race to which he belonged, but he insisted upon going into a coach used by the race to which he did not belong. Neither in the information nor plea was his particular race or color averred.

The petition for the writ of prohibition averred that petitioner was seven eighths Caucasian and one eighth African blood; that the mixture of colored blood was not discernible in him, and that he was entitled to every right, privilege and immunity secured to citizens of the United States of the white race; and that, upon such theory, he took possession of a vacant seat in a coach where passengers of the white race were accommodated, and was ordered by the conductor to vacate said coach and take a seat in another assigned to persons of the colored race, and having refused to comply with such demand he was forcibly ejected with the aid of a police officer, and imprisoned in the parish jail to answer a charge of having violated the above act.

The constitutionality of this act is attacked upon the ground that it conflicts both with the Thirteenth Amendment of the Constitution, abolishing slavery, and the Fourteenth Amendment, which prohibits certain restrictive legislation on the part of the States . . . .

A statute which implies merely a legal distinction between the white and colored races—a distinction which is founded in the color of the two races, and which must always exist so long as white men are distinguished from the other race by color—has no tendency to destroy the legal equality of the two races, or reestablish a state of involuntary servitude. Indeed, we do not understand that the Thirteenth Amendment is strenuously relied upon by the plaintiff in error in this connection. . . .

The object of the [Fourteenth] amendment was undoubtedly to enforce the absolute equality of the two races before the law, but in the nature of things it could not have been intended to abolish distinctions based on color, or to enforce social, as distinguished from political equality, or a commingling of the two races upon terms unsatisfactory to either. Laws permitting, and even requiring, their separation in places where they are liable to be brought into contact do not necessarily imply the inferiority of either race to the other, and have been generally, if not universally, recognized as within the competency of the state legislatures in the exercise of their police power. The most common instance of this is connected with the establishment of separate schools for white and colored children, which has been held to be a valid exercise of the legislative power even by courts of States where the political rights of the colored race have been longest and most earnestly enforced. . . .

The distinction between laws interfering with the political equality of the negro and those requiring the separation of the two races in schools, theatres and railway carriages has been frequently drawn by this court. Thus in *Strauder* v. *West Virginia,* 100 U.S. 303, it was held that a law of West Virginia limiting to white male persons, 21 years of age and citizens of the State, the right to sit upon juries, was a discrimination which implied a legal inferiority in civil society, which lessened the security of the right of the colored race, and was a step toward reducing them to a condition of servility. Indeed, the right of a colored man that, in the selection of jurors to pass upon his life, liberty and property, there shall be no exclusion of his race, and no discrimination against them because of color, has been asserted in a number of cases. *Virginia* v. *Rives,* 100 U.S. 313; *Neal* v. *Delaware,* 103 U.S. 370; *Bush* v. *Kentucky,* 107 U.S. 110; *Gibson* v. *Mississippi,* 162 U.S. 565. So, where the laws of a particular locality or the charter of a particular railway corporation has provided that no person shall be excluded from the cars on account of color, we have held that this meant that persons of color should travel in the same car as white ones, and that the enactment was not satisfied by the company's providing cars assigned exclusively to people of color, though they were as good as those which they assigned exclusively to white persons. *Railroad Company* v. *Brown,* 17 Wall. 445.

. . . . Where a statute of Louisiana required those engaged in the transportation of passengers among the States to give to all persons travelling within that State, upon vessels employed in that business, equal rights and privileges in all parts of the vessel, without distinction on account of race or color, and subjected to an action for damages the owner of such a vessel, who excluded colored passengers on account of their color from the cabin set aside by him for the use of whites, it was held to be so far as it applied to interstate commerce, unconstitutional and void. *Hall* v. *DeCuir,* 95 U.S. 485. The court in this case however, expressly disclaimed that it had anything whatever to do with the statute as a regulation of internal commerce, or affecting anything else than commerce among the States. . . .

It is claimed by the plaintiff in error that, in any mixed community, the reputation of belonging to the dominant race, in this instance the white race, is property, in the same sense that a right of action, or of inheritance, is property. Conceding this to be so, for the purposes of this case, we are unable to see how this statute deprives him of, or in any way affects his right to, such property. If he be a white man and assigned to a colored coach, he may have his action for damages against the company for being deprived of his so called property. Upon the other hand, if he be a colored man and be so assigned, he has been deprived of no property, since he is not lawfully entitled to the reputation of being a white man.

In this connection, it is also suggested by the learned counsel for the plaintiff in error that the same argument that will justify the state legislature in requiring railways to provide separate accommodations for the two races will also authorize them to require separate cars to be provided for people whose hair is of a certain color, or who are aliens, or who belong to certain nationalities, or to enact laws requiring colored people to walk upon one side of the street, and white people upon the other, or requiring white men's houses painted white, and colored men's black, or their vehicles or business signs to be of different colors. Upon the theory that one side of the street is as good as the other, or that a house or vehicle of one color is as good as one of another color. The reply to all this is that every exercise of the police power must be reasonable, and extend only to such laws as are enacted in good faith for the promotion for the public good, and not for the annoyance or oppression of a particular class. . . .

So far, then, as a conflict with the Fourteenth Amendment is concerned, the case reduces itself to the question whether the statute of Louisiana is a reasonable regulation, and with respect to this there must necessarily be a large discretion on the part of the legislature. In determining the question of reasonableness it is at liberty to act with reference to the established usages, customs and traditions of the people, and with a view to the promotion of their comfort, and the preservation of the public peace and good order. Gauged by this standard, we cannot say that a law which authorizes or even requires the separation of the two races in public conveyances is unreasonable, or more obnoxious to the Fourteenth Amendment than the acts of Congress requiring separate schools for colored children in the District of Columbia, the constitutionality of which does not seem to have been questioned, or the corresponding acts of state legislatures.

We consider the underlying fallacy of the plaintiff's argument to consist in the assumption that the enforced separation of the two races stamps the colored race with a badge of inferiority. If this be so, it is not by reason of anything found in the act, but solely because the colored race chooses to put that construction upon it. The argument necessarily assumes that if, as has been more than once the case, and is not likely to be so again, the colored race should become the dominant power in the state legislature, and should enact a law in precisely similar terms, it would thereby relegate the white race to an inferior position. We imagine that the white race, at least, would not acquiesce in this assumption. The argument also assumes that social prejudices may be overcome by legislation, and that equal rights cannot be secured to the negro except by an enforced commingling of the two races. We cannot accept this proposition. If the two races are to meet upon terms of social equality, it must be the result of natural affinities, a mutual appreciation of each other's merits and a voluntary consent of individuals. As was said by the Court of Appeals of New York in *People* v. *Gallagher,* 93 N.Y. 438, 448, "this end can neither be accomplished nor promoted by laws which conflict with the general sentiment of the community upon whom they are designed to operate. When the government, therefore, has secured to each of its citizens equal rights before the law and equal opportunities for improvement and progress, it has accomplished the end for which it was organized and performed all of the functions respecting social advantages with which it is endowed." Legislation is powerless to eradicate racial instincts or to abolish distinctions based upon physical differences, and the attempt to do so can only result in accentuating the difficulties of the present situation. If the civil and political rights of both races be equal one cannot be inferior to the other socially, the Constitution of the United States cannot put them upon the same plane. . . .

Affirmed.

MR. JUSTICE HARLAN dissenting.
. . . However apparent the injustice of such legislation may be, we have only to consider whether it is consistent with the Constitution of the United States. . . .

If a white man and a black man choose to occupy the same public conveyance on a public highway, it is their right to do so, and no government, proceeding alone on grounds of race, can prevent it without infringing the personal liberty of each. . . .

The white race deems itself to be the dominant race in this country. And so it is, in prestige, in achievements, in education, in wealth and in power. So, I doubt not, it will continue to be for all time, if it remains true to its great heritage and holds fast to the principles of constitutional liberty. But in view of the Constitution, in the eye of the law, there is in this country no superior, dominant, ruling class of citizens. There is no caste here. Our Constitution is color-blind, and neither knows nor tolerates classes among citizens. In respect of civil rights, all citizens are equal before the law. The humblest is the peer of the most powerful. The law regards man as man, and takes no account of his surroundings or of his color when his civil rights as guaranteed by the supreme law of the land are involved. It is, therefore, to be regretted that this high tribunal, the final expositor of the fundamental law of the land, has reached the conclusion that it is competent for a State to regulate the enjoyment by citizens of their civil rights solely upon the basis of race.

In my opinion, the judgment this day rendered will, in time, prove to be quite as pernicious as the decision made by this tribunal in the *Dred Scott* case. It was adjudged in that case that the descendants of Africans who were imported into this country and sold as slaves were not included nor intended to be included under the word "citizen" in the Constitution, and could not claim any of the rights and privileges which that instrument provided for and secured to citizens of the United States; that at the time of the adoption of the Constitution they were "considered as a subordinate and inferior class of beings, who had been subjugated by the dominant race, and, whether emancipated or not, yet remained subject to their authority, and had no rights or privileges but such as those who held the power and the government might choose to grant them." 19 How. 393, 404. The recent amendments of the Constitution, it was supposed, had eradicated these principles from our institutions. But it seems that we have yet, in some of the States, a dominant race— a superior class of citizens, which assumes to regulate the enjoyment of civil rights, common to all citizens, upon the basis of race. The present decision, it may well be apprehended, will not only stimulate aggressions, more or less brutal and irritating, upon the admitted rights of colored citizens, but will encourage the belief that it is possible, by means of state enactments, to defeat the beneficient purposes which the people of the United States had in view when they adopted the recent amendments of the Constitution, by one of which the blacks of this country were made citizens of the United States and of the States in which they respectively reside, and whose privileges and immunities, as citizens, the States are forbidden to abridge. Sixty millions of whites are in no danger from the presence here of eight million blacks. The destinies of the two races, in this country, are indissolubly linked together, and the interests of both require that the common government of all shall not permit the seeds of race hate to be planted under the sanction of law. What can more certainly arouse race hate, what more certainly create and perpetuate a feeling of distrust between these races, than state enactments, which, in fact, proceed on the ground that colored citizens are so inferior and degraded that they cannot be allowed to sit in public coaches occupied by white citizens? That, as all will admit, is the real meaning of such legislation as was enacted in Louisiana. . . .

I am of opinion that the Statute of Louisiana is inconsistent with the personal liberty of citizens, white and black, in that State, and hostile to both the spirit and letter of the Constitution of the United States. If laws of like character should be enacted in the several States of the Union, the effect would be in the highest degree mischievous. Slavery, as an institution tolerated by the law would, it is true, have disappeared from our country, but there would remain a power in the States, by sinister legislation, to interfere with the full enjoyment of the blessings of freedom; to regulate civil rights, common to all citizens, upon the basis of race; and to place in a condition of legal inferiority a large body of American citizens, now constituting a part of the political community called the People of the United States, for whom, and by whom through representatives, our government is administered. Such a system is inconsistent with the guarantee given by the Constitution to each State of a republican form of government, and may be stricken down by Congressional action, or by the courts in the discharge of their solemn duty to maintain the supreme law of the land, anything in the constitution or laws of any State to the contrary notwithstanding.

For the reasons stated, I am constrained to withhold my assent from the opinion and judgment of the majority.

Brown v. *Board of Education of Topeka,*
Supreme Court of the United States 347 U.S. 483 (1954)

MR. CHIEF JUSTICE WARREN delivered the opinion of the Court.

These cases come to us from the States of Kansas, South Carolina, Virginia, and Delaware. They are premised on different facts and different local conditions, but a common legal question justifies their consideration together in this consolidated opinion.[1]

In each of the cases, minors of the Negro race, through their legal representatives, seek the aid of the courts in obtaining admission to the public schools of their community on a nonsegregated basis. In each instance, they had been denied admission to schools attended by white children under laws requiring or permitting segregation according to race. This segregation was alleged to deprive the plaintiffs of the equal protection of the laws under the Fourteenth Amendment. In each of the cases other than the Delaware case, a three-judge federal district court denied relief to the plaintiffs on the so-called "separate but equal" doctrine announced by this Court in *Plessy* v. *Ferguson*, 163 U.S. 537. Under that doctrine, equality of treatment is accorded when the races are provided substantially equal facilities, even though these facilities be separate. In the Delaware case, the Supreme Court of Delaware adhered to that doctrine, but ordered that the plaintiffs be admitted to the white schools because of their superiority to the Negro schools.

The plaintiffs contend that segregated public schools are not "equal" and cannot be made "equal," and that hence they are deprived of the equal protection of the laws. Because of the obvious importance of the question presented, the Court took jurisdiction.[2] Argument was heard in the 1952 Term, and reargument was heard this Term on certain questions propounded by the Court.[3]

Reargument was largely devoted to the circumstances surrounding the adoption of the Fourteenth Amendment in 1868. It covered exhaustively consideration of the Amendment in Congress, ratification by the states, then existing practices in racial segregation, and the views of proponents and opponents of the Amendment. This discussion and our own investigation convince us that, although these sources cast some light, it is not enough to resolve the problem with which we are faced. At best, they are inconclusive. The most avid proponents of the post-War Amendments undoubtedly intended them to remove all legal distinctions among "all persons born or naturalized in the United States." Their opponents, just as certainly, were antagonistic to both the letter and the spirit of the Amendments and wished them to have the most limited effect. What others in Congress and the state legislatures had in mind cannot be determined with any degree of certainty.

An additional reason for the inconclusive nature of the Amendment's history, with respect to segregated schools, is the status of public education at that time.[4] In the South, the movement toward free common schools, supported by general taxation, had not yet taken hold. Education of white children was largely in the hands of private groups. Education of Negroes was almost nonexistent, and practically all of the race were illiterate. In fact, any education of Negroes was forbidden by law in some states. Today, in contrast, many Negroes have achieved outstanding success in the arts and sciences as well as in the business and professional world. It is true that public school education at the time of the Amendment had advanced further in the North, but the effect of the Amendment on Northern States was generally ignored in the congressional debates. Even in the North, the conditions of public education did not approximate those existing today. The curriculum was usually rudimentary; and compulsory school attendance was virtually unknown. As a consequence, it is not surprising that there should be so little in the history of the Fourteenth Amendment relating to its intended effect on public education.

In the first cases in this Court construing the Fourteenth Amendment, decided shortly after its adoption, the Court interpreted it as proscribing all state-imposed discriminations against the Negro race.[5] The doctrine of "separate but equal" did not make its appearance in this Court until 1896 in the case of *Plessy* v. *Ferguson, supra,* involving not education but transportation.[6] American courts have since labored with the doctrine for over half a century. In this Court, there have been six cases involving the "separate but equal" doctrine in the field of public education.[7] In *Cumming* v. *County Board of Education,* 175 U.S. 528, and *Gong Lum* v. *Rice,* 275 U.S. 78, the validity of the doctrine itself was not challenged.[8] In more recent cases, all on the graduate school level, inequality was found in that specific benefits enjoyed by white students were denied to Negro students of the same educational qualifications. *Missouri ex rel. Gaines* v. *Canada,* 305 U.S. 337; *Sipuel* v. *Oklahoma,* 332 U.S. 631; *Sweatt* v. *Painter,* 339 U.S. 629; *McLaurin* v. *Oklahoma State Regents,* 339 U.S. 637. In none of these cases was it necessary to re-examine the doctrine to grant relief to the Negro plaintiff. And in *Sweatt* v. *Painter, supra,* the Court expressly reserved decision on the question whether *Plessy* v. *Ferguson* should be held inapplicable to public education.

In the instant cases, that question is directly presented. Here, unlike *Sweatt* v. *Painter,* there are findings below that the Negro and white schools involved have been equalized, or are being equalized, with respect to buildings, curricula, qualifications and salaries of teachers, and other "tangible" factors.[9] Our decision, therefore, cannot turn on merely a comparison of these tangible factors in the Negro and white schools involved in each of the cases. We must look instead to the effect of segregation itself on public education.

In approaching this problem, we cannot turn the clock back to 1868 when the Amendment was adopted, or even to 1896 when *Plessy* v. *Ferguson* was written. We must consider public education in the light of its full development and its present place in American life throughout the Nation. Only in this way can it be determined if segregation in public schools deprives these plaintiffs of the equal protection of the laws.

Today, education is perhaps the most important function of state and local governments. Compulsory school attendance laws and the great expenditures for education both demonstrate our recognition of the importance of education to our democratic society. It is required in the performance of our most basic public responsibilities, even service in the armed forces. It is the very foundation of good citizenship. Today it is a principal instrument in awakening the child to cultural values, in preparing him for later professional training, and in helping him to adjust normally to his environment. In these days, it is doubtful that any child may reasonably be expected to succeed in life if he is denied the opportunity of an education. Such an opportunity, where the state has undertaken to provide it, is a right which must be made available to all on equal terms.

We come then to the question presented: Does segregation of children in public schools solely on the basis of race, even though the physical facilities and other "tangible" factors may be equal, deprive the children of the minority group of equal educational opportunities? We believe that it does.

In *Sweatt* v. *Painter, supra,* in finding that a segregated law school for Negroes could not provide them equal educational opportunities, this Court relied in large part on "those qualities which are incapable of objective measurement but which make for greatness in a law school." In *McLaurin* v. *Oklahoma State Regents, supra,* the Court, in requiring that a Negro admitted to a white graduate school be treated like all other students, again resorted to intangible considerations: ". . . his ability to study, to engage in discussions and exchange views with other students, and, in general, to learn his profession." Such considerations apply with added force to children in grade and high schools. To separate them from others of similar age and qualifications solely because of their race generates a feeling of inferiority as to their status in the community that may effect their hearts and minds in a way unlikely ever to be undone. The effect of this separation on their educational opportunities was well stated by a finding in the Kansas case by a court which nevertheless felt compelled to rule against the Negro plaintiffs:

> Segregation of white and colored children in public schools has a detrimental effect upon the colored children. The impact is greater when it has the sanction of the law; for the policy of separating the races is usually interpreted as denoting the inferiority of the Negro group. A sense of inferiority affects the motivation of a child to learn. Segregation with the sanction of law, therefore, has a tendency to (retard) the educational and

mental development of negro children and to deprive them of some of the
benefits they would receive in a racial(ly) integrated school system.[10]

Whatever may have been the extent of psychological knowledge at the time of
Plessy v. *Ferguson,* this finding is amply supported by modern authority.[11] Any
language in *Plessy* v. *Ferguson* contrary to this finding is rejected.

We conclude that in the field of public education the doctrine of "separate
but equal" has no place. Separate educational faciilties are inherently unequal.
Therefore, we hold that the plaintiffs and others similarly situated for whom
the actions have been brought are, by reason of the segregation complained of,
deprived of the equal protection of the laws guaranteed by the Fourteenth
Amendment. This disposition makes unnecessary any discussion whether such
segregation also violates the Due Process Clause of the Fourteenth Amendment.[12]

Because these are class actions, because of the wide applicability of this
decision, and because of the great variety of local conditions, the formulation
of decrees in these cases presents problems of considerable complexity. On
reargument, the consideration of appropriate relief was necessarily subordi-
nated to the primary question—the constitutionality of segregation in public
education. We have now announced that such segregation is a denial of the
equal protection of the laws. In order that we may have the full assistance of
the parties in formulating decrees, the cases will be restored to the docket, and
the parties are requested to present further argument on Questions 4 and 5
previously propounded by the Court for the reargument this Term.[13] The
Attorney General of the United States is again invited to participate. The
Attorneys General of the states requiring or permitting segregation in public
education will also be permitted to appear as *amici curiae* upon request to do
so by September 15, 1954, and submission of briefs by October 1, 1954.[14]

It is so ordered.

Notes

Brown vs. *Board of Education*

1. In the Kansas case, *Brown* v. *Board of Education,* the plaintiffs are Negro children
of elementary school age residing in Topeka. They brought this action in the United
States District Court for the District of Kansas to enjoin enforcement of a Kansas
statute which permits, but does not require, cities of more than 15,000 population to
maintain separate school facilities for Negro and white students. Kan. Gen. Stat. §72-
1724 (1949). Pursuant to that authority, the Topeka Board of Education elected to
establish segregated elementary schools. Other public schools in the community, however, are operated on a nonsegregated basis. The three-judge District Court, convened
under 28 U.S.C. §§2281 and 2284, found that segregation in public education has a
detrimental effect upon Negro children, but denied relief on the ground that Negro
and white schools were substantially equal with respect to buildings, transportation,

curricula, and educational qualifications of teachers. 98F. Supp. 797. The case is here on direct appeal under 28 U.S.C. §1253.

In the South Carolina case, *Briggs* v. *Elliott,* the plaintiffs are Negro children of both elementary and high school age residing in Clarendon County. They brought this action in the United States District Court for the Eastern District of South Carolina to enjoin enforcement of provisions in the state constitution and statutory code which require the segregation of Negroes and whites in public schools. S.C. Const., Art. XI, §7; S.C. Code §5377 (1942). The three-judge District Court, convened under 28 U.S.C. §§2281 and 2284, denied the requested relief. The court found that the Negro schools were inferior to the white schools and ordered the defendants to begin immediately to equalize the facilities. But the court sustained the validity of the contested provisions and denied the plaintiffs admission to the white schools during the equalization program. 98 F. Supp. 529. This Court vacated the District Court's judgment and remanded the case for the purpose of obtaining the court's views on a report filed by the defendants concerning the progress made in the equalization program. 342 U.S. 350. On remand, the District Court found that substantial equality had been achieved except for buildings and that the defendants were proceeding to rectify this inequality as well. 103 F. Supp. 920. The case is again here on direct appeal under 28 U.S.C. §1253.

In the Virginia case, *Davis* v. *County School Board,* the plaintiffs are Negro children of both elementary and high school age residing in New Castle County. They brought this action in the Delaware Court of Chancery to enjoin enforcement of provisions in the state constitution and statutory code which require the segregation of Negroes and whites in public schools. Del. Const., Art. X, §2; Del. Rev. Code §2631 (1935). The Chancellor gave judgment for the plaintiffs and ordered their immediate admission to schools previously attended only by white children, on the ground that the Negro schools were inferior with respect to teacher training, pupil-teacher ratio, extracurricular activities, physical plant, and time and distance involved in travel. 87 A. 2d 862. The Chancellor also found that segregation itself results in an inferior education for Negro children (see note 10, *infra*), but did not rest his decision on that ground. *Id.,* at 865. The Chancellor's decree was affirmed by the Supreme Court of Delaware, which intimated, however, that the defendants might be able to obtain a modification of the decree after equalization of the Negro and white schools had been accomplished. 91 A. 2d 137, 152. The defendants, contending only that the Delaware courts had erred in ordering the immediate admission of the Negro plaintiffs to the white schools, applied to this Court for certiorari. The writ was granted, 344 U.S. 891. The plaintiffs, who were successful below, did not submit a cross-petition.

2. 344 U.S. 1, 141, 891.

3. 345 U.S. 972. The Attorney General of the United States participated both Terms as *amicus curiae.*

4. For a general study of the development of public education prior to the Amendment, *see* Butts and Cremin, *A History of Education in American Culture* (1953), Pts. I, II; Cubberley, *Public Education in the United States* (1934 ed.), cc. II-XII. School practices current at the time of the adoption of the Fourteenth Amendment are described in Butts and Cremin, *supra,* at 269–275; Cubberley, *supra* at 288–339, 408–431; Knight, *Public Education in the South* (1922), cc. VIII, IX. *See also* H. Ex. Doc. No. 315, 41st Cong., 2d Sess. (1871). Although the demand for free public schools followed substantially the same pattern in both the North and the South, the development in

the South did not begin to gain momentum until about 1850, some twenty years after that in the North. The reasons for the somewhat slower development in the South (e.g., the rural character of the South and the different regional attitudes toward state assistance) are well explained in Cubberley, *supra*, at 408–423. In the country as a whole, but particularly in the South, the War virtually stopped all progress in public education. *Id.*, at 427–428. The low status of Negro education in all sections of the country, both before and immediately after the War, is described in Beale, *A History of Freedom of Teaching in American Schools* (1941), 112–132, 175–195. Compulsory school attendance laws were not generally adopted until after the ratification of the Fourteenth Amendment, and it was not until 1918 that such laws were in force in all the states. Cubberley, *supra*, at 563–565.

5. *Slaughter-House Cases*, 16 Wall. 36, 67–72 (1873); *Strauder* v. *West Virginia*, 100 U.S. 303, 307–308 (1880): "It ordains that no State shall deprive any person of life, liberty, or property, without due process of law, or deny to any person within its jurisdiction the equal protection of the laws. What is this but declaring that the law in the States shall be the same for black as for white; that all persons, whether colored or white, shall stand equal before the laws of the States, and, in regard to the colored race, for whose protection the amendment was primarily designed, that no discrimination shall be made against them by law because of their color? The words of the amendment, it is true, are prohibitory, but they contain a necessary implication of a positive immunity, or right, most valuable to the colored race,—the right to exemption from unfriendly legislation against them distinctively as colored,—exemption from legal discriminations, implying inferiority in civil society, lessening the security of their enjoyment of the rights which others enjoy, and discriminations which are steps towards reducing them to the condition of a subject race." See also *Virginia* v. *Rives,* 100 U.S. 313, 318 (1880); *Ex parte Virginia* 100 U.S. 339, 344–345 (1880).

6. The doctrine apparently originated in *Roberts* v. *City of Boston,* 59 Mass. 198, 206 (1850), upholding school segregation against attack as being violative of a state constitutional guarantee of equality. Segregation in Boston public schools was eliminated in 1855. Mass Acts 1855, c. 256. But elsewhere in the North segregation in public education has persisted in some communities until recent years. It is apparent that such segregation has long been a nationwide problem, not merely one of sectional concern.

7. *See also Berea College* v. *Kentucky,* 211 U.S. 45 (1908).

8. In the *Cumming* case, Negro taxpayers sought an injunction requiring the defendant school board to discontinue the operation of a high school for white children until the board resumed operation of a high school for Negro children. Similarly, in the *Gong Lum* case, the plaintiff, a child of Chinese descent, contended only that state authorities had misapplied the doctrine by classifying him with Negro children and requiring him to attend a Negro school.

9. In the Kansas case, the court below found substantial equality as to all such factors. 98 F. Supp. 797, 798. In the South Carolina case, the court below found that the defendants were proceeding "promptly and in good faith to comply with the court's decree." 103 F. Supp. 920, 921. In the Virginia case, the court below noted that the equalization program was already "afoot and progressing" (103 F. Supp. 337, 341); since then, we have been advised, in the Virginia Attorney General's brief on reargument, that the program has now been completed. In the Delaware case, the court

below similarly noted that the state's equalization program was well under way. 91 A. 2d 137, 149.

10. A similar finding was made in the Delaware case: "I conclude from the testimony that in our Delaware society, State-imposed segregation in education itself results in the Negro children, as a class, receiving educational opportunities which are substantially inferior to those available to white children otherwise similarly situated." 87 A. 2d 862, 865.

11. K. B. Clark, *Effect of Prejudice and Discrimination on Personality Development* (Midcentury White House Conference on Children and Youth, 1950); Witmer and Kotinsky, *Personality in the Making* (1952), c. VI; Deutscher and Chein, "The Psychological Effects of Enforced Segregation: A Survey of Social Science Opinion," 26 *J. Psychol.* 259 (1948); Chein, "What are the Psychological Effects of Segregation Under Conditions of Equal Facilities?," 3 *Int. J. Opinion and Attitude Res.* 229 (1949); Brameld, *Educational Costs, in Discrimination and National Welfare* (MacIver, ed., 1949), 44–48; Frazier, *The Negro in the United States* (1949), 674–681. And see generally Myrdal, *An American Dilemma* (1944).

12. *See Bolling* v. *Sharpe, post,* p. 497, concerning the Due Process Clause of the Fifth Amendment.

13. "4. Assuming it is decided that segregation in public schools violates the Fourteenth Amendment.

"(a) would a decree necessarily follow providing that, within the limits set by normal geographic school districting, Negro children should forthwith be admitted to schools of their choice, or

"(b) may this Court, in the exercise of its equity powers, permit an effective gradual adjustment to be brought about from existing segregated systems to a system not based on color distinctions?

"5. On the assumption on which questions 4 (a) and (b) are based, and assuming further that this Court will exercise its equity powers to the end described in question 4 (b),

"(a) should this Court formulate detailed decrees in these cases;

"(b) if so, what specific issues should the decrees reach;

"(c) should this Court appoint a special master to hear evidence with a view to recommending specific terms for such decrees;

"(d) should this Court remand to the courts of first instance with directions to frame decrees in these cases, and if so what general directions should the decrees of this Court include and what procedures should the courts of first instance follow in arriving at the specific terms of more detailed decrees?"

14. *See* Rule 42, Revised Rules of this Court (effective July 1, 1954).

1964 Civil Rights Act

TITLE VII—EQUAL EMPLOYMENT OPPORTUNITY

DEFINITIONS

SEC. 701. For the purposes of this title—

(a) The term "person" includes one or more individuals, labor unions, partnerships, associations, corporations, legal representatives, mutual companies, joint-stock companies, trusts, unincorporated organizations, trustees, trustees in bankruptcy, or receivers.

(b) The term "employer" means a person engaged in an industry affecting commerce who has twenty-five or more employees for each working day in each of twenty or more calendar weeks in the current or preceding calendar year, and any agent of such a person, but such term does not include (1) the United States, a corporation wholly owned by the Government of the United States, an Indian tribe, or a State or political subdivision thereof, (2) a bona fide private membership club (other than a labor organization) which is exempt from taxation under section 501(c) of the Internal Revenue Code of 1954: *Provided,* That during the first year after the effective date prescribed in subsection (a) of section 716, persons having fewer than one hundred employees (and their agents) shall not be considered employers, and, during the second year after such date, persons having fewer than seventy-five employees (and their agents) shall not be considered employers, and, during the third year after such date, persons having fewer than fifty employees (and their agents) shall not be considered employers: *Provided further,* That it shall be the policy of the United States to insure equal employment opportunites for Federal employees without discrimination because of race, color, religion, sex or national origin and the President shall utilize existing authority to effectuate this policy.

(c) The term "employment agency" means any person regularly undertaking with or without compensation to procure employees for an employer or to procure for employees opportunities to work for an employer and includes an agent of such a person; but shall not include an agency of the United States, or an agency of a State or political subdivision of a State, except that such term shall include the United States Employment Service and the system of State and local employment services receiving Federal assistance.

(d) The term "labor organization" means a labor organization engaged in an industry affecting commerce, and any agent of such an organization, and includes any organization of any kind, any agency, or employee representation committee, group, association, or plan so engaged in which employees participate and which exists for the purpose, in whole or in part, of dealing with employers concerning grievances, labor disputes, wages, rates of pay, hours, or other terms or conditions of employment, and any conference, general committee, joint or system board, or joint council so engaged which is subordinate to a national or international labor organization.

(e) A labor organization shall be deemed to be engaged in an industry affecting commerce if (1) it maintains or operates a hiring hall or hiring office which procures employees for an employer or procures for employees opportunities to work for an employer, or (2) the number of its members (or, where it is a labor organization composed of other labor organizations or their representatives, if the aggregate number of the members of such other labor organization) is (A) one hundred or more during the first year after the effective date prescribed in subsection (a) of section 716, (B) seventy-five or more during the second year after such date or fifty or more during the third year, or (C) twenty-five or more thereafter, and such labor organization—

(1) is the certified representative of employees under the provisions of the National Labor Relations Act, as amended, or the Railway Labor Act, as amended;

(2) although not certified, is a national or international labor organization or a local labor organization recognized or acting as the representative of employees of an employer or employers engaged in an industry affecting commerce; or

(3) has chartered a local labor organization or subsidiary body which is representing or actively seeking to represent employees of employers within the meaning of paragraph (1) or (2); or

(4) has been chartered by a labor organization representing or actively seeking to represent employees within the meaning of paragraph (1) or (2) as the local or subordinate body through which such employees may enjoy membership or become affiliated with such labor organization; or

(5) is a conference, general committee, joint or system board, or joint council subordinate to a national or international labor organization, which includes a labor organization engaged in an industry affecting commerce within the meaning of any of the preceding paragraphs of this subsection.

(f) The term "employee" means an individual employed by an employer.

(g) The term "commerce" means trade, traffic, commerce, transportation, transmission, or communication among the several States; or between a State and any place outside thereof; or within the District of Columbia, or a possession of the United States; or between points in the same State but through a point outside thereof.

(h) The term "industry affecting commerce" means any activity, business, or industry in commerce or in which a labor dispute would hinder or obstruct commerce or the free flow of commerce and includes any activity or industry "affecting commerce" within the meaning of the Labor-Management Reporting and Disclosure Act of 1959.

(i) The term "State" includes a State of the United States, the District of Columbia, Puerto Rico, the Virgin Islands, American Samoa, Guam, Wake Island, the Canal Zone, and Outer Continental Shelf lands defined in the Outer Continental Shelf Lands Act.

EXEMPTION

SEC. 702. This title shall not apply to an employer with respect to the employment of aliens outside any State, or to a religious corporation, association, or society with respect to the employment of individuals of a particular religion to perform work connected with the carrying on by such corporation, association, or society of its religious activities or to an educational institution with respect to the employment of individuals to perform work connected with the educational activities of such institution.

DISCRIMINATION BECAUSE OF RACE, COLOR, RELIGION, SEX, OR NATIONAL ORIGIN

SEC. 703. (a) It shall be an unlawful employment practice for an employer—

(1) to fail or refuse to hire or to discharge any individual, or otherwise to discriminate against any individual with respect to his compensation, terms, conditions, or privileges of employment, because of such individual's race, color, religion, sex, or national origin; or

(2) to limit, segregate, or classify his employees in any way which would deprive or tend to deprive any individual of employment opportunities or otherwise adversely affect his status as an employee, because of such individual's race, color, religion, sex, or national origin.

(b) It shall be an unlawful employment practice for an employment agency to fail or refuse to refer for employment, or otherwise to discriminate against, any individual because of his race, color, religion, sex, or national origin, or to classify or refer for employment any individual on the basis of his race, color, religion, sex, or national origin.

(c) It shall be an unlawful employment practice for a labor organization—

(1) to exclude or to expel from its membership, or otherwise to discriminate against, any individual because of his race, color, religion, sex, or national origin;

(2) to limit, segregate, or classify its membership, or to classify or fail or refuse to refer for employment any individual, in any way which would deprive or tend to deprive any individual of employment opportunities, or would limit such employment opportunities or otherwise adversely affect his status as an employee or as an applicant for employment, because of such individual's race, color, religion, sex, or national origin; or

(3) to cause or attempt to cause an employer to discriminate against an individual in violation of this section.

(d) It shall be an unlawful employment practice for any employer, labor organization, or joint labor-management committee controlling apprenticeship or other training or retraining, including on-the-job training programs to discriminate against any individual because of his race, color, religion, sex, or national origin in admission to, or employment in, any program established to provide apprenticeship or other training.

(e) Notwithstanding any other provision of this title, (1) it shall not be an unlawful employment practice for an employer to hire and employ employees, for an employment agency to classify, or refer for employment any individual, for a labor organization to classify its membership or to classify or refer for employment any individual, or for an employer, labor organization, or joint labor-management committee controlling apprenticeship or other training or retraining programs to admit or employ any individual in any such program, on the basis of his religion, sex, or national origin in those certain instances where religion, sex, or national origin is a bona fide occupational qualification reasonably necessary to the normal operation of that particular business or enterprise, and (2) it shall not be an unlawful employment practice for a school, college, university, or other educational institution or institution of learning to hire and employ employees of a particular religion if such school, college, university, or other educational institution or institution of learning is, in whole or in substantial part, owned, supported, controlled, or managed by a particular religion or by a particular religious corporation, association, or society, or if the curriculum of such school, college, university, or other educational institution or institution of learning is directed toward the propagation of a particular religion.

(f) As used in this title, the phrase "unlawful employment practice" shall not be deemed to include any action or measure taken by an employer, labor organization, joint labor-management committee, or employment agency with respect to an individual who is a member of the Communist Party of the United States or of any other organization required to register as a Communist-action or Communist-front organization by final order of the Subversive Activities Control Board pursuant to the Subversive Activities Control Act of 1950.

(g) Notwithstanding any other provision of this title, it shall not be an unlawful employment practice for an employer to fail or refuse to hire and employ any individual for any position, for an employer to discharge any individual from any position, or for an employment agency to fail or refuse to refer any individual for employment in any position, or for a labor organization to fail or refuse to refer any individual for employment in any position, if—

    (1) the occupancy of such position, or access to the premises in or upon which any part of the duties of such position is performed or is to be performed, is subject to any requirement imposed in the interest of the national security of the United States under any security program in effect pursuant to or administered under any statute of the United States or any Executive order of the President; and

    (2) such individual has not fulfilled or has ceased to fulfill that requirement.

(h) Notwithstanding any other provision of this title, it shall not be an unlawful employment practice for an employer to apply different standards of compensation, or different terms, conditions, or privileges of employment pursuant to a bona fide seniority or merit system, or a system which measures earnings by quantity or quality of production or to employees who work in different locations, provided that such differences are not the result of an intention to discriminate because of race, color, religion, sex, or national origin, nor shall it be an unlawful employment practice for an employer to give and to act upon the results of any professionally developed ability test provided that such test, its administration or action upon the results is not designed, intended or used to discriminate because of race, color, religion, sex or national origin. It shall not be an unlawful employment practice under this title for any employer to differentiate upon the basis of sex in determining the amount of the wages or compensation paid or to be paid to employees of such employer if such differentiation is authorized by the provisions of section 6(d) of the Fair Labor Standards Act of 1938, as amended (29 U.S.C. 206(d)).

(i) Nothing contained in this title shall apply to any business or enterprise on or near an Indian reservation with respect to any publicly announced employment practice of such business or enterprise under which a preferential treatment is given to any individual because he is an Indian living on or near a reservation.

(j) Nothing contained in this title shall be interpreted to require any employer, employment agency, labor organization, or joint labor-management committee subject to this title to grant preferential treatment to any individual or to any group because of the race, color, religion, sex, or national origin of such individual or group on account of an imbalance which may exist with respect to the total number or percentage of persons of any race, color, religion, sex, or national origin employed by any employer, referred or classified for employment by any employment agency or labor organization, admitted to membership or classified by any labor organization, or admitted to, or employed in, any apprenticeship or other training program, in comparison with the total number or percentage of persons of such race, color, religion, sex, or national origin in any community, State, section, or other area, or in the available work force in any community, State, section, or other area.

OTHER UNLAWFUL EMPLOYMENT PRACTICES

SEC. 704. (a) It shall be an unlawful employment practice for an employer to discriminate against any of his employees or applicants for employment, for an employment agency to discriminate against any individual, or for a labor organization to discriminate against any member thereof or applicant for membership, because he has opposed any practice made an unlawful employment practice by this title, or because he has made a charge, testified, assisted, or participated in any manner in an investigation, proceeding, or hearing under this title.

(b) It shall be an unlawful employment practice for an employer, labor organization, or employment agency to print or publish or cause to be printed or published any notice or advertisement relating to employment by such an employer or membership in or any classification or referral for employment by such a labor organization, or relating to any classification or referral for employment by such an employment agency, indicating any preference, limitation, specification, or discrimination, based on race, color, religion, sex, or national origin, except that such a notice or advertisement may indicate a preference, limitation, specification, or discrimination based on religion, sex, or national origin when religion, sex, or national origin is a bona fide occupational qualification for employment.

SEC. 705. (a) There is hereby created a Commission to be known as the Equal Employment Opportunity Commission, which shall be composed of five members, not more than three of whom shall be members of the same political party, who shall be appointed by the President by and with the advice and consent of the Senate. One of the original members shall be appointed for a term of one year, one for a term of two years, one for a term of three years, one for a term of four years, and one for a term of five years, beginning from the date of enactment of this title, but their successors shall be appointed for terms of five years each, except that any individual chosen to fill a vacancy shall be appointed only for the unexpired term of the member whom he shall succeed. The President shall designate one member to serve as Chairman of the Commission, and one member to serve as Vice Chairman. The Chairman shall be responsible on behalf of the Commission for the administrative operations of the Commission, and shall appoint, in accordance with the civil service laws, such officers, agents, attorneys, and employees as it deems necessary to assist it in the performance of its functions and to fix their compensation in accordance with the Classification Act of 1949, as amended. The Vice Chairman shall act as Chairman in the absence or disability of the Chairman or in the event of a vacancy in that office.

(b) A vacancy in the Commission shall not impair the right of the remaining members to exercise all the powers of the Commission and three members thereof shall constitute a quorum.

(c) The Commission shall have an official seal which shall be judicially noticed.

(d) The Commission shall at the close of each fiscal year report to the Congress and to the President concerning the action it has taken; the names, salaries, and duties of all individuals in its employ and the moneys it has disbursed; and shall make such further reports on the cause of and means of eliminating discrimination and such recommendations for further legislation as may appear desirable.

(e) The Federal Executive Pay Act of 1956, as amended (5 U.S.C. 2201–2209), is further amended—

(1) by adding to section 105 thereof (5 U.S.C. 2204) the following clause: "(32) Chairman, Equal Employment Opportunity Commission"; and

(2) by adding to clause (45) of section 106(a) thereof (5 U.S.C. 2205(a)) the following: "Equal Employment Opportunity Commission (4)."

(f) The principal office of the Commission shall be in or near the District of Columbia, but it may meet or exercise any or all its powers at any other place. The Commission may establish such regional or State offices as it deems necessary to accomplish the purpose of this title.

(g) The Commission shall have power—

(1) to cooperate with and, with their consent, utilize regional, State, local, and other agencies, both public and private, and individuals;

(2) to pay to witnesses whose depositions are taken or who are summoned before the Commission or any of its agents the same witness and mileage fees as are paid to witnesses in the courts of the United States;

(3) to furnish to persons subject to this title such technical assistance as they may request to further their compliance with this title or an order issued thereunder;

(4) upon the request of (i) any employer, whose employees or some of them, or (ii) any labor organization, whose members or some of them, refuse or threaten to refuse to cooperate in effectuating the provisions of this title, to assist in such effectuation by conciliation or such other remedial action as provided by this title;

(5) to make such technical studies as are appropriate to effectuate the purposes and policies of this title and to make the results of such studies available to the public;

(6) to refer matters to the Attorney General with recommendations for intervention in a civil action brought by an aggrieved party under section 706, or for the institution of a civil action by the Attorney General under section 707, and to advise, consult, and assist the Attorney General on such matters.

(h) Attorneys appointed under this section may, at the direction of the Commission, appear for and represent the Commission in any case in court.

(i) The Commission shall, in any of its educational or promotional activities, cooperate with other departments and agencies in the performance of such educational and promotional activities.

(j) All officers, agents, attorneys, and employees of the Commission shall be subject to the provisions of section 9 of the Act of August 2, 1939, as amended (the Hatch Act), notwithstanding any exemption contained in such section.

PREVENTION OF UNLAWFUL EMPLOYMENT PRACTICES

SEC. 706. (a) Whenever it is charged in writing under oath by a person claiming to be aggrieved, or a written charge has been filed by a member of the Commission where he has reasonable cause to believe a violation of this title has occurred (and such charge sets forth the facts upon which it is based) that an employer, employment agency, or labor organization has engaged in an unlawful employment practice, the Commission shall furnish such employer, employment agency, or labor organization (hereinafter referred to as the "respondent") with a copy of such charge and shall make an investigation of such charge, provided that such charge shall not be made public by the Commission. If the Commission shall determine, after such investigation, that there is reasonable cause to believe that the charge is true, the Commission shall endeavor to eliminate any such alleged unlawful employment practice by informal methods of conference, conciliation, and persuasion. Nothing said or done during and as a part of such endeavors may be made public by the Commission without the written consent of the parties, or used as evidence in a subsequent proceeding. Any officer or employee of the Commission, who shall make public in any manner whatever any information in violation of this subsection shall be deemed guilty of a misdemeanor and upon conviction thereof shall be fined not more than $1,000 or imprisoned not more than one year.

(b) In the case of an alleged unlawful employment practice occurring in a State, or political subdivision of a State, which has a State or local law prohibiting the unlawful employment practice alleged and establishing or authorizing a State or local authority to grant or seek relief from such practice or to institute criminal proceedings with respect thereto upon receiving notice thereof, no charge may be filed under subsection (a) by the person aggrieved before the expiration of sixty days after proceedings have been commenced under the State or local law, unless such proceedings have been earlier terminated, provided that such sixty-day period shall be extended to one hundred and twenty days during the first year after the effective date of such State or local law. If any requirement for the commencement of such proceedings is imposed by a State or local authority other than a requirement of the filing of a written and signed statement of the facts upon which the proceeding is based, the proceeding shall be deemed to have been commenced for the purposes of this subsection at the time such statement is sent by registered mail to the appropriate State or local authority.

(c) In the case of any charge filed by a member of the Commission alleging an unlawful employment practice occurring in a State or political subdivision of a State, which has a State or local law prohibiting the practice alleged and establishing or authorizing a State or local authority to grant or seek relief from such practice or to institute criminal proceedings with respect thereto upon receiving notice thereof, the Commission shall, before taking any action with respect to such charge, notify the appropriate State or local officials and, upon request, afford them a reasonable time, but not less than sixty days (provided that such sixty-day period shall be extended to one hundred and twenty days during the first year after the effective day of such State or local law), unless a shorter period is requested, to act under such State or local law to remedy the practice alleged.

(d) A charge under subsection (a) shall be filed within ninety days after the alleged unlawful employment practice occurred, except that in the case of an unlawful employment practice with respect to which the person aggrieved has followed the procedure set out in subsection (b), such charge shall be filed by the person aggrieved within two hundred and ten days after the alleged unlawful employment practice occurred, or within thirty days after receiving notice that the State or local agency has terminated the proceedings under the State or local law, whichever is earlier, and a copy of such charge shall be filed by the Commission with the State or local agency.

(e) If within thirty days after a charge is filed with the Commission or within thirty days after expiration of any period of reference under subsection (c) (except that in either case such period may be extended to not more than sixty days upon a determination by the Commission that further efforts to secure voluntary compliance are warranted), the Commission has been unable to obtain voluntary compliance with this title, the Commission shall so notify the person aggrieved and a civil action may, within thirty days thereafter, be brought against the respondent named in the charge (1) by the person claiming to be aggrieved, or (2) if such charge was filed by a member of the Commission, by any person whom the charge alleges was aggrieved by the alleged unlawful employment practice. Upon application by the complainant and in such circumstances as the court may deem just, the court may appoint an attorney for such complainant and may authorize the commencement of the action without the payment of fees, costs, or security. Upon timely application, the court may, in its discretion, permit the Attorney General to intervene in such civil action if he certifies that the case is of general public importance. Upon request, the court may, in its discretion, stay further proceedings for not more than sixty days pending the termination of State or local proceedings described in subsection (b) or the efforts of the Commission to obtain voluntary compliance.

(f) Each United States district court and each United States court of a place subject to the jurisdiction of the United States shall have jurisdiction of actions brought under this title. Such an action may be brought in any judicial district in the State in which the unlawful employment practice is alleged to have been committed, in the judicial district in which the employment records relevant to such practice are maintained and administered, or in the judicial district in which the plaintiff would have worked but for the alleged unlawful employment practice, but if the respondent is not found within any such district, such an action may be brought within the judicial district in which the respondent has his principal office. For purposes of sections 1404 and 1406 of title 28 of the United States Code, the judicial district in which the respondent has his principal office shall in all cases be considered a district in which the action might have been brought.

(g) If the court finds that the respondent has intentionally engaged in or is intentionally engaging in an unlawful employment practice charged in the complaint, the court may enjoin the respondent from engaging in such unlawful employment practice, and order such affirmative action as may be appropriate, which may include reinstatement or hiring of employees, with or without back pay (payable by the employer, employment agency, or labor organization, as the case may be, responsible for the unlawful employment practice). Interim earnings or amounts earnable with reasonable diligence by the person or persons discriminated against shall operate to reduce the back pay otherwise allowable. No order of the court shall require the admission or reinstatement of an individual as a member of a union or the hiring, reinstatement, or promotion of an individual as an employee, or the payment to him of any back pay, if such individual was refused admission, suspended, or expelled or was refused employment or advancement or was suspended or discharged for any reason other than discrimination on account of race, color, religion, sex or national origin or in violation of section 704(a).

(h) The provisions of the Act entitled "An Act to amend the Judicial Code and to define and limit the jurisdiction of courts sitting in equity, and for other purposes," approved March 23, 1932 (29 U.S.C. 101–115), shall not apply with respect to civil actions brought under this section.

(i) In any case in which an employer, employment agency, or labor organization fails to comply with an order of a court issued in a civil action brought under subsection (e), the Commission may commence proceedings to compel compliance with such order.

(j) Any civil action brought under subsection (e) and any proceedings brought under subsection (i) shall be subject to appeal as provided in sections 1291 and 1292, title 28, United States Code.

(k) In any action or proceeding under this title the court, in its discretion, may allow the prevailing party, other than the Commission or the United States, a reasonable attorney's fee as part of the costs, and the Commission and the United States shall be liable for costs the same as a private person.

Sec. 707. (a) Whenever the Attorney General has reasonable cause to believe that any person or group of persons is engaged in a pattern or practice of resistance to the full enjoyment of any of the rights secured by this title, and that the pattern or practice is of such a nature and is intended to deny the full exercise of the rights herein described, the Attorney General may bring a civil action in the appropriate district court of the United States by filing with it a complaint (1) signed by him (or in his absence the Acting Attorney General), (2) setting forth facts pertaining to such pattern or practice, and (3) requesting such relief, including an application for a permanent or temporary injunction, restraining order or other order against the person or persons responsible for such pattern or practice, as he deems necessary to insure the full enjoyment of the rights herein described.

(b) The district courts of the United States shall have and shall exercise jurisdiction of proceedings instituted pursuant to this section, and in any such proceeding the Attorney General may file with the clerk of such court a request that a court of three judges be convened to hear and determine the case. Such request by the Attorney General shall be accompanied by a certificate that, in his opinion, the case is of general public importance. A copy of the certificate and request for a three-judge court shall be immediately furnished by such clerk to the chief judge of the circuit (or in his absence, the presiding circuit judge of the circuit) in which the case is pending. Upon receipt of such request it shall be the duty of the chief judge of the circuit or the presiding circuit judge, as the case may be, to designate immediately three judges in such circuit, of whom at least one shall be a circuit judge and another of whom shall be a district judge of the court in which the proceeding was instituted, to hear and determine such case, and it shall be the duty of the judges so designated to assign the case for hearing at the earliest practicable date, to participate in the hearing and determination thereof, and to cause the case to be in every way expedited. An appeal from the final judgment of such court will lie to the Supreme Court.

In the event the Attorney General fails to file such a request in any such proceeding, it shall be the duty of the chief judge of the district (or in his absence, the acting chief judge) in which the case is pending immediately to designate a judge in such district to hear and determine the case. In the event that no judge in the district is available to hear and determine the case, the chief judge of the district, or the acting chief judge, as the case may be, shall certify this fact to the chief judge of the circuit (or in his absence, the acting chief judge) who shall then designate a district or circuit judge of the circuit to hear and determine the case.

It shall be the duty of the judge designated pursuant to this section to assign the case for hearing at the earliest practicable date and to cause the case to be in every way expedited.

EFFECT ON STATE LAWS

SEC. 708. Nothing in this title shall be deemed to exempt or relieve any person from any liability, duty, penalty, or punishment provided by any present or future law of any State or political subdivision of a State, other than any such law which purports to require or permit the doing of any act which would be an unlawful employment practice under this title.

INVESTIGATIONS, INSPECTIONS, RECORDS, STATE AGENCIES

SEC. 709. (a) In connection with any investigation of a charge filed under section 706, the Commission or its designated representative shall at all reasonable times have access to, for the purposes of examination, and the right to copy any evidence of any person being investigated or proceeded against that relates to unlawful employment practices covered by this title and is relevant to the charge under investigation.

(b) The Commission may cooperate with State and local agencies charged with the administration of State fair employment practices laws and, with the consent of such agencies, may for the purpose of carrying out its functions and duties under this title and within the limitation of funds appropriated specifically for such purpose, utilize the services of such agencies and their employees and, notwithstanding any other provision of law, may reimburse such agencies and their employees for services rendered to assist the Commission in carrying out this title. In furtherance of such cooperative efforts, the Commission may enter into written agreements with such State or local agencies and such agreements may include provisions under which the Commission shall refrain from processing a charge in any cases or class of cases specified in such agreements and under which no person may bring a civil action under section

706 in any cases or class of cases so specified, or under which the Commission shall relieve any person or class of persons in such State or locality from requirements imposed under this section. The Commission shall rescind any such agreement whenever it determines that the agreement no longer serves the interest of effective enforcement of this title.

(c) Except as provided in subsection (d), every employer, employment agency, and labor organization subject to this title shall (1) make and keep such records relevant to the determinations of whether unlawful employment practices have been or are being committed, (2) preserve such records for such periods, and (3) make such reports therefrom, as the Commission shall prescribe by regulation or order, after public hearing, as reasonable, necessary, or appropriate for the enforcement of this title or the regulations or orders thereunder. The Commission shall, by regulation, require each employer, labor organization, and joint labor-management committee subject to this title which controls an apprenticeship or other training program to maintain such records as are reasonably necessary to carry out the purpose of this title, including, but not limited to, a list of applicants who wish to participate in such program, including the chronological order in which such applications were received, and shall furnish to the Commission, upon request, a detailed description of the manner in which persons are selected to participate in the apprenticeship or other training program. Any employer, employment agency, labor organization, or joint labor-management committee which believes that the application to it of any regulation or order issued under this section would result in undue hardship may (1) apply to the Commission for an exemption from the application of such regulation or order, or (2) bring a civil action in the United States district court for the district where such records are kept. If the Commission or the court, as the case may be, finds that the application of the regulation or order to the employer, employment agency, or labor organization in question would impose an undue hardship, the Commission or the court, as the case may be, may grant appropriate relief.

(d) The provisions of subsection (c) shall not apply to any employer, employment agency, labor organization, or joint labor-management committee with respect to matters occurring in any State or political subdivision thereof which has a fair employment practice law during any period in which such employer, employment agency, labor organization, or joint labor-management committee is subject to such law, except that the Commission may require such notations on records which such employer, employment agency, labor organization, or joint labor-management committee keeps or is required to keep as are necessary because of differences in coverage or methods of enforcement between the State or local law and the provisions of this title. Where an employer is required by Executive Order 10925, issued March 6, 1961, or by any other Executive order prescribing fair employment practices for Government contractors and subcontractors, or by rules or regulations issued thereunder, to file reports relating to his employment practices with any Federal agency or committee, and he is substantially in compliance with such requirements, the Commission shall not require him to file additional reports pursuant to subsection (c) of this section.

(e) It shall be unlawful for any officer or employee of the Commission to make public in any manner whatever any information obtained by the Commission pursuant to its authority under this section prior to the institution of any proceeding under this title involving such information. Any officer or employee of the Commission who shall make public in any manner whatever any information in violation of this subsection shall be guilty of a misdemeanor and upon conviction thereof, shall be fined not more than $1,000, or imprisoned not more than one year.

INVESTIGATORY POWERS

SEC. 710. (a) For the purposes of any investigation of a charge filed under the authority contained in section 706, the Commission shall have authority to examine witnesses under oath and to require the production of documentary evidence relevant or material to the charge under investigation.

(b) If the respondent named in a charge filed under section 706 fails or refuses to comply with a demand of the Commission for permission to examine or to copy evidence in conformity with the provisions of section 709(a), or if any person required to comply with the provisions of section 709 (c) or (d) fails or refuses to do so, or if any person fails or refuses to comply with a demand by the Commission to give testimony under oath, the United States district court for the district in which such person is found, resides, or transacts business, shall, upon application of the Commission, have jurisdiction to issue to such person an order requiring him to comply with the provisions of section 709 (c) or (d) or to comply with the demand of the Commission, but the attendance of a witness may not be required outside the State where he is found, resides, or transacts business and the production of evidence may not be required outside the State where such evidence is kept.

(c) Within twenty days after the service upon any person charged under section 706 of a demand by the Commission for the production of documentary evidence or for permission to examine or to copy evidence in conformity with the provisions of section 709(a), such person may file in the district court of the United States for the judicial district in which he resides, is found, or transacts business, and serve upon the Commission a petition for an order of such court modifying or setting aside such demand. The time allowed for compliance with the demand in whole or in part as deemed proper and ordered by the court shall not run during the pendency of such petition in the court. Such petition shall specify each ground upon which the petitioner relies in seeking such relief, and may be based upon any failure of such demand to comply with the provisions of this title or with the limitations generally applicable to compulsory process or upon any constitutional or other legal right or privilege of such person. No objection which is not raised by such a petition may be urged in the defense to a proceeding initiated by the Commission under subsection (b) for enforcement of such a demand unless such proceeding is commenced by the Commission prior to the expiration of the twenty-day period, or unless the court determines that the defendant could not reasonably have been aware of the availability of such ground of objection.

(d) In any proceeding brought by the Commission under subsection (b), except as provided in subsection (c) of this section, the defendant may petition the court for an order modifying or setting aside the demand of the Commission.

NOTICES TO BE POSTED

SEC. 711. (a) Every employer, employment agency, and labor organization, as the case may be, shall post and keep posted in conspicuous places upon its premises where notices to employees, applicants for employment, and members are customarily posted a notice to be prepared or approved by the Commission setting forth excerpts from or, summaries of, the pertinent provisions of this title information pertinent to the filing of a complaint.

(b) A willful violation of this section shall be punishable by a fine of not more than $100 for each separate offense.

VETERANS' PREFERENCE

SEC. 712. Nothing contained in this title shall be construed to repeal or modify any Federal, State, territorial, or local law creating special rights or preference for veterans.

RULES AND REGULATIONS

SEC. 713. (a) The Commission shall have authority from time to time to issue, amend, or rescind suitable procedural regulations to carry out the provisions of this title. Regulations issued under this section shall be in conformity with the standards and limitations of the Administrative Procedure Act.

(b) In any action or proceeding based on any alleged unlawful employment practice, no person shall be subject to any liability or punishment for or on account of (1) the commission by such person of an unlawful employment practice if he pleads and proves that the act or omission complained of was in good faith, in conformity with, and in reliance on any written interpretation or opinion of the Commission, or (2) the failure of such person to publish and file any information required by any provision of this title if he pleads and proves that he failed to publish and file such information in good faith, in conformity with the instructions of the Commission issued under this title regarding the filing of such information. Such a defense, if established, shall be a bar to the action or proceeding, notwithstanding that (A) after such act or omission, such interpretation or opinion is modified or rescinded or is determined by judicial authority to be invalid or of no legal effect, or (B) after publishing or filing the description and annual reports, such publication or filing is determined by judicial authority not to be in conformity with the requirements of this title.

SEC. 714. The provisions of section 111, title 18, United States Code, shall apply to officers, agents, and employees of the Commission in the performance of their official duties.

SEC. 715. The Secretary of Labor shall make a full and complete study of the factors which might tend to result in discrimination in employment because of age and of the consequences of such discrimination on the economy and individuals affected. The Secretary of Labor shall make a report to the Congress not later than June 30, 1965, containing the results of such study and shall include in such report such recommendations for legislation to prevent arbitrary discrimination in employment because of age as he determines advisable.

SEC. 716. (a) This title shall become effective one year after the date of its enactment.

(b) Notwithstanding subsection (a), sections of this title other than sections 703, 704, 706, and 707 shall become effective immediately.

(c) The President shall, as soon as feasible after the enactment of this title, convene one or more conferences for the purpose of enabling the leaders of groups whose members will be affected by this title to become familiar with the rights afforded and obligations imposed by its provisions, and for the purpose of making plans which will result in the fair and effective administration of this title when all of its provisions become effective. The President shall invite the participation in such conference or conferences of (1) the members of the President's Committee on Equal Employment Opportunity, (2) the members of the Commission on Civil Rights, (3) representatives of State and local agencies engaged in furthering equal employment opportunity, (4) representatives of private agencies engaged in furthering equal employment opportunity, and (5) representatives of employers, labor organizations, and employment agencies who will be subject to this title.

Appendix B

Executive Orders

Executive Order 8802

Reaffirming Policy of Full Participation in the Defense Program by All Persons, Regardless of Race, Creed, Color, or National Origin, and Directing Certain Action in Furtherance of Said Policy

Whereas it is the policy of the United States to encourage full participation in the national defense program by all citizens of the United States, regardless of race, creed, color, or national origin, in the firm belief that the democratic way of life within the Nation can be defended successfully only with the help and support of all groups within its borders; and

Whereas there is evidence that available and needed workers have been barred from employment in industries engaged in defense production solely because of considerations of race, creed, color, or national origin, to the detriment of workers' morale and of national unity:

Now, therefore, by virtue of the authority vested in me by the Constitution and the statutes, and as a prerequisite to the successful conduct of our national defense production effort, I do hereby reaffirm the policy of the United States that there shall be no discrimination in the employment of workers in defense industries or government because of race, creed, color, or national origin, and I do hereby declare that it is the duty of employers and of labor organizations, in furtherance of said policy and of this order, to provide for the full and equitable participation of all workers in defense industries, without discrimination because of race, creed, color, or national origin;

And it is hereby ordered as follows:

1. All departments and agencies of the Government of the United States concerned with vocational and training programs for defense production shall take special measures appropriate to assure that such programs, are administered without discrimination because of race, creed, color, or national origin;

2. All contracting agencies of the Government of the United States shall include in all defense contracts hereafter negotiated by them a provision obligating the contractor not to discriminate against any worker because of race, creed, color, or national origin;

317

3. There is established in the Office of Production Management a Committee on Fair Employment Practice, which shall consist of a chairman and four other members to be appointed by the President. The Chairman and members of the Committee shall serve as such without compensation but shall be entitled to actual and necessary transportation, subsistence and other expenses incidental to performance of their duties. The Committee shall receive and investigate complaints of discrimination in violation of the provisions of this order and shall take appropriate steps to redress grievances which it finds to be valid. The Committee shall also recommend to the several departments and agencies of the Government of the United States and to the President all measures which may be deemed by it necessary or proper to effectuate the provisions of this order.

FRANKLIN D. ROOSEVELT
June 25, 1941

Executive Order 9980

Regulations Governing Fair Employment Practices
Within the Federal Establishment

WHEREAS the principles on which our Government is based require a policy of fair employment through the Federal establishment, without discrimination because of race, color, religion, or national origin; and

WHEREAS it is desirable and in the public interest that all steps be taken necessary to insure that this long-established policy shall be more effectively carried out:

NOW, THEREFORE, by virtue of the authority vested in me as President of the United States, by the Constitution and the laws of the United States, it is hereby ordered as follows:

1. All personnel actions taken by Federal appointing officers shall be based solely on merit and fitness; and such officers are authorized and directed to take appropriate steps to insure that in all such actions there shall be no discrimination because of race, color, religion, or national origin.

2. The head of each department in the executive branch of the Government shall be personally responsible for an effective program to insure that fair employment policies are fully observed in all personnel within his department.

3. The head of each department shall designate an official thereof as Fair Employment Officer. Such Officer shall be given full operating responsibility, under the immediate supervision of the department head, for carrying out the fair-employment policy herein stated. Notice of the appointment of such Officer shall be given to all officers and employees of the department. The Fair Employment Officer shall, among other things—

(a) Appraise the personnel actions of the department at regular intervals to determine their conformity to the fair-employment policy expressed in this order.

(b) Receive complaints or appeals concerning personnel actions taken in the department on grounds of alleged discrimination because of race, color, religion, or national origin.

(c) Appoint such central or regional deputies, committees, or hearing boards, from among the officers of employees of the department, as he may find necessary or desirable on a temporary or permanent basis to investigate, or to receive, complaints of discrimination.

(d) Take necessary corrective or disciplinary action, in consultation with, or on the basis of delegated authority from, the head of the department.

4. The findings or action of the Fair Employment Officer shall be subject to direct appeal to the head of the department. The decision of the head of the department on such appeal shall be subject to appeal to the Fair Employment Board of the Civil Service Commission, hereinafter provided for.

5. There shall be established in the Civil Service Commission a Fair Employment Board (hereinafter referred to as the Board) of not less than seven persons, the members of which shall be officers or employees of the Commission. The Board shall—

(a) Have authority to review decisions made by the head of any department which are appealed pursuant to the provisions of this order, or referred to the Board by the head of the department for advice, and to make recommendations to such head. In any instance in which the recommendation of the Board is not promptly and fully carried out the case shall be reported by the Board to the President, for such action as he finds necessary.

(b) Make rules and regulations, in consultation with the Civil Service Commission, deemed necessary to carry out the Board's duties and responsibilities under this order.

(c) Advise all departments on problems and policies relating to fair employment.

(d) Disseminate information pertinent to fair-employment programs.

(e) Coordinate the fair-employment policies and procedures of the several departments.

(f) Make reports and submit recommendations to the Civil Service Commission for transmittal to the President from time to time, as may be necessary to the maintenance of the fair-employment program.

6. All departments are directed to furnish to the Board all information needed for the review of personnel actions or for the compilation of reports.

7. The term "department" as used herein shall refer to all departments and agencies of the executive branch of the Government, including the Civil Service Commission. The term "personnel action," as used herein, shall include failure to act. Persons failing of appointment who allege a grievance relating to discrimination shall be entitled to the remedies herein provided.

8. The means of relief provided by this order shall be supplemental to those provided by existing statutes, Executive orders, and regulations. The Civil Service Commission shall have authority, in consultation with the Board, to make such additional regulations, and to amend existing regulations, in such manner as may be found necessary or desirable to carry out the purposes of this order.

HARRY S. TRUMAN
July 26, 1948

Executive Order 10308

Improving the Means for Obtaining Compliance with the Nondiscrimination Provisions of Federal Contracts

WHEREAS existing Executive orders require the contracting agencies of the United States Government to include in their contracts a provision obligating the contractor not to discriminate against any employee or applicant for employment because of race, color, creed, or national origin and obligating him to include a similar provision in all subcontracts; and

WHEREAS it is necessary and desirable to improve the means for obtaining compliance with such nondiscrimination provisions:

NOW THEREFORE, by virtue of the authority vested in me by the Constitution and statutes, and as President of the United States, including the authority conferred by the Defense Production Act of 1950, as amended, and pursuant to the authority conferred by and subject to the provisions of section 214 of the act of May 3, 1945, 59 Stat. 134 (31 U.S.C. 691), it is ordered as follows:

Section 1. The head of each contracting agency of the Government of the United States shall be primarily responsible for obtaining compliance by any contractor or subcontractor with the said nondiscrimination provisions of any contract entered into, amended, or modified by his agency and of any subcontract thereunder, and shall take appropriate measures to bring about the said compliance.

Section 2. There is hereby established the Committee on Government Contract Compliance hereinafter referred to as the Committee. The Committee shall be composed of eleven members as follows:

(a) One representative of each of the following named agencies (hereinafter referred to as the participating agencies), who shall be designated by the respective heads of the participating agencies: the Department of Defense, the Department of Labor, the Atomic Energy Commission, the General Services Administration, and the Defense Materials Procurement Agency.

(b) Six other members, who shall be designated by the President. The Committee shall have a chairman and a vice-chairman, both of whom shall be designated by the President from among its members.

Section 3. The Committee is authorized on behalf of the President to examine and study the rules, procedures, and practices of the contracting agencies of the Government as they relate to obtaining compliance with Government contract provisions prohibiting the discrimination referred to above in order to determine in what respects such rules, procedures, and practices may be strengthened and improved. The Committee shall confer and advise with the appropriate officers of the various contracting agencies and with other persons concerned with a view toward the prevention and elimination of such discrimination, and may make to the said officers recommendations which in the judgment of the Committee will prevent or eliminate discrimination. When deemed necessary by the Committee it may submit any of these recommendations to the Director of Defense Mobilization, and the Director shall, when he deems it appropriate, forward such recommendations to the President, accompanied by a statement of his views as to the relationship thereof to the mobilization effort. The Committee shall establish such rules as may be necessary for the performance of its functions under this order.

Section 4. All contracting agencies of the Government are authorized and directed to cooperate with the Committee and, to the extent permitted by law, to furnish the Committee such information and assistance as it may require in the performance of its functions under this order. The participating agencies shall defray such necessary expenses of the Committee as may be authorized by law, including section 214 of the act of May 3, 1945, 59 Stat. 134 (31 U.S.C. 691).

HARRY S. TRUMAN
December 3, 1951

Executive Order 10479

Establishing the Government Contract Committee

WHEREAS it is in the interest of the Nation's economy and security to promote the fullest utilization of all available manpower; and

WHEREAS it is the policy of the United States Government to promote equal employment opportunity for all qualified persons employed or seeking employment on government contracts because such persons are entitled to fair and equitable treatment in all aspects of employment on work paid for from public funds; and

WHEREAS it is the obligation of the contracting agencies of the United States Government and government contractors to insure compliance with, and successful execution of, the equal employment opportunity program of the United States Government; and

WHEREAS existing Executive orders require the government contracting agencies to include in their contracts a provision obligating the government contractor not to discriminate against any employee or applicant for employment because of race, creed, color, or national origin and obligating the government contractor to include a similar provision in all subcontracts; and

WHEREAS a review and analysis of existing practices and procedures of government contracting agencies show that the practices and procedures relating to compliance with the nondiscrimination provisions must be revised and strengthened to eliminate discrimination in all aspects of employment:

NOW, THEREFORE, by virtue of the authority vested in me by the Constitution and statutes, and as President of the United States, and pursuant to the authority conferred by and subject to the provisions of section 214 of the act of May 3, 1954, 59 Stat. 134, (U.S.C. 691), it is ordered as follows:

Section 1. The head of each contracting agency of the Government of the United States shall be primarily responsible for obtaining compliance by any contractor or subcontractor with the said nondiscrimination provisions of any contract entered into, amended, or modified by his agency and of any subcontract thereunder, and shall take appropriate measures to bring about the said compliance.

Section 2. The head of each contracting agency shall take appropriate measures, including but not limited to the establishment of compliance procedures, to carry out the responsibility set forth in section 1 hereof.

Section 3. There is hereby established the Government Contract Committee, hereinafter referred to as the Committee. The Committee shall be composed of fourteen members as follows:

(a) One representative of the following-named agencies to be designated by the respective heads of such agencies: the Atomic Energy Commission, the Department of Commerce, the Department of Defense, the Department of Justice, the Department of Labor, and the General Services Administration.

(b) Eight other members to be appointed by the President. The Chairman and Vice Chairman shall be designated by the President.

Section 4. The Committee shall make recommendations to the contracting agencies for improving and making more effective the nondiscrimination provisions of government contracts. All contracting agencies of the Government are directed and authorized to cooperate with the Committee and, to the extent permitted by law, to furnish the Committee such information and assistance as it may require in the performance of its functions under this order. The Committee shall establish such rules as may be necessary for the performance of its functions under this order, and shall make annual or semiannual reports on its progress to the President.

Section 5. The Committee may receive complaints of alleged violations of the nondiscrimination provisions of government contracts. Complaints received shall be transmitted by the Committee to the appropriate contracting agencies to be processed in accordance with the agencies' procedures for handling such complaints. Each contracting agency shall report to the Committee the action taken with respect to all complaints received by the agency, including those transmitted by the Committee. The Committee shall review and analyze the reports submitted to it by the contracting agencies.

Section 6. The Committee shall encourage the furtherance of an educational program by employer, labor, civic, educational, religious, and other voluntary non-governmental groups in order to eliminate or reduce the basic causes and costs of discrimination in employment.

Section 7. The Committee is authorized to establish and maintain cooperative relationships with agencies of state and local governments, as well as with nongovernmental bodies, to assist in achieving the purpose of this order.

Section 8. The government agencies (except the Department of Justice) designated in section 3 (a) of this order shall defray such necessary expenses of the Committee as may be authorized by law, including section 214 of the act of May 3, 1945, 59 Stat. 134 (31 U.S.C. 691); provided that no agency shall supply more than 50% of the funds necessary to carry out the purposes of this order. The Department of Labor shall provide necessary space and facilities for the Committee. In the case of the Department of Justice the contribution shall be limited to the rendering of legal services.

Section 9. Executive Order No. 10308 of December 5, 1951 (16 F.R. 12303) is hereby revoked and the Committee on Government Contract Compliance established thereby is abolished. All records and property of the said Committee are transferred to the Government Contract Committee. The latter Committee shall wind up any outstanding affairs of the abolished Committee.

> DWIGHT D. EISENHOWER
> August 13, 1953

Executive Order 10557

Approving the Revised Provision in Government Contracts Relating To Nondiscrimination in Employment

WHEREAS the contracting agencies of the United States Government are required by existing Executive orders to include in all contracts executed by them a provision obligating the contractor not to discriminate against any employee or applicant for employment because of race, creed, color, or national origin, and obligating the contractor to include a similar clause in all subcontracts, and

WHEREAS the Committee on Government Contracts is authorized by Executive Order 10479, as amended, to make recommendations to the contracting agencies for improving and making more effective the nondiscrimination provision of Government contracts, and

WHEREAS the Committee on Government Contracts, in consultation with the principal contracting agencies of the Government, has recommended that in the future the contracting agencies of the Government include in place of, and as a means of better explaining, the present nondiscrimination provision of Government contracts, the following provision:

> In connection with the performance of work under this contract, the contractor agrees not to discriminate against any employee or applicant for employment because of race, religion, color, or national origin. The aforesaid provision shall include, but not be limited to, the following: employment, upgrading, demotion, or transfer; recruitment or recruitment advertising; layoff or termination; rates of pay or other forms of compensation; and selection for training including apprenticeship. The contractor agrees to post hereafter in conspicuous places, available for employees and applicants for employment, notices to be provided by the contracting officer setting forth the provisions of the nondiscrimination clause.
>
> The contractor further agrees to insert the foregoing provision in all subcontracts hereunder, except subcontracts for standard commercial supplies or raw materials.

NOW, THEREFORE, by virtue of the authority vested in me by the Constitution and statutes, and as President of the United States, and in order to clarify the provisions of the existing orders, it is ordered as follows:

Section 1. The contract provision relating to nondiscrimination in employment recommended by the Committee on Government Contracts, is hereby approved.

Section 2. The contracting agencies of the Government shall hereafter include the approved nondiscrimination provision in all contracts executed by them on and after a date 90 days subsequent to the date of this order, except:

a. Contracts and subcontracts to be performed outside the United States where no recruitment of workers within the limits of the United States is involved; and

b. Contracts and subcontracts to meet other special requirements or emergencies, if recommended by the Committee on Government Contracts.

Section 3. The General Services Administration shall take appropriate action to revise the standard Government contract forms to accord with the provisions of this order.

DWIGHT D. EISENHOWER
September 3, 1954

Executive Order 10925

Establishing the President's Committee
On Equal Employment Opportunity

WHEREAS discrimination because of race, creed, color, or national origin is contrary to the Constitutional principles and policies of the United States; and

WHEREAS it is the plain and positive obligation of the United States Government to promote and ensure equal opportunity for all qualified persons, without regard to race, creed, color, or national origin, employed or seeking employment with the Federal Government and on government contracts; and

WHEREAS it is the policy of the executive branch of the Government to encourage by positive measures equal opportunity for all qualified persons within the Government; and

WHEREAS it is in the general interest and welfare of the United States to promote its economy, security, and national defense through the most efficient and effective utilization of all available manpower; and

WHEREAS a review and analysis of existing Executive orders, practices, and government agency procedures relating to government employment and compliance with existing nondiscrimination contract provisions reveal an urgent need for expansion and strengthening of efforts to promote full equality of employment opportunity; and

WHEREAS a single governmental committee should be charged with responsibility for accomplishing these objectives:

NOW, THEREFORE, by virtue of the authority vested in me as President of the United States by the Constitution and statutes of the United States, it is ordered as follows:

Part I Establishment of the President's Committee on Equal Employment Opportunity.

Section 101. There is hereby established the President's Committee on Equal Employment Opportunity.

Section 102. The Committee shall be composed as follows:

(a) The Vice President of the United States who is hereby designated Chairman of the Committee and who shall preside at meetings of the Committee.

(b) The Secretary of Labor who is hereby designated Vice Chairman of the Committee and who shall act as Chairman in the absence of the Chairman. The Vice Chairman shall have general supervision and direction of the work of the Committee and of the execution and implementation of the policies and purposes of this order.

(c) The Chairman of the Atomic Energy Commission, the Secretary of Commerce, the Attorney General, the Secretary of Defense, the Secretaries of the

Army, Navy and Air Force, the Administrator of General Services, the Chairman of the Civil Service Commission, and the Administrator of the National Aeronautics and Space Administration. Each such member may designate an alternate to represent him in his absence.

(d) Such other members as the President may from time to time appoint.

(e) An Executive Vice Chairman, designated by the President, who shall be *ex officio* a member of the Committee. The Executive Vice Chairman shall assist the Chairman, the Vice Chairman and the Committee. Between meetings of the Committee he shall be primarily responsible for carrying out the functions of the Committee and may act for the Committee pursuant to its rules, delegations, and other directives. Final action in individual cases or classes of cases may be taken and final orders may be entered on behalf of the Committee by the Executive Vice Chairman when the Committee so authorizes.

Section 103. The Committee shall meet upon the call of the Chairman and at such other times as may be provided by its rules and regulations. It shall

(a) consider and adopt rules and regulations to govern its proceedings;

(b) provide generally for the procedures and policies to implement this order;

(c) consider reports as to progress under this order;

(d) consider and act, where necessary or appropriate, upon matters which may be presented to it by any of its members; and

(e) make such reports to the President as he may require or the Committee shall deem appropriate. Such reports shall be made at least once annually and shall include specific reference to the actions taken and results achieved by each department and agency. The Chairman may appoint sub-committees to make special studies on a continuing basis.

Part II Nondiscrimination in Government Employment

Section 201. The President's Committee on Equal Employment Opportunity established by this order is directed immediately to scrutinize and study employment practices of the Government of the United States, and to consider and recommend additional affirmative steps which should be taken by executive departments and agencies to realize more fully the national policy of nondiscrimination within the executive branch of the Government.

Section 202. All executive departments and agencies are directed to initiate forthwith studies of current government employment practices within their responsibility. The studies shall be in such form as the Committee may prescribe and shall include statistics on current employment patterns, a review of current procedures, and the recommendation of positive measures for the elimination of any discrimination, direct or indirect, which now exists. Reports and recommendations shall be submitted to the Executive Vice Chairman of the Committee no later than sixty days from the effective date of this order, and the Committee, after considering such reports and recommendations, shall report to the President on the current situation and recommend positive measures to accomplish the objectives of this order.

Section 203. The policy expressed in Executive Order No. 10590 of January 18, 1955 (20 F.R. 409), with respect to the exclusion and prohibition of discrimination against any employee or applicant for employment in the Federal Government because of race, color, religion, or national origin is hereby reaffirmed.

Section 204. The President's Committee on Government Employment Policy, established by Executive Order No. 10590 of January 18, 1955 (20 F.R. 409), as amended by Executive Order No. 10722 of August 5, 1957 (22 F.R. 6287), is hereby abolished, and the powers, functions and duties of that Committee are hereby transferred to, and henceforth shall be vested in, and exercised by the President's Committee on Equal Employment Opportunity in addition to the powers conferred by this order.

Part III Obligations of Government Contractors and Subcontractors

Subpart A—Contractors' Agreements

Section 301. Except in contracts exempted in accordance with section 303 of this order, all government contracting agencies shall include in every government contract hereafter entered into the following provisions:

"In connection with the performance of work under this contract, the contractor agrees as follows:

"(1) The contractor will not discriminate against any employee or applicant for employment because of race, creed, color, or national origin. The contractor will take affirmative action to ensure that applicants are employed, and that employees are treated during employment without regard to their race, creed, color, or national origin. Such action shall include, but not be limited to the following: employment, upgrading, demotion or transfer; recruitment or recruitment advertising; layoff or termination; rates of pay or other forms of compensation; and selection for training, including apprenticeship. The contractor agrees to post in conspicuous places, available to employees and applicants for employment, notices to be provided by the contracting officer setting forth the provisions of this nondiscrimination clause.

"(2) The contractor will, in all solicitations or advertisements for employees placed by or on behalf of the contractor, state that all qualified applicants will receive consideration for employment without regard to race, creed, color, or national origin.

"(3) The contractor will send to each labor union or representative of workers with which he has a collective bargaining agreement or other contract or understanding, a notice to be provided by the agency contracting officer, advising the said labor union or workers' representative of the contractor's commitments under this section, and shall post copies of the notice in conspicuous places available to employees and applicants for employment.

"(4) The contractor will comply with all provisions of Executive Order No. 10925 of March 6, 1961, and of the rules, regulations, and relevant orders of the President's Committee on Equal Employment Opportunity created thereby.

"(5) The contractor will furnish all information and reports required by Executive Order No. 10925 of March 6, 1961, and by the rules, regulations, and orders of the said Committee, or pursuant thereto, and will permit access to his books, records, and accounts by the contracting agency and the Committee for purposes of investigation to ascertain compliance with such rules, regulations, and orders.

"(6) In the event of the contractor's non-compliance with the nondiscrimination clauses of this contract or with any of the said rules, regulations, or orders, this contract may be cancelled in whole or in part and the contractor may be declared ineligible for further government contracts in accordance with procedures authorized in Executive Order No. 10925 of March 6, 1961, and such other sanctions may be imposed and remedies invoked as provided in the said Executive order or by rule, regulation, or order of the President's Committee on Equal Employment Opportunity, or as otherwise provided by law.

"(7) The contractor will include the provisions of the foregoing paragraphs (1) through (6) in every subcontract or purchase order unless exempted by rules, regulations, or orders of the President's Committee on Equal Employment Opportunity issued pursuant to section 303 of Executive Order No. 10925 of March 6, 1961, so that such provisions will be binding upon each subcontractor or vendor. The contractor will take such action with respect to any subcontract or purchase order as the contracting agency may direct as a means of enforcing such provisions including sanctions for non-compliance: Provided, however, that in the event the contractor becomes involved in, or is threatened with, litigation with a subcontractor or vendor as a result of such direction by the contracting agency, the contractor may request the United States to enter into such litigation to protect the interests of the United States."

Section 302.

(a) Each contractor having a contract containing the provisions prescribed in section 301 shall file, and shall cause each of its subcontractors to file, Compliance Reports with the contracting agency, which will be subject to review by the Committee upon its request. Compliance Reports shall be filed within such times and shall contain such information as to the practices, policies, programs, and employment statistics of the contractor and each subcontractor, and shall be in such form, as the Committee may prescribe.

(b) Bidders or prospective contractors or subcontractors may be required to state whether they have participated in any previous contract subject to the provisions of this order, and in that event to submit on behalf of themselves and their proposed subcontractors, Compliance Reports prior to or as an initial part of their bid or negotiation of a contract.

(c) Whenever the contractor or subcontractor has a collective bargaining agreement or other contract or understanding with a labor union or other representative of workers, the Compliance Report shall include such information as to the labor union's or other representative's practices and policies affecting compliance as the Committee may prescribe: Provided, that to the extent such information is within the exclusive possession of a labor union or other workers' representative and the labor union or representative shall refuse to furnish such information to the contractor, the contractor shall so certify to the contracting agency as part of its Compliance Report and shall set forth what efforts he has made to obtain such information.

(d) The Committee may direct that any bidder or prospective contractor or subcontractor shall submit, as part of his Compliance Report, a statement in writing, signed by an authorized officer or agent of any labor union or other workers' representative with which the bidder or prospective contractor deals, together with supporting information, to the effect that the said labor union's or representative's practices and policies do not discriminate on the grounds of race, color, creed, or national origin, and that the labor union or representative either will affirmatively cooperate, within the limits of his legal and contractual authority, in the implementation of the policy and provisions of this order or that it consents and agrees that recruitment, employment, and the terms and conditions of employment under the proposed contract shall be in accordance with the purposes and provisions of the order. In the event that the union or representative shall refuse to execute such a statement, the Compliance Report shall so certify and set forth what efforts have been made to secure such a statement.

Section 303. The Committee may, when it deems that special circumstances in the national interest so require, exempt a contracting agency from the requirement of including the provisions of section 301 of this order in any specific contract, subcontract, or purchase order. The Committee may, by rule or regulation, also exempt certain classes of contracts, subcontracts, or purchase orders (a) where work is to be or has been performed outside the United States and no recruitment of workers within the limits of the United States is involved; (b) for standard commercial supplies or raw materials; or (c) involving less than specified amounts of money or specified numbers of workers.

Subpart B—Labor Unions and Representatives of Workers

Section 304. The Committee shall use its best efforts, directly and through contracting agencies, contractors, state and local officials and public and private agencies, and all other available instrumentalities, to cause any labor union, recruiting agency or other representative of workers who is or may be engaged in work under Government contracts to cooperate with, and to comply in the implementation of, the purposes of this order.

Section 305. The Committee may, to effectuate the purposes of section 304 of this order, hold hearings, public or private, with respect to the practices and policies of any such labor organization. It shall from time to time submit special reports to the President concerning discriminatory practices and policies of any such labor organization, and may recommend remedial action if, in its judgment, such action is necessary or appropriate. It may also notify any Federal, state, or local agency of its conclusions and recommendations with respect to any such labor organization which in its judgment has failed to cooperate with the Committee, contracting agencies, contractors, or subcontractors in carrying out the purposes of this order.

Subpart C—Powers and Duties of the President's Committee on Equal Employment Opportunity and of Contracting Agencies

Section 306. The Committee shall adopt such rules and regulations and issue such orders as it deems necessary and appropriate to achieve the purposes of this order, including the purposes of Part II hereof relating to discrimination in Government employment.

Section 307. Each contracting agency shall be primarily responsible for obtaining compliance with the rules, regulations, and orders of the Committee with respect to contracts entered into by such agency or its contractors or affecting its own employment practices. All contracting agencies shall comply with the Committee's rules in discharging their primary responsibility for securing compliance with the provisions of contracts and otherwise with the terms of this Executive order and of the rules, regulations, and orders of the Committee pursuant hereto. They are directed to cooperate with the Committee, and to furnish the Committee such information and assistance as it may require in the performance of its functions under this order. They are further directed to appoint or designate, from among the agency's personnel, compliance officers. It shall be the duty of such officers to seek compliance with the objectives of this order by conference, conciliation, mediation, or persuasion.

Section 308. The Committee is authorized to delegate to any officer, agency, or employee in the executive branch of the Government any function of the Committee under this order, except the authority to promulgate rules and regulations of a general nature.

Section 309.

(a) The Committee may itself investigate the employment practices of any Government contractor or subcontractor, or initiate such investigation by the appropriate contracting agency or through the Secretary of Labor to determine whether or not the contractual provisions specified in section 301 of this order have been violated. Such investigation shall be conducted in accordance with the procedures established by the Committee, and the investigating agency shall report to the Committee any action taken or recommended.

(b) The Committee may receive and cause to be investigated complaints by employees or prospective employees of a Government contractor or subcontractor which allege discrimination contrary to the contractual provisions specified in section 301 of this order. The appropriate contracting agency or the Secretary of Labor, as the case may be, shall report to the Committee what action has been taken or is recommended with regard to such complaints.

Section 310.

(a) The Committee, or any agency or officer of the United States designated by rule, regulation, or order of the Committee, may hold such hearings, public or private, as the Committee may deem advisable for compliance, enforcement, or educational purposes.

(b) The Committee may hold, or cause to be held, hearings in accordance with subsection (a) of this section prior to imposing, ordering, or recommending the imposition of penalties and sanctions under this order, except that no order for debarment of any contractor from further government contracts shall be made without a hearing.

Section 311. The Committee shall encourage the furtherance of an educational program by employer, labor, civic, educational, religious, and other nongovernmental groups in order to eliminate or reduce the basic causes of discrimination in employment on the grounds of race, creed, color, or national origin.

Subpart D—Sanctions and Penalties

Section 312. In accordance with such rules, regulations or orders as the Committee may issue or adopt, the Committee or the appropriate contracting agency may:

(a) Publish, or cause to be published, the names of contractors or unions which it has concluded have complied or have failed to comply with the provisions of this order or of the rules, regulations, and orders of the Committee.

(b) Recommend to the Department of Justice that, in cases where there is substantial or material violation or the threat of substantial or material violation of the contractual provisions set forth in section 301 of this order, appropriate proceedings be brought to enforce those provisions, including the enjoining, within the·limitations of applicable law, of organizations, individuals or groups who prevent directly or indirectly, or seek to prevent directly or indirectly, compliance with the aforesaid provisions.

(c) Recommend to the Department of Justice that criminal proceedings be brought for the furnishing of false information to any contracting agency or to the Committee as the case may be.

(d) Terminate, or cause to be terminated, any contract, or any portion or portions thereof, for failure of the contractor or subcontractor to comply with the nondiscrimination provisions of the contract. Contracts may be terminated absolutely or continuance of contracts may be conditioned upon a program for future compliance approved by the contracting agency.

(e) Provide that any contracting agency shall refrain from entering into further contracts, or extensions or other modifications of existing contractor, until such contractor has satisfied the Committee that he has established and will carry out personnel and employment policies in compliance with the provisions of this order.

(f) Under rules and regulations prescribed by the Committee, each contracting agency shall make reasonable efforts within a reasonable time limitation to secure compliance with the contract provisions of this order by methods of conference, conciliation, mediation, and persuasion before proceedings shall be instituted under paragraph (b) of this section, or before a contract shall be terminated in whole or in part under paragraph (d) of this section for failure of a contractor or subcontractor to comply with the contract provisions of this order.

Section 313. Any contracting agency taking any action authorized by this section, whether on its own motion, or as directed by the Committee, or under the Committee's rules and regulations, shall promptly notify the Committee of such action or reasons for not acting. Where the Committee itself makes a determination under this section, it shall promptly notify the appropriate contracting agency of the action recommended. The agency shall take such action and shall report the results thereof to the Committee within such time as the Committee shall provide.

Section 314. If the Committee shall so direct, contracting agencies shall not enter into contracts with any bidder or prospective contractor unless the bidder or prospective contractor has satisfactorily complied with the provisions of this order or submits a program for compliance acceptable to the Committee or, if the Committee so authorizes, to the contracting agency.

Section 315. Whenever a contracting agency terminates a contract, or whenever a contractor has been debarred from further Government contracts, because of noncompliance with the contractor provisions with regard to nondiscrimination, the Committee, or the contracting agency involved, shall promptly notify the Comptroller General of the United States.

Subpart E—Certificates of Merit

Section 316. The Committee may provide for issuance of a United States Government Certificate of Merit to employers or employee organizations which are or may hereafter be engaged in work under Government contracts, if the Committee is satisfied that the personnel and employment practices of the employer, or that the personnel, training, apprenticeship, membership, grievance and representation, upgrading and other practices and policies of the employee organization, conform to the purposes and provisions of this order.

Section 317. Any Certificate of Merit may at any time be suspended or revoked by the Committee if the holder thereof, in the judgment of the Committee, has failed to comply with the provisions of this order.

Section 318. The Committee may provide for the exemption of any employer or employee organization from any requirement for furnishing information as to compliance if such employer or employee organization has been awarded a Certificate of Merit which has not been suspended or revoked.

Part IV—Miscellaneous

Section 401. Each contracting agency (except the Department of Justice) shall defray such necessary expenses of the Committee as may be authorized by law, including section 214 of the act of May 3, 1945, 59 Stat. 134 (31 U.S.C. 691): Provided, that no agency shall supply more than fifty percent of the funds necessary to carry out the purposes of this order. The Department of Labor shall provide necessary space and facilities for the Committee. In the case of the Department of Justice, the contribution shall be limited to furnishing legal services.

Section 402. This order shall become effective thirty days after its execution. The General Services Administration shall take appropriate action to revise the standard Government contract forms to accord with the provisions of this order and of the rules and regulations of the Committee.

Section 403. Executive Order No. 10479 of August 13, 1953 (18 F.R. 4899), together with Executive Orders Nos. 10482 of August 15, 1953 (18 F.R. 4944), and 10733 of October 10, 1957 (22 F.R. 8135), amending that order, and Executive Order No. 10557 of September 3, 1954 (19 F.R. 5655), are hereby revoked, and the Government Contract Committee established by Executive Order No. 10479 is abolished. All records and property of or in the custody of the said Committee are hereby transferred to the President's Committee on Equal Employment Opportunity, which shall wind up the outstanding affairs of the Government Contract Committee.

JOHN F. KENNEDY
March 6, 1961

Executive Order 11246

Under and by virtue of the authority vested in me as President of the United States by the Constitution and statutes of the United States, it is ordered as follows:

PART I Nondiscrimination in Government Employment

[Secs. 101–105, barring discrimination in federal employment on account of race, color, religion, sex or national origin, were superseded by Executive Order 11478. These provisions called for affirmative-action programs for equal opportunity at the agency level under general supervision of the Civil Service Commission; establishment of complaint procedures at each agency with appeal to the Commission; and promulgation of regulations by CSC.]

PART II Nondiscrimination in Employment by Government Contractors and Subcontractors

SUBPART A—Duties of the Secretary of Labor

Sec. 201. The Secretary of Labor shall be responsible for the administration of Parts II and III of this Order and shall adopt such rules and regulations and issue such orders as he deems necessary and appropriate to achieve the purposes thereof.

SUBPART B—Contractors' Agreements

Sec. 202. Except in contracts exempted in accordance with Section 204 of this Order, all Government contracting agencies shall include in every Government contract hereafter entered into the following provisions:

"During the performance of this contract, the contractor agrees as follows:

"(1) The contractor will not discriminate against any employee or applicant for employment because of race, color, religion, sex or national origin. The contractor will take affirmative action to ensure that applicants are employed, and that employees are treated during employment, without regard to their race, color, religion, sex, or national origin. Such action shall include, but not be limited to the following: employment, upgrading, demotion, or transfer; recruitment or recruitment advertising; layoff or termination; rates of pay or other forms of compensation; and selection for training, including apprenticeship. The contractor agrees to post in conspicuous places, available to employees and applicants for employment, notices to be provided by the contracting officer setting forth the provisions of this nondiscrimination clause.

"(2) The contractor will, in all solicitations or advertisements for employees placed by or on behalf of the contractor, state that all qualified applicants will receive consideration for employment without regard to race, color, religion, sex, or national origin.

"(3) The contractor will send to each labor union or representative of workers with which he has a collective bargaining agreement or other contract or understanding, a notice, to be provided by the agency contracting officer, advising the labor union or workers' representative of the contractor's commitments under Section 202 of Executive Order No. 11246 of September 24, 1965, and shall post copies of the notice in conspicuous places available to employees and applicants for employment.

"(4) The contractor will comply with all provisions of Executive Order No. 11246 of September 24, 1965, and of the rules, regulations, and orders of the Secretary of Labor.

"(5) The contractor will furnish all information and reports required by Executive Order No. 11246 of September 24, 1965, and by the rules, regulations, and orders of the Secretary of Labor, or pursuant thereto, and will permit access to his books, records, and accounts by the contracting agency and the Secretary of Labor for purposes of investigation to ascertain compliance with such rules, regulations, and orders.

"(6) In the event of the contractor's noncompliance with the nondiscrimination clauses of this contract or with any of such rules, regulations, or orders this contract may be cancelled, terminated, or suspended in whole or in part and the contractor may be declared ineligible for further Government contracts in accordance with procedures authorized in Executive Order No. 11246 of September 24, 1965, and such other sanctions may be imposed and remedies invoked as provided in Executive Order No. 11246 of September 24, 1965, or by rule, regulation, or order of the Secretary of Labor or as otherwise provided by law.

"(7) The contractor will include the provisions of Paragraphs (1) through (7) in every subcontract or purchase order unless exempted by rules, regulations, or orders of the Secretary of Labor issued pursuant to Section 204 of Executive Order No. 11246 of September 24, 1965, so that such provisions will be binding upon each subcontractor or vendor. The contractor will take such action with respect to any subcontract or purchase order as the contracting agency may direct as a means of enforcing such provisions including sanctions for noncompliance: Provided, however, That in the event the contractor becomes involved in, or is threatened with, litigation with a subcontractor or vendor as a result of such direction by the contracting agency, the contractor may request the United States to enter into such litigation to protect the interest of the United States."

Sec. 203.

(a) Each contractor having a contract containing the provisions prescribed in Section 202 shall file, and shall cause each of his subcontractors to file, Compliance Reports with the contracting agency or the Secretary of Labor as may be directed. Compliance Reports shall be filed within such times and shall contain such information as to the practices, policies, programs, and employment policies, programs, and employment statistics of the contractor and each subcontractor, and shall be in such form, as the Secretary of Labor may prescribe.

(b) Bidders or prospective contractors or subcontractors may be required to state whether they have participated in any previous contract subject to the provisions of this Order, or any preceding similar executive order, and in that event to submit, on behalf of themselves and their proposed subcontractors, Compliance Reports prior to or as an initial part of their bid or negotiation of a contract.

(c) Whenever the contractor or subcontractor has a collective bargaining agreement or other contract or understanding with a labor union or an agency referring workers or providing or supervising apprenticeship or training for such workers, the Compliance Report shall include such information as to such labor union's or agency's practices and policies affecting compliance as the

Secretary of Labor may prescribe: Provided, That to the extent such information is within the exclusive possession of a labor union or an agency referring workers or providing or supervising apprenticeship or training and such labor union or agency shall refuse to furnish such information to the contractor, the contractor shall so certify to the contracting agency as part of its Compliance Report and shall set forth what efforts he has made to obtain such information.

(d) The contracting agency or the Secretary of Labor may direct that any bidder or prospective contractor or subcontractor shall submit, as part of his Compliance Report, a statement in writing, signed by an authorized officer or agent on behalf of any labor union or any agency referring workers or providing or supervising apprenticeship or other training, with which the bidder or prospective contractor deals, with supporting information, to the effect that the signer's practices and policies do not discriminate on the grounds of race, color, religion, sex, or national origin, and that the signer either will affirmatively cooperate in the implementation of the policy and provisions of this Order or that it consents and agrees that recruitment, employment, and the terms and conditions of employment under the proposed contract shall be in accordance with the purposes and provisions of the Order. In the event that the union or the agency shall refuse to execute such a statement, the Compliance Report shall so certify and set forth what efforts have been made to secure such a statement and such additional factual material as the contracting agency or the Secretary of Labor may require.

Sec. 204. The Secretary of Labor may, when he deems that special circumstances in the national interest so require, exempt a contracting agency from the requirement of including any or all of the provisions of Section 202 of this Order in any specific contract, subcontract, or purchase order. The Secretary of Labor may, by rule or regulation, also exempt certain classes of contracts, subcontracts, or purchase orders (1) whenever work is to be or has been performed outside the United States and no recruitment of workers within the limits of the United States is involved; (2) for standard commercial supplies or raw materials; (3) involving less than specified amounts of money or specified numbers of workers; or (4) to the extent that they involve subcontracts below a specified tier. The Secretary of Labor may also provide, by rule, regulation, or order, for the exemption of facilities of a contractor which are in all respects separate and distinct from activities of the contractor related to the performance of the contract: Provided, That such an exemption will not interfere with or impede the effectuation of the purposes of this Order: And provided further, That in the absence of such an exemption all facilities shall be covered by the provisions of this Order.

SUBPART C—Powers and Duties of the Secretary of Labor and the Contracting Agencies

Sec. 205. Each contracting agency shall be primarily responsible for obtaining compliance with the rules, regulations, and orders of the Secretary of Labor with respect to contracts entered into by such agency or its contractors. All contracting agencies shall comply with the rules of the Secretary of Labor in discharging their primary responsibility for securing compliance with the provisions of contracts and otherwise with the terms of this Order and of the rules, regulations, and orders of the Secretary of Labor issued pursuant to this Order. They are directed to cooperate with the Secretary of Labor and to furnish the Secretary of Labor such information and assistance as he may require in the performance of his functions under this Order. They are further directed to appoint or designate, from among the agency's personnel, compliance officers. It shall be the duty of such officers to seek compliance with the objectives of this Order by conference, conciliation, mediation, or persuasion.

Sec. 206.

(a) The Secretary of Labor may investigate the employment practices of any Government contractor or subcontractor, or initiate such investigation by the appropriate contracting agency, to determine whether or not the contractual provisions specified in Section 202 of this Order have been violated. Such investigation shall be conducted in accordance with the procedures established by the Secretary of Labor and the investigating agency shall report to the Secretary of Labor any action taken or recommended.

(b) The Secretary of Labor may receive and investigate or cause to be investigated complaints by employees or prospective employees of a Government contractor or subcontractor which allege discrimination contrary to the contractual provisions specified in Section 202 of this Order. If this investigation is conducted for the Secretary of Labor by a contracting agency, that agency shall report to the Secretary what action has been taken or is recommended with regard to such complaints.

Sec. 207. The Secretary of Labor shall use his best efforts, directly and through contracting agencies, other interested Federal, State, and local agencies, contractors, and all other local agencies, contractors, and all other available instrumentalities to cause any labor union engaged in work under Government contracts or any agency referring workers or providing or supervising apprenticeship or training for or in the course of such work to cooperate in the implementation of the purposes of this Order. The Secretary of Labor shall, in appropriate cases, notify the Equal Employment Opportunity Commission, the Department of Justice, or other appropriate Federal agencies whenever it has reason to believe that the practices of any such labor organization or agency violate Title VI or Title VII of the Civil Rights Act of 1964 or other provision of Federal law.

Sec. 208. (a) The Secretary of Labor, or any agency, officer, or employee in the executive branch of the Government designated by rule, regulation, or order of the Secretary, may hold such hearings, public or private, as the Secretary may deem advisable for compliance, enforcement, or educational purposes.

(b) The Secretary of Labor may hold, or cause to be held, hearings in accordance with Subsection (a) of this Section prior to imposing, ordering, or recommending the imposition of penalties and sanctions under this Order. No order for debarment of any contractor from further Government contracts under Section 209 (a)(6) shall be made without affording the contractor an opportunity for a hearing.

SUBPART D—Sanctions and Penalties

Sec. 209. (a) In accordance with such rules, regulations, or orders as the Secretary of Labor may issue or adopt, the Secretary or the appropriate contracting agency may:

(1) Publish, or cause to be published, the names of contractors or unions which it has concluded have complied or have failed to comply with the provisions of this Order or the rules, regulations, and orders of the Secretary of Labor.

(2) Recommend to the Department of Justice that, in cases in which there is substantial or material violation or the threat of substantial or material violation of the contractual provisions set forth in Section 202 of this Order, appropriate proceedings be brought to enforce these provisions, including the enjoining, within the limitations of applicable law, of organizations, individuals, or groups who prevent directly or indirectly, or seek to prevent directly or indirectly, compliance with the provisions of this Order.

(3) Recommend to the Equal Employment Opportunity Commission or the Department of Justice that appropriate proceedings be instituted under Title VII of the Civil Rights Act of 1964.

(4) Recommend to the Department of Justice that criminal proceedings be brought for the furnishing of false information to any contracting agency or to the Secretary of Labor as the case may be.

(5) Cancel, terminate, suspend, or cause to be cancelled, terminated, or suspended, any contract, or any portion or portions thereof, for failure of the contractor or subcontractor to comply with the nondiscrimination provisions of the contract. Contracts may be cancelled, terminated, or suspended absolutely or continuance of contracts may be conditioned upon a program for future compliance approved by the contracting agency.

(6) Provide that any contracting agency shall refrain from entering into further contracts, or extensions or other modifications of existing contracts, with any noncomplying contractor, until such contractor has satisfied the Secretary of Labor that such contractor has established and will carry out personnel and employment policies in compliance with the provisions of this Order.

(b) Under rules and regulations prescribed by the Secretary of Labor, each contracting agency shall make reasonable efforts within a reasonable time limitation to secure compliance with the contract provisions of this Order by methods of conference, conciliation, mediation, and persuasion before proceedings shall be instituted under Subsection (a)(2) of this Section, or before a contract shall be cancelled or terminated in whole or in part under Subsection (a)(5) of this Section for failure of a contractor or subcontractor to comply with the contract provisions of this Order.

Sec. 210. Any contracting agency taking any action authorized by this Subpart whether on its own motion, or as directed by the Secretary of Labor, or under the rules and regulations of the Secretary, shall promptly notify the Secretary of such action. Whenever the Secretary of Labor makes a determination under this Section, he shall promptly notify the appropriate contracting agency of the action recommended. The agency shall take such action and shall report the results thereof to the Secretary of Labor within such time as the Secretary shall specify.

Sec. 211. If the Secretary shall so direct, contracting agencies shall not enter into contracts with any bidder or prospective contractor unless the bidder or prospective contractor has satisfactorily complied with the provisions of this Order or submits a program for compliance acceptable to the Secretary of Labor or, if the Secretary so authorizes, to the contracting agency.

Sec. 212. Whenever a contracting agency cancels or terminates a contract or whenever a contractor has been debarred from further Government contracts, under Section 209 (a) (6) because of noncompliance with the contract provisions with regard to nondiscrimination, the Secretary of Labor or the contracting agency involved shall promptly notify the Comptroller General of the United States. Any such debarment may be rescinded by the Secretary of Labor or by the contracting agency which imposed the sanction.

SUBPART E—Certificates of Merit

Sec. 213. The Secretary of Labor may provide for issuance of a United States Government Certificate of Merit to employers or labor unions, or other agencies which are or may hereafter be engaged in work under Government contracts, if the Secretary is satisfied that the personnel and employment practices of the employer, or that the personnel training, apprenticeship, membership, grievance and representation, upgrading, and other practices and policies of the labor union or other agency conform to the purposes and provisions of this Order.

Sec. 214. Any Certificate of Merit may at any time be suspended or revoked by the Secretary of Labor if the holder thereof, in the judgment of the Secretary, has failed to comply with the provisions of this Order.

Sec. 215. The Secretary of Labor may provide for the exemption of any employer, labor union, or other agency from any reporting requirements imposed under or pursuant to this Order if such employer, labor union, or other agency has been awarded a Certificate of Merit which has not been suspended or revoked.

PART III Nondiscrimination Provisions in Federally Assisted Construction Contracts

Sec. 301. Each executive department and agency which administers a program involving Federal financial assistance shall require as a condition for the approval of any grant, contract, loan, insurance, or guarantee thereunder, which may involve a construction contract, that the applicant for Federal assistance undertake and agree to incorporate, or cause to be incorporated, into all construction contracts paid for in whole or in part with funds obtained from the Federal Government or borrowed on the credit of the Federal Government pursuant to such grant, contract, loan, insurance, or guarantee, or undertaken pursuant to any Federal program involving such grant, contract, loan, insurance, or guarantee, the provisions prescribed for Government contracts by Section 203 of this Order or such modification thereof, preserving in substance the contractor's obligations thereunder, as may be approved by the Secretary of Labor, together with such additional provisions as the Secretary deems appropriate to establish and protect the interest of the United States in the enforcement of those obligations. Each such applicant shall also undertake and agree (1) to assist and cooperate actively with the administering department or agency and the Secretary of Labor in obtaining the compliance of contractors and subcontractors with those contract provisions and with the rules, regulations, and relevant orders of the Secretary, (2) to obtain and to furnish the administering department or agency and to the Secretary of Labor such information as they may require for the supervision of such compliance, (3) to carry out sanctions and penalties for violation of such obligations imposed upon contractors and subcontractors by the Secretary of Labor or the administering department or agency pursuant to Part II, Subpart D, of this Order, and (4) to refrain from entering into any contract subject to this Order, or extension or other modification of such a contract with a contractor debarred from Government contracts under Part II, Subpart D, of this Order.

Sec. 302. (a) "Construction contract" as used in this Order means any contract for the construction, rehabilitation, alteration, conversion, extension, or repair of buildings, highways, or other improvements to real property.

(b) The provisions of Part II of this Order shall apply to such construction contracts, and for purposes of such application the administering department or agency shall be considered the contracting agency referred to therein.

(c) The term "applicant" as used in this Order means an applicant for Federal assistance or, as determined by agency regulation, other program participant, with respect to whom an application for any grant, contract, loan, insurance, or guarantee is not finally acted upon prior to the effective date of this Part, and it includes such an applicant after he becomes a recipient of such Federal assistance.

Sec. 303. (a) Each administering department and agency shall be responsible for obtaining the compliance of such applicants with their undertaking under this Order. Each administering department and agency is directed to cooperate with the Secretary of Labor, and to furnish the Secretary such information and assistance as he may require in the performance of his functions under this Order.

(b) In the event an applicant fails and refuses to comply with his undertakings, the administering department or agency may take any or all of the following actions: (1) cancel, terminate, or suspend in whole or in part the agreement contract, or other arrangement with such applicant with respect to which the failure and refusal occurred; (2) refrain from extending any further assistance to the applicant under the program with respect to which the failure or refusal occurred until satisfactory assurance of future compliance has been received from such applicant; and (3) refer the case to the Department of Justice for appropriate legal proceedings.

(c) Any action with respect to an applicant pursuant to Subsection (b) shall be taken in conformity with Section 602 of the Civil Rights Act of 1964 (and the regulations of the administering department or agency issued thereunder), to the extent applicable. In no case shall action be taken with respect to an applicant pursuant to Clause (1) or (2) of Subsection (b) without notice and opportunity for hearing before the administering department or agency.

Sec. 304. Any executive department or agency which imposes by rule, regulation, or order requirements of nondiscrimination in employment, other than requirements imposed pursuant to this Order may delegate to the Secretary of Labor by agreement such responsibilities with respect to compliance standards, reports, and procedures as would tend to bring the administration of such requirements into conformity with the administration of requirements imposed under this Order: Provided, That actions to effect compliance by recipients of Federal financial assistance with requirements imposed pursuant to Title VI of the Civil Rights Act of 1964 shall be taken in conformity with the procedures and limitations prescribed in Section 602 thereof and the regulations of the administering department or agency issued thereunder.

PART IV Miscellaneous

Sec. 401. The Secretary of Labor may delegate to any office, agency, or employee in the Executive branch of the Government, any function or duty of the Secretary under Parts II and III of this Order, except authority to promulgate rules and regulations of a general nature.

Sec. 402. The Secretary of Labor shall provide administrative support for the execution of the program known as the "Plans for Progress."

Sec. 403. (a) Executive Orders Nos. 10590 (January 18, 1955), 10722 (August 5, 1957), 10925 (March 6, 1961), 11114 (June 22, 1963), and 11162 (July 28, 1964) are hereby superseded and the President's Committee on Equal Employment Opportunity established by Executive Order No. 10925 is hereby abolished.

(All records and property in the custody of the Committee shall be transferred to the Civil Service Commission and the Secretary of Labor, as appropriate.)

(b) Nothing in this Order shall be deemed to relieve any person of any obligation assumed or imposed under or pursuant to any executive order superseded by this Order. All rules, regulations, orders, instructions, designations, and other directives issued by the President's Committee on Equal Employment Opportunity and those issued by the heads of various departments or agencies under or pursuant to any of the executive orders superseded by this Order, shall, to the extent that they are not inconsistent with this Order, remain in full force and effect unless and until revoked or superseded by appropriate authority. References in such directives to provisions of the superseded orders shall be deemed to be references to the comparable provisions of this Order.

Sec. 404. The General Services Administration shall take appropriate action to revise the standard Government contract forms to accord with the provisions of this Order and of the rules and regulations of the Secretary of Labor.

Sec. 405. This Order shall become effective 30 days after the date of this Order.

LYNDON B. JOHNSON
September 24, 1965

REVISED ORDER, NUMBER 4

U. S. DEPARTMENT OF LABOR
OFFICE OF FEDERAL CONTRACT COMPLIANCE
Washington, D. C. 20210

CHAPTER 60—Office of Federal Contract Compliance,
Equal Employment Opportunity, Department of Labor

(Reprint from FEDERAL REGISTER, VOL. 36, NO. 234—
SATURDAY, DECEMBER 4, 1971)

TITLE 41—PUBLIC CONTRACTS AND PROPERTY MANAGEMENT
Chapter 60—Office of Federal Contract Compliance, Equal Employment Opportunity, Department of Labor

PART 60-2—AFFIRMATIVE ACTION PROGRAMS

On August 31, 1971, notice of proposed rule making was published in the FEDERAL REGISTER (36 F.R. 17444) with regard to amending Chapter 60 of Title 41 of the Code of Federal Regulations by adding a new Part 60-2, dealing with affirmative action programs. Interested persons were given 30 days in which to submit written comments, suggestions, or objections regarding the proposed amendments.

Having considered all relevant material submitted, I have decided to, and do hereby amend Chapter 60 of Title 41 of the Code of Federal Regulations by adding a new Part 60-2, reading as follows:

Subpart A—General

Sec.

60-2.1   Title, purpose and scope.
60-2.2   Agency action.

Subpart B—Required Contents of Affirmative Action Programs

60-2.10   Purpose of affirmative action program.
60-2.11   Required utilization analysis.
60-2.12   Establishment of goals and timetables.
60-2.13   Additional required ingredients of affirmative action programs.
60-2.14   Compliance status.

Subpart C—Methods of Implementing the Requirements of Subpart B

60-2.20   Development or reaffirmation of the equal employment opportunity policy.
60-2.21   Dissemination of the policy.
60-2.22   Responsibility for implementation.
60-2.23   Identification of problem areas by organization unit and job classification.
60-2.24   Development and execution of programs.
60-2.25   Internal audit and reporting systems.
60-2.26   Support of action programs.

Subpart D—Miscellaneous

60-2.30   Use of goals.
60-2.31   Preemption.
60-2.32   Supersedure.

AUTHORITY: The provisions of this Part 60-2 issued pursuant to sec. 201, Executive Order 11246 (30 F.R. 12319).

Subpart A—General

§60-2.1 Title, purpose and scope.

This part shall also be known as "Revised Order No. 4," and shall cover non-construction contractors. Section 60-1.40 of this Chapter, Affirmative Action Compliance Programs, requires that within 120 days from the commencement of a contract each prime contractor or subcontractor with 50 or more employees and a contract of $50,000 or more develop a written affirmative action compliance program for each of its establishments, and such contractors are now further required to revise existing written affirmative action programs to include the changes embodied in this order within 120 days of its publication in the FEDERAL REGISTER. A review of agency compliance surveys indicates that many contractors do not have affirmative action programs on file at the time an establishment is visited by a compliance investigator. This part details the agency contractor's failure to develop and maintain an affirmative action program and then set forth detailed guidelines to be used by contractors and Government agencies in developing and judging these programs as well as the good faith effort required to transform the programs from paper commitments to equal employment opportunity. Subparts B and C are concerned with affirmative action plans only.

Relief for members of an "affected class" who, by virtue of past discrimination, continue to suffer the present effects of that discrimination must either be included in the contractor's affirmative action program or be embodied in a separate written "corrective action" program. An "affected class" problem must be remedied in order for a contractor to be considered in compliance. Section 60-2.2 herein pertaining to an acceptable affirmative action program is also applicable to the failure to remedy discrimination against members of an "affected class."

§60-2.2   Agency action.

(a) Any contractor required by §60-1.40 of this chapter to develop an affirmative action program at each of his establishments who has not complied fully with that section is not in compliance with Executive Order 11246, as amended (30 F.R. 12319). Until such programs are developed and found to be acceptable in accordance with the standards and guidelines set forth in §§60-2.10 through 60-2.32, the contractor is unable to comply with the equal employment opportunity clause.

(b) If, in determining such contractor's responsibility for an award of a contract it comes to the contracting officer's attention, through sources within his agency or through the Office of Federal Contract Compliance or other Government agencies, that the contractor has not developed an acceptable affirmative action program at each of his establishments, the contracting officer shall notify the Director and declare the contractor-bidder nonresponsible unless he can otherwise affirmatively determine that the contractor is able to comply with his equal employment obligations or, unless, upon review, it is determined by the Director that substantial issues of law or fact exist as to the contractor's responsibility to the extent that a hearing is, in his sole judgment, required prior to a determination that the contractor is nonresponsible: *Provided,* That during any pre-award conferences every effort shall be made through the processes of conciliation, mediation and persuasion to develop an acceptable affirmative action program meeting the standards and guidelines set forth in §§60-2.10 through 60-2.32 so that, in the performance of his contract, the contractor is able to meet his equal employment obligations in accordance with the equal opportunity clause and applicable rules, regulations, and orders: *Provided further,* That when the contractor-bidder is declared nonresponsible more than once for inability to comply with the equal employment opportunity clause a notice setting a timely hearing date shall be issued concurrently with the second nonresponsibility determination of § 60-1.26 proposing to declare such contractor-bidder ineligible for future contracts and subcontracts.

(c) Immediately upon finding that a contractor has no affirmative action program or that his program is not acceptable to the contracting officer, the compliance agency representative or the representative of the Office of Federal Contract Compliance, whichever has made such a finding, shall notify officials of the appropriate compliance agency and the Office of Federal Contract Compliance of such fact. The compliance agency shall issue a notice to the contractor giving him 30 days to show cause why enforcement proceedings under section 209 (b) of Executive Order 11246, as amended, should not be instituted.

(1) If the contractor fails to show good cause for his failure or fails to remedy that failure by developing and implementing an acceptable affirmative action program within 30 days, the compliance agency, upon the approval of the Director, shall immediately issue a notice of proposed cancellation or termination of existing contracts or subcontracts and debarment from future contracts and subcontracts pursuant to § 60-1.26(b), giving the contractor 10 days to request a hearing. If a request for hearing has not been received within 10 days from such notice, such contractor will be declared ineligible for future contracts and current contracts will be terminated for default.

(2) During the "show cause" period of 30 days every effort shall be made by the compliance agency through conciliation, mediation, and persuasion to resolve the deficiencies which led to the determination of nonresponsibility. If satisfactory adjustments designed to bring the contractor into compliance are not concluded, the compliance agency, with the prior approval of the Director, shall promptly commence formal proceedings leading to the cancellation or termination of existing contracts or subcontracts and debarment from future contracts and subcontracts under § 60-1.26(b) of this chapter.

(d) During the "show cause" period and formal proceedings, each contracting agency must continue to determine the contractor's responsibility in considering whether or not to award a new or additional contract.

Subpart B—Required Contents of Affirmative Action Programs

§ 60-2.10 Purpose of affirmative action program.

An affirmative action program is a set of specific and result-oriented procedures to which a contractor commits himself to apply every good faith effort. The objective of those procedures plus such efforts is equal employment opportunity. Procedures without effort to make them work are meaningless; and effort, undirected by specific and meaningful procedures, is inadequate. An acceptable affirmative action program must include an analysis of areas within which the contractor is deficient in the utilization of minority groups and women, and further, goals and timetables to which the contractor's good faith efforts must be directed to correct the deficiencies and, thus to increase materially the utilization of minorities and women, at all levels and in all segments of his work force where deficiencies exist.

§ 60-2.11   Required utilization analysis.

Based upon the Government's experience with compliance reviews under the Executive order programs and the contractor reporting system, minority groups are most likely to be underutilized in departments and jobs within departments that fall within the following Employer's Information Report (EEO-1) designations: officials and managers, professionals, technicians, sales workers, office and clerical and craftsmen (skilled). As categorized by the EEO-1 designations, women are likely to be underutilized in departments and jobs within departments as follows: officials and managers, professionals, technicians, sales workers (except over-the-counter sales in certain retail establishments), craftsmen (skilled and semi-skilled). Therefore, the contractor shall direct special attention to such jobs in his analysis and goal setting for minorities and women. Affirmative action programs must contain the following information:

(a) An analysis of all major job classifications at the facility, with explanation if minorities or women are currently being under-utilized in any one or more job classifications (job "classification" herein meaning one or a group of jobs having similar content, wage rates and opportunities). "Underutilization" is defined as having fewer minorities or women in a particular job classification than would reasonably be expected by their availability. In making the work force analysis, the contractor shall conduct such analysis separately for minorities and women.

(1) In determining whether minorities are being underutilized in any job classification the contractor will consider at least all of the following factors:

(i) The minority population of the labor area surrounding the facility;

(ii) The size of the minority unemployment force in the labor area surrounding the facility;

(iii) The percentage of the minority work force as compared with the total work force in the immediate labor area;

(iv) The general availability of minorities having requisite skills in the immediate labor area;

(v) The availability of minorities having requisite skills in an area in which the contractor can reasonably recruit;

(vi) The availability of promotable and transferable minorities within the contractor's organization;

(vii) The existence of training institutions capable of training persons in the requisite skills; and

(viii) The degree of training which the contractor is reasonably able to undertake as a means of making all job classes available to minorities.

(2) In determining whether women are being underutilized in any job classification, the contractor will consider at least all of the following factors:

(i) The size of the female unemployment force in the labor area surrounding the facility;

(ii) The percentage of the female workforce as compared with the total workforce in the immediate labor area;

(iii) The general availability of women having requisite skills in the immediate labor area;

(iv) The availability of women having requisite skills in an area in which the contractor can reasonably recruit;

(v) The availability of women seeking employment in the labor or recruitment area of the contractor;

(vi) The availability of promotable and transferable female employees within the contractor's organization;

(vii) The existence of training institutions capable of training persons in the requisite skills; and

(viii) The degree of training which the contractor is reasonably able to undertake as a means of making all job classes available to women.

§ 60-2.12   Establishment of goals and timetables.

(a) The goals and timetables developed by the contractor should be attachable in terms of the contractor's analysis of his deficiencies and his entire affirmative action program. Thus, in establishing the size of his goals and the length of his timetables, the contractor should consider the results which could reasonably be expected from his putting forth every good faith effort to make his overall affirmative action program work. In determining levels of goals, the contractor should consider at least the factors listed in § 60-2.11.

(b) Involve personnel relations staff, department and division heads, and local and unit managers in the goal setting process.

(c) Goals should be significant, measurable and attainable.

(d) Goals should be specific for planned results, with timetables for completion.

(e) Goals may not be rigid and inflexible quotas which must be met, but must be targets reasonably attainable by means of applying every good faith effort to make all aspects of the entire affirmative action program work.

(f) In establishing timetables to meet goals and commitments, the contractor will consider the anticipated expansion, contraction and turnover of and in the work force.

(g) Goals, timetables and affirmative action commitments must be designed to correct any identifiable deficiencies.

(h) Where deficiencies exist and where numbers or percentages are relevant in developing corrective action, the contractor shall establish and set forth specific goals and timetables separately for minorities and women.

(i) Such goals and timetables, with supporting data and the analysis thereof shall be a part of the contractor's written affirmative action program and shall be maintained at each establishment of the contractor.

(j) Where the contractor has not established a goal, his written affirmative action program must specifically analyze each of the factors listed in §60-2.11 and must detail his reason for a lack of a goal.

(k) In the event it comes to the attention of the compliance agency or the Office of Federal Contract Compliance that there is a substantial disparity in the utilization of a particular minority group of men or women of a particular· minority group, the compliance agency or OFCC may require separate goals and timetables for such minority group and may further require, where appropriate, such goals and timetables by sex for such group for such job classifications and organizational units specified by the compliance agency or OFCC.

(l) Support data for the required analysis and program shall be compiled and maintained as part of the contractor's affirmative action program. This data will include but not be limited to progression line charts, seniority rosters, applicant flow data, and applicant rejection ratios indicating minority and sex status.

(m) Copies of affirmative action programs and/or copies of support data shall be made available to the compliance agency or the Office of Federal Contract Compliance, at the request of either, for such purposes as may be appropriate to the fulfillment of their responsibilities under Executive Order 11246, as amended.

§ 60-2.13   Additional required ingredients of affirmative action programs.

Effective affirmative action programs shall contain, but not necessarily be limited to, the following ingredients:

(a) Development of reaffirmation of the contractor's equal employment opportunity policy in all personnel actions.

(b) Formal internal and external dissemination of the contractor's policy.

(c) Establishment of responsibilities for implementation of the contractor's affirmative action program.

(d) Identification of problem areas (deficiencies) by organizational units and job classification.

(e) Establishment of goals and objectives by organizational units and job classification, including timetables for completion.

(f) Development and execution of action oriented programs designed to eliminate problems and further designed to attain established goals and objectives.

(g) Design and implementation of internal audit and reporting systems to measure effectiveness of the total program.

(h) Compliance or personnel policies and practices with the Sex Discrimination Guidelines (41 CFR Part 60-20).

(i) Active support of local and national community action programs and community service programs, designed to improve the employment opportunities of minorities and women.

(j) Consideration of minorities and women not currently in the workforce having requisite skills who can be recruited through affirmative action measures.

§ 60-2.14 Compliance status.

No contractor's compliance status shall be judged alone by whether or not he reaches his goals and meets his timetables. Rather, each contractor's compliance posture shall be reviewed and determined by reviewing the contents of his program, the extent of his adherence to this program, and his good faith efforts to make his program work toward the realization of the program's goals within the timetables set for completion. There follows an outline of examples of procedures that contractors and Federal agencies should use as a guideline for establishing, implementing, and judging an acceptable affirmative action program.

Subpart C—Methods of Implementing the Requirements of Subpart B

§ 60-2.20 Development or reaffirmation of the equal employment opportunity policy.

(a) The contractor's policy statement should indicate the chief executive officers' attitude on the subject matter, assign overall responsibility and provide for a reporting and monitoring procedure. Specific items to be mentioned should include, but not be limited to:

(1) Recruit, hire, train, and promote persons in all job classifications, without regard to race, color, religion, sex, or national origin, except where sex is a bona fide occupational qualification. The term "bona fide occupational qualification" has been construed very narrowly under the Civil Rights Act of 1964. Under Executive Order 11246 as amended and this part, this term will be construed in the same manner.

(2) Base decisions on employment so as to further the principle of equal employment opportunity.

(3) Insure that promotion decisions are in accord with principles of equal employment opportunity by imposing only valid requirements for promotional opportunities.

(4) Insure that all personnel actions such as compensation, benefits, transfers, layoffs, return from layoffs, company sponsored training, education, tuition assistance, social and recreation programs, will be administered without regard to race, color, religion, sex, or national origin.

§ 60-2.21 Dissemination of the policy.

(a) The contractor should disseminate his policy internally as follows:

(1) Include it in contractor's policy manual.

(2) Publicize it in company newspaper, magazine, annual report and other media.

(3) Conduct special meetings with executive management, and supervisory personnel to explain intent of policy and individual responsibility for effective implementation, making clear the chief executive officer's attitude.

(4) Schedule special meetings with all other employees to discuss policy and explain individual responsibility for effective implementation, making clear the chief executive officer's attitude.

(5) Discuss the policy thoroughly in both employee orientation and management training programs.

(6) Meet with union officials to inform them of policy, and request their cooperation.

(7) Include nondiscrimination clauses in all union agreements, and review all contractual provisions to ensure they are nondiscriminatory.

(8) Publish articles covering EEO programs, progress reports, promotions, etc., of minority and female employees, in company publications.

(9) Post the policy on company bulletin boards.

(10) When employees are featured in product or consumer advertising, employee handbooks or similar publications both minority and nonminority, men and women should be pictured.

(11) Communicate to employees the existence of the contractors affirmative action program and make available such elements of his program as will enable such employees to know of and avail themselves of its benefits.

(b) The contractor should disseminate his policy externally as follows:

(1) Inform all recruiting sources verbally and in writing of company policy, stipulating that these sources actively recruit and refer minorities and women for all positions listed.

(2) Incorporate the Equal Opportunity clause in all purchase orders, leases, contracts, etc., covered by Executive Order 11246, as amended, and its implementing regulations.

(3) Notify minority and women's organizations, community agencies, community leaders, secondary schools and colleges, of company policy, preferably in writing.

(4) Communicate to prospective employees the existence of the contractor's affirmative action program and make available such elements of his program as will enable such prospective employees to know of and avail themselves of its benefits.

(5) When employees are pictured in consumer or help wanted advertising, both minorities and nonminority men and women should be shown.

(6) Send written notification of company policy to all subcontractors, vendors and suppliers requesting appropriate action on their part.

§ 60-2.22   Responsibility for implementation.

(a) An executive of the contractor should be appointed as director or manager of company Equal Opportunity Programs. Depending upon the size and geographical alignment of the company, this may be his or her sole responsibility. He or she should be given the necessary top management support and staffing to execute the assignment. His or her identity should appear on all in ternal and external communications on the company's Equal Opportunity Programs. His or her responsibilities should include, but not necessarily be limited to:

(1) Developing policy statements, affirmative action programs, internal and external communication techniques.

(2) Assisting in the identification of problem areas.

(3) Assisting line management in arriving at solutions to problems.

(4) Designing and implementing audit and reporting systems that will:

(i) Measure effectiveness of the contractor's programs.

(ii) Indicate need for remedial action.

(iii) Determine the degree to which the contractor's goals and objectives have been attained.

(5) Serve as liaison between the contractor and enforcement agencies.

(6) Serve as liaison between the contractor and minority organizations, women's organizations and community action groups concerned with employment opportunities of minorities and women.

(7) Keep management informed of latest developments in the entire equal opportunity area.

(b) Line responsibilities should include, but not be limited to, the following:

(1) Assistance in the identification of problem areas and establishment of local and unit goals and objectives.

(2) Active involvement with local minority organizations, women's organizations, community action groups and community service programs.

(3) Periodic audit of training programs, hiring and promotion patterns to remove impediments to the attainment of goals and objectives.

(4) Regular discussions with local managers, supervisors and employees to be certain the contractor's policies are being followed.

(5) Review of the qualifications of all employees to insure that minorities and women are given full opportunities for transfers and promotions.

(6) Career counseling for all employees.

(7) Periodic audit to insure that each location is in compliance in area such as:

(i) Posters are properly displayed.

(ii) All facilities, including company housing, which the contractor maintains for the use and benefit of his employees, are in fact desegregated, both in policy and use. If the contractor provides facilities such as dormitories, locker rooms and rest rooms, they must be comparable for both sexes.

(iii) Minority and female employees are afforded a full opportunity and are encouraged to participate in all company sponsored educational, training, recreational and social activities.

(8) Supervisors should be made to understand that their work performance is being evaluated on the basis of their equal employment opportunity efforts and results, as well as other criteria.

(9) It shall be a responsibility of supervisors to take actions to prevent harassment of employees placed through affirmative action efforts.

§ 60-2.23   Identification of problem areas by organizational units and job classifications.

(a) An in-depth analysis of the following should be made, paying particular attention to trainees and those categories listed in § 60-2.11(d).

(1) Composition of the work force by minority group status and sex.

(2) Composition of applicant flow by minority group status and sex.

(3) The total selection process including position descriptions, position titles, worker specifications, application forms, interview procedures, test administration, test validity, referral procedures, final selection process, and similar factors.

(4) Transfer and promotion practices.

(5) Facilities, company sponsored recreation and social events, and special programs such as educational assistance.

(6) Seniority practices and seniority provisions of union contracts.

(7) Apprenticeship programs.

(8) All company training programs, formal and informal.

(9) Work force attitude.

(10) Technical phases of compliance, such as poster and notification to labor unions, retention of applications, notification to subcontractors, etc.

(b) If any of the following items are found in the analysis, special corrective action should be appropriate.

(1) An "underutilization" of minorities or women in specific work classifications.

(2) Lateral and/or vertical movement of minority or female employees occurring at a lesser rate (compared to work force mix) than that of nonminority or male employees.

(3) The selection process eliminates a significantly higher percentage of minorities or women than nonminorities or men.

(4) Application and related preemployment forms not in compliance with Federal legislation.

(5) Position descriptions inaccurate in relation to actual functions and duties.

(6) Tests and other selection techniques not validated as required by the OFCC Order on Employee Testing and other Selection Procedures.

(7) Test forms not validated by location, work performance and inclusion of minorities and women in sample.

(8) Referral ratio of minorities or women to the hiring supervisor or manager indicates a significantly higher percentage are being rejected as compared to nonminority and male applicants.

(9) Minorities or women are excluded from or are not participating in company sponsored activities or programs.

(10) De facto segregation still exists at some facilities.

(11) Seniority provisions contribute to overt or inadvertent discrimination,

i.e., a disparity by minority group status or sex exists between length of service and types of job held.

(12) Nonsupport of company policy by managers, supervisors or employees.

(13) Minorities or women underutilized or significantly underrepresented in training or career improvement programs.

(14) No formal techniques established for evaluating effectiveness of EEO programs.

(15) Lack of access to suitable housing inhibits recruitment efforts and employment of qualified minorities.

(16) Lack of suitable transportation (public or private) to the work place inhibits minority employment.

(17) Labor unions and subcontractors not notified of their responsibilities.

(18) Purchase orders do not contain EEO clause.

(19) Posters not on display.

§ 60-2.24   Development and execution of programs.

(a) The contractor should conduct detailed analyses of position descriptions to insure that they accurately reflect position functions, and are consistent for the same position from one location to another.

(b) The contractor should validate worker specifications by division, department, location or other organizational unit and by job category using job performance criteria. Special attention should be given to academic, experience and skill requirements to insure that the requirements in themselves do not constitute inadvertent discrimination. Specifications should be consistent for the same job classification in all locations and should be free from bias as regards to race, color, religion, sex, or national origin, except where sex is a bona fide occupational qualification. Where requirements screen out a disproportionate number of minorities or women such requirements should be professionally validated to job performance.

(c) Approved position descriptions and worker specifications, when used by the contractor, should be made available to all members of management involved in the recruiting, screening, selection, and promotion process. Copies should also be distributed to all recruiting sources.

(d) The contractor should evaluate the total selection process to insure freedom from bias and, thus, aid in the attainment of goals and objectives.

(1) All personnel involved in the recruiting, screening, selection, promotion, disciplinary, and related processes should be carefully selected and trained to insure elimination of bias in all personnel actions.

(2) The contractor shall observe the requirements of the OFCC Order pertaining to the validation of employee tests and other selection procedures.

(3) Selection techniques other than tests may also be improperly used so as to have the effect of discriminating against minority groups and women. Such techniques include but are not restricted to, unscored interviews, unscored or casual application forms, arrest records, credit checks, considerations of marital

status or dependency or minor children. Where there exist data suggesting that such unfair discrimination or exclusion of minorities or women exists, the contractor should analyze his unscored procedures and eliminate them if they are not objectively valid.

(e) Suggested techniques to improve recruitment and increase the flow of minority or female applicants follow:

(1) Certain organizations such as the Urban League, Job Corps, Equal Opportunity Programs, Inc., Concentrated Employment Programs, Neighborhood Youth Corps, Secondary Schools, Colleges, and City Colleges with high minority enrollment, the State Employment Service, specialized employment agencies, Aspira, LULAC, SER, the G.I. Forum, the Commonwealth of Puerto Rico are normally prepared to refer minority applicants. Organizations prepared to refer women with specific skills are: National Organization for Women, Welfare Rights Organizations, Women's Equity Action League, Talent Bank from Business and Professional Women (including 26 women's organizations), Professional Women's Caucus, Intercollegiate Association of University Women, Negro Women's sororities and service groups such as Delta Sigma Theta, Alpha Kappa Alpha, and Zeta Phi Beta; National Council of Negro Women, American Association of University Women, YWCA, and sectarian groups such as Jewish Women's Groups, Catholic Women's Groups and Protestant Women's Groups, and women's colleges. In addition, community leaders as individuals shall be added to recruiting sources.

(2) Formal briefing sessions should be held, preferably on company premises, with representatives from these recruiting sources. Plant tours, presentations by minority and female employees, clear and concise explanations of current and future job openings, position descriptions, worker specifications, explanations of the company's selection process, and recruiting literature should be an integral part of the briefings. Formal arrangements should be made for referral of applicants, followup with sources, and feedback on disposition of applicants.

(3) Minority and female employees, using procedures similar to subparagraph (2) of this paragraph, should be actively encouraged to refer applicants.

(4) A special effort should be made to include minorities and women on the Personnel Relations staff.

(5) Minority and female employees should be made available for participation in Career Days, Youth Motivation Programs, and related activities in their communities.

(6) Active participation in "Job Fairs" is desirable. Company representatives so participating should be given authority to make on-the-spot commitments.

(7) Active recruiting programs should be carried out at secondary schools, junior colleges, and colleges with predominantly minority or female enrollments.

(8) Recruiting efforts at all schools should incorporate special efforts to reach minorities and women.

(9) Special employment programs should be undertaken whenever possible.

Some possible programs are:

(i) Technical and nontechnical co-op programs with predominantly Negro and women's colleges.

(ii) "After school" and/or work-study jobs for minority youths, male and females.

(iii) Summer jobs for underprivileged youth, male and female.

(iv) Summer work-study programs for male and female faculty members of the predominantly minority schools and colleges.

(v) Motivation, training and employment programs for the hard-core unemployed, male and female.

(10) When recruiting brochures pictorially present work situations, the minority and female members of the work force should be included, especially when such brochures are used in school and career programs.

(11) Help wanted advertising should be expanded to include the minority news media and women's interest media on a regular basis.

(f) The contractor should insure that minority and female employees are given equal opportunity for promotion. Suggestions for achieving this result include:

(1) Post or otherwise announce promotional opportunities.

(2) Make an inventory of current minority and female employees to determine academic, skill and experience level of individual employees.

(3) Initiate necessary remedial, job training and workstudy programs.

(4) Develop and implement formal employee evaluation programs.

(5) Make certain "worker specifications" have been validated on job performance related criteria. (Neither minority nor female employees should be required to possess higher qualifications than those of the lowest qualified incumbent.)

(6) When apparently qualified minority or female employees are passed over for upgrading, require supervisory personnel to submit written justification.

(7) Establish formal career counseling programs to include attitude development, education aid, job rotation, buddy system and similar programs.

(8) Review seniority practices and seniority clauses in union contracts to insure such practices or clauses are nondiscriminatory and do not have a discriminatory effect.

(g) Make certain facilities and company-sponsored social and recreation activities are desegregated. Actively encourage all employees to participate.

(h) Encourage child care, housing and transportation programs appropriately designed to improve the employment opportunities for minorities and women.

§ 60-2.25   Internal audit and reporting systems.

(a) The contractor should monitor records of referrals, placements, transfers, promotions and terminations at all levels to insure nondiscriminatory policy is carried out.

(b) The contractor should require formal reports from unit managers on a schedule basis as to degree to which corporate or unit goals are attained and timetables met.

(c) The contractor should review report results with all levels of management.

(d) The contractor should advise top management of program effectiveness and submit recommendations to improve unsatisfactory performance.

§ 60-2.26   Support of action programs.

(a) The contractor should appoint key members of management to serve on Merit Employment Councils, Community Relations Boards and similar organizations.

(b) The contractor should encourage minority and female employees to participate actively in National Alliance of Businessmen programs for youth motivation.

(c) The contractor should support Vocational Guidance Institutes, Vestibule Training Programs and similar activities.

(d) The contractor should assist secondary schools and colleges in programs designed to enable minority and female graduates of these institutions to compete in the open employment market on a more equitable basis.

(e) The contractor should publicize achievements of minority and female employees in local and minority news media.

(f) The contractor should support programs developed by such organizations as National Alliance of Businessmen, the Urban Coalition and other organizations concerned with employment opportunities for minorities or women.

Subpart D—Miscellaneous

§ 60-2.30   Use of goals.

The purpose of a contractor's establishment and use of goals is to insure that he meet his affirmative action obligation. It is not intended and should not be used to discriminate against any applicant or employee because of race, color, religion, sex, or national origin.

§ 60-2.31   Preemption.

To the extent that any State or local laws, regulations or ordinances, including those which grant special benefits to persons on account of sex, are in conflict with Executive Order 11246, as amended, or with the requirements of this part, we will regard them as preempted under the Executive order.

§ 60-2.32   Supersedure.

All orders, instructions, regulations, and memoranda of the Secretary of Labor, other officials of the Department of Labor and contracting agencies are hereby superseded to the extent that they are inconsistent herewith, including a previous "Order No. 4" from this Office dated January 30, 1970. Nothing in this

part is intended to amend 41 CFR 60-3 published in the FEDERAL REGIS-
TER on October 2, 1971 or Employee Testing and Other Selection Procedures
or 41 CFR 60-20 on Sex Discrimination Guidelines.

Effective date. This part shall become effective on the date of its publication
in the FEDERAL REGISTER (12-4-71).

Signed at Washington, D. C., this 1st day of December 1971.

J. D. HODGSON,
Secretary of Labor

HORACE E. MENASCO,
Acting Assistant Secretary for
Employment Standards

JOHN L. WILKS,
Director, Office of Federal
Contract Compliance

[FR Doc. 71-17789 Filed 12-3-71; 8:51 a.m.]

Appendix C

Format for Development of an Affirmative Action Plan
by Institutions of Higher Education
U.S. Department of Health, Education, and Welfare,
Office for Civil Rights, 1975

Format for Development of an Affirmative Action
Plan by Institutions of Higher Education

On December 4, 1971, the Office of Federal Contract Compliance (OFCC), U.S. Department of Labor, issued regulations regarding contractor's obligations to develop Affirmative Action Programs (41 CFR Part 60-2, known as Revised Order No. 4). Several revisions and amendments have been made to those regulations since that time.

These regulations, because they apply to all contractors, regardless of industry or geographic location, are of necessity, general in nature. Because there are unique problems in certain industries, whole industries or multi-facility contractors often will want to adopt national formats. The regulations provide for agreements between government and industry applying the basic requirements of Order No. 4 to individual industry or company situations. (*See* 41 CFR 60-60.3)

The following format applies the requirements of Order No. 4 to colleges and universities. The format is an approved method for development and implementation of affirmative action programs in the university setting. Universities may choose, however, to continue the use of job groupings, analytical procedures and goal setting techniques which depart from this format, provided such departures are not in violation of Order No. 4.

Attaining the objectives of equal employment opportunity in higher education requires affirmative action programs that reflect both the characteristics of these institutions as a group, and the substantial variations among them. The development, maintenance, and improvement of high-quality academic faculties is a vital, complex, and often fragile process. Affirmative action can be a positive assistance in developing and strengthening the quality of academic faculties. This format, intended only to provide relatively detailed guidance conceining the application of 41 CFR Part 60-2 to higher education institutions, should be understood and implemented within this framework of objectives.

Industry Format—Colleges and Universities
A. *Work Force Analysis.*

A work force analysis is basic to the adequacy of any program, and forms the foundation from which the university develops its subsequent actions. This requirement is contained in 41 CFR 60-2.11(a) (as revised), which states:

> Workforce analysis . . . is defined as a listing of each job title as appears in applicable collective bargaining agreements or payroll records (not job group) ranked from the lowest paid to the highest paid within each department or other similar organizational unit including departmental or unit supervision. If there are separate work units or lines of progression within a department a separate list must be provided for each such work unit, or line, including unit supervisors. For lines of progression there must be indicated the order of jobs in the line through which an employee could move to the top of the line. Where there are no formal progression lines or usual promotional sequences, job titles should be listed by department job families, or disciplines, in order of wages rates or salary ranges. For each job title the total number of incumbents, the total number of male and female incumbents, and the total number of male and female incumbents in each of the following groups must be given: Blacks, Spanish-surnamed Americans, American Indians, and Orientals.* The wage rate or salary range for each job title must be given. All job titles, including all managerial job title, must be listed.

On May 29, 1975, the Equal Employment Opportunity Commission published in final form the Higher Education Staff Information Report (EEO-6), a joint requirement of the EEOC, Office for Civil Rights, HEW, and the Office of Federal Contract Compliance. This report requires certain job groupings within EEO-6 primary occupational activities by wage or salary intervals. Such report must initially be made by all public and private institutions and campuses in November 1975.

To minimize workload for the university, an acceptable method of arranging data is by title, by appropriate organizational unit within these *EEO-6 categories*. Since EEO-6 will not be operational until November 1975, as an acceptable alternate, universities may arrange data by job title, by appropriate organizational unit, within *EEO-1 categories* until January 1, 1976, provided salary data is included. If EEO-6 categories are used, the work force array should be shown by salary steps within each title in each category. (If salary

* Minority group titles from EEO-1. EEO-6 minority titles may be used instead.

information is separately programmed, such data may be submitted in a separate document, provided the job titles and organizational units are arranged similarly to the work force display.)

Two major groupings of jobs must be considered: Faculty and Other Instructional Staff, and Non-Instructional Positions.

(a) *Faculty and Other Instructional Staffs.*

All persons in this major group fall in the EEO-6 category *Faculty* or EEO-1 category *Professional*. Each faculty or other instructional position must be presented by department, with the following subcategories:

(1) Ladder Rank Faculty
(2) Non-Ladder Rank Instructional Staff (non-student)
(3) Student Teaching Assistants

If chairman is a separate title, this job title must be listed. The analysis should indicate whether the incumbents are tenured or non-tenured.

(b) *Non-Instructional Positions.*

These positions fall in EEO-6 categories Executive/Administrative/Managerial, Professional Non-Faculty, Office and Clerical, Technical and Paraprofessional, Crafts, Service and Maintenance, or equivalent EEO-1 categories. Job titles in each category must be shown by department or other organizational unit for ease of comparison with availability data. Student Research Assistants must also be shown. In those cases where there are formal lines of progression (which may cover more than one EEO-6 category), the individual job titles must be listed in such progression order. So far as feasible, all other job titles should be listed in order of EEO-6 salary groupings and such groupings identified for each title. In those cases in which salary ranking of titles is not feasible, due to wide variations of the salaries of incumbents in individual titles, some other method of ordering may be adopted. *Attachment 2* reflects an acceptable work force display by EEO-6 category; *Attachment 3* reflects an acceptable arrangement for progression line jobs.

B. *Availability and Utilization Analysis.*

The second basic requirement in all affirmative action programs is the utilization analysis. Such an analysis consists of combining non-student job titles into job groups determining the availability of minorities and women for each group, in light of skill requirements, recruitment area, promotable individuals, etc., and then determining if minorities and women in job groups correspond to their availability. (*See* 41 CFR 60-2.11(b), as revised)

The following approach to the utilization analyses is suggested:

(1) *Combining Job Titles and Departments into Job Groups.*

(a) *Faculty and Other Instructional Positions (Non-Student)*

Departments having similar disciplines should generally be combined. Department size and institutional organizations will vary, but aggregations of departments should usually be based on factors of common administrative control (e.g., under a single dean) and relatedness of academic discipline and similarity in percentage of female or minority availability. An example of an appropriate aggregation would be "Physical Sciences," which would include the following departments:

Astronomy
Astrophysics
Chemistry
Geology
Physics

In addition, a more specific, or secondary job grouping, within the primary aggregation, is also essential. Secondary job groupings must be divided as indicated below, and may be further subdivided in order to reflect institutional employment patterns.

(1) Ladder Rank Faculty

(2) Non-Ladder Rank Instructional Staff (non-student)

(b) *Non-Instructional Positions.*

To further minimize the university workload, and to facilitate data processing, the primary and secondary job groupings, used in EEO-6, will satisfy the requirements of 41 CFT 60-2.11 (b) (as amended) as it applies to non-instructional positions. In this regard the primary job groupings are:

1. Executive/Administrative/Managerial
2. Professional Non-Faculty
3. Secretarial/Clerical
4. Technical/Paraprofessional
5. Skilled Crafts
6. Service/Maintenance

As a further example, the secondary job groups for Secretarial/Clerical are:

(a) Below $5,000
(b) $5,000–$7,499
(c) $7,500–$9,999
(d) $10,000–$12,999
(e) $13,000–$15,999
(f) $16,000 and above

Alternately, institutions may form within EEO categories, groups of related job titles, provided each title is placed in one of these groupings. Because availability will vary depending on profession, *Professional Non-Faculty* job grouping should be by department or other organizational unit(s) which reflect similarity of availability. Other primary and secondary job groupings may be grouped university wide rather than subdivided within organizational units unless a significant disparity of utilization is identified.

(2) *Determining Availability and Underutilization.*

For each of the job groups for both faculty and non-instructional positions, a comparison must be made of the percentage of each minority and total women available in the appropriate recruiting areas having requisite skills for the group compared, considering all the factors in 41 CFR 60-2.11(b). Whenever the percentage of such persons available in that job group is less than the percentage available within the applicable labor area, the affirmative action program must specifically state that underutilization exists in that group.

(a) *Faculty and Other Instructional Positions.*

While availability of complete data remains a problem, both HEW and DOL are working to develop improved data. In addition, as data from EEO-6 submissions are obtained and consolidated, such information will be a significant aid to universities in their availability analysis. The university should develop the best possible information based upon a variety of sources available using all factors in 41 CFR 60-2.11(b). In addition, the following sources should be consulted:

(1) "Summary Report 1973 Doctorate Recipients from United States Universities," prepared by the Commission on Human Resources, National Academy of Sciences, May 1974. This survey is annual, 2,500 copies are printed and one is distributed to each graduate Dean. Other copies are available free upon request while the supply lasts. The survey for 1974 is in press.

(2) 1973 Survey of Doctoral Scientists and Engineers from the *Roster of Doctoral Scientists and Engineers.* Included in *Doctoral Scientists and Engineers in the United States: 1973 Profile.* Published by the Commission on Human Resources, National Academy of Sciences. Available upon request.

(3) *Professional Women and Minorities: A Manpower Data Resources Service,* prepared by Betty M. Vetter and Eleanor L. Babco of the Scientific Manpower Commission, 1776 Massachusetts Avenue, N.W., Washington, D.C. 20036. (This is a complete survey and summary of sources of availability data for professional women and minorities, available for a charge in a loose-leaf notebook with updating service.)

All the foregoing sources provide information on social sciences, humanities, and some professional fields, in addition to the physical and biological sciences and engineering.

For women, *Earned Degree Conferred,* an annual publication by the U.S. Office of Education, should be consulted. Currently, such data is shown by sex, but not by race, and is reported both by individual discipline and, in some cases, by subfield within the discipline.

One aceptable compilation of availability data for women for faculty positions requiring the doctorate is presentation of the number and percent of women doctorate recipients in feeder institutions by major field for the most recent 3–5 year period for which data are available. "Availability" in such a compilation will be the percent of women doctorate recipients by field in those institutions taken together. "Feeder Schools" are those graduate schools from which the university normally hires, and may be defined by the university, so long as the selection is not limited to institutions admitting disproportionate numbers of one sex or the other. *(See Attachment 4.)*

Until comparable data for minorities as that for women are available, one acceptable compilation of availability data for minorities for faculty positions requiring the doctorate, is presentation by general field (e.g., social science) of the average of (a) the percentage of minority recipients of the doctorate in the most recent year for which data are available *(see* Item 1 above), and (b) the percentage of minorities of total holders of the doctorate in a recent year *(see* Item 2 above). For format, *see Attachment 5.*

For faculty positions not requiring a Ph.D., surveys of female and minority college graduates, with and/or without advanced degrees, should be reviewed. In addition, Table 3 of the State Employment Service Guidelines furnishes percentages of teachers and administrators in elementary and secondary schools which may be of some assistance.

(b) *Non-Instructional Positions.*

In determining availability of minorities and women for non-instructional positions, all criteria listed in 41 CFT 60-2.11 should be analyzed.

Analysis should also consider local State Employment Security Agencies' *Manpower Information for Affirmative Action Programs* data which is now available in most localities. The specific figures shown in Table I, II, and III in those releases can be used in the analysis of population, work force, unemployment, skill availability. Current occupations of employed persons indicated in Table III should be considered a minimum basis for utilization, but additional opportunities afforded through training and recruitment should also be considered. When other data are available for specific skills, they may be used.

The labor market in which the university normally recruits should be considered in identifying appropriate geographical area.

C. *Goals and Timetables.*

Where underutilization exists, and the increase in the number of persons in a job group necessary to eliminate underutilization is .5 persons or greater, each program must contain goals which satisfy each of the following requirements:

(1) *Ultimate Goals.*

An ultimate goal must be established for each job group in which underutilization exists and must be designed to correct the underutilization by the application of every good faith effort. The ultimate goal must be stated as

(a) a percentage of the total employees in the job group and must be equal to the percentage of minorities or women available for work in the job group in the applicable labor market, and (b) a whole number, representing the total minorities and total women necessary to be employed to reach full utilization.

A single goal for minorities for each job group is acceptable, unless, through the university's evaluation it is determined that one minority is underutilized in a substantially disparate manner, to other minority groups, in which case separate goals and timetables for such minority groups may be required indi- vidually. It may further be required, where appropriate, that separate goals be established within the minority group by sex. (*See* 41 CFR 60-2.11(k)) For example, if a department or group significantly underutilizes one or more minority groups, but not all, the goal must address itself to the particular group or groups underutilized and is not satisfied by hiring additional minorities from ethnic groups not underutilized.

(2) *Interim Goals.*

(a) *Faculty and Other Instructional Staff Job Groups.*

Because availability of minorities or women is very low and the projected number of opportunities, due to low turnover and lack of expansion, for each year, is limited, annual goals often result in small numbers. For each faculty and other instructional staff job group in which underutilization exists, the uni- versity must project rate of hiring and/or promoting minorities and women until underutilization is eliminated. However, these rates may be established for three-year periods unless special circumstances, such as the expectancy of high turnover and significant availability warrant the establishment of shorter term interim goals.

Compliance officers shall evaluate the success or failure to meet these goals at the end of each three-year period (or lesser period, if applicable). How- ever, there must be good faith hiring efforts year by year. These rates should be maximum rates that can be achieved through putting forth a very good faith effort, including the use of available recruitment and training facilities, and must not be lower than the percentage rates set as representing the percentage availability of women and minorities in the applicable labor market.

(b) *Non-Instructional Job Groups.*

Annual goals must be established for all job groups where underutiliza- tion exists. Such goals should reflect the maximum hiring and/or promotion rates than can be achieved through putting forth every good faith effort and must not be lower than the ultimate goal.

(3) *Timetables.*

(a) *Faculty and Other Instructional Staff Job Groups.*

In the case of faculty and other instructional staff job groups, be- cause of small sizes of job units, slow rates of turnover due to tenure, and difficulties in projecting trends in minority and female supply, timetables will often represent both very rough estimates and long durations of time. For these reasons, timetables which reach beyond six years for reaching full utilization are not required for these job groups. The university must commit itself to at least annual review and updating of goals and timetables, until underutilization is eliminated and it is expected that, as additional minorities and females come into the labor market, the timetables will be shortened.

(b) *Non-Instructional Job Groups.*

For each non-instructional job group in which underutilization exists, a specific timetable must be established which projects the minimum feasible time period for eliminating underutilization.

(4) In all cases, determination of availability and adequacy of goals must be reviewed annually in order to give full consideration to changes in minority and female supply.

(5) Each program must contain specific and detailed action-oriented programs, including recruitment and training programs, which comply with Revised Order No. 4. Among other requirements, these programs must commit the university to undertake every good faith effort to contact and make use of relevant recruitment and training resources available in the community and to use its own resources for recruiting and training minorities and women to fill positions in job groups where underutilization exists.

(6) An acceptable format for displaying utilization data and goals for faculty and other instructional staff is shown in *Attachment 6.* A format for non-instructional employees is shown in *Attachment 7.*

(D) *Implementation of an Affirmative Action Program.*

Revised Order No. 4 sets forth the mandatory contents of written affirmative action programs in Subpart B ("Required Contents of Affirmative Action Programs"). Each affirmative action program (AAP) must contain the elements described in that Subpart, although there may be some variations from contractor to contractor, based on variations ir personnel structure and emplovment practices .

One important part of an AAP is the identification of problem areas *(see* para. 60-2.13(d)). The primary tools for identification of problem areas are the work force analysis and the utilization analysis These statistics should reveal areas where minorities or women are concentrated or are not working, as well as disparities in compensation and awarding of tenure. Other problem areas may come to the university's attention through other means, such as complaints of disparities in research grants or teaching assignments.

Once a university determines that a problem exists, it should attempt to identify the sources of the problem, and take appropriate action to correct it. A contractor's good faith efforts under para. 60-2.10 will be judged, in part, on whether such an investigation and corrective action have been undertaken to implement the AAP.

An AAP, however, is only a document with no substance unless it is fully implemented. After setting forth what must be included in each AAP, therefore, Order No. 4 continues: "There follows as outlines of examples of procedures that contractors and Federal agencies should use as a guideline for establishing and implementing and judging an acceptable affirmative action program." (Para. 60-2.14) In general, Subpart C, entitled "Methods of Implementing the Requirements of Subpart B," is designed to give guidance and provide examples of methods of taking corrective action to deal with problem areas identified in the AAP itself. It is not intended to impose specific mandatory requirements on all contractors without regard to the existence of identified problems. Furthermore, nothing in Subpart C should be construed as requiring institution-wide presentation in the AAP of statistical data developed as a means of investigating the cause of specific Problems.

DATED: *AUGUST 18, 1975*

MARTIN H. GERRY,
Acting Director
Office for Civil Rights

Appendix D

*Basic Model Used in Chapter Seven for
Projecting Future Supply of Faculty Members*

Discussion of Model Used to Make
Basic Projections

The Model

1. $F(0) = \overline{F}$; $FBPD(0) = \overline{FBPD}$; $FBM(0) = \overline{FBM}$
2. $H(T) = f(T + 1) \, E(T + 1) - [1 - q(T)]F(T)$
3. $F(T + 1) = F(T) + H(T) - q(T)F(T)$
4. $HPHD(T) = p(T)H(T)$
5. $HM(T) = [1 - P(T)]H(T)$
6. $HBPD(T) = d(T)HPHD(T), \, d(T) = \dfrac{GBPD(T)}{GPD(T)}$
7. $HBM(T) = M(T) \, HM(T), \, M(T) = \dfrac{GBM(T)}{GM(T)}$
8. $FBPD(T + 1) = FBPD(T) + HBPD(T) - [1 - qB(T)]FBPD(T)$
9. $FBM(T + 1) = FBM(T) + HBM(T) - [1 - qB(T)]FBM(T)$
10. $FBT[T + 1] = FBPD(T + 1) + FBM(T + 1)$

The model used to derive the basic projections discussed in the text is presented in the above equations. The model is solved iteratively moving from one time period to the next. The model may be thought of as a stock adjustment model where the stock of faculty is adjusted to the desired level in each time period by new hires and faculty exits. It is assumed throughout the projection period that there is no discrepancy between projected enrollment and actual enrollments. It is also assumed that the stock is completely adjusted to the desired level during each time period.

The model starts with a set of initial conditions as given in equation 1. These conditions describe the stocks which exist at the initial period. Given these initial stocks and enrollment projections equation 2 is used to determine hiring during the first period. The hiring is such that the actual stock will become equal to the desired stock. The desired stock is determined by multiplying the desired faculty-student ratio in the next time period by the expected enrollment. From this is subtracted the current stock minus faculty exits. Then in equation 3 the stock in the next period is calculated by adding together the new hiring determined in equation 2 and the previous stock and subtracting out the faculty exits.

Continuing on, equations 4 and 5 allocate the total hiring between hiring at the Ph.D. and non-Ph.D. level. This is accomplished in these equations by multiplying the total hiring by the proportion of that hiring which will be Ph.D.-level hiring during that time period. The remainder of hiring is then non-Ph.D. hiring.

Equations 6 and 7 are then utilized to determine the level of black hiring, given the level of total hiring. The parameter d(T) is used to allocate the Ph.D.-level hiring. In this usage the parameter is determined by the black availability. Similarly, a parameter based on non-Ph.D. availability is used to allocate the non-Ph.D. hiring. In this usage availability is measured by the proportion of blacks among Ph.D. graduates for Ph.D.-level hiring, and the proportion of blacks among master's graduates for non-Ph.D.-level hiring.

Given the hiring estimates from equations 6 and 7, equations 8 and 9 are used to determine the next year's stock of black faculty. These equations are used in the same way as equation 3. The next year's stock is determined by adding the new hirings and subtracting the exits.

Finally, equation 10 is used to derive the total black faculty in the coming period. This estimate simply aggregates the estimates for the two categories of black faculty. In order to derive the next year's estimates, return to equation two.

The model can be implemented once values or functions are established for each parameter and enrollment projection. The derivations and justifications of the parameter values or functions used in the projections are discussed in the main text.

The model also must be constrained in usage to make sure that hiring for any category never exceeds total availability within any time period. A restriction was imposed that disallowed negative hiring. The model is flexible and easily adaptable to a variety of assumptions about availabilities, the effect of equal opportunity, growth in enrollments, changes in composition of faculties, and changes in faculty-student ratios.

Definition of Symbols

$F(T)$ = Total faculty at time T.

$FBPD(T)$ = Black doctorate-level faculty at time T.

$FBM(T)$ = Black nondoctorate faculty at time T.

H(T)	= Total hiring at time T.
E	= Enrollment.
HPHD	= Total hiring of Ph.D.'s.
HBPD	= Black doctorate-level hiring at time T.
HM	= Hiring of Masters.
HBM	= Black non-doctorate-level hiring at time T.
q(T)	= Faculty exit value at time T.
qB(T)	= Black faculty exit value at time T.
p(T)	= Proportion of hiring that is doctorate-level at time T.
d(T)	= The proportion that black doctorate-level hiring is to total doctorate-level hiring at time T.
M(T)	= The proportion that black nondoctorate-level hiring at time T.
0	= At time zero at the initial time.
GPD	= Total doctorate-level graduates at time T.
GBPD	= Black doctorate-level graduates at time T.
GM	= Total nondoctorate-level graduates at time T.
GBM	= Black nondoctorate-level graduates at time T.

Notes

Chapter 2

1. Allen B. Ballard, "Academia's Record of 'Benign Neglect'," *Change*, March 1973, p. 27.

2. I. E. Taylor, "Negro Teachers in White Colleges," *School and Society*, 24 May 1947, p. 369.

3. Taylor, "Negro Teachers," p. 370; Horace Mann Bond, *Black American Scholars: A Study of Their Beginnings* (Detroit: Balamp Publishing, 1972), p. 26.

4. Dorothy B. Porter, "Edward Christopher Williams," *Phylon 8* (Fourth Quarter 1947): 315–321; *Evening Star* (Washington), 26 December 1929, p. 7.

5. Rayford W. Logan, ed., *W. E. B. DuBois: A Profile* (New York: Hill and Wang, 1971), pp. xix–xxii.

6. W. E. B. DuBois, "My Evolving Program for Negro Freedom," in *What the Negro Wants*, ed. Rayford W. Logan (Chapel Hill: University of North Carolina Press, 1944), p. 44.

7. Elliott M. Rudwick, *W. E. B. DuBois: Propagandist of the Negro Past* (New York: Atheneum, 1968), pp. 31–34.

8. James Allen Moss, "Negro Teachers in Predominantly White Colleges," *Journal of Negro Education* 27 (Fall 1958): 453.

9. W. Montague Cobb, "William A. Hinton, M.D., 1883–," *Journal of the National Medical Association* 49 (November 1957): 427–28.

10. E. Franklin Frazier, *The Negro in the United States* (New York: Macmillan Co., 1949), p. 478, quoted from Moss, "Negro Teachers in Predominantly White Colleges," p. 454.

11. Christopher Jencks and David Riesman, *The Academic Revolution* (Garden City, N.Y.: Doubleday Co. 1968), p. 420.

12. Taylor, "Negro Teachers," p. 370.

13. Obituary in the *Chicago Tribune,* 17 November 1963, p. 26.

14. "Negroes on White College Faculties," *Negro College Quarterly* 4 (December 1946): 184.

15. Fred G. Wale, "Chosen for Ability," *Atlantic Monthly*, July 1947, p. 83; R. B. Atwood, H. S. Smith, and Catherine O. Vaughn, "Negro Teachers in Northern Colleges and Universities in the United States," *Journal of Negro Education* 18 (October 1949): 565–66.

16. *See* G. Franklin Edward's chapter on Frazier in *Black Sciologists: Historical and Contemporary Perspectives,* ed. James Blackwell and Morris Janowitz (Chicago: University of Chicago Press, 1974), pp. 85–117.

17. A. Gilbert Belles, "The College Faculty, the Negro Scholar, and the Julius Rosenwald Fund," *Journal of Negro History* 54 (October 1969): 384–85.

18. Ibid., pp. 385–86.

19. Ibid., pp. 387–88.

20. Wale, "Chosen for Ability," p. 82.

21. Ibid.

22. Ibid.

23. F. L. Marcuse, "Some Attitudes toward Employing Negroes as Teachers in a Northern University," *Journal of Negro Education* 17 (January 1948): 19, 23.

24. "Biographical Sketch of Rayford Whittingham Logan" in *Fourth Annual Rayford W. Logan Lecture* (Washington, D.C.: Department of History, Howard University, 1973). Rayford W. Logan, John Hope Franklin, and Benjamin Quarles are the only Negro historians listed in *Who's Who in the World.*

25. Herbert M. Morais, *International Library of Negro Life and History,* (New York: Publishers Co. 1970), 4: 107–9.

26. *New York Times,* 22 April 1975, p. 30; *Washington Post,* 21 April 1975, p. 65.

27. "Current Trends and Events of National Importance in Negro Education," *Journal of Negro Education* 18 (Spring 1949): 173–179.

28. Charles H. Thompson, Editorial Comment, *Journal of Negro Education* 25 (Spring 1956): 91.

29. Moss, "Negro Teachers in Predominantly White Colleges," pp. 451–62.

30. Theodore Caplow and Reece J. McGee, *The Academic Marketplace* (New York: Basic Books, 1958), pp. 226–27, quoted in Harold M. Rose, "An Appraisal of the Negro Educator's Situation in the Academic Marketplace," *Journal of Negro Education* 23 (Winter 1966): 19; Atwood, Smith, and Vaughn, "Negro Teachers in Northern Colleges and Universities," pp. 559–67.

31. Harold M. Rose, "The Market for Negro Educators in College and Universities Outside of the South," *Journal of Negro Education* 30 (Autumn 1961): 432.

32. Jencks and Riesman, *The Academic Revolution,* p. 432.

33. Rose, "The Market for Negro Educators," p. 432.

34. Rose, "An Appraisal of the Negro Educator's Situation," p. 21.

35. A. Gilbert Belles, "Negroes Are Few on College Faculties," *Southern Education Report* 4 (July/August 1968): 23–25.

36. Ibid.

37. Thomas Sowell, *Affirmative Action Reconsidered: Was It Necessary in Academia?* (Washington, D.C.: American Enterprise Institute for Public Policy Research, 1975), p. 15.

38. Rose, "An Appraisal of the Negro Educator's Situation," p. 20.

39. Alan E. Bayer, *Teaching Faculty in Academe 1972–73* (Washington, D.C.: American Council on Education, 1973), p. 14.

40. Paul E. Wisdom and Kenneth A. Shaw, "Black Challenge to Higher Education," in *The Campus and Racial Crisis*, ed. David C. Nichols and Olive Mills (Washington, D.C.: American Council on Education, 1970), pp. 100–101.

41. Ibid., pp. 101–5.

42. National Board on Graduate Education, *Minority Group Participation in Graduate Education* (Washington, D.C.: National Board On Graduate Education, 1976), p. 3.

43. Ibid., p. 1.

44. Carnegie Council on Policy Studies in Higher Education, *Selective Admissions in Higher Education* (San Francisco: Jossey-Bass Publishers, 1977), p. 83.

45. Institute for the Study of Educational Policy, *Equal Educational Opportunity: More Promise than Progress* (Washington, D.C.: Howard University Press, forthcoming), chap. 1.

46. *New York Times*, 21 October 1969, p. 24; 22 July 1971, p. 30; 18 October 1970, p. 92; 10 October 1971, p. 81.

47. National Board on Graduate Education, *Minority Group Participation*, p. 13.

48. Ibid., p. 69; *See also* Institute for the Study of Educational Policy, *Equal Educational Opportunity for Blacks in U.S. Higher Education: An Assessment* (Washington, D.C.: Howard University Press, 1976), p. 83.

49. National Board on Graduate Education, *Minority Group Participation*, p. 5.

50. National Research Council, *Summary Report 1975 Doctorate Recipients from United States Universities* (Washington, D.C.: National Academy of Sciences), table 5, p. 22; National Research Council, *Summary Report 1976 Doctorate Recipients from United States Universities* (Washington, D.C.: National Academy of Sciences, 1977), table 5, p. 24.

51. Institute for the Study of Educational Policy, *More Promise than Progress*, chap. 2.

52. Ibid., Appendix B.

53. Ibid.

54. Ibid., chap. 2.

55. National Research Council, *Summary Report 1976 Doctorate Recipients from United States Universities*.

56. National Board on Graduate Education, *Minority Group Participation*, p. 55.

57. Ibid., p. 196.

58. Ibid., p. 24.

59. Ibid.

60. Ibid., p. 194.

61. Institute for the Study of Educational Policy, *Equal Educational Opportunity*, chap. 2.

62. Ibid., chap. 1.

63. National Board on Graduate Education, *Minority Group Participation*, p. 13.

64. Malcolm J. Sherman, "Affirmative Action and the AAUP," *AAUP Bulletin* 61 (December 1975): 293–303.

65. "Controversy," *AAUP Bulletin* 62 (Autumn 1976): 326–32.

66. Ibid.

67. Ibid.

68. Ibid.

69. Rose, "An Appraisal of the Negro Educator's Situation," p. 26.

Chapter 3

1. *United Jewish Organization of Williamsburg* v. *Carey*, 97 S. Ct. 996 (1977); But, cf *McDonald* v. *Santa Fe Trail Transportation Co.*, 427 U.S. 273 (1976).

2. John Hart Ely, "The Constitutionality of Reverse Racial Discrimination," *University of Chicago Law Review* 41 (Summer 1974): 723, 727.

3. Civil Rights Act of 1866, 14 Stat. 27.

4. Kenneth S. Tollett, "Black Lawyers, Their Education, and the Black Community," *Howard Law Journal* 17 (1972): 326, 340.

5. *Jones* v. *Alfred H. Mayer Co.*, 392 U.S. 409 (1968).

6. *Scott* v. *Sanford*, 19 How. (60 U.S.) 393 (1857).

7. *The Slaughter House Cases*, 83 U.S. (16 Wall) 36, 71, 81 (1873).

8. 14 Stat. 428 (1867).

9. 14 Stat. 50 (1866).

10. 14 Stat. 546 (1867), 8 U.S.C.A. §56 (1942).

11. 16 Stat. 140 (1870).

12. 16 Stat. 433 (1871).

13. 17 Stat. 13 (1871).

14. 18 Stat. 335 (1875).

15. *Swann* v. *Charlotte-Mecklenburg Board of Education*, 402 U.S. 1 (1971).

16. *Gallagher* v. *Carter*, 406 U.S. 950 (1972), denying cert. to 452 F. 2d 315 (1971).

17. *Norwalk CORE* v. *Norwalk Redevelopment Agency*, 395 F. 2d 920 (1968); *FCC* v. *TV9 Inc.* 495 F. 2d 929 (1973).

18. *Loving* v. *Virginia*, 388 U.S. 1, 11 (1967).

19. *Shapiro* v. *Thompson*, 394 U.S. 618, 634 (1969).

20. *Green* v. *County School Board*, 391 U.S. 430 (1968) at 442.

21. *DeFunis* v. *Odegaard*, 416 U.S. 312 (1974).

22. Robert M. O'Neil, "Racial Preference and Higher Education. The Larger Context," *Virginia Law Review* 60 (October 1974): 928.

23. This second argument appears to run counter to the constitutional principle that life, liberty, and other fundamental rights may not be submitted to the vote: "constitutional rights can hardly be infringed simply because a majority of the people choose that it be." *Lucas* v. *Forty-Fourth General Assembly*, 377 U.S. 713 (1964). *Lucas* was a state reapportionment case dealing with the fundamental right to vote. The Colorado legislature was already being elected upon a debatable apportionment basis and it proposed two amendments. One retained the bad features of the existing scheme and the other apportioned the state senate in such a way that it departed to the ex-

treme from population-based representation. In a referendum in which the two apportionment schemes were submitted to the people for adoption, they were hardly given a choice to vote on a scheme which was consistent with the one person, one vote mandate of the Supreme Court. The undiluted right to vote is preservative of all other rights. Furthermore, it is most difficult to perceive what legitimate interest a state could have in weighting the votes of one group more than another. Moreover, a malapportioned legislature raises a problem concerning a republican form of government which is guaranteed to every state by Article IV, Section 4 of the Constitution. Although the Court has shied away from enforcing this provision, because it labels the issue raised by it as a political question, obviously the guarantee clause also implies one person, one vote. *See* Kenneth Tollett, "Political Questions and the Law," *University of Detroit Law Journal* 42 (April 1965): 439. Finally, the referendum proposals were not designed to correct past and present injustices perpetrated against a minority but to perpetuate the representative advantage of a minority of voters.

24. *See* Amici Curiae Brief of Deans of the University of California Law School.

25. Barton J. Bernstein, "The New Deal: The Conservative Achievements of Liberal Reform," in *Towards a New Past: Dissenting Essays in American History*, ed. Barton J. Bernstein (New York: Random House, 1968), p. 279.

26. Rayford W. Logan, *The Negro in the United States* (New York: Van Nostrand Reinhold Co., 1970), pp. 95–96.

27. Bernstein, "America in War and Peace: The Test of Liberalism," in *Toward a New Past*, p. 298.

28. Bernstein, "The Ambiguous Legacy: The Truman Administration and Civil Rights," in *Politics and Policies of the Truman Administration*, ed. Barton J. Bernstein (Chicago: Quadrangle Books, 1972), p. 274.

29. Howard Zinn, *Postwar America: 1945–1971* (Indianapolis: Bobbs-Merrill Co. 1973), p. 122.

30. Bernstein, "The Ambiguous Legacy," p. 298.

31. Ibid., *See* Ibid., p. 312, note 51.

32. Ibid., p. 299.

33. Alonzo L. Hamby, *Beyond the New Deal: Harry Truman and American Liberalism* (New York: Columbia University Press, 1973), p. 446.

34. Bernstein, "The Ambiguous Legacy," p. 299.

35. Herbert S. Parmet, *Eisenhower and the American Crusades* (New York: Macmillan Co., 1972), p. 439.

36. Executive Order 10479, "Establishing the Government Contract Committee," *Code of Federal Regulations, Title 3—The President, 1949–1953 Compilation* (Washington, D.C.: U.S. Government Printing Office, 1960), p. 961.

37. Ibid., pp. 961–62.

38. Executive Order 10557, "Approving the Revised Provision in Government Contracts Relating to Nondiscrimination in Employment," *Code of Federal Regulations, Title 3—The President, 1954–1958 Compilation* (Washington, D.C.: U.S. Government Printing Office, 1961), p. 203.

39. Parmet, *Eisenhower and the American Crusades*, p. 555.

40. Civil Rights Act of 1957, 71 Stat. 634.

41. John Hope Franklin, *Racial Equality in America,* (Chicago: University of Chicago Press, 1976), pp. 88–89.

42. Potomac Institute, *Affirmative Action: The Unrealized Goal* (Washington, D.C.: Potomac Institute, 1973), p. 8.

43. Executive Order 10925, "Establishing the President's Committee on Equal Employment Opportunity," *Code of Federal Regulations, Title 3—The President, 1959–1963 Compilation* (Washington, D.C.: U.S. Government Printing Office, 1964), p. 448.

44. Ibid., p. 452.

45. "Statement by the President Upon Signing Order Establishing the President's Committee on Equal Employment Opportunity," 7 March 1961, in *Public Papers of the Presidents, John F. Kennedy, 1961* (Washington, D.C.: U.S. Government Printing Office, 1964), p. 150.

46. Ibid.

47. Allan Wolk, *The Presidency and Black Civil Rights: Eisenhower to Nixon* (Rutherford, N.J.: Fairleigh Dickenson University Press, 1971), p. 35.

48. 42 U.S.C. 2000e et seq.

49. George Cooper, Harriet Rabb, and Howard J. Rubin, *Fair Employment Litigation* (Saint Paul: West Publishing Co., 1975), p. 28.

50. Potomac Institute, *Affirmative Action,* p. 12.

51. *Higher Education Guidelines.* (Washington, D.C.: U.S. Department of Health, Education, and Welfare, Office of the Secretary, Office for Civil Rights, 1972), p. 3.

52. U.S. Equal Employment Opportunity Commission, *Affirmative Action and Equal Employment, A Guidebook for Employees,* vol. 1. (Washington, D.C.: U.S. Government Printing Office, 1974), p. 4.

53. "Statement by the President on the Signing of Equal Employment Agreements by Major Government Contractors," 12 July 1961, in *Public Papers of the Presidents, John F. Kennedy, 1961,* p. 504.

54. *Carter* v. *Gallagher,* 452 F. 2d 315 (1971).

55. *NAACP* v. *Allen,* 493 F. 2d 614 (1974).

56. *Quarles* v. *Philip Morris, Inc.,* 279 F. Supp. 505 (1968).

57. *Asbestos Workers* v. *Vogler,* 407 F. 2d 1047 (1969).

58. *United Papermakers* v. *United States,* 416 F. 2d 980 (1969).

59. *United States* v. *Sheet Metal Workers, Local No. 36,* 416 F. 2d 123 (1969).

60. *United States* v. *IBEW, Local No. 38,* 428 F. 2d 144 (1970).

61. *United Papermakers, supra* note 58, at 989.

62. *See* Paul Brest, "The Supreme Court 1975 Term—Foreword: In Defense of the Antidiscrimination Principle," *Harvard Law Review* 90 (November 1976): 32; Judith Caditz, *White Liberals in Transition: Current Dilemmas of Ethnic Integration* (New York: Spectrum Publications, 1976), p. 26; Natalie C. Gillette, "Current Decisions," *William and Mary Law Review* 12 (Summer 1971): 918–21; William Gould, *Black Workers in White Unions: Job Discrimination in the United States* (Ithaca, N.Y.: Cornell University Press, 1977), p. 92; Leslie D. King, "Current Decisions," *Texas*

Southern University Law Review 2 (Fall 1971): 155–59; August Meier and Elliott Rudwick, *From Plantation to Ghetto*, 3d ed (New York: Hill and Wang, 1976), p. 337; Rowland L. Young, "Supreme Court Report," *American Bar Association Journal* 57 (June 1971): 609–10.

63. *Griggs* v. *Duke Power Co.*, 401 U.S. 424 (1971).

64. Ibid., 429–30.

65. *United States* v. *Ironworkers, Local 86*, 443 F. 2d 544 (1971).

66. Ibid., 353.

67. *Swann, supra*, note 15. In this landmark case, the Supreme Court upheld a North Carolina District Court's use of "mathematical ratio" based upon race in the assignment of students to school. According to the Supreme Court, "the use made of mathematical ratio was no more than a starting point in the process of shaping a remedy, rather than an inflexible requirement." (p. 25.) This decision has served as an important precedent for several of the cases considered in this section have referred to this part of the *Swann* decision in upholding and in ordering "ratio" hiring, "affirmative hiring relief," or "quota relief."

68. *Carter, supra*, note 54.

69. *Stamps* v. *Detroit Edison Co.*, 365 F. Supp. 87 (1973).

70. *United States* v. *Wood, Wire, and Metal Lathers International Union, Local No. 46*, 471 F. 2d 408 (1973).

71. *Morrow* v. *Crisler*, 491 F. 2d 1053 (1974).

72. *NAACP* v. *Allen*, 493 F. 2d 614 (1974).

73. *Carter, supra*, note 54 at 328, 329, 330.

74. *Stamps, supra*, note 69 at 109, 122.

75. *United States, supra*, note 70 at 413.

76. *Morrow, supra*, note 71 at 1056.

77. *NAACP, supra*, note 72 at 618–19.

78. Ibid., 619.

79. *United States* v. *Elevator Constructors, Local 5*, 13 FEP Cases 80 (1976).

80. Ibid., 87.

81. The major exception to the court's favorable interpretations of Executive Order 11246 and affirmative action plans has been *Cramer* v. *Virginia Commonwealth University* 415 F. Supp. (1976) in which a Virginia District Court held that the university's affirmative action plan resulted in "reverse discrimination" based on sex. The Executive Order, according to the court, "could not serve as basis for justifying 'affirmative action' plan of university insofar as such plan resulted in reverse sex discrimination by adoption of 'quotas' or 'goals' for hiring of minorities which violated Civil Rights Act of 1964." (*Cramer* v. *V.C.U.*, 674).

82. *Weiner* v. *Cuyahoga Community College District*, 249 N.E. 2d 907 (1964).

83. Ibid., 910.

84. *Joyce* v. *McCrane*, 320 F. Supp. 1284 (1970).

85. Ibid., 1291.

86. *Contractors Association of Eastern Pennsylvania* v. *Secretary of Labor*, 442 F. 2d 159 (1971).

87. Ibid., 164, 173.

88. Ibid., 175.

89. Ibid., 175, 176–77.

90. *Southern Illinois Builders Association* v. *Ogilvie*, 471 F. 2d 680 (1972).

91. Ibid., 686.

92. *Associated General Contractors of Massachusetts, Inc.* v. *Altshuler*, 490 F. 2d '1973), 9.

93. Ibid., 12, 13, 14.

94. Ibid., 16.

95. Ibid., 18.

Chapter 4

1. "Affirmative Action Program," §60–2.12(e) *Federal Register*, 36, no. 234, Saturday, 4 December 1971.

2. *New York Times*, 26 August 1973, Section IV, p. 11; Carnegie Council on Policy Studies in Higher Education, *Making Affirmative Action Work in Higher Education: An Analysis of Institutional and Federal Policies with Recommendations* (San Francisco: Jossey-Bass Publishers, 1975), p. 29.

3. U.S. Equal Employment Opportunity Commission, "Higher Educational Staff Information (EEO-6): National Employment Data—1975," Washington, D.C., July 1977.

4. While there is uniformity in the critics' attacks on affirmative action, there are differences in approach and style. Some critics are harsher in their attacks than others. These critics are "hard-core" critics of affirmative action. Generally, this type of critic sees nothing positive at all occurring from affirmative action as presently implemented. Moreover, such a critic offers no alternative other than the status quo to bring more blacks, women, and other minorities into academia. Representative of this type of critic are George Roche, Paul Seabury, Thomas Sowell, Nathan Glazer, Sidney Hook, Irving Kristol, Miro Todorovich, Allen C. Ornstein, Malcolm J. Sherman, Charles J. Frankel, Edward Shils, and Ernest Van Den Haag.

There is a second type of critic who is more amenable to affirmative action and does offer viable alternatives. However, this type of critic is overshadowed by the more vocal hard-liners. Richard Lester, author of *Anti-Bias Regulations*, and John Bunzel reflect this type of critic.

5. "Red Tape Blues," *Newsweek*, 30 August 1976, p. 77; Dallin H. Oaks, "Universities as Government Plantations," *Learning and the Law* 4 (Spring 1977): 48.

6. U.S. Congress, House, Special Subcommittee on Education, *Federal Higher Education Programs Institutional Eligibility—Part 2A Civil Rights Obligations: Hearings*, 93d Cong., 2d sess., 1974, p. 455.

7. Thomas Sowell, "Affirmative Action Reconsidered." *Public Interest* 42 (Winter 1976): 47–65; *Affirmative Action Reconsidered: Was It Necessary in Academia?* (Wash-

ington, D.C.: American Enterprise Institute for Public Policy Research, 1975); "A Black 'Conservative' Dissents," *New York Times Magazine*, 8 August 1976, p. 14.

8. William Moore, Jr. and Lonnie H. Wagstaff, *Black Educators in White Colleges* (San Francisco: Jossey-Bass Publishers, 1974), p. 74.

9. Edward Shils, "Academic Appointment, University Autonomy, and the Federal Government," *Minerva* (April 1971): 167–68.

10. Sidney Hook, "Discrimination Against the Qualified?" *New York Times*, 5 November 1971, p. 43.

11. Ibid.

12. Ibid.

13. George C. Roche, III, Testimony Before the U.S. Commission on Civil Rights, Washington, D.C., 10 September 1975, p. 5.

14. Thomas Sowell, *Affirmative Action Reconsidered*, p. 15.

15. Kent G. Mommsen, "Career Patterns of Black American Doctorates," (Ph.D. diss., Florida State University, 1972), p. 88.

16. Ibid., p. 121.

17. Ibid., p. 124.

18. Andrew Billingsley, "The Black Presence in American Higher Education," in *What Black Educators Are Saying*, ed. Nathan Wright, Jr. (New York: Hawthorn Books, 1970), p. 130.

19. Ibid.

20. Walter Goodman, "The Return to the Quota System," *New York Times Magazine*, 10 September 1972, p. 118.

21. Paul Seabury, "HEW and the Universities," *Commentary*, February 1972, p. 41; Sowell, "Affirmative Action Reconsidered," p. 64.

22. *See* Victor S. Navasky, "The Greening of Griffin Bell," *New York Times Magazine*, 27 February 1977, p. 44; *New York Times*, 18 March 1977, pp. A1, A16; *Pittsburgh Courier*, 27 August 1977, p. 2.

23. Thomas Sowell, *Black Education: Myths and Tragedies* (New York: David McKay Co., 1974), pp. 292–93; Hook, "Discrimination Against the Qualified?," p. 43; Seabury, "HEW and the Universities," p. 39.

24. It appears that the Carter administration is beginning to assert its power in denying contracts or funds to contractors and school districts that engage in racial or sexual discrimination. In August 1977 the Labor Department barred two companies, the Arnastasi Brothers Corporation and the Ingersoll Milling Machine Company, from receiving federal contracts because of discrimination against minorities and women *(New York Times*, 27 August 1977, p. 44). In December 1977, HEW threatened the withholding of federal funds from twenty-two school districts and colleges because of their refusal to sign pledges not to practice sex discrimination *(Washington Post*, 10 December 1977, p. A7).

25. Phone call from Don McLearn, public information officer, OCR, 21 October 1977 to Gerald Gill. Mr. McLearn pointed out that these plans are all from colleges and universities that hold at least one million dollar contracts.

26. *See* John Searle, "Two Concepts of Academic Freedom," in *The Concept of*

Academic Freedom, ed. Edmund L. Pincoffs (Austin, Tex.: University of Texas Press, 1975), pp. 86–96.

27. Charles Frankel, "Epilogue: Reflections on a Worn-Out Model," in *Universities in the Western World,* ed. Paul Seabury (New York: The Free Press, 1975), p. 286; Alexander M. Bickel, "The Aims of Education and the Proper Standards of the University," in *Universities in the Western World,* p. 3; Leon D. Epstein, *Governing the University* (San Francisco: Jossey-Bass Publishers, 1974), p. 126.

28. This writer attended a conference by the University Centers for Rational Alternatives in December 1976. The conference's theme was "The University and the State: The Proper Role of Government in Higher Education" with sessions devoted to "The Government as Patron of Higher Education," "The Costs of Government Regulation," "Government Regulation and Academic Freedom," and "The University and the State Claims and Expectations." However, affirmative action was the conference's "whipping boy" as speaker after speaker denounced affirmative action as "quotas," "discrimination against white males," and as a "bureaucratization of the bathos of the 1960s."

29. The substance of this statement is borne out by the comments of one of the participants in the UCRA conference mentioned in note 28. This participant mentioned that he was being sued under the Buckley Amendment by a former student for whom he had written an unfavorable recommendation. Yet, none of the critics considered in this chapter has addressed this issue.

30. Frankel, "Epilogue," p. 286; Seabury, "HEW and the Universities," p. 42; Sowell, *Affirmative Action Reconsidered,* p. 38.

31. George Will, "Common Sense on Race," *Newsweek* 24 January 1977, p. 80.

32. George Will, "Sympathetic Justice," *Washington Post,* 5 May 1977, p. A23.

33. Quoted from Glickstein, Howard A., "Statement of Howard A. Glickstein, Director, Notre Dame Center for Civil Rights Before the Department of Labor Fact-Finding Hearing on Contract Compliance by Institutions of Higher Education," Washington, D.C., 20 August 1975, p. 9.

34. As the section, "Affirmative Action and the Courts," in chapter three has indicated, the argument of "goals as quotas" originated prior to the application of the Executive Order to colleges and universities.

35. "The Ladd-Lipset Survey," *Chronicle of Higher Education,* 24 May 1976, p. 16.

36. J. Stanley Pottinger, "The Drive Toward Equality," *Change,* October 1972, p. 24.

37. Walter J. Leonard, "A Step Toward Equality: Affirmative Action and Equal Employment Opportunity," *Black Law Journal* 4 (Fall 1974): 233; Vernon E. Jordan, Jr., "Blacks and Higher Education—Some Reflections," *Daedalus* 104 (Winter 1975): 161.

38. George C. Roche, III, *The Balancing Act: Quota Hiring in Higher Education* (La Salle, Ill.: Open Court Publishing Co., 1974), p. 20. John Bunzel, "The Quota Mentality," *Freedom at Issue,* November–December 1972, cited in U.S., Congress, House, Special Subcommittee on Education, *Civil Rights Obligations*—Part 2B, 1975, pp. 1172–1179; U.S. Congress, House, Special Subcommittee on Education, *Hearings,* p. 457.

39. Pottinger, "The Drive Toward Equality," p. 29.

40. U.S. Department of Health, Education, and Welfare, Office for Civil Rights,

Peter Holmes, Memorandum to College and University Presidents, December 1974, Washington, D.C., p. 4.

41. Navasky, "The Greening of Griffin Bell," p. 44.

42. *New York Times*, 6 June 1977, p. A1.

43. U.S. Commission on Civil Rights, "Statement on Affirmative Action," Clearinghouse Publication 54, October 1977, pp. 6–7.

44. U.S. Congress, House, Special Subcommittee on Education, *Hearings*, pp. 456–57; Thomas Sowell, "The Plight of Black Students in the United States," *Daedalus* 103 (Spring 1974): 185–86.

45. Jordan, "Blacks and Higher Education," p. 161.

46. Pottinger, "The Drive Toward Equality," p. 29.

47. Shils, "Academic Appointment, University Autonomy, and the Federal Government," pp. 167–68; Sowell, "The Plight of Black Students in the United States," p. 185.

48. Paul Seabury, "The Idea of Merit," *Commentary*, December 1972, p. 41.

49. U.S., Congress, House, Special Subcommittee on Education, *Hearings*, p. 455; John Bunzel, "Do Colleges Practice Reverse Bias?" *Wall Street Journal*, 27 July 1972, p. 10.

50. Robert Staples, "The Black Scholar in Academe," *Change*, November 1972, p. 46.

51. "The Ladd-Lipset Survey," *Chronicle of Higher Education*, 1 March 1976, p. 12.

52. Mary F. Berry, "The Mythology of Equal Treatment," *Learning and the Law* 2 (Spring 1975): 24.

53. John Bunzel, "The Politics of Quotas," *Change*, October 1972, p. 30.

54. Bernard Rosenberg and Irving Howe, "Are American Jews Turning Toward the Right?" in *The New Conservatives: A Critique from the Left*, eds. Lewis A. Coser and Irving Howe (New York: Quadrangle Books, 1974), p. 84.

55. Jordan, "Blacks and Higher Education," p. 160.

56. Seabury, "The Idea of Merit," p. 43.

57. Brewster C. Denny, "The Decline of Merit," *Science* 186 (December 1974): 875.

58. The origin of the term "reverse discrimination" has not been ascertained, but the term "discrimination in reverse" was used as early as 1963, *before* the passage of the Civil Rights Act of 1964. *See* Carl M. Brauer. *John F. Kennedy and the Second Reconstruction* (New York: Columbia University Press, 1977), p. 284.

59. "Minority Hiring Again: A Big Issue for Colleges," *U.S. News and World Report*, 22 July 1974, p. 54; "Faculty Backlash," *Newsweek*, 4 December 1972, p. 127.

60. Tom Wicker, "The Real Reverse of Racism," *New York Times*, 11 January 1975, Section IV, p. 19.

61. Roche, *The Balancing Act*, p. 6; Ralph Kinney Bennett, "Colleges Under the Federal Gun," *Reader's Digest*, May 1976, p. 128; James J. Kilpatrick, "Negative Affirmative," *New York Post*, 25 May 1977, p. 47.

62. U.S. Department of Health, Education, and Welfare, Office for Civil Rights, Holmes, Memorandum, p. 2.

63. Roche, Testimony, p. 4; Sidney Hook and Miro Todorovich, "The Tyranny of Reverse Discrimination," *Change*, Winter 1975–1976, p. 43.

64. Bunzel, "Do Colleges Practice Reverse Bias?," cited in U.S., Congress, House, Special Subcommittee on Education, *Federal Higher Education Programs Institutional Eligibility—Part 2B Appendix*, 1975, p. 1170; Ralph K. Winter, Jr., Statement, *Affirmative Action: The Answer to Discrimination*, (Washington, D.C.: American Enterprise Institute for Public Policy Research, 28 May 1975), p. 39. More recently, the critics have used another type of letter as evidence of "reverse discrimination." One would-be job seeker received a letter stating:

> It is with considerable regret that I have to let you know that we are not offering you the position in our department. As you know, there is considerable pressure from HEW to hire members of minority groups. We have offered the place to Ms. [   ], the one who was here just a few days before you arrived.
>
> We all felt, of all the candidates we had checked into, you and Ms. [   ] were at the top of the list. You have had more experience in teaching and already have your doctoral degree in hand. Her teaching is rather limited, and she will not get her degree until sometime this fall. Yet, under the circumstances, it was thought wise to offer her the position.

See Hook and Todorovich, "The Tyranny of Reverse Discrimination," p. 43.

65. James A. Goodwin, "Playing Games with Affirmative Action," *Chronicle of Higher Education*, 28 April 1975, p. 24.

66. U.S. Congress, House, Special Subcommittee on Education, *Hearings*, p. 457.

67. Sowell, "Affirmative Action Reconsidered," p. 58.

68. Ibid.

69. Edward Hecht, Letter to the Editor, *Chronicle of Higher Education*, 27 June 1977, p. 11.

70. Roche, Testimony, p. 7; Edward Shils, "The Academic Ethic under Strain," in *Universities in the Western World*, p. 39.

71. Horace Mann Bond, *Black American Scholars: A Study of Their Beginnings* (Detroit: Balamp Publishing, 1972), pp. 73–75; Kent G. Mommsen, "Black Ph.Ds in the Academic Marketplace: Supply, Demand, and Price," *Journal of Higher Education* 45 (April 1974): 256.

72. Moore and Wagstaff, *Black Educators in White Colleges*, p. 95.

73. Ibid., 78.

74. Sowell, "A Black 'Conservative' Dissents," p. 15.

75. Ibid.

76. Carl T. Rowan, *Just Between Us Blacks* (New York: Random House, 1974), p. 10.

77. William B. Gould, Paper delivered at the conference "Equality in America: A Color-Blind Constitution?" sponsored by the Equal Employment Litigation Clinic of the Howard University School of Law, Washington, D.C., 18 March 1977.

78. Nathan Glazer, *Affirmative Discrimination: Ethnic Inequality and Public Policy* (New York: Basic Books, 1975), p. 197.

79. "Affirmative Action Programs" §60–2.24 (e) (9) (ii), *Federal Register* 36, no. 234, Saturday, 4 December 1971.

80. Ibid., §60–2.24 (e) (9) (v).

81. Sowell, *Affirmative Action Reconsidered*, p. 40.

82. Sowell, *Black Education*, p. 292.

83. Roche, *The Balancing Act*, pp. 40–42; U.S. Congress, House, Special Subcommittee on Education, *Hearings*, pp. 458–59; Seymour Martin Lipset, "The American University, 1964–1974; From Activism to Austerity," in *Universities in the Western World*, p. 149.

84. Sowell, *Black Education*, p. 69.

85. As an example, *see* Charles V. Willie, "An Examination of the Future in Relation to the Past: A Personal History of Affirmative Action," Consultation on Affirmative Action, U.S. Civil Rights Commission, Washington, D.C., 9 September 1975, p. 24.

86. W. Arthur Lewis, "The Road to the Top Is Through Higher Education—Not Black Studies," *New York Times Magazine*, 11 May 1969, p. 34; "The Black Mood on Campus," *Newsweek*, 10 February 1969, pp. 57, 59.

87. Robert M. O'Neil, *Discriminating Against Discrimination: Preferential Admissions and the DeFunis Case* (Bloomington, Ind.: Indiana University Press, 1975), p. 141.

88. Sowell, "Affirmative Action Reconsidered," p. 57.

89. Ibid.

90. *New York Times*, 26 August 1973, Section IV, p. 11.

91. Richard B. Freeman, *Black Elite: The New Market for Highly Educated Black Americans* (New York: McGraw-Hill, 1976), p. 200.

92. Carnegie Council, *Making Affirmative Action Work in Higher Education*, p. 29.

93. U.S. Equal Employment Opportunity Commission, "Higher Educational Staff Information (EEO-6); phone calls by Gerald Gill to James S. Neal, Chief Information Branch, Research Division, EEOC, 19 July 1977 and 28 July 1977.

94. Roche, *The Balancing Act*, pp. 39–40.

95. Mommsen, "Career Patterns of Black American Doctorates," p. 75.

96. *New York Times*, 6 April 1975, Section IV, p. 5; Andrew Billingsley, Letter to the Editor, *New York Times*, 11 December 1976, p. 22; Leonard, "A Step Toward Equality," pp. 214–23; Hugh Gloster, Paper on Affirmative Action on the panel "Affirmative Action and Reverse Discrimination" at the 61st Annual Convention of the Association for the Study of Afro-American Life and History, Washington, D.C., 15 October 1977.

97. Sowell, *Affirmative Action Reconsidered*, p. 38; Kilpatrick, "Negative Affirmative," p. 47; Seabury, "HEW and the Universities," p. 44; Allan C. Ornstein, "Affirmative Action and the Education Industry," in *Policy Issues in Education*, eds. Allan C. Ornstein and Steven I. Miller (Lexington, Mass.: D. C. Heath and Co., 1976), p. 143.

98. Sowell, "Affirmative Action Reconsidered," p. 57; Kilpatrick, "Negative Affirmative," p. 47.

99. "Red Tape Blues," p. 77.

100. *Washington Post*, 5 July 1977, p. A8; *New York Times*, 4 December 1977, p. 24.

101. Carol Van Alystyne and Sharon L. Coldren, *The Costs of Implementing Federally Mandated Social Programs at Colleges and Universities* (Washington, D.C.: American Council on Education, 1976), pp. 14, 28.

102. U.S. Congress, House, Special Subcommittee on Education, *Hearings*, p. 459.

103. Moore and Wagstaff, *Black Educators in White Colleges*, p. 87.

104. U.S. Congress, House, Special Subcommittee on Education, *Appendix*, p. 1311.

105. Roche, *The Balancing Act*, p. 46.

106. Sowell, "The Plight of Black Students in the United States," p. 193.

107. U.S. Congress, House, Special Subcommittee on Education, *Hearings*, pp. 359–60.

108. Sidney Hook, "Racial and Sexual Quotas: They're Not Only Illegal; They're Immoral," *Daily News* (New York), 27 March 1977, p. 64.

109. John Bunzel, "The Quota Mentality," *Freedom at Issue*, November–December 1972, cited in U.S., Congress, House, Special Subcommittee on Education, *Appendix*, p. 1178.

110. Ibid.

111. Stephen J. Wright, "Redressing the Imbalance of Minority Groups in the Professions," *Journal of Higher Education* 43 (March 1972): 239–48.

Chapter 5

1. U.S. Department of Health, Education, and Welfare, *Higher Education Guidelines* (Washington, D.C.: Department of Health, Education, and Welfare, 1 October 1972), p. 3.

2. *See* Executive Order 11246 in Appendix B.

3. U.S. General Accounting Office. *The Equal Employment Opportunity Program for Federal Nonconstruction Contractors Can Be Improved* (Washington, D.C., 29 April 1975), pp. 2, 4, 5.

4. U.S. General Accounting Office, *The Equal Employment Opportunity Program;* p. 5; U.S. Department of Health, Education, and Welfare, *Higher Education Guidelines*, p. 1.

5. U.S. Comptroller General of the United States, "A Report to Senator Bayh," (Washington, D.C., 30 March 1977), p. 2.

6. Ibid.; On 1 October 1977 construction compliance was transferred to the Department of Housing and Urban Development.

7. U.S. Department of Health, Education, and Welfare, *Higher Education Guidelines*, p. 1.

8. U.S. Commission on Civil Rights, *The Federal Civil Rights Enforcement Effort*, (Washington, D.C., 1974) 3: 200–203.

9. Ibid.; Institute for the Study of Educational Policy Questionnaire, 18 April 1977; Interview with William Thomas, OCR.

10. U.S. Commission on Civil Rights, *The Federal Civil Rights Enforcement Effort*, 3: 207–8.

11. U.S. Comptroller General of the United States, "A Report to Senator Bayh"; Questionnaire from the Institute for the Study of Educational Policy to Albert T. Hamlin, HEW, 18 April 1977. According to an article in the *Washington Post*, 30 December 1977, p. A1, the Carter administration has agreed to hire 898 new employees for OCR in an effort to eliminate its complaint backlog.

12. Institute for the Study of Educational Policy, Questionnaire, 18 April 1977.

13. Interviews with John Hodgdon, Burt Taylor, and Walter Bailey, OCR, 4 May 1977.

14. U.S. Commission on Civil Rights, *The Federal Civil Rights Enforcement Effort* 3:. 211; Institute for the Study of Educational Policy, Questionnaire, 18 April 1977.

15. *See* Executive Order 11246, as amended, included in Appendix B.

16. U.S. Department of Health, Education, and Welfare, Office for Civil Rights, J. Stanley Pottinger, Memorandum to College and University Presidents, 1 October 1972, Washington, D.C.

17. *See* Title 41 CFR 60–1—Obligations of Contractors; and Title 41 CRF 60–2—Affirmative Action Programs, cited in *Higher Education Guidelines*, Tables B and C.

18. U.S. Department of Health, Education, and Welfare, Office for Civil Rights, Peter E. Holmes, Memorandum to College and University Presidents, December 1974, Washington, D.C.

19. Interviews with Hodgdon, Taylor, and Bailey; U.S. Department of Health, Education, and Welfare, Office for Civil Rights, "Format for Development of an Affirmative Action Plan by Institutions of Higher Education" August 1975.

20. This is an estimate John Hodgdon made for the HEW-DOL Advisory Committee for Higher Education Equal Opportunity Program.

21. Interviews with OCR higher education staff in Atlanta, Chicago, and San Francisco.

22. U.S. General Accounting Office, *More Assurances Needed that Colleges and Universities with Government Contracts Provide Equal Employment Opportunity* (Washington, D.C., 25 August 1975), p. 7; U.S. Department of Health, Education, and Welfare, "List of Approved Affirmative Action Plans," April 1975.

23. Institute for the Study of Educational Policy, Questionnaire, 18 April 1977; Telephone conversation with Don McLearn, Public Information Officer, OCR, 21 October 1977.

24. U.S. General Accounting Office, *More Assurances Needed*, pp. 8, 11, 12.

25. U.S. Department of Health, Education, and Welfare, *Higher Education Guidelines*, pp. C1, C2.

26. U.S. Commission on Civil Rights, *The Federal Civil Rights Enforcement Effort*, 3: 276–78.

27. *Chronicle of Higher Education*, 23 June 1975, pp. 1, 6.

28. Institute for the Study of Educational Policy, Questionnaire, 18 April 1977.

29. Ibid.; Interview with Thomas; U.S. General Accounting Office, *More Assurances Needed*, p. 12.

30. U.S. Department of Health, Education, and Welfare, *Higher Education Guidelines*, p. C1, C2.

31. Institute for the Study of Educational Policy, Questionnaire, 18 April 1977.

32. U.S. Commission on Civil Rights, *The Federal Civil Rights Enforcement Effort*, 3: 308.

33. Institute for the Study of Educational Policy, Questionnaire, 18 April 1977.

34. Interview with Thad Heath, OFCCP, 20 May 1977.

35. Ibid., Interviews with Hodgdon, Taylor, and Bailey.

36. U.S. General Accounting Office, *More Assurances Needed*, pp. 8, 9.

37. U.S. Commission on Civil Rights, *The Federal Civil Rights Enforcement Effort*, 3: 279–81.

38. Institute for the Study of Educational Policy, Questionnaire, 18 April 1977.

39. U.S. Department of Health, Education, and Welfare, *Higher Education Guidelines*, p. A6.

40. Ibid.

41. Carnegie Council on Policy Studies in Higher Education, *Making Affirmative Action Work in Higher Education: An Analysis of Institutional and Federal Policies with Recommendations*. (San Francisco: Jossey-Bass Publishers, 1975), p. 180.

42. U.S. Commission on Civil Rights, *The Federal Civil Rights Enforcement Effort*, 3: 229–32.

43. Interview with Heath; Interviews with Hodgdon, Taylor, and Bailey.

44. U.S. Department of Health, Education, and Welfare, Office for Civil Rights, Martin H. Gerry, Memorandum requesting for Organizational Change, 31 December 1975, Washington, D.C.

45. U.S. Department of Health, Education, and Welfare, Office for Civil Rights, Reorganization Plan for Office for Civil Rights Regional Offices Addendum to 31 December 1975, OCR Reorganizational Memorandum, 27 February 1976, Washington, D.C.

46. U.S. General Accounting Office, *More Assurances Needed*, 25, August 1975, p. 24.

47. Interviews with Hodgdon, Taylor, and Bailey.

48. Interview with Heath.

49. U.S. Department of Labor, Office for Federal Contract Compliance Programs Task Force, *Preliminary Report on the Revitalization of the Federal Contract Compliance Program* (Washington, D.C., 1977), p. x.

50. *See* Volume 5 of U.S. Commission on Civil Rights, *The Federal Civil Rights Enforcement Effort—1974* (Washington, D.C., July 1975).

Sources

Chapter 6

Persons Interviewed at
Florida State University

Dr. Stanley Marshall, President
Dr. Freddie L. Groomes, Assistant to the President
Mr. Robert Bichel, University Counsel
Dr. Daisy Flory, Dean of the Faculties
Dr. Wallace Woodard, Associate Professor
Ms. Rebecca Jones, Graduate Student
Mr. Scott Kent, Assistant Vice-President
Mr. Rick Robinson, Personnel Director
Dr. Paul Puryear, Provost
Dr. William Gamble, Assistant Professor
Dr. Wallace Gatewood, Assistant Professor

Other Sources

Florida State University. *Affirmative Action Program for Equal Opportunities.* Talla-hassee, Fla.: Florida State University, July 1973.

Florida State University. *Supplemental Data to FSU Affirmative Action Plan.*

Florida State University. *Manual for Affirmative Action Program Development and Implementation in Higher Education Institutions,* Tallahassee, Fla.: Florida State University, May 1974.

Florida State University. *Project Opportunity.* Tallahassee, Fla.: Florida State University, January 1975.

Florida State University. *Affirmative Action Program Update: A Plan for Continuous Equal Opportunity.* Tallahassee, Fla.: Florida State University, July 1975.

Florida State University System. *Equal Employment Opportunity Grants-in-Aid for 1977–78.*

Groomes, Freddie L. "Placement and the Role of the Affirmative Action Officer." Affirmative Action Officers Conference, Austin, Texas, 21 April 1975.

U.S. Department of Health, Education, and Welfare. Office for Civil Rights. Problem Areas, Questions, and Requests Pertaining to the Affirmative Action Plan and the Compliance (with Executive Order 11246) Program of Florida State University.

Persons Interviewed at Harvard

Mr. Daniel Steiner	University Counsel
Mr. Walter Leonard	Special Assistant to the President
Dr. Blenda Wilson	Senior Associate Dean Graduate School of Education
Dr. George Lombard	Senior Associate Dean Graduate School of Business Administration
Dr. Phylis Keller	Assistant Dean Faculty of Arts and Sciences
Mr. Carl Cooper	Research Fellow School of Law
Dr. Orlando Patterson	Professor of Sociology Department of Sociology
Mr. Robert Shinton	Secretary to the Corporation
Dr. William Capron	Associate Dean John F. Kennedy School of Government
Dr. Ephraim Isaacs	Associate Professor Afro-American Studies Department
Dr. John Kain	Chairman Department of Urban and Regional Planning Graduate School of Design
Dr. Michael Spence	Professor Department of Economics Chairman of the Faculty Senate Committee
Mr. Walter Patterson, Jr.	Civil Rights Specialist OCR Regional Office, Boston Department of Health, Education, and Welfare
Ms. Marilyn Taylor	Doctoral Student Graduate School of Business Administration

Other Sources

"Affirmative Action Report on Faculty Shows Improvement in Hiring Patterns." *Harvard Crimson.* 21 May 1976.

Barron's Profiles. *Harvard College,* Woodbury, N.Y.: Barron's Educational Series, 1974.

"EEOC Investigates Racism in Isaacs Tenure Case." *Harvard Crimson,* 17 April 1976.

"FAS Report Shows Affirmative Action Making Progress." *Harvard Gazette,* 21 May 1976.

Fletcher, William. "Affirmative Action at Harvard." *Harvard Gazette,* 24 February 1976.

Freedberg, Robin. "Women Urge More Affirmative Action." *Harvard Crimson,* 5 March 1973.

————. "University Hiring Plan Faces Unfavorable Review by HEW." *Harvard Crimson,* 17 May 1973.

Handie, Peter, and Jacobs, Bruce. "On the Brink: Afro-American Studies at Harvard." *Harvard Crimson,* 18 January 1977.

Harvard University. Affirmative Action Quarterly Report to the Office for Civil Rights.

Harvard University. Afro-American Studies Department. "A Statement of the Afro-American Studies Department on Tenure and the Ephraim Isaacs Case," 29 October 1975.

Harvard University. Department of City and Regional Planning. "Faculty Appointments and Affirmative Action: Report for 1975–76," 20 May 1976.

Harvard University. Harvard University Affirmative Action Plan, 31 July 1973.

Harvard University. Memorandum Discussing Ephraim Isaacs's Tenure Case on the Harassment and Suspension of Sherman Halcombe from the Task Force on Affirmative Action.

Harvard University. Memorandum on Information for the Dean Regarding Nontenure Teaching Appointments, Revised, September 1976.

Harvard University. Revised Affirmative Action Plan and Status Report, December 1976.

Harvard University. Task Force on Affirmative Action. Memorandum to John G. Bynoe, Regional Director, Office for Civil Rights. 23 February 1976. (Discusses the Harvard Affirmative Action Plan).

"HEW Reveals Sex Bias in GSD Hiring Practices." *Harvard Crimson,* 25 September 1972.

Isaacs, Ephraim. "The Case for Academic Fairness." *Harvard Crimson.* 22 February 1972.

Isaacs, Ephraim to Derek Bok, 12 October 1975, personal communication.

Leonard, Walter J. to John G. Bynoe, Director Region 1, Office for Civil Rights. 28 February 1975.

Luxenberg, Steven. "HEW Investigation Prompts Renewed Concern with Quotas." *Harvard Crimson,* 25 September 1972.

"President Bok: Universities must not Abandon Afro-American Studies Field." *Harvard Gazette,* 15 November 1974.

"President Issues Progress Report on Affirmative Action." *Harvard Gazette,* 12 December 1975.

Rivera, George. Letter to the Editor. *Harvard Crimson,* 7 June 1976.

Rosovsky, Henry. Supplementary Instruction for the Preparation of Materials for Ad

Hoc Committees on Permanent Appointments, Memorandum to Department Chairman," 25 August 1975.

Seligman, Nicole R. "More Black Students Will Enter GSAS Despite Failure of Recruiting Drive." *Harvard Crimson,* 14 June 1976.

Swanson, David. "Dan Steiner: New Man with the Bullhorn." *Harvard Crimson,* 13 October 1972.

"Tenure Ephraim Isaacs." *Harvard Crimson,* May 1976.

Persons Interviewed at Oberlin College

Mr. Emil C. Danenberg, President

Dr. Carolyn D. Spatta, Assistant to the President; Secretary of the College

Dr. Dan Mittleman, Director, Computing Center

Mr. Dayton E. Livingston, Vice-President for Business and Finance

Ms. Marjorie Gerlach, Director of Foundation and Corporate Support

Mr. James G. Lubetkin, Director of College Information

Mr. Carl W. Bewig, Director of Admissions

Mr. Emanuel Harris, Jr., Director of Personnel

Mr. Herbert F. Johnson, Librarian

Dr. W. Bruce Richards, Associate Professor

Mr. Carl G. Breuning, Superintendent of Building and Grounds

Dr. Samuel C. Carrier, Associate Dean

Dr. Paula L. Goldsmid, Associate Dean

Mr. David S. Boe, Dean of the Conservatory of Music

Mr. Booker C. Peek, Assistant Professor

Mr. Michael Weaver, Part-Time Instructor

Other Sources

Barron's Profiles. *Oberlin College,* Woodbury, N.Y.: Barron's Educational Series, 1974.

Carl W. Bewig to Oberlin College Community. Interoffice Memorandum, 6 May 1976.

Fletcher, Robert Samuel. *A History of Oberlin College from Its Foundation Through the Civil War,* 2 vols., Oberlin, Ohio: Oberlin College, 1943.

Ikeda, K.; Rich, R.; and, Rossi, Peter, Report on Costs and Returns to Investment in the Form of Student Attainments and Institutional Development of the 1971 Commitment, Revised, 1976.

Oberlin College. *Affirmative Action Plan,* 20 April 1976.

Oberlin College. *Bulletin and Course Catalog, 1976–77.*

Oberlin College. *Student Regulations, 1975–76.*

Spatta, Carolyn D., to John E. Fleming, 7 July 1977, personal communication.

Persons Interviewed at Merritt

Dr. Donald H. Godbold, President
Mr. Antonio Latorre, Professor
Mr. Gary Howard, Division Chairman
Ms. Alice Rupchan, Staff
Mr. Gary Howard, Division Chairman
Mr. George Herring, Assistant Dean
Ms. Carolyn A. Schuetz, Director, Cooperative Education
Mr. Harry Shortess, Assistant Dean
Mr. Wilfred Desrosiers, Jr., Dean
Mr. Lloyd G. Baysdorfer, Dean
Ms. Pearlina Hill, Professor
Dr. John Sommersette, Professor
Mr. Finis Minns, Student Body President

Other Sources

Axtell, Dayton. "Academic Performance of Merritt College Transfer." Report No. 1, December 1971; Report No. 2, May 1973; Report No. 4, May 1974.
Merritt College. *Affirmative Action Hiring Guidelines.*
Merritt College. *Affirmative Action Program,* 11 April 1974.
Merritt College. *Bulletin,* 1975–1976.
Merritt College. *Merritt Community College HEW Special Services Project, Proposal.*
Merritt College. *Procedures for Employment of Certified Personnel* (contract).
Merritt College. *Procedures for Employment of Certified Personnel* (hourly).
Peralta Community College District. *Affirmative Action Report of Certified Contract Personnel, 1972–73.*
Zelays, G. R., and Collins, Pat. *Report on the Transfer Program, the Basic Skills Learning Center, and the Career Guidance Center: 1975–1976.*

Chapter 7

1. Alan E. Bayer, *Teaching Faculty in Academe, 1972–1973* (Washington, D.C.: American Council on Education, 1973), p. 14.
2. U.S. Department of Commerce, Bureau of the Census, *Characteristics of the Population—1970,* Part 1 Section 2 (Washington, D.C.: Government Printing Office, June 1973).
3. William Moore, Jr., and Lonnie H. Wagstaff, *Black Educators in White Colleges* (San Francisco: Jossey-Bass Publishers, 1974), chapter 5, esp. pp. 147–183.
4. Ibid., passim.

5. Commission on Human Resources of the National Research Council, *Minority Groups Among United States Doctorate Level Scientists, Engineers, and Scholars, 1973* (Washington, D.C.: National Academy of Sciences, 1974), p. 27.

6. James W. Bryant, *A Survey of Black American Doctorates* (New York: Ford Foundation, Special Projects in Education, 1970), p. 3.

7. National Research Council, *Summary Report 1973: Doctorate Recipients from United States Universities* (Washington, D.C.: National Academy of Sciences, 1974), p. 4.

8. Commission on Human Resources of the National Research Council, *Minority Groups*, pp. 21–23.

9. ISEP calculations based on Bayer, *Teaching Faculty in Academe*, p. 26.

10. Ibid.

11. Ibid., p. 16.

12. Moore and Wagstaff, *Black Educators in White Colleges*, p. 46.

13. Ibid., p. 56.

14. Ibid., p. 35.

15. Kent G. Mommsen, "Black Ph.D's in the Academic Marketplace: Supply, Demand, and Price." *Journal of Higher Education* 45 (April 1974): 261.

16. Wagstaff and Moore, *Black Educators in White Colleges*, p. 56.

17. Ibid., p. 189.

18. Richard B. Freeman, "The Implications of the Changing Labor Market for Members of Minority Groups," in *Higher Education and the Labor Market*, ed. Margaret S. Gordon (New York: McGraw-Hill Book Co., 1974), pp. 83–109.

19. Quoted in *A Fact Book on Higher Education*, Third Issue 1976 (Washington, D.C.: American Council on Education, 1977), pp. 76, 155.

20. Based on National Center for Education Statistics data quoted in *The Condition of Education, 1977 Edition* (Washington, D.C.: U.S. Government Printing Office, 1977) 3: 52.

21. Roy Radner and Leonard S. Miller, et. al. *Demand and Supply in U.S. Higher Education* (New York: McGraw-Hill, 1975), pp. 315–351.

22. U.S. Department of Health, Education, and Welfare, National Center for Education Statistics, *Projections of Education Statistics to 1983–84*, 1974 Edition (Washington, D.C.: U.S. Government Printing Office, 1975), p. 71.

23. *See* Richard B. Freeman, *The Market for College-Trained Manpower* (Cambridge, Mass.: Harvard University Press, 1971).

24. Quoted in: Fred E. Crossland, *Graduate Education and Black Americans* (New York: Ford Foundation Special Projects in Education, 1968); Frank Brown and Madelon D. Stent, *Minorities in U.S. Institutions of Higher Education* (New York: Praeger Publishers, 1977), p. 83.

25. *See* discussion in Chapter 2.

26. Brown and Stent, p. 83.

27. Ibid., p. 85.

28. Institute for the Study of Educational Policy, *Equal Educational Opportunity:*

More Promise than Progress (Washington, D.C.: Howard University Press, forthcoming).

29. Commission on Human Resources of the National Research Council, *Summary Report 1974: Doctorate Recipients from United States Universities* (Washington, D.C.: National Academy of Sciences, 1975), p. 22.

30. *See* discussion of data problems in Institute for the Study of Educational Policy, *Equal Educational Opportunity for Blacks in U.S. Higher Education: An Assessment* (Washington, D.C.: Howard University Press, 1976), pp. 9–18.

31. U.S. Department of Commerce, Bureau of the Census, *Projections of the Population of the United States: 1977 to 2050* (Washington, D.C.: U.S. Government Printing Office, 1977), p. 50.

32. Radner and Miller, et. al., *Demand and Supply*, pp. 336–38.

33. For a recent analysis of the changing racial climate, see Faustine C. Jones, *The Changing Mood in America: Eroding Commitment?* (Washington, D.C.: Howard University Press, 1977).

34. *See* Richard B. Freeman, *The Overeducated American* (New York: Academic Press, 1976).

35. Radner and Miller, et. al., *Demand and Supply*, p. 320.

Selected Bibliography

Books and Monographs

American Enterprise Institute. *Affirmative Action: The Answer to Discrimination?* Washington, D.C.: American Enterprise Institute for Public Policy Research, 28 May 1976.

Bayer, Alan E. *Teaching Faculty in Academe 1972–73.* Washington, D.C.: American Council on Education, 1973.

Bernstein, Barton J., ed. *Towards a New Past: Dissenting Essays in American History.* New York: Random House, 1968.

————, ed. *Politics and Policies of the Truman Administration.* Chicago: Quadrangle Books, 1972.

Blackwell, James and Janowitz, Morris, eds. *Black Sociologists: Historical and Contemporary Perspectives.* Chicago: University of Chicago Press, 1974.

Bond, Horace Mann. *Black American Scholars: A Study of Their Beginnings.* Detroit: Balamp Publishing, 1972.

Brauer, Carl M. *John F. Kennedy and the Second Reconstruction.* New York: Columbia University Press, 1977.

Brown, Frank, and Stent, Madelon D. *Minorities in U.S. Institutions of Higher Education.* New York: Praeger Publishers, 1977.

Bryant, James W. *A Survey of Black American Doctorates.* New York: Ford Foundation Special Projects in Education, 1970.

Caditz, Judith. *White Liberals in Transition: Current Dilemmas of Ethnic Integration.* New York: Spectrum Publications, 1976.

Caplow, Theodore, and McGee, Reece J. *The Academic Marketplace.* New York: Basic Books, 1958.

Carnegie Council on Policy Studies in Higher Education. *Making Affirmative Action Work in Higher Education: An Analysis of Institutional and Federal Policies With Recommendations.* San Francisco: Jossey-Bass Publishers, 1975.

————. *Selective Admissions in Higher Education.* San Francisco: Jossey-Bass Publishers, 1977.

Commission on Human Resources of the National Research Council. *Minority Groups Among United States Doctorate Level Scientists, Engineers, and Scholars, 1973.* Washington, D.C.: National Academy of Sciences, 1974.

Cooper, George; Rabb, Harriet; and Rubin, Howard J. *Fair Employment Litigation.* Saint Paul: West Publishing Company, 1975.

Coser, Lewis A., and Howe, Irving, eds. *The New Conservatives: A Critique from the Left.* New York: Quadrangle Books, 1974.

Crossland, Fred E. *Graduate Education and Black Americans.* New York: Ford Foundation Special Projects in Education, 1968.

Epstein, Benjamin R., and Forster, Arnold. *Preferential Treatment and Quotas.* New York: Anti-Defamation League of B'nai B'rith, 1974.

Epstein, Leon D. *Governing The University.* San Francisco: Jossey-Bass Publishers, 1974.

Fleming, John E. *The Lengthening Shadow of Slavery: A Historical Justification for Affirmative Action.* Washington, D.C.: Howard University Press, 1976.

Franklin, John Hope. *From Slavery to Freedom.* Fourth Edition. New York: Alfred A. Knopf, 1974.

———. *Racial Equality in America.* Chicago: University of Chicago Press, 1976.

Frazier, E. Franklin. *The Negro in the United States.* New York: The Macmillan Company, 1949.

Freeman, Richard B. *The Market for College-Trained Manpower.* Cambridge, Mass.: Harvard University Press, 1971.

———. *The Overeducated American.* New York: Academic Press, 1976.

———. *Black Elite: The New Market for Highly Educated Black Americans.* New York: McGraw-Hill, 1976.

Gans, Herbert J. *More Equality.* New York: Pantheon Books, 1973.

Glazer, Nathan. *Affirmative Discrimination: Ethnic Inequality and Public Policy.* New York: Basic Books, 1975.

Gordon, Margaret, ed. *Higher Education and the Labor Market.* New York: McGraw-Hill, 1974.

Gould, William. *Black Workers in White Unions: Job Discrimination in the United States.* Ithaca, New York: Cornell University Press, 1977.

Gross, Barry, ed. *Reverse Discrimination.* Buffalo, New York: Prometheus Books, 1977.

Hamby, Alonzo L. *Beyond the New Deal: Harry Truman and American Liberalism.* New York: Columbia University Press, 1973.

Institute for the Study of Educational Policy. *Equal Educational Opportunity for Blacks in U.S. Higher Education: An Assessment.* Washington, D.C.: Howard University Press, 1976.

————. *Equal Educational Opportunity: More Promise Than Progress.* Washington, D.C.: Howard University Press, forthcoming, 1978.

Jencks, Christopher, and Reisman, David. *The Academic Revolution.* Garden City, New York: Doubleday and Company, Inc., 1968.

Jones, Faustine C. *The Changing Mood in America: Eroding Commitment?* Washington, D.C.: Howard University Press, 1977.

Lester, Richard. *Anti-Bias Regulations of Universities.* New York: McGraw-Hill, 1974.

Logan, Rayford W. *The Negro in the United States.* New York: Van Nostrand Reinhold Company, 1970.

————, ed. *What the Negro Wants.* Chapel Hill: University of North Carolina Press, 1944.

————, ed. *W. E. B. DuBois: A Profile.* New York: Hill and Wang, 1971.

Meier, August, and Rudwick, Elliott. *From Plantation to Ghetto.* 3rd edition. New York: Hill and Wang, 1976.

Moore, William Jr., and Wagstaff, Lonnie H. *Black Educators in White Colleges.* San Francisco: Jossey-Bass Publishers, 1974.

Morais, Herbert M. *International Library of Negro Life and History,* vol. 4. New York: Publishers Co., 1967–1970.

National Board on Graduate Education. *Minority Group Participation in Graduate Education.* Washington, D.C.: National Board on Graduate Education, 1976.

National Research Council. *Summary Report, 1973, Doctorate Recipients from United States Universities.* National Academy of Sciences: Washington, D.C., 1974.

————. *Summary Report, 1974, Doctorate Recipients from United States Universities.* National Academy of Sciences: Washington, D.C., 1975.

————. *Summary Report, 1975, Doctorate Recipients from United States Universities.* National Academy of Sciences: Washington, D.C., 1976.

————. *Summary Report, 1976, Doctorate Recipients from United States Universities.* National Academy of Sciences: Washington, D.C., 1977.

Nichols, David C., and Mills, Olive, eds. *The Campus and Racial Crisis.* Washington, D.C.: American Council on Education, 1970.

O'Neil, Robert M. *Discriminating Against Discrimination: Preferential Admissions and the DeFunis Case.* Bloomington, Ind.: Indiana University Press, 1975.

Ornstein, Allan C., and Miller, Steven I., eds. *Policy Issues in Education.* Lexington, Mass.: D. C. Heath and Co., 1976.

Parmet, Herbert S. *Eisenhower and The American Crusades.* New York: The Macmillan Company, 1972.

Pincoffs, Edmund L., ed. *The Concept of Academic Freedom.* Austin, Texas: University of Texas Press, 1975.

Potomac Institute. *Affirmative Action: The Unrealized Goal.* Washington, D.C.: Potomac Institute, 1973.

Radner, Roy, and Miller, Leonard S., et al. *Demand and Supply in U.S. Higher Education.* New York: McGraw-Hill, 1975.

Roche, George C., III. *The Balancing Act: Quota Hiring in Higher Education.* LaSalle, Illinois: Open Court Publishing Company, 1974.

Rowan, Carl T. *Just Between Us Blacks.* New York: Random House, 1974.

Rudwick, Elliott M. *W. E. B. DuBois: Propagandis' of the Negro Past.* New York: Atheneum, 1968.

Seabury, Paul, ed. *Universities in the Western World.* New York: The Free Press, 1975.

Sowell, Thomas. *Black Education: Myths and Tragedies.* New York: David McKay Company, Inc., 1974.

———. *Affirmative Action Reconsidered: Was It Necessary in Academia?* Washington, D.C.: American Enterprise Institute for Public Policy Research, 1975.

Van Alstyne, Carol, and Coldren, Sharon L. *The Costs of Implementing Federally Mandated Social Programs At Colleges and Universities.* Washington, D.C.: American Council on Education, 1976.

Wolk, Allan. *The Presidency and Black Civil Rights: Eisenhower to Nixon.* Rutherford, New Jersey: Fairleigh Dickenson University Press, 1971.

Wright, Nathan Jr., ed. *What Black Educators Are Saying.* New York: Hawthorn Books, 1970.

Zinn, Howard. *Postwar America: 1945–1971.* Indianapolis: Bobbs-Merrill, 1973.

Articles

"Affirmative Action in Higher Education: A Report by the Council Commission On Discrimination." *AAUP Bulletin* 59 (June 1973): 178–183.

"Affirmative Action: The Negative Side." *Time,* 15 June 1974, p. 86.

Andrulis, Dennis P.; Iscoe, Ira; Sikes, Melvin P.; and Friedman, Thomas. "Black Professionals in Predominantly White Institutions of Higher Education—An Examination of Some Demographic and Mobility Characteristics." *Journal of Negro Education* 44 (Winter 1975): 6–11.

Atwood, R. B.; Smith, H. S.; and Vaughn, Catherine O. "Negro Teachers in Northern Colleges and Universities in the United States." *Journal of Negro Education* 18 (Fall 1949): 559–567.

Ballard, Allen B. "Academia's Record of 'Benign Neglect'." *Change,* March 1973, pp. 27–33.

Bayles, Michael D. "Reparations to Wronged Groups." *Analysis* 33 (June 1973): 182–184.

Belles, A. Gilbert. "Negroes Are Few on College Faculties." *Southern Education Report* 4 (July/August 1968): 23–25.

———. "The College Faculty, The Negro Scholar and the Julius Rosenwald Fund." *Journal of Negro History* 54 (October 1969): 383–392.

Bennett, Ralph Kinney. "Colleges Under the Federal Gun." *Reader's Digest,* May 1976, pp. 126–130.

Berry, Mary F. "The Mythology of Equal Treatment." *Learning and the Law* 2 (Spring 1975): 23–25.

"Biographical Sketch of Rayford Whittingham Logan." In the *Fourth Annual Rayford W. Logan Lecture.* Washington, D.C. Department of History, Howard University, 1973.

"The Black Mood on Campus." *Newsweek,* 10 February 1969, pp. 53–59.

Brest, Paul. "The Supreme Court 1975 Term—Foreword: In Defense of the Antidiscrimination Principle." *Harvard Law Review* 90 (November 1976): 1–54.

Bunzel, John. "The Politics of Quotas." *Change,* October 1972, pp. 25, 30–35.

Cobb, W. Montague. "William A. Hinton, M.D., 1883– ." *Journal of the National Medical Association* 49 (November 1957): 427–428.

"Controversy." *AAUP Bulletin* 62 (Autumn 1976): 326–332.

"Current Trends and Events of National Importance in Negro Education." *Journal of Negro Education* 18 (Spring 1949): 173–179.

Denny, Brewster C. "The Decline of Merit." *Science* 186 (December 1974): 875.

Ely, John Hart. "The Constitutionality of Reverse Racial Discrimination." *University of Chicago Law Review* 41 (Summer 1974): 723–741.

"Faculty Backlash." *Newsweek,* 4 December 1972, pp.127–128.

Fein, Leonard J. "Thinking About Quotas." *Midstream,* March 1973, pp. 13–17.

Fuerst, J. S. "Quotas as an Instrument of Public Interest." *Society,* January 1976, pp. 11, 18–21.

Galbraith, John Kenneth; Kuh, Edwin; and Thurow, Lester C. "The Galbraith Plan to Promote the Minorities." *New York Times Magazine,* 22 August 1971, pp. 9, 35, 38, 40.

Garcia, Ricardo L. "Affirmative Action Hiring: Some Perceptions." *Journal of Higher Education* 45 (April 1974): 268–272.

Gillette, Natalie C. "Current Decisions." *William and Mary Law Review* 12 (Summer 1971): 918–921.

Goldman, Allan H. "Affirmative Action." *Philosophy and Public Affairs* 5 (Winter 1976): 178–195.

Golightly, Cornelius L. "Justice and 'Discrimination For' in Higher Education." *Philosophic Exchange* 1 (Summer 1974): 5–14.

Goodman, Walter. "'The Return to the Quota System." *New York Times Magazine*, 10 September 1972, pp. 28–29, 103–106, 108, 112, 114, 118.

Havighurst, Robert J. "Individual and Group Rights in a Democracy." *Society*, January 1976, pp. 13, 25–28.

Hook, Sidney, and Todorovich, Miro. "The Tyranny of Reverse Discrimination." *Change*, Winter 1975, pp. 42–43.

"In Job-Bias Test, Colleges Get Passing Grade." *U.S. News and World Report*, 18 August 1975, pp. 73–75.

Jones, Edward, and Jones, Virginia L. "Negro Teachers on White College Faculties." *Negro College Quarterly* 4 (December 1946): 184–186, 237–238.

Jordan, Vernon E., Jr. "Blacks and Higher Education—Some Reflections." *Daedalus* 104 (Winter 1975): 160–165.

King, Leslie D. "Current Decisions." *Texas Southern University Law Review* 2 (Fall 1971): 155–159.

Leonard, Walter J. "A Step Toward Equality: Affirmative Action and Equal Employment Opportunity." *Black Law Journal* 4 (Fall 1974): 214–223.

Lewis, W. Arthur. "The Road to the Top is Through Higher Education—Not Black Studies." *New York Times Magazine*, 11 May 1969, pp. 34–35, 40, 42, 44, 46, 49, 50, 52, 54.

Marcuse, F. L. "Some Attitudes Toward Employing Negroes as Teachers in a Northern University." *Journal of Negro Education* 17 (Winter 1948): 18–26.

"Minority Hiring Again: A Big Issue for Colleges." *U.S. News and World Report*, 22 July 1974, pp. 53–54.

Mommsen, Kent G. "Black Ph.Ds in the Academic Marketplace: Supply, Demand, and Price." *Journal of Higher Education* 45 (April 1974): 253–267.

Moss, James Allen. "Negro Teachers in Predominantly White Colleges." *Journal of Negro Education* 27 (Fall 1958): 451–462.

Nash, Peter G. "Affirmative Action Under Executive Order 11246." *New York University Law Review* 46 (April 1971): 225–261.

Navasky, Victor S. "The Greening of Griffin Bell." *New York Times Magazine*, 27 February 1977, pp. 41–42, 44, 46, 50.

"Negroes on White College Faculties." *Negro College Quarterly* 4 (December 1946): 184–186, 237–238.

Nickel, James W. "Discrimination and Morally Relevant Characteristics." *Analysis* 32 (March 1972): 113–114.

———. "Should Reparations Be to Individuals or to Groups?" *Analysis* 34 (April 1974): 154–160.

O'Neil, Robert M. "Racial Preference and Higher Education: The Larger Context." *Virginia Law Review* 60 (October 1974): 925–954.

Oaks, Dallin H. "Universities as Government Plantations." *Learning and the Law* 4 (Spring 1977): 20–23, 48–51.

Ornstein, Allan C. "Quality, Not Quotas." *Society*, January 1976, pp. 10, 14–17.

Porter, Dorothy B. "Edward Christopher Williams." *Phylon* 8 (Fourth Quarter 1947): 315–321.

Pottinger, J. Stanley. "The Drive Toward Equality." *Change* (October 1972): 24, 26–29.

"The Pottinger Papers." *Commentary*, May 1972, pp. 10–12, 14–16, 21–24, 26–28.

Rafky, David M. "The Black Scholar in the Academic Marketplace." *Teachers College Record* 74 (December 1972): 225–260.

Record, Jane Cassels, and Record, Wilson. "Ethnic Studies and Affirmative Action: Ideological Roots and Implications for the Quality of American Life." *Social Science Quarterly* 55 (September 1974): 502–519.

"Red Tape Blues." *Newsweek*, 30 August 1976, p. 77.

Ringer, Benjamin B. "Affirmative Action, Quotas, and Meritocracy." *Society*, January 1976, pp. 12, 22–25.

Rose, Harold M. "The Market of Negro Educators in College and Universities Outside of the South." *Journal of Negro Education* 30 (Autumn 1961): 432–435.

———. "An Appraisal of the Negro Educator's Situation on the Academic Marketplace." *Journal of Negro Education* 35 (Winter 1966): 18–26.

Seabury, Paul. "HEW and the Universities." *Commentary*, February 1972, pp. 38–44.

———. "The Idea of Merit." *Commentary*, December 1972, pp. 41–45.

Sher, George. "Justifying Reverse Discrimination in Employment." *Philosophy and Public Affairs* 4 (Winter 1975): 159–170.

Sherman, Malcolm J. "'Affirmative Action and the AAUP." *AAUP Bulletin* 61 (December 1975): 293–303.

Shils, Edward. "Academic Appointment, University Autonomy and the Federal Government." *Minerva*, April 1971, pp. 161–170.

Silvestri, Marco J., and Kane, Paul L. "How Affirmative Is the Action for Administrative Positions in Higher Education?" *Journal of Higher Education* 46 (July/August 1975): 445–450.

Solomon, Lewis D., and Heeter, Judith S. "The Case for Preferential Hiring." *Change*, June 1977, pp. 6–7, 64.

Sowell, Thomas. "The Plight of Black Students in the United States." *Daedalus* 103 (Spring 1974): 179–196.

———. "Affirmative Action Reconsidered." *Public Interest* 42 (Winter 1976): 47–65.

———. "A Black 'Conservative' Dissents." *New York Times Magazine,* 8 August 1976, pp. 14–15, 43, 45–46.

Staples, Robert. "The Black Scholar in Academe." *Change,* November 1972, pp. 42–48.

Steele, Claude M., and Green, Stephen G. "Affirmative Action and Academic Hiring: A Case Study of a Value Conflict." *Journal of Higher Education* 47 (July/August 1976): 413–435.

Strickland, Edward. "Black Faculty Members at Multiracial Campuses: Some Problems of Modeling Roles." *Journal of Black Studies* 6 (December 1975): 200–207.

Sugnet, Charles J. "The Uncertain Progress of Affirmative Action." *Change,* May 1974, pp. 37–42.

Taylor, I. E. "Negro Teachers in White Colleges." *School and Society,* May 24, 1947, pp. 369–372.

Taylor, Paul W. "Reverse Discrimination and Compensatory Justice." *Analysis* 33 (June 1973): 177–182.

Tenzer, Morton J., and Coser, Rose Laub. "A Debate on Affirmative Action." *Dissent* 23 (Spring 1976): 207–210.

Thalberg, Irving. "Reverse Discrimination and the Future." *Philosophical Forum* 5 (Fall 1973–Winter 1974): 294–308.

Thompson, Charles H. "Editorial Comment." *Journal of Negro Education* 25 (Spring 1956): 91–94.

Todorovich, Miro, and Glickstein, Howard. "Discrimination in Higher Education: A Debate on Faculty Employment." *Civil Rights Digest,* Spring 1975, pp. 3–7, 9–21.

Tollett, Kenneth S. "Black Lawyers, Their Education, and the Black Community." *Howard Law Journal* 17 (Number 2, 1972): 326–357.

———. "Political Questions and the Law." *University of Detroit Law Journal* 42 (April 1965): 439–471.

Van Den Haag, Ernest. "Reverse Discrimination: A Brief Against It." *National Review,* 29 April 1977, pp. 492–495.

Wale, Fred G. "Chosen for Ability." *Atlantic Monthly,* July 1947, pp. 81–85.

Wasserstrom, Richard. "The University and the Case for Preferential Treatment." *American Philosophical Quarterly* 13 (April 1976): 165–170.

Will, George. "Common Sense on Race." *Newsweek,* 24 January 1977, p. 80.

"Will Government Patronage Kill the Universities?" *Change,* Winter 1975–1976, pp. 10–13, 60–61.

Winston, Michael R. "Through the Back Door: Academic Racism and the Negro Scholar in Historical Perspective." *Daedalus* 100 (Summer 1971): 678–714.

Wright, Stephen J. "Redressing the Imbalance of Minority Groups in the Professions." *Journal of Higher Education* 43 (March 1972): 239–248.

Wubnig, Judy. "The Merit Criterion of Employment: An Examination of Some Current Arguments Against Its Use." *Humanist,* September–October 1976, pp. 36–39.

Young, Rowland L. "Supreme Court Report." *American Bar Association Journal* 57 (June 1971): 609–610.

Newspapers

Chicago Tribune, 17 November 1963.
Chronicle of Higher Education, 1975–1977.
Evening Star (Washington), 26 December 1929.
New York Post, 1977.
New York Times, 1973–1977.
Pittsburgh Courier, 27 August 1977.
Wall Street Journal, 1976–1977.
Washington Afro-American, 1976–1977.
Washington Post, 1973–1977.
Washington Star, 1975–1977.

Signed Newspaper Articles

Bunzel, John H. "Do Colleges Practice Reverse Bias?" *Wall Street Journal,* 27 July 1972, p. 10.

Ezorsky, Gertrude. "Hiring Faculty Women." *New York Times,* 11 October 1976, p. 27.

Goodwin, James A. "Playing Games with Affirmative Action." *Chronicle of Higher Education,* 28 April 1975, p. 24.

Hook, Sidney. "Discrimination Against the Qualified?" *New York Times,* 5 November 1971, p. 43.

Hook, Sidney. "Racial and Sexual Quotas: They're Not Only Illegal; They're Immoral." *Daily News* (New York), 27 March 1977, p. 64.

Kilpatrick, James J. "Negative Affirmative," New York Post, 25 May 1977, p. 47.

Roche, John P. "Affirmative Action: Every Legitimate Break." Washington Star, 11 December 1976, p. A15.

St. Antoine, Theodore J. "Affirmative Action, a 'Heroic' Measure." New York Times, 26 November 1976, p. A23.

Wicker, Tom. "A Misplaced Anger." New York Times, 30 June 1974, Sec. IV, p. 19.

———. "The Real Reverse of Racism." New York Times, 11 January 1975, Section IV, p. 19.

Will, George. "Sympathetic Justice." Washington Post, 5 May 1977, p. A23.

U.S. Government Publications

United States Commission on Civil Rights. Statement on Affirmative Action for Equal Employment Opportunities. Washington, D.C.: U.S. Government Printing Office, February 1973.

———. Federal Civil Rights Enforcement Effort. 5 vols. Washington, D.C., 1971–1975.

———. "Statement on Affirmative Action." Clearinghouse Publication 54. Washington, D.C., 1977.

U.S. Comptroller General of the United States. "A Report to Senator Bayh." Washington, D.C., 30 March 1977.

U.S. Congress, House, Special Subcommittee on Education. Federal Higher Education Programs Institutional Eligibility—Parts 2A and 2B, 93d Cong., 2d sess., 1974. Washington, D.C.: Government Printing Office, 1975.

U.S. Department of Commerce Bureau of the Census. Characteristics of the Population—1970, Part 1, Section 2. Washington, D.C.: Government Printing Office, June 1973.

U.S. Department of Commerce, Bureau of the Census, Projections of the Population of the United States: 1977 to 2050, Washington, D.C.: U.S. Government Printing Office, 1977.

U.S. Department of Health, Education, and Welfare, National Center for Education Statistics. Projections of Education Statistics to 1981–82, 1972 Edition. Washington, D.C.: Government Printing Office, 1973.

———. Projections of Education Statistics to 1983–84, 1974 Edition. Washington, D.C.: Government Printing Office, 1975.

———. The Condition of Education, 1977 Edition. Washington, D.C.: Government Printing Office, 1977.

———. Office for Civil Rights. "Format for Development of an Affirmative Action Plan by Institutions of Higher Education." Washington, D.C., 1975.

———. *Higher Education Guidelines*. Washington, D.C., 1972.

———. Gerry, Martin H. Memorandum Requesting for Organizational Change. Washington, D.C., 3 December 1975.

———. Holmes, Peter. Memorandum to College and University Presidents. Washington, D.C., December 1974.

———. Problem Areas, Questions, and Requests Pertaining to the Affirmative Action Plan and the Compliance (with Executive Order 11246) Program of Florida State University.

———. Reorganization Plan for Office for Civil Rights Regional Offices, Addendum to the 31 December 1975, OCR Reorganizational Memorandum. Washington, D.C., 27 February 1976.

U.S. Department of Labor, Office for Federal Contract Compliance Programs Task Force. *Preliminary Report on the Revitalization of the Federal Contract Compliance Program*. Washington, D.C., 1977.

U.S. Equal Employment Opportunity Commission. *Affirmative Action and Equal Employment, A Guidebook for Employers*. Washington, D.C., 1974.

———. "Higher Educational Staff Information (EEO-6): National Employment Data—1975." Washington, D.C., July 1977.

The Federal Register, 36, no. 234. 4 December 1971.

U.S. General Accounting Office. *The Equal Employment Opportunity Program for Federal Nonconstruction Contracts Can Be Improved*. Washington, D.C., 1975.

———. *More Assurances Needed That Colleges and Universities with Government Contracts Provide Equal Employment Opportunity*. Washington, D.C., 1975.

Special Reports

"Affirmative Action Report on Faculty Shows Improvement in Hiring Patterns." *Harvard Crimson*. 21 May 1976.

Axtell, Dayton. "Academic Performance of Merritt College Transfers.' Report No. 1, December 1971; Report No. 2, May 1973; Report No. 4, May 1974.

Barron's Profiles. *Harvard College*. Woodbury, N.Y.: Barron's Educational Series, 1974.

———. *Oberlin College*. Woodbury, N.Y.: Barron's Educational Series, 1974.

Bewig, Carl W., to Oberlin College Community. Interoffice Memorandum, 6 May 1976.

"EEOC Investigates Racism in Isaacs's Tenure Case." *Harvard Crimson*. 17 April 1976.

"FAS Report Shows Affirmative Action Making Progress." *Harvard Gazette*, 21 May 1976.

Fletcher, Robert Samuel. *A History of Oberlin College from Its Foundation Through the Civil War*. 2 vols. Oberlin, Ohio: Oberlin College, 1943.

Fletcher, William. "Affirmative Action at Harvard." *Harvard Gazette*. 24 February 1976.

Florida State University. *Affirmative Action Program for Equal Opportunities*. July 1973.

————. *Affirmative Action Program Update: A Plan for Continuous Equal Opportunity*. July 1975.

————. *Manual for Affirmative Action Program Development and Implementation in Higher Education Institutions*. May 1974.

————. *Project Opportunity*. January 1975.

————. *Supplemental Data to FSU Affirmative Action Plan*.

(Florida) State University System. *Equal Employment Opportunity Grants-in-Aid for 1977–78*.

Freedberg, Robin. "University Hiring Plan Faces Unfavorable Review by HEW." *Harvard Crimson*. 17 May 1973.

————. "Women Urge More Affirmative Action." *Harvard Crimson*. 5 March 1973.

Handie, Peter, and Jacobs, Bruce. "On the Brink: Afro-American Studies at Harvard." *Harvard Crimson*. 18 January 1977.

Harvard University. Affirmative Action Quarterly Report to the Office for Civil Rights.

————. Afro-American Studies Department. "A Statement of the Afro-American Studies Department on Tenure and the Ephraim Isaacs Case." 29 October 1975.

————. Department of City and Regional Planning. "Faculty Appointments and Affirmative Action: Report for 1975–1976." 20 May 1976.

————. Harvard University Affirmative Action Plan. 31 July 1973.

————. Memorandum Discussing Ephraim Isaacs's Tenure Case on the Harassment and Suspension of Sherman Halcombe from the Task Force on Affirmative Action.

————. Memorandum on "Information for the Dean Regarding Nontenure Teaching Appointments," Revised September 1976.

————. Revised Affirmative Action Plan and Status Report. December 1976.

————. Task Force on Affirmative Action. Memorandum to John G. Bynoe, Regional Director, Office for Civil Rights. 23 February 1976. (Discusses the Harvard Affirmative Action Plan).

"HEW Reveals Sex Bias in GSD Hiring Practices." *Harvard Crimson.* 25 September 1972.

Ikeda, K.; Rich, R.; and Rossi, Peter. Report on Costs and Returns to Investment in the Form of Student Attainments and Institutional Development of the 1971 Commitment. Revised. 1976.

Institute for the Study of Educational Policy, Questionnaire, 18 April 1977.

Isaacs, Ephraim. "The Case for Academic Fairness." *Harvard Crimson.* 22 February 1972.

————. to Derek Bok. 12 October 1975.

Leonard, Walter J. to John G. Bynoe, Director, Region 1, Office for Civil Rights. 28 February 1975.

Luxenberg, Steven M. "HEW Investigation Prompts Renewed Concern with Quotas." *Harvard Crimson.* 25 September 1972.

Merritt College. *Affirmative Action Hiring Guidelines.*

————. *Affirmative Action Program.* 11 April 1974.

————. *Bulletin.* 1975–1976.

————. *Merritt Community College HEW Special Services Project, Proposal.*

————. *Procedure for Employment of Certified Personnel* (hourly).

————. *Procedure for Employment of Certified Personnel* (contract).

Oberlin College. *Affirmative Action Plan.* 20 April 1976.

————. *Bulletin and Course Catalog,* 1976–1977.

————. *Student Regulation, 1975–1976.*

Peralta Community College District. *Affirmative Action Report of Certified Contract Personnel, 1972–73.*

"President Bok: Universities Must Not Abandon Afro-American Studies Field." *Harvard Gazette.* 15 November 1974.

"President Issues Progress Report on Affirmative Action." *Harvard Gazette.* 12 December 1975.

Rivera, George. Letter to the Editor. *Harvard Crimson.* 7 June 1976.

Rosovsky, Henry. "Supplementary Instruction for the Preparation of Materials for Ad Hoc Committees on Permanent Appointments." Memorandum to Department Chairmen. 25 August 1975.

Seligman, Nicole R. "More Black Students Will Enter GSAS Despite Failure of Recruiting Drive." *Harvard Crimson.* 14 June 1976.

Spatta, Carolyn D. to John E. Fleming. 7 July 1977.

Swanson, David. "Dan Steiner: New Man with the Bullhorn." *Harvard Crimson.* 13 October 1972.

"Tenure Ephraim Isaacs." *Harvard Crimson.* May 1976.

Zelays, G. R., and Collins, Pat. *Report* on the Transfer Program, the Basic Skills Learning Center, and the Career Guidance Center: 1975–1976.

Unpublished Works

Flemming, Arthur S. "Statement Before Fact-Finding Hearing Convened by the Secretary of Labor on the Implementation of Executive Order 11246 Affirmative Action Requirements As Applied to Employment at Institutions of Higher Education." Washington, D.C., 12 November 1975.

Glickstein, Howard A. "Statement of Howard A. Glickstein, Director, Notre Dame Center for Civil Rights Before the Department of Labor Fact-Finding Hearing on Contract Compliance by Institutions of Higher Education." Washington, D.C., 20 August 1975.

Gloster, Hugh. Paper on Affirmative Action on the panel, "Affirmative Action and Reverse Discrimination," at the 61st Annual Convention of the Association for the Study of Afro-American Life and History. Washington, D.C., 15 October 1977.

Groomes, Freddie. "Placement and the Role of the Affirmative Action Officer." American Association for Affirmative Action Officers Conference, Austin, Texas, 21 April 1975.

Gould, William B. Paper delivered at the conference, "Equality in America: A Color-Blind Constitution?" at the Second Annual Conference of the Equal Employment Litigation Clinic of the Howard University School of Law. Washington, D.C., 18 March 1977.

Hook, Sidney. "Statement Before the Fact-Finding Hearings of the Office of Federal Contract Compliance of the Department of Labor." Washington, D.C., 30 October 1975.

Mommsen, Kent G. "Career Patterns of Black American Doctorates." Ph.D. dissertation, Florida State University, 1972.

Roche, George S. "Testimony Before the U.S. Commission on Civil Rights." Washington, D.C., 10 September 1975.

Taylor, George D. "Affirmative Action as a Model for Social Change." n.d.

Willie, Charles V. "An Examination of the Future in Relations to the Past: A Personal History of Affirmative Action." Consultation on Affirmative Action, U.S. Civil Rights Commission. Washington, D.C., 9 September 1975.

Civil Rights Acts

The Civil Rights Act of 1866, 14 Stat. 27

The Civil Rights Act of 1867, 14 Stat. 428

The Civil Rights Act of 1867, 14 Stat. 546
The Civil Rights Act of 1870, 16 Stat. 140
The Civil Rights Act of 1871, 16 Stat. 433
The Civil Rights Act of 1871, 17 Stat. 13
The Civil Rights Act of 1875, 18 Stat. 335
The Civil Rights Act of 1957, 71 Stat. 634
The Civil Rights Act of 1964, 42 U.S.C. 2000e seq.
Equal Employment Opportunity Act of 1972, P.L. 92-261, 86 Stat. 103

Executive Orders

Executive Order 8802, June 25, 1941
Executive Order 9346, May 27, 1943
Executive Order 9980, July 26, 1948
Executive Order 10308, December 3, 1951
Executive Order 10479, August 13, 1953
Executive Order 10557, September 3, 1954
Executive Order 10925, March 6, 1961
Executive Order 11246, September 24, 1965
Executive Order 11375, October 13, 1967
Executive Order 11478, August 8, 1969

Court Cases

Asbestos Workers v. *Vogler,* 407 F. 2d 1047 (1969).
Associated General Contractors of Massachusetts, Inc. v. *Altshuler,* 490 F. 2d (1973).
Bakke v. *The Regents of the University of California,* 553 P. 2d 1152 (1976).
Carter v. *Gallagher,* 452 F. 315 (1971).
Contractors Association of Eastern Pennsylvania v. *Secretary of Labor,* 442 F. 2d 159 (1971).
Cramer v. *Virginia Commonwealth University,* 415 F. Supp. 673 (1976).
DeFunis v. *Odegaard,* 416 U.S. 312 (1974).
Green v. *County School Board,* 391 U.S. 430 (1968).
Griggs v. *Duke Power Co.,* 401 U.S. 424 (1971).
Jones v. *Alfred H. Mayer Co.,* 392 U.S. 409 (1968).
Joyce v. *McCrane,* 320 F. Supp. 1284 (1970).

Loving v. *Virginia*, 388 U.S. 1 (1967).

McDonald v. *Santa Fe Trail Transportation Co.*, 427 U.S. 273 (1976).

Morrow v. *Crisler*, 491 F. 2d 1053 (1974).

NAACP v. *Allen*, 493 F. 2d 614 (1974).

Norwalk CORE v. *Norwalk Redevelopment Agency*, 395 F.2d 920 (1968).

Quarles v. *Philip Morris, Inc.*, 279 F. Supp. 505 (1968).

Scott v. *Sanford*, 61 U.S. (19 How.) 393 (1857).

Shapiro v. *Thompson*, 394 U.S. 618 (1969).

The Slaughter House Cases, 83 U.S. (16 Wall) 36 (1873).

Southern Illinois Builders Association v. *Ogilvie*, 471 F. 2d 680 (1972).

Stamps v. *Detroit Edison Co.*, 365 F. Supp. 87 (1973).

Swann v. *Charlotte-Mecklenburg Board of Education*, 402 U.S. 1 (1971).

United Jewish Organization of Williamsburg v. *Carey*, 97 S. Ct. 996 (1977).

United Papermakers v. *United States*, 416 F.2d 980 (1969).

United States v. *Elevator Constructors, Local 5*, 13 FEP Cases 80 (1976).

United States v. *IBEW, Local No. 38*, 428 F. 2d 144 (1970).

United States v. *Ironworkers Local 86*, 443 F. 2d 544 (1971).

United States v. *Sheet Metal Workers, Local No. 36*, 416 F. 2d 123 (1969).

United States v. *Wood, Wire, and Metal Lathers International Union, Local No. 46*, 471 F. 2d 408 (1973).

Weiner v. *Cuyahoga Community College District*, 249 N.E. 2d 907 (1969).

Oral Interviews

HEW, Office for Civil Rights
  Bailey, Mr. Walter, Equal Opportunity Specialist, Washington, D.C.
  Brown, Mr. Robert, Program Manager, San Francisco.
  Bryson, Mr. Lou, Chief of Higher Education, Atlanta.
  Hodgdon, Mr. John, Chief of Policy for Higher Education and Secondary Education, Washington, D.C.
  King, Ms. Pat, Deputy Director, Washington, D.C.
  Lee, Ms. Ki, Equal Opportunity Specialist, Washington, D.C.
  Lemon, Mr. James, Equal Opportunity Specialist, Washington, D.C
  Lepper, Dr. Mary, Division Director, Higher Education, Washington, D.C.
  McLearn, Mr. Don, Public Information Officer, Washington, D.C.
  Patterson, Mr. Walter Jr., Civil Rights Specialist, Boston
  Taylor, Mr. Burton, Chief of Operations, Higher Education Division, Washington, D.C.
  Thomas, Mr. William H., OCR Regional Office, Atlanta.

Tyson, Mr. Herb, Acting Director, Higher Education Division, Washington, D.C.

Equal Employment Opportunity Commission
Neal, Mr. James, Chief, Information Branch, Research Division.

DOL, Office of Federal Contract Compliance Program
Heath, Mr. Thad, Equal Opportunity Officer

Florida State University
Bichel, Mr. Robert, University Counsel
Flory, Dr. Daisy, Dean of the Faculties
Gamble, Dr. William, Assistant Professor
Gatewood, Dr. Wallace, Assistant Professor
Groomes, Dr. Freddie L., Assistant to the President
Jones, Ms. Rebecca, Graduate Student
Kent, Mr. Scott, Assistant Vice-President
Marshall, Dr. Stanley, President
Puryear, Dr. Paul, Provost
Robinson, Mr. Rick, Personnel Director
Woodard, Dr. Wallace, Associate Professor

Harvard University
Capron, Dr. William, Associate Dean, John F. Kennedy School of Government
Cooper, Mr. Carl, Research Fellow, School of Law
Isaacs, Dr. Ephraim, Associate Professor, Afro-American Studies
Kain, Dr. John, Chairman, Department of Urban and Regional Planning, Graduate School of Design
Keller, Dr. Phylis, Assistant Dean, Faculty of Arts and Sciences
Lombard, Dr. George, Senior Associate Dean, Graduate School of Business Administration
Leonard, Mr. Walter, Special Assistant to the President
Patterson, Dr. Orlando, Professor of Sociology, Department of Sociology
Shinton, Mr. Robert, Secretary to the Corporation
Spence, Dr. Michael, Professor, Department of Economics, Chairman of the Faculty Senate Committee
Steiner, Mr. Daniel, University Counsel
Taylor, Ms. Marilyn, Doctoral Student, Graduate School of Business Administration
Wilson, Dr. Blenda, Senior Associate Dean, Graduate School of Education

Oberlin College
Bewig, Mr. Carl W., Director of Admissions
Boe, Mr. David S., Dean of the Conservatory of Music
Breuning, Mr. Carl G., Superintendent of Buildings and Grounds
Carrier, Dr. Samuel C., Associate Dean

Danenberg, Mr. Emil C., President
Gerlach, Ms. Marjorie, Director of Foundation and Corporate Support
Goldsmid, Dr. Paula L., Associate Dean
Harris, Mr. Emanuel, Jr., Director of Personnel
Johnson, Mr. Herbert F., Librarian
Livingston, Mr. Dayton E., Vice-President for Business and Finance
Lubetkin, Mr. James G., Director of College Information
Mittleman, Dr. Dan, Director, Computer Center
Peek, Mr. Booker C., Assistant Professor
Richards, Dr. W. Bruce, Associate Professor
Spatta, Dr. Carolyn D., Assistant to the President; Secretary to the College
Weaver, Mr. Michael, Part-Time Instructor

Merritt College
Barroca, Dr. Manuel R. B., Chairman
Baysdorfer, Mr. Lloyd G., Dean
Desrosiers, Mr. Wilfred, Jr., Dean
Godbold, Dr. Donald H., President
Herring, Mr. George, Assistant Dean
Hill, Ms. Pearlina, Professor
Howard, Mr. Gary, Division Chairperson
Latorre, Mr. Antonio, Professor
Minns, Mr. Finis, Student Body President
Ropchan, Ms. Alice, Staff
Schuetz, Ms. Carolyn A., Director, Cooperative Education
Shortess, Mr. Harry, Assistant Dean
Sommersette, Dr. John, Professor

Index

Adelbert College, 21
Affirmative action
  and Equal Employment Opportunity
      Commission, 66–67
  and impact of educational programs,
      53, 55
  and President's Committee on Equal
      Employment Opportunity, 65
  controversial aspects of, 53–54
  defined, 7
  educators' criticism of, 78, 79–100
  educators' criticism refuted, 78–79, 82,
      83, 84–100
  employers' obligations under, 6
  estimated impact on future black
      faculty employment, 209–12, 237,
      239–55, 256–63, 367–69
  federal government
      policy and procedures, 5, 12, 105–6
      programs, 67–70
      regulations governing, 109–16
      responsibility for, 9, 103–4
  goals of, 7–8
  higher education case studies of
      at Florida State University, 135,
          136–58
      at Harvard University, 135, 158–77
      at Merritt College, 135, 192–204
      at Oberlin College, 135, 177–92
      conclusions of, 204–6
  historical justification for, 3, 4, 54
  legal bases for, 48–51, 56–59
  legal decisions opposing, 51
  legal decisions supporting, 52
  necessity for, 272–75
  Office for Civil Rights as administrator
      of, 118–33
  procedures for enforcing, 11–12
  purpose of, 4, 5–6, 53, 94
  suggested public policies for hiring
      black faculty, 263–71
  white educators' attitudes toward, 44–
      45, 46–47

      See also Executive Order 11246; Office
          for Civil Rights (OCR), HEW
Alabama Department of Public Safety,
      73
American Council on Education (ACE),
      95, 97, 231
American Missionary Association, 19
Anti-Ku Klux Klan Act. *See* Enforcement
      Act (1871)
Armstrong, Samuel Chapman, 19–20
Asbestos Workers v. *Vogler,* 70
*Associated General Contractors of Massa-
      chusetts, Inc.* v. *Altshuler,* 76
Atlanta Compromise Address (1895), 20
Atlanta University, 24, 43

Bakke, Allan, 274
Bakke v. *Regents of the University of
      California,* 4, 53, 54, 55, 274–75
Bayer, Alan E., 79, 95, 213, 214, 219, 226
Bell, Griffin, 87
Berea College v. *Kentucky,* 300
Bernstein, Barton J., 60
Berry, Mary F., 89
Billingsley, Andrew, 82–83, 96
Black Codes, 49
Bolling v. *Sharpe,* 301
Bond, Horace Mann, 32
"Boston Plan," 76
Briggs v. *Elliott,* 299
Brown, Sterling, 32
Brown v. *Board of Education of Topeka,*
      3, 32, 33–34, 46, 64, text of, 295–301
Buckley Amendment. *See* Family Educa-
      tional Rights and Privacy Act (1974)
Bunche, Ralph J., 32
Bunzel, John, 79–99 *passim*
Bureau of Education, U.S., 23
Bureau of Indian Affairs, U.S., 18
Bureau of Refugees, Freedmen, and
      Abandoned Land, 17
Burger, Warren, 71
Bush v. *Kentucky,* 291

Califano, Joseph A., Jr., 87
Caliver, Ambrose, 32
Caplow, Theodore, 35
Carnegie Corporation, 85
Carnegie Council on Policy Studies in
    Higher Education, 79, 95, 129
Carter, Hodding, 35
Carter, James E. (Jimmy), 3
Carter v. *Gallagher*, 72
Cartter enrollment projections, 224–25,
    227–28
Central College (New York), 17
Cheek, James, 96
Civil Rights Act (1866), 49, 50
Civil Rights Act (1875), 51
Civil Rights Act (1957), 57, 64
Civil Rights Act (1964), 5, 59, 69, 70, 72,
    82
    Title VI, 57, 106, 107, 275
    Title VII, 57, 66, 70–76 *passim*, 107,
        112
    text of, 301–16
Civil Rights Act (1972), 69
Clark, Kenneth, 32
Cobb, W. Montague, 32
Commission on Civil Rights, U.S., 57, 64,
    108, 122, 127, 128, 129
Committee on Academic Nondiscrimina-
    tion and Integrity, 80
Committee on Equal Employment
    Opportunity. *See* Equal Employ-
    ment Opportunity, Committee on
Committee on Fair Employment Prac-
    tices. *See* Fair Employment Practices
    Commission (FEPC)
Committee on Government Compliance,
    56
Committee on Government Contract
    Compliance (CGCC), 62, 63
Committee on Government Contracts, 63
Comprehensive Alcohol Abuse and
    Alcoholism Prevention, Treatment
    and Rehabilitation Act, 106
Compromise of 1877, 18
*Contractors Association of Eastern Penn-
    sylvania* v. *Secretary of Labor*, 75
Cumming v. *County Board of Education*,
    296, 300
Curry, Jabez Lamar Monroe, 20

Davis, Arthur P., 32
Davis, John W., 32
Davis, William Allison, 27, 32
Davis v. *County School Board*, 299

DeFunis v. *Odegaard*, 52
Dred Scott v. *Sanford*, 16, 17, 50, 276–85,
    293
Drew, Charles R., 31
Discrimination
    by federal government, 22, 23, 26–27,
        49, 50–51
    in education, 14, 20–22, 23–24
    in employment, 7–8, 9–10
    U.S. historical background of, 4, 14–19
    See also Legal decisions; individual
        court case entries
Drug Abuse and Treatment Act (1972),
    106
DuBois, William Edward Burghardt, 14,
    21–22
Dunbar High School (Washington, D.C.),
    25, 26
Dykes, Eve Beatrice, 32

Education, 16–17, 19–21, 23–26, 34–35, 39
Education, higher
    affirmative action case studies
        at Florida State University, 135,
            136–58
        at Harvard University, 135–158–77
        at Merritt College, 135–, 192–204
        at Oberlin College, 135, 177–92
        conclusions of, 204–6
    affirmative action employment policies
        in, 110–12
    and employment of black faculty in
        white colleges, 14, 27–30, 32, 35–38
    and institutions' affirmative action
        obligations, 109–12
    and Order No. 4, 116–18
    enrollment projections for, 222–38
        passim
    estimated impact of affirmative action
        on future black faculty employ-
        ment, 209–12, 237, 239–55, 256–63,
        367–69
    suggested public policies for hiring
        black faculty, 263–71
Education Amendments (1972), 80, 106
Educational Testing Service, 174–231
Educators
    criticism of affirmative action, 78, 79–
        100
    criticism of affirmative action refuted,
        78–79, 82, 83, 84–100
    whites' attitudes toward affirmative
        action, 44–45, 46–47
Eisenhower, Dwight D., 56, 63
Ely, J. H., 49

Emancipation Proclamation, 285–88
Enforcement Act (1870), 50–51
Equal Employment Opportunity, Committee on, 57, 65, 68
Equal Employment Opportunity Act (1972), 58, 66
Equal Employment Commission, 58–59, 68, 70, 79, 95–96, 125, 212
Equal Pay Act, 112
Espy, Herbert G., 29
Executive Order 8802 (1941), 26–27, 55, 56, 60, 61, 62, 317–18
Executive Order 9346, 56–60, 62
Executive Order 9980, 56, 61, 318–20
Executive Order 9981 (1948), 27
Executive Order 10308, 56, 62, 320–21
Executive Order 10479, 56, 63, 321–23
Executive Order 10557, 56, 63, 323–24
Executive Order 10925, 57, 65, 325–33
Executive Order 11246, 5, 7, 8, 58, 67–91 *passim*, 121
    court cases upholding, 74–76
    implementation of, 103, 104, 105–6
    institutions regulated by, 118, 119
    text of, 333–42
    See also Affirmative action; Office for Civil Rights (OCR), HEW
Executive Order 11375, 58, 67
Executive Order 11478, 58, 67

Faculty, black, 274
    and affirmative action case studies
        at Florida State University, 138, 139–42, 143–44, 145–55
        at Harvard University, 156–67, 172–77
        at Merritt College, 193–94, 195–99
        at Oberlin College, 179–80, 181–83, 184–85, 187
        conclusions of, 204–6
    at white institutions, 27–30, 32
    EEOC report on, 95–96
    estimated future impact of affirmative action on, 209–12, 237, 239–55, 256–63, 367–69
    status in academic markets, 213–22
    suggested public hiring policies of, 263–71
Fair Employment Practices Commission (FEPC), 26–27, 55, 56, 60–63
Family Educational Rights and Privacy Act (1974), 85
Faubus, Orval, 34
Federal government
    affirmative action programs of, 67–70

and future black faculty employment, 263–71
antidiscriminatory employment policies of, 55–67
job and education responsibility of, 103–4
See also Health, Education and Welfare, U.S. Department of; Executive Orders
Fifteenth Amendment, U.S. Constitution, 3, 17, 49, 50, 51, 289–90
Fisk University, 19, 24
Florida State University, 135, 136–58
Ford Foundation, 39, 40, 216
Fourteenth Amendment, U.S. Constitution, 3, 17, 34, 48–52 *passim*, 289, 290, 292, 295
Franklin, John Hope, 32
Frazier, E. Franklin, 26, 28–29
Frederick Douglass High School (Baltimore), 26
Freeman, Richard B., 95

Gaines, Lloyd, 26
General Accounting Office, 120–21, 128
Georgetown University, 20
Gibson v. *Mississippi*, 291
Glazer, Nathan, 80, 93–94
Glidden Company (Chicago), 32
Gloster, Hugh, 96
Gong Lum v. *Rice*, 296, 300
Gould, William B., 93
Government Contracts Committee, U.S., 56
"Grandfather clause," 19
Greener, Richard, 20
Griggs v. *Duke Power Company*, 71
Groomes, Freddie, 136, 137

Haggstrom enrollment projections, 224
Hall v. *DeCuir*, 291
Hampton Normal and Agricultural Institute, 19, 20, 24
Harris, Abram L., 27–28
Harvard University, 135, 158–77
Hastie, William H., 32
Hayes, Rutherford B., 18
Healey, Patrick, 20
Health, Education and Welfare, U.S. Department of, 44, 67–68, 84, 85. *See also* Office for Civil Rights (OCR), HEW
Hershey, C. B., 29
Hillsdale College, 79
Hinton, William A., 25

Holmes, Dwight Oliver Wendell, 32
Holmes, Peter, 87, 91, 116, 157
Hook, Sidney, 80–99 *passim*
Hope, John, 32
Houston, Charles H., 32
Howard University, 24, 43, 84
Howe, Irving, 89

"Interposition," 34

Jencks, Christopher, 26, 35
Johnson, Andrew, 17
Johnson, Lyndon B., 58
Jones v. Alfred H. Mayer Company, 49
Jordan, Vernon, 87, 89–90
Josephson, Clarence E., 29
Joyce v. McCrane, 75
Julian, Percy L., 31–32
Julius Rosenwald Fund, *See* Rosenwald, Julius, Fund
Just, Ernest E., 32

Keller, Dean, 175
Kennedy, John F., 57, 65, 66
Kilson, Martin, 95
King, Martin Luther, Jr., 66, 82

Labor, U.S. Department of, 5, 65, 67–68, 80, 85, 105, 109, 120, 132. *See also* Office of Federal Contract Compliance Programs (OFCCP)
Ladd, Everett Carll, Jr., 86, 89
Legal decisions
  favoring discrimination, 3, 16, 18
  opposing discrimination, 3, 26, 32–35, 49–50, 51–52, 70–77
  See also individual court case entries
Leonard, Walter J., 96, 165, 175
Lewis, Harold O., 32
Lewis, W. Arthur, 95
Lipset, Seymour Martin, 86, 89
Locke, Alain, 14, 32
Lodge, Henry Cabot, 18, 19
Logan, Rayford W., 31
Loving v. Virginia, 52

McGee, Reece J., 35
McLaurin v. Oklahoma State Regents, 296, 297
Marshall, Stanley, 136, 137
"Massive resistance," 34
Mays, Benjamin, 32
Meharry Medical College, 43
Merritt College (California), 135, 192–204
Miller, Leonard S., 224, 225–26, 251

Miller, Samuel F., 50
Mississippi Highway Patrol, 73
Missouri ex rel. Gaines v. Canada, 296
Mommsen, Kent G., 82, 96
Moore, William, Jr., 92, 215–16, 219, 220, 221
Morehouse College, 19
Morrow v. Crisler, 73
Moss, James A., 35

National Academy of Sciences, 40, 216–17
National Association for the Advancement of Colored People (NAACP), 22, 26, 30, 32–33
NAACP v. Allen, 73
National Board on Graduate Education, 44
National Center for Education Statistics (NCES), 222–23, 226, 227
National Labor Relations Act, 112
National Research Council, 40, 42
Neal v. Delaware, 291
Niagara Movement, 22
Nixon, Richard M., 58
Nonteaching higher education personnel
  at Florida State University, 138, 139, 140, 141–42, 145–55
  at Harvard University, 167–69
  at Merritt College, 193–94, 195–99
  at Oberlin College, 180–81, 182–83, 187–88
Norwalk CORE v. Norwalk Redevelopment Agency, 52

Oberlin College, 92, 135, 177–92
Office for Civil Rights (OCR), HEW, 69, 79, 81, 86, 87
  and higher education affirmative action case studies, 144, 156–58, 159, 175, 176, 177, 192, 199
  and affirmative action plan recommendations, 205–6
  as affirmative action administrator, 118–33
"Format for Development of an Affirmative Action Plan by Institute of Higher Education," 358–66
  purpose of, 105–6
  staff and structure of, 106–9
Office of Federal Contract Compliance (OFCC), 67, 68
Office of Federal Contract Compliance Programs (OFCCP), 105, 122, 125–26, 129, 132, 133

Office of Production Management, 55, 56, 60

Ohio Gubernatorial Executive Order (5 June 1967), 74–75

O'Neil, Robert M., 95

Peabody, George, 20

Peabody Education Fund, 20

People v. *Gallagher*, 293

Phelps-Stokes Fund, 23

Philadelphia Negro, The, 21–22

"Philadelphia Plan," 75

Pifer, Alan, 85–86

Plessy v. *Ferguson*, 3, 18, 19, 20, 23, 33, 53, 290–95, 296, 298

Porter, Dorothy, 32

Porter, James A., 32

Potomac Institute, 64

Pottinger, J. Stanley, 86, 88, 109

Powell, Lewis, 274, 275

President's Committee on Equal Employment Opportunity. *See* Equal Employment Opportunity, Committee on

Public Health Service Act, 106

Public Law 93–638, 106

Quarles, Benjamin, 32

Quarles v. *Philip Morris, Inc.*, 70

Racism. *See* Discrimination

Radner, Roy, 224, 225–26, 251

Railroad Company v. *Brown*, 291

Randolph, A. Philip, 26, 55

Reason, Charles, 16–17

Rehabilitation Act (1973), 106

"Reverse discrimination," 44–45, 52, 90–92, 116, 272–73

Revised Order No. 4, 12, 68, 80–91 *passim*, 99, 342–57

Riesman, David, 26, 35

Roberts v. *City of Boston*, 300

Roche, George, 79–80, 81, 86, 90, 92, 96, 98

Roosevelt, Franklin D., 26, 55, 56, 60

Rose, Harold M., 35, 36, 46

Rosenberg, Bernard, 89

Rosenwald, Julius, Fund, 27, 29, 37

Rowan, Carl, 93

Rubaii, Sandra, 45

Seabury, Paul, 80, 83, 84, 88, 90, 92, 98

Sears, Barnas, 20

Shaw, Kenneth A., 36–38

Shaw University, 19

Sherman, Malcolm J., 44–45

Shils, Edward, 80–81

Shipherd, John J., 177

Sipuel v. *Oklahoma*, 290

Slaughter House cases, 50, 300

Snowden, Frank M., 32

Southern Association of Colleges and Secondary Schools, 24

Southern Education Reporting Service (SERS), 36, 37

Southern Illinois Builders Association v. *Ogilvie*, 75–76

Sowell, Thomas, 36, 80, 82, 83, 87, 91–98 *passim*

Spero, Sterling D., 27

Stamps v. *Detroit Edison Company*, 72

Staples, Robert, 89

State University of New York, 44–45

Stewart, Philo, 177

Students, black

  and affirmative action case studies

    at Florida State University, 138–39, 152, 155–56

    at Harvard University, 158

    at Merritt College, 194

    at Oberlin College, 177, 188–92

  graduate school enrollment of, 38–44, 230–32, 235–37, 238, 255–56, 258, 259–60

  private college enrollment of, 190

  professional school enrollment of, 40–41, 44

  undergraduate enrollment of, 231, 232–35

  white college attitudes toward, 37–38

Strauder v. *West Virginia*, 291, 300

Swann v. *Board of Education*, 52

Sweatt v. *Painter*, 296, 297

Tate, Merze, 32

Taylor, Alrutheus, 32

Thirteenth Amendment, U.S. Constitution, 3, 17, 49, 50, 288, 290

Thomas, Charles, 32

Thompson, Charles H., 34–35

Title VI. *See* Civil Rights Act (1964), Title VI

Title VII. *See* Civil Rights Act (1964), Title VII

Title VII. *See* Education Amendments (1972)

Title VII. *See* Public Health Service Act

Title VIII. *See* Public Health Service Act

Title IX. *See* Education Amendments
(1972)
Tollett, Kenneth S., 48
Trotter, William Monroe, 22
Truman, Harry S, 27, 56, 61–63

United Papermakers v. *United States,*
70–71
United States v. *Elevator Constructors,
Local 5,* 74
United States v. *IBEW, Local No. 38,* 70
United States v. *Ironworkers Local 86,* 71
United States v. *Sheet Metal Workers,
Local No. 36,* 70
United States v. *Wood, Wire, and Metal
Lathers International Union, Local
46,* 72
University of California, Davis Medical
School, 274, 275
University of Southern California, 20

Virginia, Ex parte, 300
Virginia v. *Rives,* 291, 300

Wagstaff, Lonnie H., 92, 215–16, 219, 220,
221

Wale, Fred G., 29
Warren, Earl, 34
Washington, Booker T., 20
Weiner v. *Cuyahoga Community College
District,* 74–75
Wesley, Charles H., 14, 32
White Citizens Councils, 35
Wicker, Tom, 90
Wilkinson, Frederick D., 32
Will, George F., 85
Williams, Chancellor, 32
Williams, Edward C., 21
Williams, Walter, 95
Wilson, Woodrow, 22
Wisdom, Paul E., 36–38
Women. *See* Florida State University,
Harvard University, Merritt College
and Oberlin College affirmative
action case studies
Woodson, Carter G., 14, 32
Wright, Stephen J., 99

Xavier University, 23

Zinn, Howard, 62